Communications in Computer and Information Science   **899**

Commenced Publication in 2007
Founding and Former Series Editors:
Phoebe Chen, Alfredo Cuzzocrea, Xiaoyong Du, Orhun Kara, Ting Liu,
Dominik Ślęzak, and Xiaokang Yang

More information about this series at http://www.springer.com/series/7899

Ganesh Chandra Deka · Omprakash Kaiwartya
Pooja Vashisth · Priyanka Rathee (Eds.)

Applications of Computing and Communication Technologies

First International Conference, ICACCT 2018
Delhi, India, March 9, 2018
Revised Selected Papers

Springer

Editors
Ganesh Chandra Deka
Ministry of Skill Development
Delhi
India

Omprakash Kaiwartya
School of Science and Technology
Nottingham Trent University
Nottingham
UK

Pooja Vashisth
Department of Computer Science,
Shyama Prasad Mukherji College
University of Delhi
Delhi
India

Priyanka Rathee
Department of Computer Science,
North Campus
University of Delhi
Delhi
India

ISSN 1865-0929   ISSN 1865-0937   (electronic)
Communications in Computer and Information Science
ISBN 978-981-13-2034-7   ISBN 978-981-13-2035-4   (eBook)
https://doi.org/10.1007/978-981-13-2035-4

Library of Congress Control Number: 2018951240

This Springer imprint is published by the registered company Springer Nature Singapore Pte Ltd.
The registered company address is: 152 Beach Road, #21-01/04 Gateway East, Singapore 189721, Singapore

Preface

People across globe have understood the immense potential of IT with respect to its contribution in terms of economic growth, efficient governance, and improving quality of life in general. The main objective of the International Conference on Applications of Computing and Communication Technologies 2018 (ICACCT-2018) held at Shyama Prasad Mukherji College, University of Delhi, on March 9, 2018, was a humble beginning toward the empowerment of our society through technology to create a better tomorrow.

The University of Delhi is a premier university in India with a venerable legacy and international acclaim for the highest academic standards, diverse educational programs, distinguished faculty, illustrious alumni, varied co-curricular activities, and modern infrastructure. Over the many years of its existence, the university has sustained the highest global standards and best practices in higher education. Its long-term commitment to nation building and unflinching adherence to universal human values are reflected in its motto: "Nishtha Dhriti Satyam" निष्ठा धृति सत्यम् (Dedication, Steadfastness, and Truth). Established in 1922 as a unitary, teaching, and residential university by the Act of the then Central Legislative Assembly, a strong commitment to excellence in teaching, research, and social outreach has made the university a role model and trend-setter for other universities. The President of India is the Visitor, the Vice-President is the Chancellor, and the Chief Justice of the Supreme Court of India is the Pro-Chancellor of the University. Beginning with three colleges and 750 students, it has grown as one of the largest universities in India with 16 faculties, over 80 academic departments, an equal number of colleges, and over seven lakh students.

SPM College is a well-known women's college of the University of Delhi. It was established in 1969 in the memory of distinguished academician and statesman Shyama Prasad Mukherji. It has no affiliation with any sect, religion, political group, or thinking. The college motto "tejasvi naa vadhi mastu" in Sanskrit has a profound meaning. It is derived from the Taittiriya Upanisad. It means, "Let our efforts at learning be luminous (Tejasvi) and filled with joy, and endowed with the force of purpose (Vadhi Mastu)."

This conference was successful in facilitating academics, researchers, and industry professionals to deliberate upon the latest issues and advancement in ICT and its applications. In total, 109 papers were submitted in three tracks. After a thorough review process, 30 papers were selected for oral presentation during the conference. After the oral presentation of the papers at the conference, the papers were further refined to enhance their quality.

This conference proceedings will prove beneficial for academics, researchers, and practitioners as it contains a wealth of valuable information on the recent developments in ICT.

July 2018

Ganesh Chandra Deka
Omprakash Kaiwartya
Pooja Vashisth
Priyanka Rathee

Organization

General Chairs

Jaime Lloret   Polytechnic University of Valencia, Spain
Punam Bedi   University of Delhi, India
Pooja Vashisth   University of Delhi, India
Omprakash Kaiwartya   Nottingham Trent University, UK
Priyanka Rathee   University of Delhi, India

Technical Program Committee

Ganesh Chandra Deka (Chair)	Ministry of Skill Development and Entrepreneurship, Government of India, India
Robin Singh Bhadoria (Co-chair)	IIIT Nagpur, India
Abdul Hanan Abdullah	Universiti Teknologi Malaysia (UTM), Malaysia
Shiv Prakash	Indian Institute of Information Technology (IIIT), Kottayam, India
Sushil Kumar	Jawaharlal Nehru University (JNU), New Delhi, India
Akshansh Gupta	Jawaharlal Nehru University (JNU), New Delhi, India
Virendra Ranga	National Institute of Technology, Kurukshetra, India
Yue Cao	Northumbria University, Newcastle, UK
A. K. Verma	Thapar University, India
Somayajulu D. V. L. N.	National Institute of Technology, Warangal, Telangana, India
Sudhakar Tripathi	National Institute of Technology, Patna, India
Sujata Pal	IIT Ropar, India
R. K. Aggrawal	Jawaharlal Nehru University, Delhi, India
R. K. Sharma	Thapar University, India
Rajiv Ratn Shah	Singapore Multimedia University, Singapore
Sangram Ray	National Institute of Technology, Sikkim, India
S. B. Bhattacharya	Indian Association for Medical Informatics, India
Bhaskar Mandal	National Institute of Technology, Jamshedpur, India
Kashif Naseer	Bahria University, Islamabad, Pakistan
Koushlendra Kumar Singh	Jamia Millia Islamia, India
M. Nizamuddin	National Institute of Technology, Jamshedpur, Jharkhand, India
Manoranjan Mohanty	New York University Abu Dhabi, UAE
Meenakshi Tripathi	Malviya National Institute of Technology, Jaipur, India
Navjot Singh	National Institute of Technology, Uttrakhand, India
Neeraj Kumar	Thapar University, India

Neetesh Kumar	Indian Institute of Information Technology (IIIT), Gwalior, India
Nitin Kumar	National Institute of Technology, Uttrakhand, India
Pinaki Mitra	National Institute of Technology, Guwahati, India
Pradeep Singh	National Institute of Technology, Raipur, India
Deepak Garg	Bennett University School of Engineering and Applied Sciences, India
Dilip Singh Sisodia	National Institute of Technology, Raipur, India
Ditipriya Sinha	National Institute of Technology, Patna, India
Geetali Banerji	IITM, Delhi, India
Anjali Thukral	University of Delhi, India
Gyanendra Verma	National Institute of Technology, Kurukshetra, India
Harmeet Kaur	University of Delhi, India
Bhawna	University of Delhi, India
Biri Arun	National Institute of Technology, Sikkim, India
Biplav Srivastava	IBM
Brij Gupta	National Institute of Technology, Kurukshetra, India
Chandresh Kumar Maurya	IBM Research Center, Bangalore, India
Daya Gupta	Indira Gandhi Delhi Technical University, India
Deepa Anand	CMR Institute of Technology, Bangalore, India
Deepak Gupta	NIT Arunachal Pradesh, Yupia, India
Harsha Ratnani	Jagannath International Management School, Delhi, India
Hema Banati	University of Delhi, India
Mohd Ansari	Jamia Millia Islamia, India
Mohammad Yahya H. Al-Shamri	King Khalid University, Abha, Saudi Arabia
Monica Arora	Apeejay School of Management, Delhi, India
Mukesh Saini	IIT Ropar, India
Pinaki Mitra	IIT Guwahati, India
Prerna Mahajan	IITM, Delhi, India
Raveesh	University of Delhi, India
Richa Sharma	University of Delhi, India
Rinkle Rani	Thapar University, India
Sandeep Marwaha	ICASR, India
Udai Pratap Rao	S.V. National Institute of Technology, Surat, India
V. B. Singh	University of Delhi, India
A. K. Mohapatra	IGDTUW, India
Shefalika Ghosh Samaddar	NIT Sikkim, India
Vinay Kumar	Vivekananda Institute of Professional Studies (VIPS), India
Deepali Kamthania	Vivekananda Institute of Professional Studies (VIPS), India
Judhistir Mahapatro	National Institute of Technology, Uttarakhand, India

Advisory Committee

Abdul Hanan Abdullah	Universiti Teknologi Malaysia (UTM), Malaysia
Ao Lei	University of Surrey, UK
Bingpeng Zhou	Hong Kong University of Sciences Technology, SAR China
Chandra K. Jaggi	University of Delhi, India
D. K. Lobiyal	Jawaharlal Nehru University, New Delhi, India
Jaime Lloret	Polytechnic University of Valencia, Spain
K. K. Bharadwaj	Jawaharlal Nehru University, New Delhi, India
Kusum Deep	IIT Roorkee, India
Manoranjan Mohanty	New York University Abu Dhabi, UAE
M. D. Asri Bin Ngadi	Universiti Teknologi Malaysia (UTM), Malaysia
Mukesh Prasad	University of Technology, Sydney, Australia
Paresh Virparia	Sardar Patel University, Gujarat, India
Prakash C. Jha	University of Delhi, India
Rajiv Ratn Shah	Singapore Management University, Singapore
Saroj Kaushik	Indian Institute of Technology, Delhi, India
Subhash Bhalla	University of Aarhus, Denmark
Tiaohao Guo	Queen Mary University of London, UK
Vasudha Bhatnagar	University of Delhi, India
Vibhakar Mansotra	University of Jammu, India
Xiaokang Zhou	Shiaga University, Japan
Xu Zhang	Xi'an University of Technology, China
Yue Cao	Northumbria University, UK

Local Organizing Committee

Ram Shringar Raw	Indira Gandhi National Tribal University, India
Reema Thareja	SPMC, University of Delhi, India
Jaya Gera	SPMC, University of Delhi, India
Baljeet Kaur	SPMC, University of Delhi, India
Shweta Tyagi	SPMC, University of Delhi, India
Pratibha	SPMC, University of Delhi, India
Mansi Sood	SPMC, University of Delhi, India
Anuradha Singhal	SPMC, University of Delhi, India
Sonia Kumari	SPMC, University of Delhi, India
Shaheen	SPMC, University of Delhi, India
Akanksha Bansal Chopra	SPMC, University of Delhi, India
Seema Rani	SPMC, University of Delhi, India

Student Coordinators

Manisha Vashisth
Pooja Garg
Anchal Dua
Deepali Singhal
Vaishali Wahi

Contents

Application and Services

Communication and System Technologies

Trending Pattern Analysis of Twitter Using Spark Streaming

Prachi Garg$^{(\boxtimes)}$, Rahul Johari, Hemang Kumar, and Riya Bhatia

Wireless Adhoc Network Group of Engineering and Research (WANGER) Lab,
University School of Information, Communication and Technology (USICT),
Guru Gobind Singh Indraprastha University, Sector – 16C,
Dwarka 110078, Delhi, India
prachi333l@gmail.com, rahul.johari.in@ieee.org,
hemangsk@gmail.com, riyabhatia26@gmail.com

Abstract. A method had been adopted to predict the trending patterns on the twitter in near-real time environment. These trending patterns help the companies to know their customers and to predict their brand awareness. The pattern was recognized by analyzing the tweets fetched in real time environment and by examining the most popular hashtags on the twitter platform in past few seconds. The work was implemented using a big data technology 'Spark Streaming'. These hashtag patterns allow the people to follow the discussions on particular brand, event or any promotion. These hashtags are used by many companies as a signature tag to gain popularity of their brand on social networking platforms.

Keywords: Twitter patterns · Twitter trends · Popular hashtags
Spark Streaming · DStream

1 Introduction

Pattern recognition is the task of identifying similarities within a dataset. Twitter is a social networking platform where people find and follow certain hashtags related to an event, brand or any kind of promotion. The world is getting smaller and smaller day by day through internet and usage of social sites. Data is growing exponentially as the number of users and activities over the web are increasing rapidly [1]. The consumer market is becoming competitive and the need to keep a tab on trends is a must. These trends are the patterns being followed by most of the people. Twitter is a micro blogging site that provides an opportunity for performing analysis on expressed opinions and to predict the popular hashtags denoting a trend in the market [2]. In this work, pattern recognition [3] of twitter trends was performed where tweets were fetched on three consecutive days at same time every day. The tweets were processed and the popular hashtags were computed separately for each day. These popular hashtags denote the pattern on each day which is being followed by the people. While posting a tweet, a user can mention a hashtag anywhere in the tweet text. Therefore only the hashtags were extracted from each tweet and the count of each unique hashtag was

© Springer Nature Singapore Pte Ltd. 2018
G. C. Deka et al. (Eds.): ICACCT 2018, CCIS 899, pp. 3–13, 2018.
https://doi.org/10.1007/978-981-13-2035-4_1

maintained. This count denoted the number of occurrences of the respective hashtag. The pattern so formed is used further as awareness analysis.

Twitter is a social networking platform [4], where users posts, can retweet others' post and can interact using twitter messages called tweets. Data across twitter application is growing exponentially as the number of users and activities over the web are increasing rapidly. People take over to twitter to present their opinions related to any issue. Hashtags is usually a label used by many people to emphasize the theme of their tweet content [5]. It makes it easier for other users to find and follow the content related to such themes as highlighted by these tags. This work adopted the approach of analyzing such hashtags to evaluate the theme or trending pattern being followed currently by the various people on social sites. Different social networking sites uses these hashtags to evaluate the inclination of various users and comes out with the trends being followed. Different companies uses this analysis process to identify the perspectives of different people about their brand and predicts the reach of their products to users. This helps the companies to perform the awareness analysis of their respective products. Exploiting this approach in this work, the pattern of trending was evaluated [6]. The work was performed in near-real time. Companies follows the same task for larger intervals of time to come up with large patterns, but such huge computations are not possible on a single node (standalone).

2 Problem Definition

This work focused on performing pattern recognition of trends being followed on the twitter. The tweets are important for analysis because data arrive at a high frequency and algorithms that process them must do so under very strict constraints of storage and time. All public tweets posted on twitter are freely available through a set of APIs provided by Twitter. Using streaming APIs, the streaming context object [7] (created for every task of streaming in Spark) established the connection of the spark master to the twitter. The fetching of tweets occurred in near-real time since Spark involves micro- batch processing wherein the fetched data is stored in the form of batches at regular intervals of time [8]. The pattern was recognized using the hashtags to predict the trending pattern. Different companies perform the same task of pattern recognition and trending analysis for large intervals of time. The gist of this task used by many companies was being showcased in this work.

Today the data is generating in exponentially huge amount across different platforms. Different companies uses such data to analyze the reach of their product to people and the views about their product. It is impossible to manually process such a huge amount of data. This is where the need of automatic analyzing process becomes evident. That is why, the tool 'Spark' fits in here correctly. Spark has in-memory processing, due to which the processing speed of datasets is quite high. It works using Resilient Distributed Datasets (RDDs), which have partitions to store the data. This involves parallel processing. Therefore, Spark core API called Spark Streaming was used to implement the work.

Twitter allows users to post messages, find and follow hashtags and provides its data in real time for the researchers to perform any kind of analysis on it. The messages known as 'tweets' are streamed in near-real time in this work, as it included the micro-batch processing wherein different batches were formed containing tweets, at regular intervals. Such a huge amount of data can be efficiently used for social network studies and analysis to gain useful and meaningful results. A user follows a set of people, and has a set of followers. When that user sends an update out, that update is seen by all of his followers. User can also retweet other user's updates. Users find and follow the hashtags on twitter. Hashtags are the tags, defined using a symbol of hash, which are used by people to emphasize the theme of their tweet content [2]. These labels are used by users to easily find the messages with a specific theme or content. Different social networking platforms uses these hashtags to predict the trending and to identify the pattern of the popular hashtags. Companies implement this at large scale to predict the awareness, about their respective products, among people. Since the tweets are fetched in real time, therefore an ecosystem having high processing speed was required.

3 Proposed System

To improve the scalability, efficiency and processing speed, it was proposed to implement the application on Spark. Since, spark provides in-memory processing, the computational and processing speed of Spark is quite high. Spark uses the core API known as Spark Streaming. Spark streaming works by creating DStreams (Discretized Streams). While fetching the data, the data is stored only at regular intervals of time. Therefore, a dataset known as RDD is used, which stores the data being streamed during an interval of time. As the interval finishes, the data is streamed but will only be stored, after the commencement of next interval, in new RDD. This process creates a group of RDDs. This collection of RDDs is stated as DStream. The interval at which the batch is formed is known as micro-batch processing intervals. The processing of this DStream is also done at regular intervals of time. This interval is defined as window interval. Window interval states that how many RDDs have to be taken from a DStream, to process the data. Therefore at each interval, it defines a certain window containing a number of RDDs, on which the computations will be applied to process the data contained in those RDDs. This is how Spark Streaming works as depicted in Fig. 1.

3.1 Twitter Streaming APIs

Twitter enables users to fetch the twitter data in real time using special streaming APIs. These APIs helps the application to establish a connection between the twitter and the sink. Twitter provides four keys: 'Consumer Key', 'Consumer Secret key', 'Access Token' and 'Access Token Secret'. These keys are treated as the APIs and are unique to every user. In this work, these APIs were provided at the run time using arguments. Following steps were being followed to generate the streaming APIs:

- An application was created by the user by visiting the twitter site, after logging into twitter account.

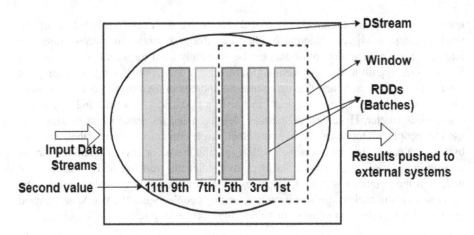

Fig. 1. Mechanism of streaming using Spark

- The newly created application generates a unique set of Consumer key and Consumer Secret key.
- Along with this, a set of Access Token key and Access Token Secret key was generated.

These keys are passed as arguments at run-time while executing the application. Further these APIs are used to set the system properties so that twitter4j library can use them to generate the OAuth credentials. This library is used by twitter stream to establish the connection between twitter and the sink and finally create the stream to fetch the data. To set the system properties, following command was used:

```
System.setProperty("twitter4j.oauth.consumerKey",
consumerKey)
```

Similarly for other keys, the system properties were defined.

4 Methodology Adopted

4.1 Creating a Spark Streaming Context Object

This object is created by passing the Spark configuration object and the interval in micro- batch processing. To create this object, following command was executed:

```
val sparkConf=new
SparkConf().setAppName("TwitterPopularT
ags").setMaster("local[2]")
```

Here setAppName() method defines the application name. setMaster() defines the cluster on which the spark will run. In this work, local mode was used as the cluster and 2 threads were used to implement it.

Spark Streaming uses this object to establish a connection between the source (from where the live data has to be streamed) and the sink (where the live data will be stored).

This object acts as the entry point for all streaming functionality. The Streaming Context object is created after the initialization of Spark Configuration object and the Spark Context object which are require to start the spark shell. Spark configuration object also defines the cluster on which the application should be executed. There are three possible clusters (master node) available in Spark which are 'Mesos Cluster', 'Yarn Cluster' and the 'Local Mode'. This local mode is the standalone mode where the application executes on the single node.

```
val ssc=new StreamingContext(sparkConf, Seconds(1))
```

Here Seconds(1) is the micro-batch interval that is, the batch would be formed at regular intervals of 1 s.

4.2 Creating a DStream

Spark streaming is a core Spark API which enables the live data stream processing. Internally, this API transforms the live data streams being fetched into various batches. Therefore, spark streaming never processes record by record of the fetched data, instead it processes the whole batch at once. These batches are created at regular intervals of time, and are stored as RDDs (Resilient Distributed Dataset). The collection of these batches is known as DStreams (Discretized Streams). A group of batches are processed in each interval. These groups of batches are defined using the window interval being defined during the initialization of DStreams. Interval for creating the batches at regular intervals is also defined in initialization phase. In this work, the interval for creating batches was 1 s and the window interval was set as 5 s. This state that batches will be formed at intervals of 1 s and the processing of DStreams (collection of batches) is done at intervals of 5 s. This means that the processing will be done on the data being fetched in last 5 s. This batch interval is known as micro-batch processing interval. Spark Streaming works by creating an object called Spark Streaming Context. Sometimes, a filter can be applied while fetching the tweets, which would then stream only the tweets containing that particular filter keyword in the tweet text. The streaming of tweets and the formation of batches occurs using the createStream() method. The Streaming Context object and the filter (if there) is passed as arguments to it. Since this whole process is executed on batches, and batches are formed only at regular intervals of time, therefore this kind of streaming is stated as near-real time streaming.

```
val stream= TwitterUtils.createStream(ssc, None,filters)
```

Here 'stream' is the DStream formed for streaming the tweets. The 'filters' passed as an argument in createStream() method is the filter if used to fetch the tweets. This filter is used to target and fetch only those tweets, which have this value of filter being used, in the tweet text. Therefore, only the tweets containing this word (value of filter) would be fetched and stored in the DStream created. TwitterUtils is the class used as the utility file to perform the real-time streaming of tweets.

4.3 Filtering the Hashtags

The tweets being fetched undergoes the split() method. This method splits the tweet text into words, where each word was analyzed whether it starts from a hashtag or not. If the word starts with the hashtag, then that particular word was retained and rest of the words of the whole tweet text were discarded. The splitting of the tweet was done using " " delimiter.

```
val
hashTags=stream.flatMap(status=>status.getText.split("
").filter(_.startsWith("#")))
```

In this process, on every tweet fetched, split() method was executed using the " " delimiter. This divided each tweet text into words. Finally, the words beginning with # were retained and rest of the words were discarded. Finally, 'hashTags' is the DStream storing only the words starting with #.

4.4 Computing Popular Hashtags Using Window Interval

For each tweet streamed, hashtags were retained if present. Words other than hashtags were discarded. Now the window was created which contained the hashtags of only some particular time interval. This resulted in a collection of hashtags in that particular window. In this work, the window of 5 s was used. This interval states that the window would contain the hashtags identified out of tweets in last 5 s only. Any further processing can now only be done individually on these windows. This was how the processing of the tweets fetched in last 5 s was done. Now the count of each unique hashtag was made which resulted in the number of occurrences of each hashtag across the window set of hashtags. The hashtags were sorted based on the number of occurrences (count value) and were finally displayed. Finally, the 10 most popular hashtags (based on their number of occurrences) were displayed at each interval of 5 s.

```
val
topCounts10=hashTags.map((_,1)).reduceByKeyAndWindow(_+_,
Seconds(5)).mapcase(topic,count)=>(count,topic).transform
(_.sortByKey(false))
```

Here the count of each unique hashtag was computed that is, how many number of times a hashtag was used by different users. Finally the hashtags were sorted, using sortByKey() method, in decreasing order based on the count value. In this command the 'Seconds(5)' defines the window interval. A window was created which considers a certain number of RDDs at a time. This window was formed at regular intervals of time that is, at intervals of 5 s. Now the processing of RDDs would be done only at intervals of 5 s. Therefore, RDDs lying in a particular window would be considered together while processing.

4.5 Simulation Performed

The approach followed in this work is explained below in Algorithm 1.

Algorithm 1:- Obtaining the hashtags and their respective count from twitter

---

Input: Twitter APIs

Output: Hashtags with their number of occurrences

Initialization: Initialize micro-batch interval $(MB_{seconds})$. Set few keywords to filter the streaming (K). Initialize window interval $(Wnd_{seconds})$.

```
1.     sparkConf ← new SparkConf( )
2.     ssc ← new StreamingContext(sparkConf, MBseconds)
3.     stream ← createStream(ssc, K)
4.     let hashtags[ ] and count_hashtags[ ][ ] be new
              arrays
5.     i = 0
6.     for each tweet ∈ stream and tweet != null
7.             tokens ← tweet.split( )
8.             if(tokens.startsWith("#")) then
9.                 hashtags[i] = tokens
10.                i++
11.            end if
12.    end for
13.    count_hashtags[ ][ ] ← hashtags.map( (_ , 1)
              ).reduceByKeyAndWindow( _ + _ , Wndseconds )
14.    Sort count_hashtags[ ][ ] by count
15.    return count_hashtags[ ][ ]
```

4.6 Pattern or Trend Recognition on Twitter

The fetched tweets and the computation of the most popular hashtags resulted in the trends being followed currently. The same process was executed for three days at same time every day. This resulted in different trends or the patterns of the tweets every day [9]. This was how the pattern or the trend of twitter hashtags was predicted and recognized. These trends are used by companies to get to know their customers and the awareness of their product, brand or any promotion in market. These trends depicts patterns of the awareness among people. Out of all the hashtags, the 10 most popular hashtags were considered to form the trending pattern [10].

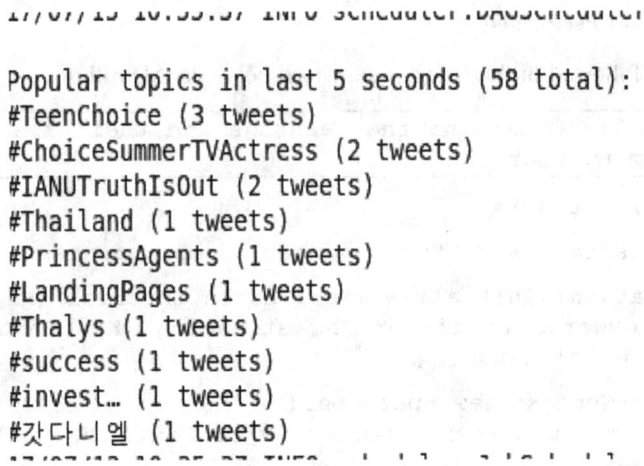

17/07/13 10:33:37 INFO scheduler.DAGScheduler:

```
Popular topics in last 5 seconds (58 total):
#TeenChoice (3 tweets)
#ChoiceSummerTVActress (2 tweets)
#IANUTruthIsOut (2 tweets)
#Thailand (1 tweets)
#PrincessAgents (1 tweets)
#LandingPages (1 tweets)
#Thalys (1 tweets)
#success (1 tweets)
#invest… (1 tweets)
#갓다니엘 (1 tweets)
```

Fig. 2. Popular hashtags identified on day 1.

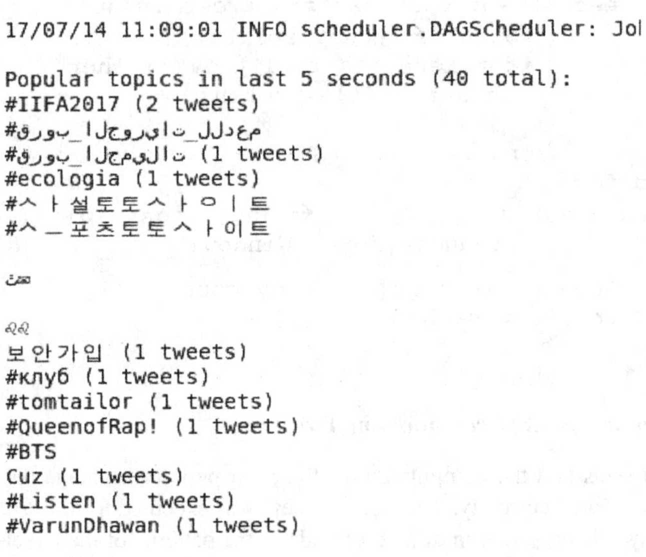

```
17/07/14 11:09:01 INFO scheduler.DAGScheduler: Jo|

Popular topics in last 5 seconds (40 total):
#IIFA2017 (2 tweets)
#قرب_الجزايرت_للدعم
#قرب_الجمليات (1 tweets)
#ecologia (1 tweets)
#ㅅㅏ설토토ㅅㅏ이트
#ㅅ_포츠토토ㅅㅏ이트

تخت

಄಄
보안가입 (1 tweets)
#клуб (1 tweets)
#tomtailor (1 tweets)
#QueenofRap! (1 tweets)
#BTS
Cuz (1 tweets)
#Listen (1 tweets)
#VarunDhawan (1 tweets)
```

Fig. 3. Popular hashtags identified on day 2.

4.7 Results

The application was executed on three consecutive days. The popular hashtags were identified on all the three days, wherein the hashtags were identified from the tweets in last 5 s. Figure 2 depicts the popular hashtags on day 1. It also defines the total number of hashtags in that interval. Figure 3 depicts the popular hashtags that were identified

```
Popular topics in last 5 seconds (97 total):
#ALDUB2getherForever (4 tweets)
#TeenChoice (3 tweets)
#ChoiceSummerGroup (2 tweets)
#themasksinger2 (2 tweets)
#KulitBerminyak (1 tweets)
#몬스타엑스 (1 tweets)
#IIFA2017 (1 tweets)
#IIFARocks (1 tweets)
#memek (1 tweets)
#ngentot (1 tweets)
```

Fig. 4. Popular hashtags identified on day 3.

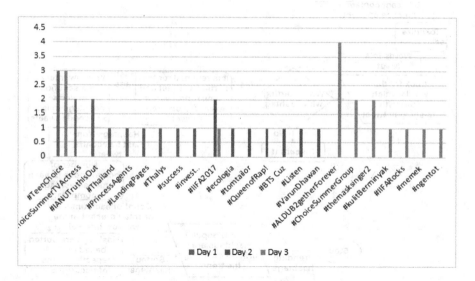

Fig. 5. Bar chart depicting the results of this application

on day 2. Similarly, the process was executed on day 3, and the hashtags were identified as depicted in Fig. 4. The Fig. 5 depicts the bar chart depicting the hashtags identified versus their respective number of occurrences on each day. Figure 6 depicts the entire flow of steps being followed to generate the set of popular hashtags.

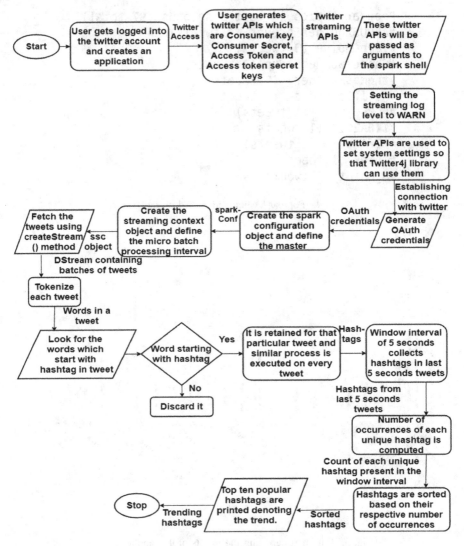

Fig. 6. Flowchart mentioning the steps being followed.

5 Conclusion

Users find and follow the hashtags on twitter to support an issue or a product. Different companies uses this method of trending as a way to compute the awareness of their product. They identify, how many people are tweeting about their product using these hashtags analysis. Companies uses it to find the reach of their product to different users. Different social networking sites are using this kind of pattern recognition to evaluate the trending patterns in real-time. Spark has the capability of in-memory processing, therefore, this tool was used to implement the system. This work is used for identifying the fake tweets being made by people to come under the top trending group.

Acknowledgments. We would like to thank our institution Guru Gobind Singh Indraprastha University for such a great exposure to accomplish such tasks and providing a strong platform to develop our skills and capabilities.

References

1. Tsai, C.-W., Yang, Y.-L., Chiang, M.-C., Yang, C.-S.: Intelligent big data analysis: a review. Int. J. Big Data Intell. **1**(4), 181–191 (2014)
2. Weller, K., Bruns, A., Burgess, J.E., Mahrt, M., Puschmann, C.: Twitter and society: an introduction. In: Twitter and Society, vol. 89, pp. xxix–xxxviii. Peter Lang, New York (2014)
3. Hatua, A., Nguyen, T., Sung, A.: An approach for pattern recognition and prediction of information diffusion model on Twitter. World Acad. Sci. Eng. Technol. Int. J. Comput. Inf. Eng. **5**(3) (2018)
4. Roberts, H., Sadler, J., Chapman, L.: The value of Twitter data for determining the emotional responses of people to urban green spaces: a case study and critical evaluation. Urban Stud. (2018). https://doi.org/10.1177/0042098017748544
5. Türker, İ., Sulak, E.E.: A multilayer network analysis of hashtags in twitter via co-occurrence and semantic links. Int. J. Mod. Phys. B **32**(4), 1850029 (2018)
6. De Cock, B., Pedraza, A.P.: From expressing solidarity to mocking on Twitter: pragmatic functions of hashtags starting with# jesuis across languages. Lang. Soc. **47**, 1–21 (2018)
7. Stypinski, M.: Apache Spark streaming (2017)
8. Shoro, A.G., Soomro, T.R.: Big data analysis: Apache spark perspective. Glob. J. Comput. Sci. Technol. (2015)
9. Li, H., Dombrowski, L., Brady, E.: Working toward empowering a community: how immigrant-focused nonprofit organizations use twitter during political conflicts. In: Proceedings of the 2018 ACM Conference on Supporting Groupwork, pp. 335–346. ACM (2018)
10. Javed, N., Muralidhara, B.L.: Semantic interpretation of tweets: a contextual knowledge-based approach for tweet analysis. In: Margret Anouncia, S., Wiil, U.K. (eds.) Knowledge Computing and Its Applications, pp. 75–98. Springer, Singapore (2018). https://doi.org/10.1007/978-981-10-6680-1_4

NPCCPM: An Improved Approach Towards Community Detection in Online Social Networks

Hilal Ahmad Khanday[✉], Rana Hashmy, and Aaquib Hussain Ganai

Department of Computer Sciences, University of Kashmir, Srinagar, India
hilalhyder@gmail.com, ranahashmy@gmail.com,
hussainaaquib332@gmail.com

Abstract. In this paper, we focus on the task community detection in social networks as it is the key aspect of complex network analysis. Lot of work has already been carried out on community detection, though most of the work done in this field is on non-overlapping communities. But in real networks, some nodes may belong to more than one community, so overlapping community detection needs more attention. The most popular technique for detecting overlapping communities is the Clique Percolation Method (CPM) which is based on the concept that the internal edges of a community are likely to form cliques due to their high density. CPM uses the term k-clique to indicate a complete sub-graph with k vertices. But it is not clear a priori which value of k one has to choose to detect the meaningful structures. Here we propose a method NO PARAMETER CORE CPM (NPCCPM) which calculates the value of k dynamically. Dynamic calculation of k makes it sure to give out the good community structure. We have developed a tool that improves the quality of simple CPM by making CPM-cover much more efficient by absorbing all the eligible nodes to communities and leaving out the bad nodes as outliers with respect to the given new detected cover.

Keywords: Social networks · Community detection · Clique · CPM
NPCCPM · Overlapping communities

1 Introduction

Social interactions have been increasing at a rapid pace, so to detect the subsets of nodes in the social networks that are intra-densely interactive is an important task of the hour. Understanding the structure of the network and making decisions in the network has gained a great attention during last few years. Nodes in networks organize into densely linked groups that are commonly referred to as network communities, clusters or modules [1, 2]. The idea of community detection is different from the simple division of network into sub-groups of members, rather it is a concrete (meaningful) division of network into sub-groups of members. Detecting these communities in the social networks is an NP Hard problem.

The understanding and models of network communities has evolved over time [3, 4]. Early works on network community detection were heavily influenced by the research on the strength of weak ties [5]. This lead researchers to think of networks as

© Springer Nature Singapore Pte Ltd. 2018
G. C. Deka et al. (Eds.): ICACCT 2018, CCIS 899, pp. 14–22, 2018.
https://doi.org/10.1007/978-981-13-2035-4_2

consisting of dense clusters that are linked by a small number of long-range ties [6]. Graph partitioning [2], betweenness centrality [6], as well as modularity [7] based methods all assume such view of network communities and thus search for edges that can be cut in order to separate the clusters. Since then a lot of work has been done in the field and later it was realized that such definition of network communities does not allow for community overlaps. In many networks a node may belong to multiple communities simultaneously which leads to overlapping community structure [8–10]. Since the interactions over the social networks are overlapped in nature [10], so using disjoint community detection approach doesn't suit best for social networks because of leaving out some overlapped natural members of communities. Therefore the natural approach for discovering the community structure in the social network is overlapped one. Figure 1 is a simple network with two overlapping communities. In the figure, node 5 and node 6 belong to both the two communities, so they are overlapping nodes.

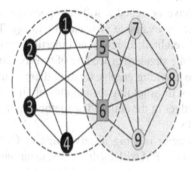

Fig. 1. Network with simple overlapped community structure

2   Related Work

Girvan and Newman's algorithm [6] provides the key idea for community detection i.e. whatever mechanism we use to detect the communities; the idea is to divide the network into subsets of nodes, thereby increasing the power of intra-closeness within the groups than between the groups. Detection of communities in social networks has two approaches: one is the disjoint community detection - in which communities have no intersected (common) members and another approach is overlapping community detection - in which communities have some intersected members.

Since then much more work has been made in this area [11, 12]. Given a social network represented by an undirected graph G with nodes n and edges m, the task of community detection is to find the groups of nodes that are much more like communities. The term community has made its existence since 1887 [6] but there is no globally concrete definition of this term yet known but for us it is a group of nodes having better intracloseness within group than intercloseness between groups [7, 8].

Many traditional community detecting methods hold that each node can only belong to one community, such as Modularity optimization [13, 14], Hierarchical clustering [6, 15], Spectral Algorithms [16, 17], methods based on statistical inference [18]. However in some real networks, communities are not independent, nodes can belong to more than one community, which will lead to overlapping communities. For example, a researcher may belong to more than one research group, or a protein may exist in multiple complex systems. Therefore, the identification of overlapping communities is of central importance.

The principal step in the direction of the overlapped community detection approach has been made by Palla et al. in 2005 whilst proposing Clique Percolation Method (CPM). CPM is based on the impression that communities tend to form cliques due to the high density of edges inside. The CPM works by detecting the cliques in the given social graph of some clique size k, where k is the number of nodes forming the clique. This CPM is able to discover a community structure that mostly makes the coverage of a minimum number of nodes under respective community cover, although there can be a vast percentage of nodes in the network that can be best members of some communities in the CPM's detected cover.

Palla and co-workers have designed a software package implementing the CPM, called cfinder, which is freely available (www.cfinder.org). The algorithm has been extended to the analysis of weighted, directed and bipartite graphs. For weighted graphs, in principle one can follow the standard procedure of thresholding the weights, and then applying the method on the resulting graphs, treating them as unweighted. Farkas et al. [10] proposed that instead of thresholding the weights of cliques, defines the geometric mean of the weights of all edges of the clique. The method has been extended to bipartite graphs by Lehmann et al. [8].

The clique size k parameter is a big disadvantage of CPM because it is unclear beforehand on what value of k, CPM will result the best meaningful community structure [1]. There is also an extended version of this CPM that has been named as extended CPM (ECPM). ECPM uses basic result cover of simple CPM as core cover uses belonging coefficient to cover all other nodes that have been left uncovered by CPM. This approach takes much more time to make the coverage of all nodes possible.

3   Proposed Method

Clique Percolation Method (CPM) is the most common technique for detecting overlapped communities. It is based on the concept that the internal edges of a community are likely to form cliques due to their high density. On the other hand, it is unlikely that intercommunity edges form cliques. Palla et al. uses the term k-clique to indicate a complete sub-graph with k vertices. But it is not clear a priori which value of k one has to choose to detect meaningful structures. Our work tries to resolve the problem of this clique size parameter k by calculating it dynamically in the given network, such that there is no difference in making choice about its value beforehand in which case one is not sure about the reliability of final community structure. We then improve the quality of CPM by using the output communities of CPM as cores and by using community conductance [10] as a measure to absorb the rest of the nodes that have been left uncovered by CPM in efficient amount of time; less its value, better is community like structure.

So follows a way of making the community detection an efficient process rather than taking it as a simple meaningless node coverage process.

We tried a lot of ways to solve the problem with parameter k, and at last we reached to an efficient solution for the problem. Our method that we call NO PARAMETER CORE CPM (NPCCPM) calculates this value of k dynamically in the given network in the following simple way:

k = integer ((Sum of degrees of all the nodes in the network) / (total number of nodes in the network)).

Mathematically we can say that

$$k = \frac{\sum_{v \in V} d(v)}{n} \tag{1}$$

where k is the clique size, V is the set of nodes, d(v) is the degree of node v and n is the number of nodes.

Our method NPCCPM calculates this value of k and catches the basic cliques using CPM. There may be some efficient nodes which remain uncovered yet. We then use these basic communities in the CPM cover as cores to find a measure called as conductance:

Conductance = total no. of edges that are outward from the community / total degree of all the nodes in the given community.

Our approach finds the conductance value for all the cores. Then each node among the left out nodes from the given network is temporarily combined to each core as:

Tc = combine (new node, each core)

Tc: Temporary community constructed by including the new node.

And then re-calculating the value of conductance for new communities (containing this node) in the following way:

If new node is sharing some edges directly with the given core then conductance is calculated simply as above, otherwise if there is no sharing between the given node and the core, then conductance is calculated differently as:

Conductance (tc) = ((total no. of outward edges of tc) − 1) / ((total degree of tc) + 1)

After calculating this conductance value for every free node against each core, a filtering comparison takes place as follows:

Nodes, whose conductance (Tc) for a given core is less than the Tc of respective core, are all accepted as new members by the given core and there by resulting in the updated community for that respective core. The procedure of filtering is repeated for all the cores.

The newly updated communities are then merged to make the detected community structure more efficient by using a coefficient called as Jaccard coefficient (Jaccard similarity) [13, 18].This coefficient is obtained by dividing the Intersection of no. of nodes among communities by the union of no. of nodes of the communities. If the value of Jaccard coefficient for a given number of communities is much high, then those participating communities are merged, otherwise no merging takes place. After this Jaccard similarity test has been performed for every permutation, the final community structure is output in the form of a cover.

Eventually we used the overlapped modularity measure by Nepsuz, for testing the efficiency of our approach as against CPM on the basis of motive: the higher the value of modularity, the more like community structure [14]. The modularity M of a local community is defined as the ratio of its internal edges and external edges

$$M = \frac{M_{in}}{M_{out}} = \frac{\frac{1}{2}\Sigma_{ij}A_{ij}\theta(i,j)}{\Sigma_{ij}A_{ij}\lambda(i,j)} \tag{2}$$

M_{in} represents the internal edges whose endpoints are both in community C and M_{out} represents the external edges which means only one of its endpoints belongs to community C. If both nodes i and j belong to community C, $\theta(i, j) = 1$, otherwise, $\theta(i, j) = 0$. $\lambda(i, j) = 1$ when just only one of nodes i and j belongs to community C and else $\lambda(i, j) = 0$. A strong community should have high value of M, which is based on the relationship between inside edges and outside edges rather than only relying on inside edges.

4 Experimentation

We did all our work in Java language by making a tool that finds an optimised community structure from a given social network. We mainly used two datasets for our study; one - Karate Club Network having 34 nodes and 78 edges, and the other Dolphin Network - having 62 nodes and 159 edges. Besides we tested our algorithm on certain synthetic datasets and found the results quite normal. We used the recursive pruning on the datasets to lower the time complexity. We did a unique implementation of CPM in our NPCCPM.

After applying the conventional CPM part to the two main datasets, only 35% of the total number of nodes came under the detected cover for Karate club network while as rest of the percentage remained uncovered. For Dolphin network only 15% of the total number of nodes got covered under the cover given by CPM, and rest remained uncovered. In case of karate club network, the proposed approach resulted in 100% node coverage under cover and in case of Dolphin network, 92% of the nodes got covered while as only remaining 8% of the nodes acted as outliers. All the nodes of the karate club have been covered in a single iteration, while as Extended CPM takes a lot of iterations for the said network to make coverage of nodes 100%.

The threshold value we have used for Jaccard similarity is 0.80. Our approach yielded two communities for each dataset, and when we see the ground truth of these two networks, both of them have two communities.

The cover that was detected for Karate Club dataset is (shown in Fig. 2):

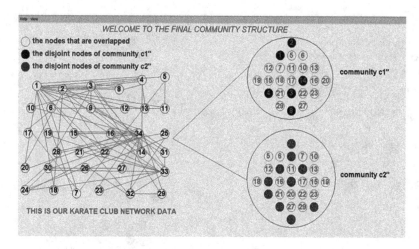

Fig. 2. Communities as found in Karate Club Network Dataset

c1'': 1,2,3,4,5,6,7,8,10,11,12,13,14,15,16,17,18,19,20,21,22,23,24,25,26,27,29

c2'':9,24,30,31,6,7,8,9,10,11,12,13,14,15,16,17,18,19,20,21,22,23,24,25,26,27,28, 29.33,34,28,32

The cover that was spotted for Dolphin network data is:

c1'':7,10,14,18,58,1,2,3,4,5,6,7,8,9,11,12,13,16,17,20,23,24,26,27,28,29,31,32,33, 35,36,37,40,41,42,43,44,45.47,48,49,50,51,53,54,55,56,57,59,60,61,62

c2'':52,19,30,46,22,25,4,5,8,9,11,12,13,17,20,23,24,26,27,32,33,36,40,42,45, 47.49.50,51,53,54,56,57,59,60,61,62

The outliers were: 15,22,34,38,39.

5   Results

We tested our algorithm on both of the above datasets: for karate club network the value of total degree of all the nodes/total no. of nodes in the network came out to be 4.588 therefore the value of k = 4. And for Dolphin network, the initial value came out to be 5.129 and hence we took value of k = 5.

We calculated the modularity for the cover that was detected by CPM on karate club network data and it came out to be 0.074 (as shown in Fig. 3). While as for our detected cover for karate club network, it was 0.1008 (as shown in Fig. 4). So we believe that our approach gives optimised values as compared to CPM.

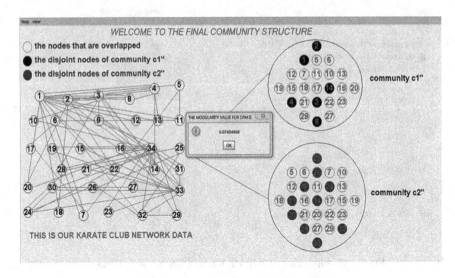

Fig. 3. Modularity value as found by CPM

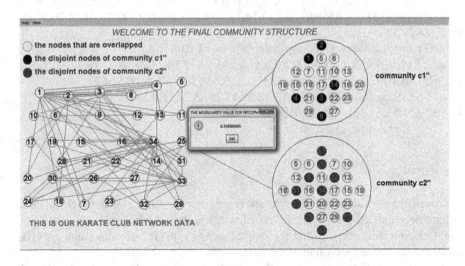

Fig. 4. Modularity value as found by NPCCPM

When we tested the modularity by Nepsuz on the cover detected by CPM on Dolphin network, it came out to be 0.059 and when we applied this measure to our detected cover by NPCCPM, modularity value came out to be 0.076 (shown in Fig. 5). So our approach is healthier than CPM.

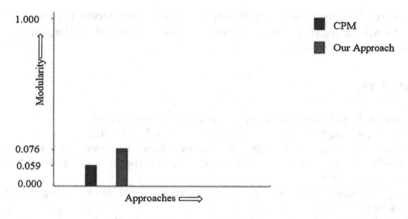

Fig. 5. Comparison of Modularity values as found on Dolphin Network Dataset by CPM and NPCCPM (Our Approach).

We tested the implementation of our algorithm on a variety of other synthetic datasets. As is shown in the graph below (Fig. 6), our results are either better than CPM or are very close to it.

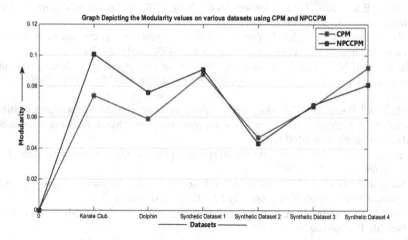

Fig. 6. Modulatory Values as obtained on various datasets using CPM and NPCCPM

6 Conclusion and Future Work

This paper presents a new approach for detecting overlapping communities which encompasses the existing clique percolation method. We made an effort to solve the problem of clique size parameter k by calculating it dynamically in the given network, so that there is no issue in making a choice about its value beforehand. Then the proposed method was used to detect the overlapping communities and it efficiently discovered overlapping communities and assured maximum node coverage for connected networks.

The quality of the community structures was evaluated using modularity measures. In future, we will focus on detecting overlapping evolving community structures in directed and weighted social networks.

References

1. Fortunato, S.: Community detection in graphs. Physics reports (2010)
2. Schaeffer, S.: Graph clustering. Comput. Sci. Rev. **1**(1), 27–64 (2007)
3. Leskovec, J., Lang, K.J., Dasgupta, A., Mahoney, M.W.: Community structure in large networks, Natural cluster sizes and the absence of large well-defined clusters. Internet Math. **6**(1), 29–123 (2009)
4. Yang, J., Leskovec, J.: Defining and evaluating network communities based on ground-truth. In: ICDM 2012 (2012)
5. Granovetter, M.S.: The strength of weak ties. Am. J. Sociol. (1973)
6. Girvan, M., Newman, M.: Community structure in social and biological networks. PNAS **99**(12), 7821–7826 (2002)
7. Newman, M.: Modularity and community structure in networks. PNAS **103**(23), 8577–8582 (2006)
8. Ahn, Y., Bagrow, J.P., Lehmann, S.: Link communities reveal multi-scale complexity in networks. Nature **466**(7307), 761 (2010)
9. Airoldi, E.M., Blei, D.M., Fienberg, S.E., Xing, E.P.: Mixed membership stochastic blockmodels. JMLR **9**, 1981–2014 (2007)
10. Palla, G., Der´enyi, I., Farkas, I., Vicsek, T.: Uncovering the overlapping community structure of complex networks in nature and society. Nature **435**(7043), 814 (2005)
11. Raghavan, U.N., Albert, R., Kumara, S.: Near linear time algorithm to detect community structures in large-scale networks. Phys. Rev. E Stat. Nonlin. Soft Matter Phys. **76**(3), 036106 (2007)
12. Subelj, S., Bajec M.: Unfolding communities in large complex networks: combining defensive and offensive label propagation for core extraction. Phys. Rev. E Stat. Nonlin. Soft Matter Phys. **83**(3), 036103 (2011)
13. Newman, M.E.J., Girvan, M.: Finding and evaluating community structure in networks. Phys. Rev. E **69**(2), 026113 (2004)
14. Shang, R.H., et al.: Community detection based on modularity and an improved genetic algorithm. Phys. a-Stat. Mech. Appl. **392**(5), 1215–1231 (2013)
15. Blondel, V.: Fast unfolding of communities in large networks. J. Stat. Mech: Theory Exp. **2008**(10), P10008 (2008)
16. Shen, H.W., Cheng, X.Q.: Spectral methods for the detection of network community structure: a comparative analysis. J. Stat. Mech: Theory Exp. **2010**(10), P10020 (2010)
17. Jiang, J.Q., Dress, A.W.M., Yang, G.K.: A spectral clustering-based framework for detecting community structures in complex networks. Appl. Math. Lett. **22**(9), 1479–1482 (2009)
18. Rosvall, M., Bergstrom, C.T.: Maps of random walks on complex networks reveal community structure. Natl. Acad. Sci. **105**(4), 1118–1123 (2008)

Financial Time Series Forecasting Using Deep Learning Network

Preeti[⊠], Ankita Dagar, Rajni Bala, and Ram Pal Singh

Department of Computer Science, Deen Dayal Upadhyaya College,
University of Delhi, New Delhi, India
p06p05@gmail.com

Abstract. The analysis of financial time series for predicting the future developments is a challenging problem since past decades. A forecasting technique based upon the machine learning paradigm and deep learning network namely Extreme Learning Machine with Auto-encoder (ELM-AE) has been proposed. The efficacy and effectiveness of ELM-AE has been compared with few existing forecasting methods like Generalized Autoregressive Conditional Heteroskedastcity (GARCH), General Regression Neural Network (GRNN), Multiple Layer Perceptron (MLP), Random Forest (RF) and Group Method of Data Handling (GRDH). Experimental results have been computed on two different time series data that is Gold Price and Crude Oil Price. The results indicate that the implemented model outperforms existing models in terms of qualitative parameters such as mean square error (MSE).

Keywords: Auto-encoder · Deep learning · ELM · Forecasting Time series

1 Introduction

Financial time series [3] are inherently noisy and nonstationary. The nonstationary time series are those where statistical parameters like mean, median, standard deviation changes over a period of time. These characteristics of time series will continuously alter the relationship between the input and output variables. It has been observed in literature that during forecasting recent observations have more impact rather distant observations. The same approach can be considered in forecasting nonstationary time series [14].

Literature survey shows that a number of models have been built upon time series data for forecasting and prediction analysis. The two widely used techniques for time series forecasting are statistical and computational methods. The statistical methods are used by economists for price forecasting studies. The popular time series forecasting techniques include exponential smoothing and autoregressive models like Autoregressive Integrated Moving Average (ARIMA) [10] and GARCH family models [18]. However, recent trend shows that machine learning algorithms have outperformed classical statistical techniques [7]. Among

© Springer Nature Singapore Pte Ltd. 2018
G. C. Deka et al. (Eds.): ICACCT 2018, CCIS 899, pp. 23–33, 2018.
https://doi.org/10.1007/978-981-13-2035-4_3

various machine learning techniques, Support Vector Regression(SVR) and Artificial Neural Network(ANN) [11] have widely been used to forecast the time series data. Oancea [10] has used ANN in forecasting crude oil price data. Another variant of ANN, i.e. Multi-layer Perceptron(MLP) have also been applied on Gold-price and Crude-Oil price data [12]. However, above mentioned methods can easily fall into local minima and it becomes difficult to achieve a global optimal solution. Other than MLP, several other techniques have also been used such as GARCH, GRNN, GMDH and RF for future prediction on time series data [12]. Apart from neural network family models, Kim et al. [8] have studied SVR technique for stock market price prediction. Furthermore, SVR technique with adaptive parameters have been used for financial forecasting and achieved good generalization performance [4]. Since financial time series data is more prone to noise, so modelling this data using SVR could lead to overfitting and uderfitting problems [4].

Recently, Deep learning(DL) [5,15] has gained more attention in pattern recognition, computer vision, natural language processing, bio-informatics and several machine learning fields since it is outperforming on a number of difficult tasks. It is evident from the study of related work that several machine learning techniques have been used for forecasting different time series but very few efforts have been made to study this problem using machine learning technique with deep learning. Kuremoto et al. [9] and Shen et al. [16] used deep belief networks in financial market prediction. However, one of the approach of deep learning namely autoencoders method have rarely been explored for time series prediction. Therefore, this paper focuses on using the combination of autoencoder with one of the machine learning techniques to build a forecasting model.

The remaining paper is structured as follows. In Sect. 2, there is a brief overview of ELM and ELM-Autoencoder with an overview of deep learning. Section 3 describes the proposed algorithm along with the description of financial time series data. In Sect. 4, experimental results have been presented and discussed. Finally, conclusions and future perspective of paper is discussed in Sect. 5.

2   Brief Theories About ELM and Auto-Encoder

This section presents an overview about the basics of Extreme Learning Machine and ELM Auto-encoder.

2.1   Extreme Learning Machine

Extreme learning machine (ELM) is an efficient learning method proposed to train single layer feed-forward neural networks (SLFNs) [6]. SLFN is a feed-forward neural network with single hidden layer connecting input layer to output layer. For past decades, Back-Propagation (BP) algorithm based upon gradient descent has been used for training SLFN. However, gradient descent based learning methods are usually very slow due to iterative learning. These algorithms might not always converge to global minima. Because of these issues in learning algorithms of feed-forward neural network, they might not lead to better generalized solution. Unlike these traditional learning algorithms, ELM trains SLFN by chossing input weights and hidden layer biases arbitrarily. So, there will not be any iterative tuning of parameters. After choosing input weights and hidden layer biases randomly, SLFN can be considered as a linear system. Then the output weights of SLFN can be determined through simple generalized inverse operation of the output matrix obtained from hidden layer.

Given a training set with N number of random samples $S = \{(x_i, t_i) \mid x_i = [x_{i1}, \cdots, x_{in}]^T \in \mathbb{R}^n,\ t_i = [t_{i1}, \cdots, t_{im}]^T \in \mathbb{R}^m,\ i = 1,\ 2,\ \cdots,\ N\}$, ELM is mathematically modeled as [6]

$$\sum_{i=1}^{\tilde{N}} \beta_i g(x_j) = \sum_{i=1}^{\tilde{N}} \beta_i g(w_i \cdot x_j + b_i) = o_j, j = 1, \cdots, N \qquad (1)$$

where $w_i = [w_{i1}, \cdots, w_{in}]^T$ is the weight vector which connects input layer and hidden layer, n is number of features, m is the number of classes, $\tilde{N}$ represents number of hidden nodes and $g(x)$ is the activation function (infinitely differentiable). In this study, radial basis function (RBF) has been used as the activation function. The steps used by ELM for training SLFN are as follows:

1. For $i = 1,\ 2,\ \cdots,\ \tilde{N}$, input weights w_i and biases b_i are chosen randomly and fixed.
2. In the nextstep, the hidden layer output matrix of neural network denoted by H is computed as follows

$$H(w_1, \cdots, w_{\tilde{N}}, b_1, \cdots, b_N, x_1, \cdots, x_N) =$$
$$\begin{bmatrix} g(w_1 \cdot x_1 + b_1) & \cdots & g(w_{\tilde{N}} \cdot x_1 + b_{\tilde{N}}) \\ \vdots & \cdots & \vdots \\ g(w_1 \cdot x_N + b_1) & \cdots & g(w_{\tilde{N}} \cdot x_N + b_{\tilde{N}}) \end{bmatrix}_{N \times \tilde{N}} \qquad (2)$$

where, the ith column of H is the output of ith hidden node with respect to inputs $x_1, x_2, \cdots, x_N$.
3. The output weight vector β connecting hidden nodes and output nodes is calculated using $\beta = H^\dagger T$ where $T = [t_{i1}, \cdots, t_{im}]^T$ and $H^\dagger$ is the Moore Penrose generalized inverse of matrix H [13].

2.2 Auto-Encoder

Artificial neural network with deep architecture has become a powerful tool to represent the high level abstract features of high dimensional data. Based on the concept of ELM, the extreme learning machine with auto-encoder (ELM-AE) [17] is proposed as an unsupervised learning algorithm. The aim of an auto-encoder is to learn new encoding for set of data using deep learning architecture. The basic idea of ELM-AE is consist of two stage process. Given a dataset

$X = [x_1^T, x_2^T, \cdots, x_N^T]$ where, N represents the number of samples. In the first stage, n_i number of input features of original data are mapped onto n_h number of hidden neurons. Now, depending upon the size of n_i and n_h, three different architectures of ELM-AE are possible: (1) compressed architecture, where $n_i > n_h$ (2) equal dimension architecture, $n_i = n_h$ (3) sparse architecture, $n_i < n_h$. The mapping of input x_i with n_i number of features to a n_h dimensional space is calculated as follows:

$$h(x_i) = g(a^T x_i + b) \tag{3}$$

where $h(x_i) \in \mathbb{R}^h$ is the hidden layer output vector with respect to x_i, a and b are input weight matrix and baises of hidden units respectively, and function $g(\cdot)$ represents an activation function which can be any non differentiable or piecewise continuous function. Finally, the output vector of auto-encoder can be calculated using

$$f(x_i) = h(x_i)^T \beta, i = 1, 2, ..., N \tag{4}$$

In the second stage of ELM-AE, the weight vector of output layer that is β is computed by minimizing the error loss function. The closed-form solution to calculate β is as follows:

$$\beta = (H^T H + I_{n_h}/C)^{-1} H^T X \tag{5}$$

where C is a regularization factor that is a penalty coefficient on the training error. Now given the original data X, new enriched data X_{new} which is the representation of X in n_h dimensional space can be obtained as $X_{new} = X\beta^T$. Further, this X_{new} dataset is used to build a model using ELM for forecasting time series.

3   Proposed Methodology

The framework followed to forecast time series data is depicted in Fig. 1. It shows the several stages followed as a flow chart to predict the forecast value of a time series.

The step-by-step procedure for forecasting financial time series using the proposed ELM-AE is described as follows. Let $Y = (y_1, y_2, \cdots, y_k, y_{k+1}, \cdots, y_N)$ be the set of N observations of a financial series recorded at time $t = (1, 2, \cdots, k, k+1, \cdots, N)$ respectively. Then the output variable that is label can be forecasted as follows:

1. Consider a memory order $M = 3$. Memory order M denotes the number of previous values on which current time t_{cur} value that is y_{cur} is dependent. Formulate the data having M number of input features and an output

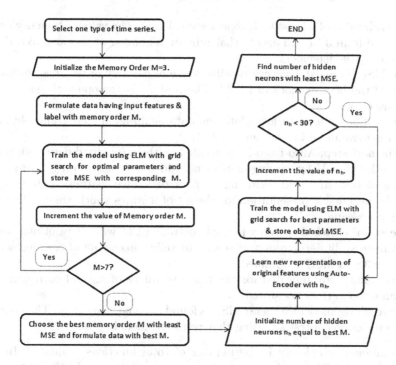

Fig. 1. System flow for forecasting financial time series.

variable/label. Where, y_{M+1} is dependent upon previous M number of series records. The exact formulation of data using given Y series is as follows:

$$
\begin{bmatrix}
 & Input features & & & Label \\
y_1 & y_2 & \cdots & y_M & y_{M+1} \\
y_2 & y_3 & \cdots & y_{M+1} & y_{M+2} \\
y_3 & y_4 & \cdots & y_{M+2} & y_{M+3} \\
\vdots & \vdots & \cdots & \vdots & \vdots \\
y_{N-M} & y_{N-M-1} & \cdots & y_{N-1} & y_N
\end{bmatrix}_{(N-M)\times(M+1)}
\tag{6}
$$

2. Normalize the obtained data in Eq. 6 in the range of [0,1]. This transformation of data is required to avoid differences in the smallest and largest value of a time series dataset.
3. The normalized dataset is divided into 80/20 partitions of training and test set respectively. Extreme learning machine algorithm is applied to obtain a model using training set. While, developing a forecasting model using ELM, a grid search has been performed to obtain the best set of values for parameters, i.e. number of hidden neurons and radial function parameter. The grid-search is performed for number of hidden neurons = $\{1,3,\cdots,99,101\}$ and activation function parameter = $\{2^{-6}, 2^{-5}, \cdots, 2^0, 2^1\}$. The obtained model is tested on test set.

4. For each value of $M = 4$ to 7, repeat steps 1 to 3. The value of memory order is varied from 3 to 7 to denote that minimum number of previous records on which y_{cur} is dependent.
5. The MSE obtained for every possible value of memory order M is compared to find the best memory order M. The best M is the one with least mean square error.
6. The best M is used to formulate the data again as in step 1 and obtained data is normalized in the range of $[0, 1]$.
7. In the next step, Auto-Encoder is applied on the normalized data with memory order best M by varying number of hidden neurons n_h ranging from the value of best M to 30. With n_h number of hidden neurons, auto-encoder results into new representation for the set of features which are used for further processing.
8. The set of enriched features is used to train ELM with the optimal set of parameters obtained from grid search to yeild forecasting of training set as in step 3 and MSE is obtained.
9. Step 7 and 8 are repeated for the range of values of n_h and corresponding mean square errors are stored.
10. The resultant model with least MSE is found at some value of n_h. Then obtain the predictions of test set using that resultant model.

Computational complexity is the number of total functions evaluated. In the proposed ELM-AE algorithm, two stage process is followed. In the first stage, autoencoder is applied whose running time is $O(mN)$, where m is the random subspace of features and N is number of training instances. Second stage includes ELM algorithm with grid searching for optimal set of parameters which takes $O(mN)$. Therefore, the total computational complexity of ELM-AE is $O(mN)$.

4   Experimental Design

In this section, there is a brief description about the various datasets used for experiments and the performance measures used for evaluation of proposed model.

4.1   Datasets Description

The datasets used for experiments are based on daily US Dollar (USD) exchange rates with respect to two different prices namely Gold and Crude Oil Price. These two datasets have been used for testing the effectiveness of proposed forecasting model. The Gold price data is obtained from [1] and Crude-Oil price data is obtained from [2]. The total number of observations in Gold-Price data are 12,630 and in Crude-Oil Price data are 7760. Each of the dataset is partitioned into both 80% Training set and 20% Test set respectively. So for Gold-Price dataset the number of records in training set are 10,104 and in test set are 2,526. And correspondingly for Crude-Oil price dataset, the partition is 6,208 and 1,552 respectively.

4.2   Data Pre-Processing

The Gold-Price data and Crude-Oil price data used for the study are pre-processed before using them with proposed model. The two major pre-processing steps performed are as follows:

1. Phase Space Reconstruction: The original time series data y is just a single column representing its closing value for time t. Where, $Y = (y_1, y_2, \cdots, y_k, y_{k+1}, \cdots, y_N)$ be the set of N number of observations at time $t = (1, 2, \cdots, k, k+1, \cdots, N)$ respectively. In this phase, the original data is converted into a set of input features given a memory order M and a label. This obtained dataset is used for further processing.
2. Normalization: Since different time series dataset may have different range of values. So after phase space reconstruction, obtained data is normalized in the range of $[0, 1]$. This normalized data is used further for training a model and to test it.

4.3   Performance Measures Used

Among several performance measures, Mean Squared Error (MSE) is the one that can be used to evaluate the performance of proposed model on time series data. It is defined as in Eq. 7

$$MSE = \frac{\sum_{i=1}^{N}(y_t - \tilde{y}_t)^2}{N} \tag{7}$$

where, N represents the total number of forecasts obtained, y_t and $\tilde{y}_t$ are actual and forecasted values at time t respectively. The MSE (see Eq. 7) measures the average of the squares of the errors or deviations from true value. It is basically the difference between estimator and estimated. MSE is useful to measure accuracy for a continuous variable. So lesser the mean square error better is the model.

5   Results and Discussion

In the previous section, we discussed about the experimental design of proposed method. This section presents the dataset-wise results obtained and discusses them.

5.1   Gold Price(USD)

At first, ELM-AE is analyzed on gold price dataset. The proposed method ELM-AE based on ELM technique is sensitive towards user defined parameter - number of hidden neurons. Figure 2 depicts the MSE obtained while predicting Gold-Price on test dataset with different number of hidden neurons. For a particular number of hidden neurons, the depicted MSE is the MSE obtained by taking average of MSE of 20 executions. As shown in Fig. 2, the minimum MSE 0.000015 for Gold Price data is obtained with 15 hidden neurons and memory order 5. Table 1 presents MSE values obtained by using different forecasting models including GARCH, MLP, GRNN, GMDH, RF, ELM and ELM-AE for both training set and test set of Gold Price (USD) dataset. It can be observed from Table 1 that our proposed models are better than other models presented in terms of MSE. Also, among the two different forecasting methods used in this study, obtained MSE with ELM-AE for test set is better than ELM method. The actual gold price index and predicted values obtained from ELM-AE model is illustrated in Fig. 3. It can be observed that the predicted value of gold price time series is very much close to its actual value. It shows the deep learning based method for time series forecasting has good predicting capability.

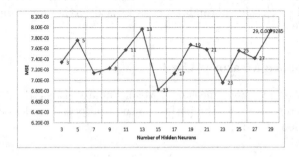

Fig. 2. MSE obtained for Gold Price data

Table 1. Comparison of results for Gold-Price data using proposed and other models

Method	Training set MSE	Test set MSE
GARCH [12]	0.000565	0.001100
MLP [12]	0.001800	0.003200
GRNN [12]	0.000451	0.000918
GMDH [12]	0.000452	0.000903
RF [12]	0.000498	0.001100
ELM	0.0000186	0.0000158
ELM-AE	0.0000192	**0.0000150**

5.2   Crude-Oil Price(USD)

The performance of proposed method ELM-AE is also evaluated on Crude-Oil price dataset. The proposed model was run for different number of hidden neurons. The MSE obtained while forecasting Crude-Oil Price test dataset with different number of hidden neurons is depicted in Fig. 4. The depicted MSE

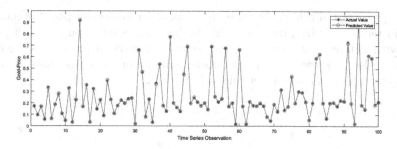

Fig. 3. Predictions of test set of Gold Price series data.

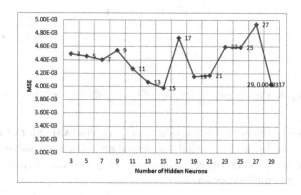

Fig. 4. MSE obtained for Crude-Oil Price data

in Fig. 4 is the average of MSE of 20 runs and minimum MSE 0.0000465 is obtained at 29 number of hidden neurons and memory order 3. Table 2 presents MSE values obtained by using different forecasting models including GARCH, MLP, GRNN, GMDH, RF, ELM and ELM-AE for both training set and test set of Crude-Oil Price (USD) dataset. It can be observed from Table 2, the two

Table 2. Comparision of results for Crude-Oil Price data using proposed and other models

Method	Training set MSE	Test set MSE
GARCH [12]	0.003527	0.002351
MLP [12]	0.005400	0.002700
GRNN [12]	0.002100	0.001800
GMDH [12]	0.002700	0.001800
RF [12]	0.003500	0.002000
ELM	0.00005263	0.00005561
ELM-AE	0.00005631	**0.00004651**

models presented in this study are better than other models proposed in related work in terms of MSE. Since, autoencoder has been applied on crude-oil price data with different number of hidden neurons to retrieve the enriched set of features. Also, it shows that the parameter number of hidden neurons used by autoencoder plays an important role in forecasting.

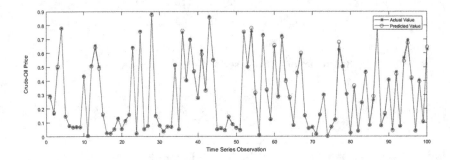

Fig. 5. Predictions of test set of crude oil price series data

Figure 5 depicts the actual price value and predicted value for crude-oil series data. It can be seen in the Fig. 5 that the actual and predicted values of crude-oil data are very close to each other. This shows that the prediction capability of proposed ELM-AE method is good.

6   Conclusion

The main aim of this paper was to study the deep learning based technique for time series prediction. This paper proposed an autoencoder based ELM algorithm, ELM-AE to forecast different time series data. The experiments have been performed on two different financial time series i.e. Gold-Price (USD) and Crude-Oil Price (USD). It is observed that the proposed ELM-AE yielded statistically significant results compared to other forecasting models such as GARCH, MLP, GRNN, GMDH and RF on two time series datasets in terms of MSE. The spectacular performance of ELM-AE is due to the presence of a deep learning approach that is autoencoder before ELM algorithm, which yeilded enriched set of features used for further modeling. The proposed model ELM-AE based on auto-encoder provides quiet promising results in forecasting. The obtained results outperform the other methods which indicate its further use in forecasting other financial or non financial time series.

References

1. http://www.quandl.com/LBMA/GOLD-Gold-Price-London-Fixing
2. http://www.quandl.com/data/FRED/DCOILBRENTEU-Crude-Oil-Prices-Brent-Europe

3. Abu-Mostafa, Y.S., Atiya, A.F.: Introduction to financial forecasting. Appl. Intell. **6**(3), 205–213 (1996)
4. Cao, L.J., Tay, F.E.H.: Support vector machine with adaptive parameters in financial time series forecasting. IEEE Trans. Neural Netw. **14**(6), 1506–1518 (2003)
5. Hinton, G.E., Salakhutdinov, R.R.: Reducing the dimensionality of data with neural networks. Science **313**(5786), 504–507 (2006)
6. Huang, G.B., Zhu, Q.Y., Siew, C.K.: Extreme learning machine: theory and applications. Neurocomputing **70**(1), 489–501 (2006)
7. Karia, A.A., Bujang, I., Ismail, A.: Forecasting on crude palm oil prices using artificial intelligence approaches. Am. J. Oper. Res. **3**(2), 259 (2013)
8. Kim, K.J.: Financial time series forecasting using support vector machines. Neurocomputing **55**(1), 307–319 (2003)
9. Kuremoto, T., Kimura, S., Kobayashi, K., Obayashi, M.: Time series forecasting using a deep belief network with restricted boltzmann machines. Neurocomputing **137**, 47–56 (2014)
10. Oancea, B., Ciucu, Ş.C.: Time series forecasting using neural networks. arXiv preprint arXiv:1401.1333 (2014)
11. Parisi, A., Parisi, F., Díaz, D.: Forecasting gold price changes: rolling and recursive neural network models. J. Multinational Financ. Manag. **18**(5), 477–487 (2008)
12. Pradeepkumar, D., Ravi, V.: Forecasting financial time series volatility using particle swarm optimization trained quantile regression neural network. Appl. Soft Comput. **58**, 35–52 (2017)
13. Rao, C.R., Mitra, S.K.: Generalized inverse of matrices and its applications (1971)
14. Refenes, A., Bentz, Y., Bunn, D.W., Burgess, A.N., Zapranis, A.D.: Financial time series modelling with discounted least squares backpropagation. Neurocomputing **14**(2), 123–138 (1997)
15. Schmidhuber, J.: Deep learning in neural networks: an overview. Neural Netw. **61**, 85–117 (2015)
16. Shen, F., Chao, J., Zhao, J.: Forecasting exchange rate using deep belief networks and conjugate gradient method. Neurocomputing **167**, 243–253 (2015)
17. Sun, K., Zhang, J., Zhang, C., Hu, J.: Generalized extreme learning machine autoencoder and a new deep neural network. Neurocomputing **230**, 374–381 (2017)
18. Zhang, G.P.: Time series forecasting using a hybrid arima and neural network model. Neurocomputing **50**, 159–175 (2003)

MapReduce Based Analysis of Sample Applications Using Hadoop

Mohd Rehan Ghazi[✉] and N. S. Raghava[✉]

Department of Electronics and Communication Engineering,
Delhi Technological University, Delhi, India
er.rehan.aras@gmail.com, nsraghava@dce.ac.in

Abstract. The rate of increase of structured, semi-structured and unstructured data is very high. To discover hidden information from different types of data is a big challenge. The two techniques, word frequency count and string matching, are applied on a single node and multi node cluster with an input data set. The results are analyzed and compared by varying MapReduce configuration of both. In this paper we have tested that for a MapReduce job how changing the number of mappers and reducers can significantly affect performance. Further, it is analyzed how Hadoop invokes number of mappers/reducers depending upon the input size and Hadoop Distributed File System (HDFS) block size. The outcome of research analysis for heterogeneous cluster configurations indicates the prospective of the framework, as well as of mappers and reducers that affect its performance.

Keywords: Big data · Cloud computing · Hadoop · HDFS · MapReduce

1 Introduction

Storing, processing, analyzing and examining huge amount of data has been a concern for a long time. If we look at all data created since the beginning of civilization up through the year 2003, it equals roughly 7 Exabytes. Today the data generated is 9.6 Exabytes on a daily basis. The rate of increase of data from different sources like e-mails, business, blogs, scientific data, etc., is very high. Processing, analyzing and Examining this enormous amount of data to extract some beneficial and valuable information there is a need and demand of setting up of storage clusters and data-intensive applications [1, 2]. Big data analytics is becoming progressively noteworthy in a variety of applications or research areas ranging from extricating business intelligence to analyze, examine and process data. Mapreduce programming model, with its scale-out architecture, is proficient in handling Big data-intensive analytic tasks and its capability to process data by multi-node clusters in a parallel manner is exceptional [3, 4]. Crucial requirements of high availability, scalability, load balancing and distribution of data, parallel processing, and fault tolerance is handled and overcome by Google after introducing the concept of Mapreduce programming model [5, 6]. MapReduce implementation on Hadoop cluster provides an advantage in processing huge amount of data in a parallel manner along with auto partition of data, distribution of data between nodes of

© Springer Nature Singapore Pte Ltd. 2018
G. C. Deka et al. (Eds.): ICACCT 2018, CCIS 899, pp. 34–44, 2018.
https://doi.org/10.1007/978-981-13-2035-4_4

a cluster, fault tolerance and load balancing management which finally results in scalable, efficient and reliable computing approach.

Mapreduce programming model and its implementation on Apache Hadoop cluster is a framework for distributed computing in scalable, reliable and parallel manner. Rather than relying on expensive systems and costly hardware for storing and processing raw data, Apache Hadoop provides efficient parallel processing of Big data [7, 8]. This immense and fast growth rate of raw data posed challenges on big corps like Facebook, WhatsApp, Google, Amazon, and Yahoo. These companies and organizations need to carry out petabytes and terabytes of raw data regularly to handle demands and deduce queries from their customers. Existing and traditional applications, software and tools are incapable to process, analyze, examine and extract some beneficial and valuable information from raw data. Apache Hadoop, with the help of its advantages, explains and answers the problem by extracting beneficial and valuable information from the enormous amount of raw data [3, 9]. Many universities, enterprises and industries works on distributed and parallel computing but for a novice of Big data and its storing, processing and analysis is not a cake walk as it wants much efforts to manage due to insufficient money and inexperience to invest in supercomputers. So it is crucial to utilize limited resources in an efficient and effective manner [10, 11]. Latency is minimized out of the Hadoop multi-node clusters wherever and whenever possible. Storage is one of the first places for latency that can be discovered and disposed of, which is why Hadoop bring the compute closer to the Data Node by using direct attached storage.

The rest of the paper is systematized as follows. Section 2 narrates the Problems overcome by Hadoop. The contribution this paper is mentioned in Sect. 3 and Sect. 4 describes implementation details and results by considering two different objectives. Section 5 presents the comparative study of the single and multi-node cluster by varying MapReduce cluster configuration. Finally, the conclusion is presented in Sect. 6.

2 Problems Overcome by Hadoop

When an enterprise needs to process a huge amount of unstructured, semi-structured and structured data per day by exploiting existing or traditional resources, it would be like hauling an elephant over a thread. The existing network would be flooded, batch processing would take weeks to complete the work of hours, the hard disks latency will increase the overhead and therefore the consequences will be harmful to the overall cost. Sometimes existing or traditional approach can be able to maintain the system architecture but how many times it will be altered and modified to the non-linear scalar solution to balance with the race of growing data.

Hence, the First problem comes in size of data, big data have increased up to terabytes and processing of this big data is not under the capability of existing or traditional systems. The second problem comes from prolonging failure and cluster growth i.e., in multi-node clusters, many nodes fail every day while storing or executing the task along with the cluster size is also not fixed and sometimes not planned also and cluster size should grow easily as the rate of Big data is increasing. The third problem is the overhead in data transportation i.e., from the location where the data is stored to its processing location, in between, there are several latencies are present which includes hard disk latency, congested network latency, etc.

For all the above-mentioned problems there is a solution available known as Hadoop distributed file system and Hadoop MapReduce i.e., the core of Apache Hadoop. For the first problem, HDFS and MapReduce distribute and parallelize the processing which means that instead of spending 10 days in order to process 200 TB of enterprise data by the only single system, the enterprise should use Hadoop cluster which dives the task and finish the tasks in hours or minutes. In Hadoop processing and input data can be scaled linearly by Hadoop over a set of low-cost commodity hardware and as the number of nodes increases the execution times can be reduced to half or less. Solution to the second problem is fault tolerance of Hadoop and its high scalability. HDFS and MapReduce have a flexible maintenance and its service availability keeps up automatically with its cluster size. So, Hadoop provides distributed storage and parallel processing power with perfect linear scalability. Hadoop tolerates faults at different levels from network to storage by accomplishing replication. For the third problem, the solution provided by the Hadoop is Data Locality which means that instead of carrying or transferring input data to application processing logic, Hadoop caries processing logic to the input data location as processing logic is comparatively much lesser in size as compared to input data to avoid latency and congestions.

3   Contribution

The contribution of this paper is to adapt the clustering method to Map and Reduce using Apache Hadoop. Two different methods have been deployed here for implementing word frequency technique and string matching using MapReduce. By clustering Hadoop using ten computers, the task execution time decreased by 85% compared to a single computer. Copy input to HDFS time, however, increases when applying Hadoop Cluster because Data Node is on every slave node and input is copied and replicated on every separate Data Node with a block size of 64 Mb. The results indicate that the high performance is achieved by combining ten separate Hadoop single node cluster and forming multi-node Hadoop cluster of ten nodes.

By controlling the number of Reducers in MapReduce, the execution time may be increased but the fault tolerance increases as if any reducer fails one can simply handle the failure. The number of mappers is set to one per HDFS block i.e., for one 64 Mb block there is one mapper because the number of map tasks for a particular task depends on the number of input splits. Thus, for 280 MB of input data and have 64 Mb HDFS block size, there will be 5 mappers.

4   Implementation Details and Results

The plan is to first execute the two applications on a single node cluster with some input data size and then the results will be checked, analyzed and compared throughout the experiments on the multi node Hadoop cluster. For a MapReduce job, changing the number of Map tasks and/or Reduce tasks can significantly affect performance, because those two settings are directly associated with the amount of cluster resources used in a job. Performance can suffer whether there is an allocation of too many resources or too few. The hurdle encountered here is how to manage the number or instances of reducer tasks launched by Hadoop's Map Reduce since it is automatically initiated and also analyze that how Hadoop invokes number of mappers depending upon the input size and HDFS block size on both single and multi-node cluster.

4.1 First Objective

First objective is to run these two applications: Word Frequency Count and String Matching on a single node cluster to analyze the ratio of their CPU execution time while managing the number or instances of reducers of Hadoop Map Reduce.

4.1.1 Setup

The single node Hadoop cluster is set up for the experiment to be carried out on a laptop for sequential execution of word frequency count and String Matching. The laptop has Intel i3 CPU running at a clock rate of 2.27 GHz with 3 GB RAM and 320 GB of the hard drive. The Hadoop and Oracle Java were installed on Linux Ubuntu 12.04 LTS; secure shell protocol (SSH) is appropriately configured as it is used by Hadoop to connect its nodes.

4.1.2 Applications

The first application is Word Frequency Count. In this, Input text files present in HDFS and Word Frequency Count Algorithm with the help of MapReduce reads these files and counts how frequently a particular word occurs generally separated by a tab/space. Input provided and output received is in text format. Each line in a text format is provided to the mapper and mapper breaks each line to words. For each word, key/value pair is generated and reducer sums the count for each word. At last single key/value pair is again generated with that particular word and sums. As a part of optimization, the reducer, on the map outputs, is also exploited as a combiner.

The second application is String Matching. The String Matching MapReduce application on Hadoop counts how often a particular matched string or regular expression is there in a file. Actually, it is the duty of mapper to count how often string appears in a single line and the reducers job is just to sum up the values. The String Matching application input will always a regular expression only and Hadoop will automatically generate number of mappers which are equal to the number of input splits. The Map Reduce operation is in two steps as shown in a Fig. 1 below.

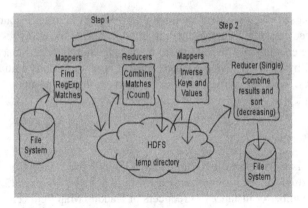

Fig. 1. String matching scenario [12]

4.1.3 Results

In Word frequency count application, allocating different and random and number of reduce tasks i.e., 1, 3, 6, and 12 to count all the words in a text file. The input was multiple textbooks together form a single text file near about 270 MB so Hadoop chooses 5 instances of mapper tasks while considering the HDFS block size and the number of input splits. This is the sequential Word Frequency count as it is on single node Hadoop cluster.

In String matching application, allocating different and random and number of instances of reducer tasks i.e., 1, 3, 6, and 12 but always the same string is searched for: "the". The input is multiple textbooks together form a single text file near about 270 MB so Hadoop chooses 5 instances of mapper tasks while considering the HDFS block size and the number of input splits. This is the sequential string matching as on single node Hadoop cluster (Fig. 2) (Table 1).

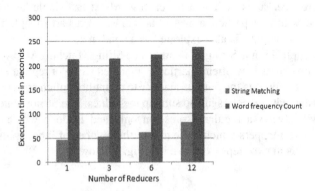

Fig. 2. Results of String Matching and Word frequency count on single node

Table 1. Result of experiments on single node

Application	Number of reducers	Execution time in seconds
String matching	1	47.5
	3	54.1
	6	62.5
	12	83.8
Word frequency count	1	213.9
	3	215.2
	6	222.6
	12	238.2

Result of experiment, on single node, of word frequency count and string matching represents that as the number of reducers increases the execution time of each experiment increases while size of input file remains the same in all cases and number of mappers invokes depend upon the input file split and HDFS block size. When searching for a particular string or regular expression takes less time compared to count all the words in a text input file. The impact of assigning more number of reducers, which results in increasing the execution time, is high in string matching compared to the case of word frequency count. In String matching the execution time almost doubled as the number of reducers changes from 1 to 12 while in the case of word frequency count the impact is comparatively less.

4.2 Second Objective

The second objective is to take benefit of the foregoing experiment on the single node Hadoop cluster in order to improve and optimize Hadoop cluster configuration for the multi node Hadoop cluster. Ultimately, the goal is to get better and preferable result as compared to single node Hadoop cluster.

4.2.1 Setup

To run the experiments, a Hadoop cluster of ten computers is set up in the university lab, each computer comprised of Intel i5 processor of 2.90 GHz and 4 GB ram with 500 GB hard drive. Ubuntu 12.04 LTS is used as an operating system on all PCs and all the computer are interconnected using a switch. Later, Hadoop is installed in a fully distributed mode in every single computer and cluster is configured as shown in Fig. 3 below:

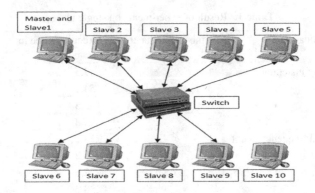

Fig. 3. Hadoop Cluster of 10 nodes

Steps followed to set up a multi node Hadoop cluster includes:

1. Install Hadoop in each computer with Ubuntu 12.04 LTS operating system as a single node Hadoop cluster.
2. Each node in the cluster has its own IP address. Now, this unique value of IP address is added in the hosts file of each node of the cluster.
3. Open SSH is used to give permission to the master node so that it can access all the other nine nodes of the cluster: This is accomplished by replicating the master node's public SSH key to the slaves.
4. The "master" and "slaves" files in hadoop folder are revised and the hostnames of the nodes are included.
5. Now, the following configuration is defined on the master node:
    i. The hostname of the master node "hadoop1" added to "masters" file of the hadoop folder.
    ii. host names of the slave nodes added to "slaves" file of the hadoop folder; which were "hadoop1" to "hadoop10".
6. The configurations of the cluster modified as now it is no longer known as "localhost" but rather as "hadoop1"; the changes were reflected across the files on all the ten nodes of the cluster.
7. Finally, the nodes of the cluster are started, from the master node (hadoop1) using two scripts: "start-dfs.sh" to start HDFS processes, and "start-mapred.sh" to start the Map Reduce processes.

4.2.2   Results

In String matching application, allocating different and random and number of instances of reducer tasks i.e., 1, 3, 6, and 12 but always the same string is searched for: "the". The input is multiple textbooks together form a single text file near about 270 MB so Hadoop chooses 5 instances of mapper tasks while considering the HDFS block size and the number of input splits. This is the parallel string matching as on multi-node Hadoop cluster (Table 2).

Table 2. Results of experiments on multinode

Application	Number of reducers	Exec. time (sec)
String matching	1	20.8
	3	24.6
	6	31.4
	12	41
Word frequency count	1	91
	3	91.6
	6	97.4
	12	104

In Word frequency count application, allocating different and random and number of reduce tasks i.e., 1, 3, 6, and 12 to count all the words in a text file. The input was multiple textbooks together form a single text file near about 270 MB so Hadoop chooses 5 instances of mapper tasks while considering the HDFS block size and the number of input splits. This is the parallel Word Frequency count as on multi-node Hadoop cluster (Fig. 4).

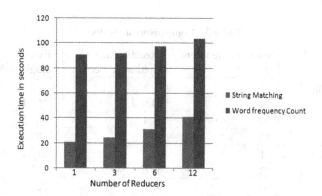

Fig. 4. Result of execution time on multi-node

Result of experiment, on multi node, of word frequency count and string matching represents that as the number of reducers increases the execution time of each experiment increases while size of input file remains the same in all cases and number of mappers invokes depend upon the input file split and HDFS block size. When searching for a particular string or regular expression takes less time compared to count all the words in a text input file. The impact of assigning more number of reducers, which results in increasing the execution time, is high in string matching compared to the case of word frequency count. In String matching the execution time almost doubled as the number of reducers changes from 1 to 12 while in the case of word frequency count the impact is comparatively less.

5 Comparative Study of Single Node and Multi-node Cluster

The overall results of the String matching and word frequency count application with different number of reducers are compared are shown in the Fig. 5 and Table 3 below-

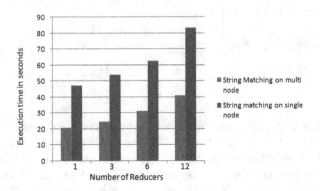

Fig. 5. Comparison of Results of execution time

Table 3. Comparison of results

Application	Number of reducers	Execution time on Multi-node (sec)	Execution time on Single node (sec)
String matching	1	20.8	47.5
	3	24.6	54.1
	6	31.4	62.5
	12	41	83.8
Word frequency count	1	91	213.9
	3	91.6	215.2
	6	97.4	222.6
	12	104	238.2

5.1 String Matching

After examining the String matching application concerning the number of reducers; the right level of parallelism is achieved by executing a program on a multi-node cluster. Figure 6 below basically shows execution time comparison, by changing the numbers of reducers, of string matching on single node and multi-node Hadoop cluster.

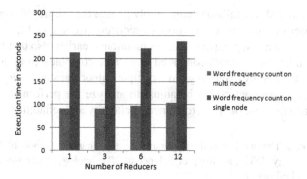

Fig. 6. Comparison of Results of execution time

Comparing the execution time, as the number of reducers increases, of string matching on single node and on multi node the execution time, in each case, increases, while size of input file remains the same in all cases and number of mappers invokes depend upon the input file split and HDFS block size. Assigning different number of reducers results in increasing the execution time is more in string matching. In String matching the execution time almost doubled as the number of reducers changes from 1 to 12.

5.2 Word Frequency Count

After examining the word frequency count application concerning the number of reducers; the right level of parallelism is achieved by executing a program on a multi-node cluster. Figure below basically shows execution time comparison, by changing the numbers of reducers, of word frequency count on single node and multi-node Hadoop cluster.

Comparing the execution time, as the number of reducers increases, of word frequency count on single node and on multi node, the execution time, in each case, increases while size of input file remains the same in all cases and number of mappers invokes depend upon the input file split and HDFS block size. Assigning different number of reducers results in increasing the execution time is more in word frequency count.

6 Conclusion

This paper shows how to operate, manage, process and analyze structured, semi-structured and unstructured data by exploiting word count and string matching applications on Hadoop by varying MapReduce configuration. Traditional and existing computing paradigms have many limitations and also it increases the cost of managing and processing data in an efficient way. To overcome these limitations Hadoop uses MapReduce and HDFS computing model. Our approach in this paper also described how Hadoop is used to achieve scalability and fault tolerance. By controlling the number of Reducers in MapReduce, the execution time may be increased but the fault tolerance increases as if any reducer fails one can simply handle the failure. In word frequency count, the impact of changing the number of reducers, from 1 to 12, is quite less as compared to string matching experiment. As mentioned earlier also that by clustering, execution time decreased by 85% compared to a single computer. In future the experiment may be elaborated by exploiting more complex algorithms on Hadoop cluster and other configuration parameters can be adjust to analyze the performance of Hadoop cluster in order to increase the fault tolerance, scalability and reliability.

Acknowledgement. This work was made possible by the financial support of Department of Science & Technology (DST), Ministry of Science and Technology, Government of India, in terms of Research Fellowship.

References

1. Hansen, C.A.: Optimizing Hadoop for the cluster, Institute for Computer Science. University of Troms, Norway 2012
2. Shelly and Raghava N.S.: Iris recognition on hadoop: a biometrics system implementation on cloud computing. In: Proceedings of IEEE CCIS, pp. 482–485, 15 September 2011
3. Benslimane, Z., Liu, Q., Hongming, Z.: Predicting hadoop parameters. In: Proceedings of the Second International Conference on Advances in Electronics and Electrical Engineering (AEEE), Seek digital library, IRED Headquarters, Santa Barbara, California USA, pp. 63–67, 6 April 2013
4. Dean, J., Ghemawat, S.: Mapreduce: simplified data processing on large clusters. In: OSDI 2004: Proceedings of the 6th Conference on Symposium on Operating Systems Design & Implementation, USENIX Association, Berkeley, CA, USA, vol. 51(1), pp. 107–113, 4 November 2004
5. Ghemawat, S., Gobioff, H., Leung, S.T.: The google file system. In: Proceedings of the 19th ACM Symposium on Operating Systems Principles, Lake George, New York, USA, vol. 37(5), pp. 29–43, 10 February 2003
6. Lam, C.: Introducing Hadoop. In: Hadoop in Action, MANNING (2011)
7. Londhe, P.D., Kumbhar, S.S., Sul, R.S., Khadse, A.J.: Processing big data using hadoop framework. In: Proceedings of 4th SARC-IRF International Conference, New Delhi, India, pp. 72–75, 27 April 2014
8. Ghazi, M.R., Gangodkar, D.: Hadoop, MapReduce and HDFS: a developers perspective. Procedia Comput. Sci. **48**, 45–50 (2015)
9. Wottrich, K., Bressoud, T.: The performance characteristics of mapreduce applications on scalable clusters. In: Proceedings of the Midstates Conference on Undergraduate Research in Computer Science and Mathematics (MCURCSM), Denison University, Granville, USA, November 2011
10. Rao, B.T., Sridevi, N.V., Reddy, V.K., Reddy, L.S.S.: Performance issues of heterogeneous hadoop clusters in cloud computing. Global J. Comput. Sci. Technol. **11**(8), 81–87 May 2011
11. Elsayed, A., Ismail, O., El-Sharkawi, M.E.: MapReduce: state-of-the-art and research directions. Int. J. Comput. Electr. Eng. **6**(1), 34–39 (2014)
12. https://ntier.wordpress.com/category/distributed/computing/hadoop/

End-to-End Security in Delay Tolerant Mobile Social Network

Rinki Rani and C. P. Katti[✉]

School of Computer & Systems Sciences, Jawaharlal Nehru University,
New Delhi 110067, India
rinki32_scs@jnu.ac.in, cpkatti@mail.jnu.ac.in

Abstract. In a Delay Tolerant Mobile Social Network (MSN) it is very difficult to maintain end-to-end security, which makes it vulnerable to various attacks like black hole attack, spoofing, modifies routing packets, packets dropping and many more. Apart from the attacks, there are various challenges in security of MSN like access control, confidentiality and intrusion detection system. Previously proposed model for security mechanism like efficient certificateless aggregate signature scheme provides security without the headache of maintaining the certificate, but the cost of signature verification is very high. So, to resolve these problems we are using HIBE (Hierarchical Identity Based Encryption) and proposing SPCRP (Secure Profile Cast Routing Protocol) which will provide end-to-end security along with the efficient key management, fine grained revocation and make sure the authorized access. We used ONE (Opportunistic Network) simulator with Profile Cast Routing protocol and observed various parameter overhead_ratio, number of messages transmitted, threshold value. We can conclude that this secure environment provides integrity, confidentiality and didn't reveal the behavioural profile of the users.

Keywords: DTN · MSN · HIBE · Routing protocol · Security

1 Introduction

In a Delay Tolerant MSN [1] network, it is very difficult to maintain end-to-end security. If the system is not end-to-end secured, then it will be vulnerable to various attacks like black hole attack, spoofing, modifies routing packets, packets dropping and many more. Previously proposed model for security mechanism like efficient certificateless aggregate signature scheme provides security without the headache of maintaining the certificate, but the cost for the length of the signature verification is very high. So, we need a mechanism which will provide security from attacks and also maintains the authenticity in the network. For building a Delay Tolerant MSN we are going to use Profile Cast Routing Protocol. This protocol builds a group of interested users based on their behaviour profile and the behavioural profile is constructed from the day to day movement. The transmission happens in between the interested users and the interested users can communicate only when they are in range of each other. But, this system does not hide the behavioural profiles of the users and anybody in the network can see it. It also has some privacy concerns. So, to resolve the entire above

© Springer Nature Singapore Pte Ltd. 2018
G. C. Deka et al. (Eds.): ICACCT 2018, CCIS 899, pp. 45–54, 2018.
https://doi.org/10.1007/978-981-13-2035-4_5

mentioned problem we are going to use HIBE (Hierarchical Identity Based Encryption) [2]. It will provide end-to-end security along with the efficient key management, fine-grained revocation and make sure the authorized access. No need to manage the keys all the time only when need can be asked to PKG (Public Key Generation) [3]. So it is easy to manage the keys and no need of certification before starting the communication. No overhead of maintaining the certificate.

We are proposing SPCRP (Secure Profile Cast Routing Protocol) which will communicate only with authenticate users without maintain keys, certificate and will provide end to end security in the network. There are various parameters which build the network. We observe how much it will affect the Traditional Profile Cast Routing Protocol. For simulation, we are going to use ONE (Opportunistic Network) [4]. After simulation and observation, we found out that our proposed model gives better results with respect to overhead ratio. The simulation result with respect to the number of messages transmitted, a number of nodes shows slightly down then the Secured profile cast routing, and this difference is very negligible. So, at the end of the dissertation we showed all the result and explained everything. At the end, we can conclude this new model provides a highly secured environment for the message transmission and also provides the advantages of HIBE. Users don't need to maintain the key for the whole session. As required by the system they can ask for the key. This secure environment provides integrity, confidentiality and didn't reveal the behavioural profile of the users.

In Sect. 2, literature review of the previous model is discussed. The design and implementation of the proposed model are presented in Sects. 3 and 4 discusses the results and analysis of the work. Finally, Sect. 5 concludes the work.

2 Related Works

Mobile social networks consist of decentralized network. While mostly present existing scheme for DTN considers one-to-one communication depends upon the user information and the aim is to deliver information efficiently and precisely. Leguay et al. [5] proposed the routing scheme for DTNs based on the mobility pattern of the two people. Validation of routing scheme is based on the high-D Euclidean environment which uses the mobility patterns of nodes called a MobySpac. Routing decision is made by MobySpace and the reliable candidate gets the custody of bundle. After getting the bundles further forwarding is done only to those nodes who have same or higher similarity with the destination node mobility pattern. Vahdat et al. [6] proposed Epidemic routing whose objective is to deliver data with high reliability even if there is loose or zero connectivity between sender and receiver. It distributes information to hosts, called carriers which are present in the connected adhoc network. Further these hosts come in contact with another host through mobility and spread the information. Through such transitive transmission of data, message reaches the destination with high probability. Daly et al. [7] model proposed a new forwarding metric based on ego network analysis to locally determine a node's centrality within the network and the node's social similarity to the destination node. Considered the complexity of the centrality metrics in populated. Further Hui et al. [8] proposed a model called Bubble which outperforms the PROPHET algorithm in terms of forwarding efficiency and doesn't forward data blindly. It is an hybrid algorithm based on the mobility traces of the user. These all proposed model are for decentralized and considers one to one communication but in Mobile social network we need to communicate one to many.

The one to many communication target on a behavioral group. Some of the proposed model [9] uses geographic information to build the communities. The data is send to the corresponding community by selecting random node in that corresponding community. Some are based on delivery probability as proposed by Lindgren et al. [10]. This model works on probability of mobility. For e.g., if we want to deliver a message from X to Z and X will never meet Z. There will be one person who will meet both X and Z. So through transitive connectivity message get delivered. Further for disconnected adhoc network Thomas et al. [11] proposed a model. In this model routing is done at the group level rather than the node level. It used the traditional concept of routing like AODV [12] by considering the group as an individual identity. It assumes that members of the group are connected to each other and they are also connected to other members of the different group. So, to communicate they used that member to communicate to other groups but these leads to privacy preserving issues. Based on the traces behavioral profile Hsu et al. [13] proposed a model, which doesn't provide security as high provided by the Hierarchical Identity Based Cryptography for end-to-end security in DTN.

One key issue for the proposed models is privacy-preserving operations and unauthorized access leads to some serious issues [14]. Liang et al. [15] proposed a model based on the profile matching for information exchange. This model reveals partial information while communicating to the initiator. Liu et al. [16] proposed a secure efficient authentication protocol for mobile ad hoc networks uses port-based vector switching and hierarchical identity based signature. But it takes some computing and signals expenses. Li et al. [17] proposed a profile matching model based on proximity. It doesn't allow the sharing of your all personal information and provides limited sharing as interest of sender. Our proposed model provides infrastructure level security and provides integrity, confidentiality and didn't reveal the behavioral profile of the users.

3 SPCRP

In this section we present our Secure Profile Cast Routing Protocol (SPCRP) providing end to end security services without certificate management and divided into two parts:

3.1 Mathematical Background

An *identity-based encryption* scheme E is specified ε by four randomized algorithms:

- **Setup:** For setting up the system parameters (params) and master keys it takes security parameter k. Given system parameters contain a description about the limited message space μ, and a cipher text space C. The generated master key is known only to the relative PKG (Public Key Generator) and the system parameter are known to everyone.

- **Extract:** It takes previously calculated params, master-key, and an ID. Params and master-key are previously generated entity while the $ID \sum\{0,1\}*$. This ID is a public key and is an arbitrary string of $0, 1$. After giving these parameters, it returns the private key corresponding to the given public key.
- **Encrypt:** The message we want to send is encrypted here. For encryption it takes 3 parameters: input params, ID, and $M \in M$. Input params were calculated in the first step. ID is a public key of the receiver and M is the message to be encrypted. After giving the input parameters, it returns encrypted message, i.e., a cipher text $C \in C$.
- **Decrypt:** After receiving data from the sender. The receiver decrypts it with the help of input params, $C \in C$, and a private key d. Here C is a ciphertext send in the previous step. The Private key is the private key of the receiver. It returns $M \in \mu$. This decrypted message should be same as the plain message.

This algorithm must satisfy the consistency by checking the decrypted message is equal to the original message or not.

$$\forall M \in \mu : Decrypt\ (params, C, d) = M, where\ C = Encrypt\ (params, ID, M).$$

3.2 SPCRP Architecture

3.2.1 System Setup

Before starting the communication we need some security parameter k, system parameter which contains the information of a predefined message space μ and cipher text information C. All these system parameters are public while the master-key s will be private and known only to "Private Key Generator" (PKG). PKG also store the information regarding system parameters. Each end point in the network who wants to send data has to get connected with the PKG and is authorized by the PKG. Each node in the network will gets the public system parameter from PKG which will be used to encrypt the message.

3.2.2 Phases in Encounters

- At source

  1. The sender is always holder of the first message in the network.
  2. Strategically, every time a sender wants to send a message to add a message holder to the network.

- At neighbouring node

  1. It searches for a dissimilar profile in the neighbourhood. When it encounters with a dissimilar behavioural profile, it encrypts the message with the help of its public key. Public keys can be made up of anything like Email id.
  2. After encrypting the message, it sends the ciphertext to the destination and senders keeps track of the behavioural profile that holds the message and all these profiles should be dissimilar.

3. If it encounters with a similar profile, a single bit is used which remember about the message holder in its neighbourhood and replicate this information to other nodes within the th_{nbr} – neighbourhood. This bit presents excessive message holder in the network.

- On receiving node

   1. The receiver receives the encrypted text from the message holder.
   2. If the receiver has its private key it will directly decrypt the message and adds the message into its buffer.
   3. If it doesn't have its private key it will request the PKG for its keys and then decrypt the message and stores in its buffer (Table 1).

A sender is always the first holder of the message. If a user X wants to transmit a message in the network. For all the nodes who encountered with the X while mobility it gets its mobility profile (MOP(Y)) and if it is not a holder of the message, it checks the similarity between its own mobility profile (MOP(X)) and encountered node Y. If similarity is less than forwarding threshold (th_{fwd}) and it is not group holder then it elect it as holder of the message in the group and mobility profile of Y is added to the holder list. Then message is encrypted with the predefine random no generated by the system and public key Y and calculated cipher text is sent to the Y. After receiving the cipher text, receiver (Y) decrypts the message with the help of its own secret key. Mobility profile of new holder of A is send in the network. We are making holder in the dissimilar group to reduce the number of copies transmitted.

If the similarity between mobility profile of holder of X and Y is greater than neighbour threshold (th_{nbr}), make the Y group holder or if the similarity between MOP(y) and MOP of X is greater then neighbour threshold then holder will remain as X. This is done to reduce the overlapping of the holder and provide the copy of messages to the intended receiver quickly. So, synchronization is done between X and Y to reduce the overlapping. If any holder again encounter it adds a bit to remember it is already a holder of the message.

If any message exists in the network for more than T time, remove all information and related information from the network. It checks for similarity between each node of Y belongs to the network except X. If the threshold value is greater than th_{nbr} set the Y as the group holder and also check for the duration of the message whether it expired or not. If it is expired remove all the relevant information from the network. In this way message get transmitted to every type of group with less overlapping of holder and minimum replication of the message with secure environment.

Table 1. Pseudocode for Secure profile cast routing protocol

```
/* MOP(X): node X mobility profile */
/* H(X): holder of node X */
/* group_holder(X): message holder in nearby of X */
/* T: Message life time */
/* siml(X, Y): similarity between X and Y */
/* e: predefined configured pairing */
/* rnd: source of randomness */
/* pk: public key */
/* sk: secret key */
/* masterKey: master key of the user created during the setup */
/* id: users' id */
/* c: cipherText */
/* th_{nbr}: threshold value of neighbourhood */
/* m: message to be send */


Setup pararmeters (e, rnd)
     return (pk, sk)
Extract (masterKey, id, rnd)
     return(pk, sk)
If message holder is node X
   Then
For each node Y encountered do
Get MOP(Y);
If Y is not a holder
then
If siml(MOP(Y), MOP(H_i(X))) < th_{fwd} ∀ i and group_holder (Y) = false
Then
select Y as holder;
Add MOP(Y) to list of holder;
Encrypt (Y , m, rnd);
Send the message;
Decrypt(c, sk);
Send MOP(H(X)), ∀ i ,
Else if siml(MOP(Y), MOP(H_i(X))) > th_{nbr} for any i
 then
Let Y set group_holder (Y)  = true;
Else
If siml (MOP(Y), MOP(H(X))) > th_{nbr}
then
 holder will be X;
Else
Synchronize  holder lists between node X and Y;

If for more than T message exists in network
then
Remove the message and related information ;

Else if group_holder(X) = true
then
For each node Y do
 then
        Obtain MOP(Y);
If siml(MOP(X), MOP(Y)) > th_{nbr} then
Let Y set group_holder(Y) = true;
If for more than T message exists in network T
then
Remove related information;
```

4 Experimental Results and Discussion

We used ONE (Opportunistic Network) with Eclipse luna based on JAVA to simulate our work. In Fig. 1 Snapshot of ONE simulator GUI interface (Table 2).

Table 2. Simulation parameters [4]

Parameters	Values
Area	15000 m × 15000 m
Simulation time	34560 s
Number of groups	2
Group threshold value	0.60
Bluetooth interface transmit speed	250 k
Bluetooth transmit range	10 m
Buffer size	2048 M

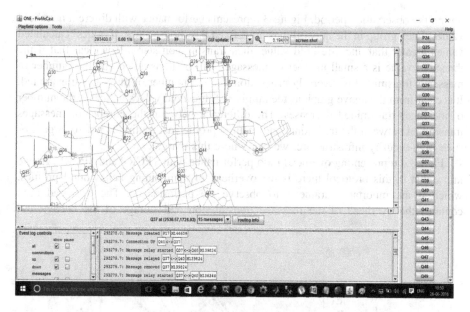

Fig. 1. ONE simulator GUI interface

Figure 2 shows the graph between the number of nodes and the number of messages transmitted. As the number of nodes increases in the Profile Cast Routing, the number of messages transmitted during the simulation time increases. From the above graph, it is clear as the number of a node increases the number of messages transmitted increases. The difference between the messages transmitted between the traditional and secured Profile Cast Routing protocol is that the drop in the number of messages is 5%

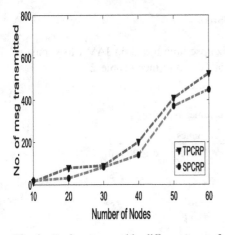

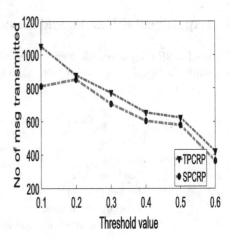

Fig. 2. Performance with different no. of nodes

Fig. 3. Performance with different threshold values

during the observation period. Figure 3 represents performance with different threshold values. Each group in the network has predefined threshold values. If nodes' calculated values greater than the threshold value, then transmission starts. It is clear that if the threshold value is a small number of messages will be transmitted and the number of messages transmitted is inversely proportional to the number of messages transmitted. It is clear from the above graph as the number of threshold values increases the number of messages transmitted decreases. The difference between the number of messages transmitted between the traditional and secured profile cast routing is not so large. For such high-security infrastructure, we can ignore this margin.

Figure 4 representing overhead ratio performance with TPCRP and SPCRP. As we know that in this protocol there is the overhead of maintaining behavioural profiles, which is an important parameter to observe the performance. The overhead ratio contains the overhead of the message transmission and storage of the behavioural

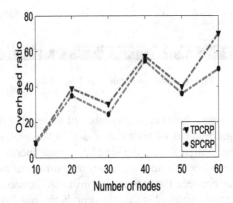

Fig. 4. Performance with respect to overhead ratio with different number of nodes

profiles. As compared to traditional profile cast routing secured profile cast routing transmit a less number of messages. So, because of less message transmission, there is less overhead in the secured profile cast routing as compared to the traditional profile cast routing. The result data set after considering different parameter is shown in Table 3.

Table 3. Data set of traditional and secured profile cast routing protocol

No. of msg transmitted after changing the number of nodes			Overhead ratio after changing the number of nodes			No. of msg transmitted after changing the threshold value		
No. of nodes	TPCRP	SPCRP	No. of nodes	TPCRP	SPCRP	Threshold value	TPCRP	SPCRP
10	14	20	10	8.5	8.0	0.1	1051	812
20	79	31	20	39.0	35.0	0.2	877	852
30	89	82	30	30.2	24.5	0.3	772	706
40	201	139	40	57.2	54.6	0.4	654	604
50	409	371	50	40.0	36.0	0.5	624	579
60	525	449	60	70.0	50.0	0.6	422	364

Data set of TPCRP and SPCRP are shown in table above. This data set was generated after implementing the TPCRP and SPCRP on ONE simulator with different number of nodes and different threshold values as shown in figure with number of nodes 10, 20, 30, 40, 50, 60. While the threshold values were 0.1, 0.2, 0.3, 0.4, 0.5, 0.6. It is clear from the table that SPCRP shows slightly low performance regarding number of messages transmitted but better performance regarding the overhead ratio.

5 Conclusions

A secured profile cast routing protocol is proposed for end-to-end security in DTN Mobile Social Network. The Profile cast routing protocol makes social groups based on the interest of the user and sends the information only to the interested users when they come in the range of communication. We provide the end-to-end security with the help of HIBE. We compare the performance of the traditional profile cast routing protocol with the secured profile cast routing protocol. For comparison with these two models we analyze the performance with (1) by changing the number of nodes and then check the number of messages delivered, (2) by changing the threshold value of the groups and observes the number of messages transmitted, (3) by observing the overhead_ratio with the changes in the number of nodes. After observing all the parameter we can conclude that secured Profile Cast Routing Protocol performance is marginally lower than traditional Profile Cast Routing Protocol.

Acknowledgement. This research has been partially supported by the Council of Scientific and Industrial Research, a research and development organization in India, with sanctioned no. 09/263(1054)/2015-EMR-I.

References

1. Nguyen, H.: Mobile social network and its open research problems. Department of Computer Science, University of Houston, Houston (2010)
2. Boneh, D., Boyen, X., Goh, E.-J.: Hierarchical identity based encryption with constant size ciphertext. In: Cramer, R. (ed.) EUROCRYPT 2005. LNCS, vol. 3494, pp. 440–456. Springer, Heidelberg (2005). https://doi.org/10.1007/11426639_26
3. Boneh, D., Franklin, M.: Identity-based encryption from the weil pairing. In: Kilian, J. (ed.) CRYPTO 2001. LNCS, vol. 2139, pp. 213–229. Springer, Heidelberg (2001). https://doi.org/10.1007/3-540-44647-8_13
4. Keränen, A., Ott, J., Kärkkäinen T.: The ONE simulator for DTN protocol evaluation. In: Proceedings of the 2nd International Conference on Simulation Tools and Techniques (2009)
5. Leguay, J., Friedman, T., Conan V.: Evaluating mobility pattern space routing for DTNs. In: Proceedings of IEEE INFOCOM (2006)
6. Vahdat, A., Becker, D.: Epidemic routing for partially connected ad hoc networks. Technical report CS-200006, Duke University (2000)
7. Daly, E., Haahr, M.: Social network analysis for routing in disconnected delay-tolerant MANETs. In: Proceedings of ACM MOBIHOC (2007)
8. Hui, P., Crowcroft, J., Yoneki, E.: Bubble rap: social-based forwarding in delay tolerant ZNetworks. In: Proceedings of ACM MOBIHOC (2008)
9. Motani, M., Srinivasan, V., Nuggehalli, P.: PeopleNet: engineering a wireless virtual social network. In: Proceedings of MOBICOM 2005 (2005)
10. Lindgren, A., Doria, A., Schelén, O.: Probabilistic routing in intermittently connected networks. In: Dini, P., Lorenz, P., de Souza, J.N. (eds.) SAPIR 2004. LNCS, vol. 3126, pp. 239–254. Springer, Heidelberg (2004). https://doi.org/10.1007/978-3-540-27767-5_24
11. Thomas, M., Gupta, A., Keshav, S.: Group based routing in disconnected ad hoc networks. In: Proceedings of 13th Annual IEEE International Conference on High Performance Computing (2006)
12. Perkins, C.E., Belding-Royer, E.M.: Ad-hoc on-demand distance vector routing. In: WMCSA, pp. 90–100 (1999)
13. Hsu, W.J., Dutta, D., Helmy, A.: CSI: a paradigm for behavior-oriented profile-cast services in mobile networks. Ad Hoc Netw. 10(8), 1586–1602 (2012)
14. Vastardis, N., Yang, K.: Mobile social networks: architectures, social properties and key research challenges. IEEE Commun. Surv. Tutor. 15(3), 1355–1371 (2013)
15. Liang, X., Li, X., Zhang, K., Lu, R., Lin, X., Shen, X.S.: Fully anonymous profile matching in mobile social networks. IEEE J. Sel. Areas Commun. 31(9), 641–655 (2013)
16. Liu, H., Liang, M.: Efficient identity-based hierarchical access authentication protocol for mobile network. Secur. Commun. Netw. 6(12), 1509–1521 (2013)
17. Li, M., Yu, S., Cao, N., Lou, W.: Privacy-preserving distributed profile matching in proximity-based mobile social networks. IEEE Trans. Wirel. Commun. 12(5), 2024–2033 (2013)

Energy Efficient Transmission in the Presence of Interference for Wireless Sensor Networks

Ajay Sikandar[1(✉)], Sushil Kumar[2], Prashant Singh[3],
Manoj Kumar Tyagi[1], and Durgesh Kumar[4]

[1] Department of Information Technology, G.L. Bajaj Institute of Technology
and Management, Greater Noida 201306, India
ajay.sikandar@gmail.com, manojankitsuhani@gmail.com
[2] Jawaharlal Nehru University, New Delhi 110067, India
skdohare@yahoo.com
[3] Northern India Engineering College, New Delhi, India
prashant.ert@gmail.com
[4] Department of Computer Science, G.L. Bajaj Institute of Technology
and Management, Greater Noida, India
durgesh.durge@gmail.com

Abstract. Minimizing Energy consumption in a wireless sensor network has become a challenging issue. Energy consumption in transmission is higher in the presence of interfering nodes due to more re-transmissions required for a successful transmission. In this paper, energy consumption model has been presented. Mathematical models for Rayleigh interference have been derived. Energy efficient algorithm for interference minimization has been investigated. The simulation result has been carried out in MATLAB. The proposed model consumes low energy and reduces interference in the presence of one interferer, two interferer and multiple interferers.

Keywords: Rayleigh interference · Signal to interference ratio
WSNs

1 Introduction

In Wireless Sensor Networks (WSNs), sensors are constrained by limited resource of memory, computation power, and energy [1]. Because of their limited battery power, energy saving is one of the prime issue in protocol designing. Therefore, energy efficient MAC protocol design is gaining attention among researchers for enhancing the lifetime of WSNs. The prime design objective of MAC protocol is to provide high throughput, to minimize collision, delay and energy usage [2]. Time division multiple access (TDMA) protocol allows some users to allocate the same frequency channel by dividing the signal into different time slots. In TDMA, each sensor is assigned a slot. The sensor turns on its radio during in the assigned time slot, and turnoff the radio when not transmitting or receiving. The time slots assignment in TDMA makes collision free multiple accesses. In this protocol, hidden terminal problem is solved because it can schedule transmission time of neighboring nodes that occur at different time.

© Springer Nature Singapore Pte Ltd. 2018
G. C. Deka et al. (Eds.): ICACCT 2018, CCIS 899, pp. 55–64, 2018.
https://doi.org/10.1007/978-981-13-2035-4_6

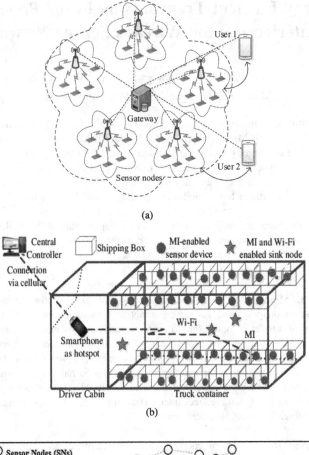

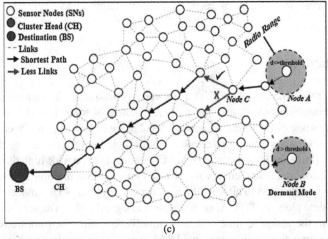

Fig. 1. Illustration of WSN: (a) mobile application oriented usage, (b) impact of sensing quality on specific WSN based product, (c) energy issue in cluster oriented routing in WSN

In order to reduce interference, time slot is assigned to every communication link, thus number of slots equal to the number of communication links of the network [3, 4]. In spite of link time slots assignments, the interference cannot be avoided completely because the transmission by a sensor node will be received by all neighboring sensor nodes [5]. It is important to have energy efficient communication because high transmit power can increase the Signal-to-Interference Noise Ratio (SINR) at the receiver. On the other hand, lower power transmission can diminish interference. The interference phenomena can be modeled mathematically by either Gaussian distribution or Rayleigh distribution. In this paper, we assume that the receiver gets no direct line to sight signal component, either from its own transmitter or from the interfering transmitter. The assumption leads us to use Rayleigh fading model for interference [6, 7]. Quality sensing and communication of boxes is illustrated. Sensors are inserted into container. During the flow of data over the internet, energy consumption is focus issue for localization, scheduling and communication in interference environment [9, 12, 17]. The illustration of WSN focusing on recent mobile application oriented usage, impact of quality of sensing in specific WSN oriented product, and energy oriented issue in WSN routing operation is presented in Fig. 1(a)–(c).

In this paper, we propose an Energy Efficient Interference Reduction Algorithm (EEIRA) to reduce wasteful transmissions due to interference. A standard energy model to represent the energy consumption in transmission and reception has been used to analyze the proposed algorithm. A mathematical formulation for the received power in presence of Rayleigh interference is given. The proposed algorithm is simulated on MATLAB platform. The rest of the paper is organized as follows: In Sect. 2 we present the overview of the related work. In Sect. 3, we present energy efficient interference reduction focusing on network model, energy model, and interference reduction algorithm. Section 4 discusses simulation result and analysis. Finally, we conclude paper in Sect. 5.

2   Related Work

Various MAC protocols have been proposed by researchers that guarantee collision free communication. Energy efficient sleep scheduling scheme was proposed for low data rate WSNs [3]. They suggest a novel interference free TDMA sleep scheduling scheme called contiguous link scheduling. In [5], authors presented distributed and centralized algorithms to find a valid link scheduling for realistic wireless network model. Authors investigate two centralized heuristic algorithms: level based scheduling and node based scheduling in [10]. Node based scheduling is adapted from classical multi hop scheduling algorithms for general ad-hoc network. Level based scheduling is novel scheduling algorithm for many to one communication in sensor networks. Energy efficiency in TDMA link scheduling was investigated with transmission power control using a realistic SINR based interference model [6]. In this scheme the works are accomplished in two folds. Firstly, express Power control and joint scheduling as a novel optimization problem that provides tunable between throughput, energy and latency. Second, author suggests both polynomial and exponential greedy based heuristic algorithm.

In [8], authors investigate TDMA scheme for energy efficiency in order to construct transmission schedule to reduce power consumption while decreasing end to end transmission time to gateway. TDMA schedule determines the length of listening period, that is as small as possible, and at the same time make sure that wake up packet collision are avoided. In [11], authors suggested a mathematical model for co-channel interferers using Rayleigh distribution. Energy oriented green computing approach has been suggested focusing on path selection and message scheduling approach. Authors suggested an energy oriented path selection and message scheduling framework for wireless sensor networks. They focus on effective cooperation between message scheduling and path selection [14]. Sensor enabled wireless network environment has been considered as application area for the green computing technique. Various energy models have been critically investigated considering model derivation and limitation identification as primary aim for cross layer approaches [15]. Energy efficient traffic prioritization scheme has been suggested focusing on medical use case of wireless sensor networks [16]. Mobile sink based adaptive immune energy efficient clustering protocol is investigated. It uses to reduce the total dissipated energy in communication and overhead packets as well as adaptive Immune Algorithm (AIA) to find the sojourn location of the mobile sink and the optimum number of cluster heads [17]. In [18], authors suggested analytical model for different deployment techniques to provide system behavior and design parameters. Mathematical model have been proposed to measure the quality of coverage, energy consumption and the network cost of geometrical deployment of pattern in term of different matrix. In these aforementioned energy efficient techniques, interference based energy oriented WSN techniques are limited.

3 Energy Efficient Interference Reduction

3.1 Network Model

In TDMA protocol, the time is divided into slots of equal length. The number of slots in each frame is fixed. The protocol has two states: active and sleep. In active state, a sensor node can receive or transmit packets. If packets are not available then node goes to idle mode. In idle mode, node doing nothing but ready to receive or transmit packet. In sleep state, sensor node turnoff its power for a period. The energy consumption of sensor node in sleep state is much less than the energy consumption in active state (cf. Fig. 2).

3.2 Energy Model

We have used radio dissipation model [13] to evaluate the performance of the proposed algorithm. In this model, energy consumption in the transmission of sensor node depends on the sum of amplifier energy and constant electronic components energy consumption proportional to distance between transmitter and receiver. In the transmission of l bits message, energy consumed by radio is given by

$$E_{Tx}(l, d) = \begin{cases} l\left(\varphi + \pi_{friss\_amp}\, d^2\right) & d \leq d_0 \\ l\left(\varphi + \pi_{two\_ray\_amp}\, d^4\right) & d > d_0 \end{cases} \tag{1}$$

Where φ constant energy consumed by electronic components, π_{friss_amp} and $\pi_{two\_ray\_amp}$ are the amount of energy per bit dissipated in the transmitter amplifiers,

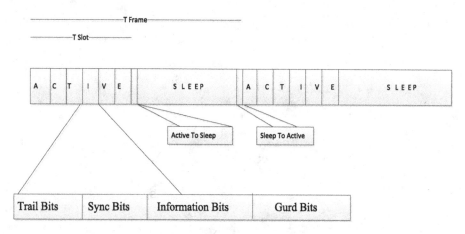

Fig. 2. TDMA active sleep model

and d distance between sender and receiver. The energy consumed $E_{Rx}(l)$ to receive the l bit message is given by

$$E_{Rx}(l) = l \times \varphi \tag{2}$$

Transmitted power of sender is to be adjusted so that the power at receiver is above a certain threshold value. During the communication between transmissions receiver's pair, the required power for transmission by the sender is a function of threshold power and the distance between the transmitter and receiver.

$$x = \begin{cases} \alpha \times P_{r\_threh}\, d^2 & d \leq d_0 \\ \beta \times P_{r\_thres}\, d^4 & d > d_0 \end{cases}, \tag{3}$$

Where x is the transmit power by the sender node.

3.3 Interference Reduction Algorithm

In this section, we present an algorithm to reduce the wasteful transmissions due to interference. Assume that all sensors use the same channel for the packets transmission and reception. The receiving sensor overhears the unwanted transmission from the nearby co-channel sensors, may cause packet loss (cf. Fig. 3). This is because of the ratio of received signal power to the interference signal power is less than a certain threshold power. The proposed algorithm sets off the nearby sensors into sleep mode such that the ratio of received signal power to the interference signal becomes greater than or equal to the threshold power. To implement the proposed idea, we assume that the interferers obey law of Rayleigh fading. In the Rayleigh fading environment, the receiver gets no direct line to sight signal component, either from its own transmitter or from the interfering transmitter. Probability density function of the corresponding received power x is given by

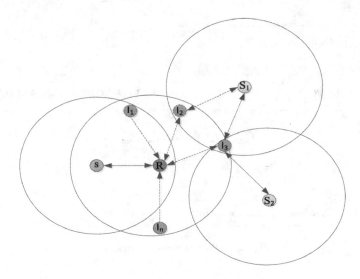

Fig. 3. Interference at receiver node

$$P(x) = \frac{1}{\alpha}e^{-\left(\frac{x}{\alpha}\right)} \tag{4}$$

where, α is the mean signal power. Similarly, the probability distribution function of interfering signal can be written as

$$P(y_1) = \frac{\beta_1}{\alpha}e^{\left(\frac{-y_1\beta_1}{\alpha}\right)} \tag{5}$$

where y_1 is the local SNR of interfering signal and β_1 is the wanted signal/interfering signal power ratio.

We derive a mathematical formula of received power at a sensor in the presence of single interfering co-channel sensor and then we generalize it for the case of multiple interfering co-channel sensors. For successful reception of packet by the receiver in the presence of single co-channel interferer, the received signal power is greater than both the desired threshold power v_0 and signal to interference protection ratio P_1. The probability of successful reception of packet at receiver in the presence of one interferer is given by

$$P^1_{succ} = prob(x > v_0, x/y_1 > P_1.)$$
$$= \int_{v_0}^{\infty} \frac{1}{\alpha}e^{-\left(\frac{x}{\alpha}\right)} * \left[\int_0^{x/P_1} \frac{\beta_1}{\alpha}e^{\left(\frac{-y_1\beta_1}{\alpha}\right)} dy_1\right] dx \tag{6}$$
$$= e^{-\left(\frac{v_0}{\alpha}\right)} - \frac{1}{1 + \frac{\beta_1}{\alpha}} * e^{\left(-\frac{v_0}{\alpha}\left(1 + \frac{\beta_1}{\alpha}\right)\right)}$$

Assume that the number of nearby co-channel sensors that interfere at receiving sensor is more than one. The probability distribution of the received signal power from n interfering co-channel sensors can be expressed as

$$P(y_n) = \frac{\beta_n}{\alpha} e^{\left(\frac{-y_n\beta_n}{\alpha}\right)} \tag{7}$$

The probability of successful reception of a packet at the receiver in the presence of n interfering sensors can expressed as

$$
\begin{aligned}
P_{succ}^n &= prob(x > v_0, x/y_n > P_{I.}) \\
&= \int_{v_0}^{\infty} P(x) \int_0^{x/P_I} P(y_1) \ldots \int_0^{x/P_I - y_1 - y_2 \ldots} {}^{y_n} P(y_n) dy_{n-1} \, dy_2 dy_1 dx \\
&= e^{-\left(\frac{v_0}{\alpha}\right)} - [pd_1 + pd_2 + pd_3 + \ldots + pd_n] \\
&= e^{-\left(\frac{v_0}{\alpha}\right)} - \gamma
\end{aligned} \tag{8}
$$

Where γ is the additional outage caused by n interferers, i.e., the difference between P_{succ}^0 and P_{succ}^n. The aforementioned network model, energy model, and interference reduction model are utilized to develop a complete set of steps for energy efficiency in WSN (see Algorithm 1).

Algorithm 1: EEIRA

Notations: x : Signal power; y: Interfering power signal; v_0: Desired signal power
   I : Number of interfering sensor; n : total number of interfering sensor
Input: x, y ,v_0 , n, I
Process:
        Begin
          1. **If** (x < v_0)
Communication abort
          2. **Else if**(x/y>P_I)
P_{succ}^0 gets satisfactory reception
          3. **Else**
          4. **For**(I=1 to n)
               Enqueue the id of all interfering sensor in non-decreasing order of SIR ratio
          5. J=1
          6. **While**(q(j)) **do**
          7. defer transmission of I_jI_j sensor
          8. **If** ($x/y_{n-j} < P_I$)
          9. increment j by 1
         10. **Else**
         11. break
         12. **Endwhile**
P_{succ}^n gets satisfactory reception
         13. **End**

---

4 Results and Discussion

4.1 Simulation Environment Setting

In this section, the outcome of simulation runs to analyze the energy efficient transmission algorithm which reduces interference, and thus the wasteful transmissions, is presented. Nodes are uniformly distributed in sensing field area of dimension 500×500 m^2. Nodes are assumed to be homogeneous in all aspect. The numbers of nodes deployed are 1200. The proposed model is simulated on MATLAB platform.

4.2 Results and Analysis

Figures 4 and 5 plot numerical computations on how the outage probability varies with Signal-to-Interference Ratio (SIR) in the presence of one interferer, multiple interferers, respectively. We obtain outage probability in the presence of Rayleigh interferer and compare with EEIRA algorithm. Where we get improve results in the different cases. In Figs. 4 and 5, show outage probability against SIR in the case of one interfering, two interfering, and multiple interfering. Algorithm is used for different cases where we get the improved result. The presence of additional interference will increase the probability of outage. It is observed that interfering sensors should be switched to sleep state to minimize the interference at receiving node that saves the power consumption of the whole networks. Energy consumption is less with less interference. As the SIR increases, outage probability increases, then system becomes more energy efficient.

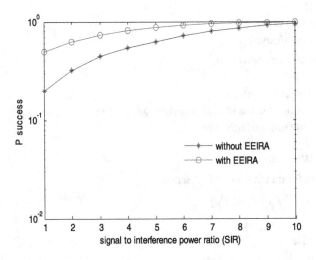

Fig. 4. Success probability with one interfering node

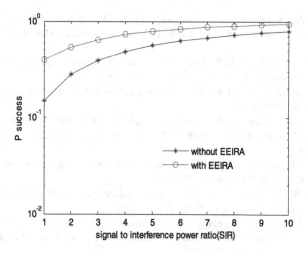

Fig. 5. Success probability with multiple interfering nodes

5 Conclusion

In this paper, we have proposed Energy efficient interference reduction algorithm. Energy consumption model was derived. Mathematical models for Minimizing Interference in Rayleigh fading environment have derived. It was observed that interfering sensors should be switched to sleep state to minimize the interference at receiving node that saves the power consumption of the whole networks.

References

1. Akyildiz, I.F., Su, W., Sankaransubramaniam, Y., Cayirci, E.: Wireless sensor network: a survey. Comput. Netw. **38**(4), 393–422 (2002)
2. Demirkol, I., Ersoy, C., Alagoz, F.: MAC protocols for wireless sensor networks: a survey. IEEE Commun. Mag. **44**(4), 115–121 (2006)
3. Ma, J., Lou, W., Wu, Y., Li, X., Chen, G.: Energy efficient TDMA sleep scheduling in wireless sensor network. In: Proceedings of IEEE Infocom, pp. 630–638 (2009)
4. Wang, W., Wang, H., Peng, D., Sarif, H.: An energy efficient pre-scheduling for hybrid CSMA/TDMA in wireless sensor network. In: 10th IEEE Singapore International Conference on Communication Systems, pp. 1–5 (2006)
5. Wang, W., Wang, Y., Li, X.Y., Song, W.Z., Frieder, O.: Efficient interference-aware TDMA link scheduling for static wireless networks. In: MOBICOM, pp. 262–273 (2006)
6. Lu, G., Krishnamachari, B.: Energy efficient joint scheduling and power control for wireless sensor network. In: 2nd Annual Conference on Sensor and Ad Hoc Communications and Networks, pp. 362–373. IEEE (2005)
7. Fang, L., Bi, G., Kot, A.C.: New method of performance analysis for diversity reception with correlated Rayleigh-fading signals. IEEE Trans. Veh. Technol. **49**(5), 1807–1812 (2000)

8. Pantazis, N.A., Vergadosb, D.J., Vergados, D.D., Douligeris, C.: Energy efficiency in wireless sensor networks using sleep mode TDMA scheduling. Ad Hoc Netw. **7**(2), 322–343 (2008)
9. Miao, G., Himayat, N., Li, G.Y., Koc, A.T., Talwar, S.: Interference-aware energy-efficient power optimization. In: Proceedings of IEEE ICC, pp. 1–5 (2009)
10. Ergen, S.C., Varaiya, P.: TDMA scheduling algorithms for wireless sensor network. Wirel. Netw. **16**(4), 985–997 (2010)
11. Sowerby, K.W., Williamson, A.G.: Outage probability calculation for a mobile radio system having multiple Rayleigh fading multiple Rayleigh interferers. IEEE Electron. Lett. **23**(11), 600–601 (1987)
12. Kumar, S., Lobiyal, D.K.: Impact of interference on coverage in wireless sensor networks. Wirel. Pers. Commun. **74**(2), 683–701 (2014)
13. Heinzelman, W.: Application-Specific Protocol Architectures for Wireless Networks. Ph.D. thesis, Massachusetts Institute of Technology (2000)
14. Farhan, L., Kharel, R., Kaiwartya, O., Hammoudeh, M., Adebisi, B.: Towards green computing for Internet of Things: energy oriented path and message scheduling approach. Sustain. Cities Soc. **38**, 195–204 (2018)
15. Kumar, K., Kumar, S., Kaiwartya, O., Cao, Y., Lloret, J., Aslam, N.: Cross-layer energy optimization for IoT environments: technical advances and opportunities. Energies **10**(12), 2073 (2017)
16. Ullah, F., Abdullah, A.H., Kaiwartya, O., Lloret, J., Arshad, M.M.: EETP-MAC: energy efficient traffic prioritization for medium access control in wireless body area networks. Telecommun. Syst., 1–23 (2017). (Online published)
17. Zahhad, M., Ahmed, S., Sabor, N., Sasaki, S.: Mobile sink- based adaptive immune energy – efficient clustering protocol for improving the lifetime and stability period of wireless sensor networks. IEEE Sens. J. **15**(18), 4576–4585 (2015)
18. Kaiwartya, O., Kumar, S., Abdullah, A.H.: Analytical model of deployment methods for application of sensors in non hostile environment. Wirel. Pers. Commun. **97**(1), 1517–1536 (2017)

Capturing User Preferences Through Interactive Visualization to Improve Recommendations

Pooja Vashisth, Purnima Khurana[✉], Punam Bedi, and Sumit Kr Agarwal

Department of Computer Science, University of Delhi, Delhi 110007, India
pk0403@gmail.com

Abstract. Recommender systems are widely used intelligent applications which assist users in a decision-making process to select one product from a huge set of alternative products or services. Recent research focus has been on developing methods for generating recommendations. We note lack of coherent research in the field of visual depictions of recommendations as well as how visualization and interactivity can aid users in use and decision-making with recommender systems. This paper proposes a novel approach to visualization of recommendations driven by preferences of the user to provide them with beneficial and persuasive recommendations. A personalized visual interface has been used considering requirements of the user and product's utility in order to provide effective recommendations to the user. The anticipated visual interface is interactive and tailored according to user's preferences. Users can alter their current necessities interactively in order to acquire the value-added recommendations from the Recommender System. It provides the users with a simple and most relevant set of recommendations as per their interest. This substantially reduces users' interaction effort, especially for a sizable and complex product domain. Precision and recall metrics have been used to measure performance of the proposed system as well as users' subjective feedback.

Keywords: Recommender system · Visualization · Interaction · Personalization
Preferences

1 Introduction

The explosive growth and variety of information available on the Web along with the rapid introduction of new e-business services (buying products, product comparison, auction, etc.) frequently overwhelmed users, leading them to make poor decisions. This is due to lack of sufficient personal experience and competence required to evaluate the overwhelming number of alternatives. The availability of choices, instead of producing a benefit, started to decrease users' well-being. It was understood that while having a choice is good, but having a number of choices may not be always better. Hence, a pressing need emerged for providing recommendations derived from filtering the whole range of available alternatives [19].

Recommender systems are widely used intelligent applications which assist users in a decision-making process to choose one item amongst a potentially overwhelming set

© Springer Nature Singapore Pte Ltd. 2018
G. C. Deka et al. (Eds.): ICACCT 2018, CCIS 899, pp. 65–76, 2018.
https://doi.org/10.1007/978-981-13-2035-4_7

of products. Recommender systems use likeness between users and recommenders or between items to form recommendation list for the user.

Various recommender systems have been developed in recent years from the very successful collaborative systems to the more recent content-based conversational systems to help online consumers find their desired products on e-commerce websites [2, 22]. When the product domain is complex, very often users are not familiar with the details of each product, or may not fully understand and appreciate the trade-offs that exist between different product attributes. It is not likely that users are able to input all their preferences precisely at one time. Thus the recommender systems need to interact with users so that they can construct their preferences gradually with a sequence of recommendation cycles. During each cycle, one or more products are recommended based on some developing model of the user's requirements, and the user has the opportunity to provide feedback in order to steer the recommender in the course of the desired product [12]. The motivation behind this research work is to provide a solution to research problems or issues faced by present day RSs. The issue under consideration is that of, "*Exposing underlying assumptions behind actions*". By tracing the evidence used to provide suggestions to the users, recommenders can expose the underlying assumptions for the user. For example, this can be done by revealing similarities between user's preferences and the product availability. This revelation is also important from a recommender's view, as it would enable exposure of reasons behind user's likes and dislikes. In addition, user's tastes are normally unstable and they keep changing on the disclosure of some new information. Hence, to resolve this issue, it is very important to understand the dynamics of modeling user preferences. This would also improve the system's understanding of a user's perspective and can be achieved using interactive user interfaces. The recommendations can be presented to the user using a personalized visual considering utility of the product and personal requirements of user [15]. These kinds of systems have the potential for significant performance benefits in terms of recommendation quality and user satisfaction.

User Interfaces for today's recommender systems are usually created in a one-interface-suits-all manner, making implicit assumptions about the needs and preferences of the user. But, user behavior is associated with an inherent uncertainty. The purpose of personalized information services is to adjust strategies of product recommendation (to fit user interests) modeled according to users' preferences. Therefore, we were motivated to propose personalized visual user interfaces for recommender systems that can not only recommend but also give rational suggestions for improving the same. These interfaces are adapted to a person's needs, preferences and can improve user satisfaction and system performance.

Visual interfaces are known to be created using icons. An icon is the unique visible element in an interactive interface, which not only bears certain information itself, but also has the function of connecting and executing in delivering messages [26]. Icons have direct influence on users' understanding, judgment and behaviour towards the interface and thus affect the process including result of interaction. Icons enhance visualization and attract the users towards recommendation systems by increasing their involvement and eagerness.

We have structured the rest of the paper as follows; related work is discussed in Sect. 2. The proposed system algorithm and the interface designs are described in detail in Sect. 3. Section 4 presents various parameters for performing user evaluation and gives the experimental results for both subjective and objective evaluation. Finally, Sect. 5 discusses conclusion and future prospects.

2   Related Work in Interactive Visual Interfaces in Recommender Systems

Though the traditional approaches to recommendation applications have solved the enormity problem of the content available and the diverse expectations of users to an extent, still there are several challenges which need attention. These challenges, in turn, have driven the increasing need for more intelligent, trustworthy and personalized applications, such as e-commerce recommender systems. The potential of these personalized and adaptive systems has been realized by industry in order to increase sales and to retain customers. Likewise, web users have come to rely on such systems to help them in finding items of interest in large information spaces more efficiently.

Three common levels in the degree of personalization were specifically identified in the work by [20]. First, when recommender applications provide identical recommendations to each customer, the application is classified as non-personalized. Second, recommenders that use current customer inputs to customize the recommendation according to the customer's current interests provide ephemeral personalization. Finally third, the most highly-personalized recommender applications use persistent personalization to create recommendations that differ for different customers, even when they are looking at the same items. Some of the ongoing research work in the field of persistent personalization is mentioned in the works [8, 11, 13, 16]. The personalized technologies aim to enhance a user's experience by taking into account users' interests, preferences, and other relevant information [24]. Personalized recommendations can be provided by using interactive visual interfaces.

There are three important issues related to the realization of interactive visual interfaces in the recommender systems. These are: adapting interfaces to user preferences [14], user interactions for eliciting preferences [2], and explaining an output. Previously, model-based interface generation systems [18] generally did not provide any mechanisms for adapting the user interface generation process to the preferences of their end users. As per survey in [10, 25], there has been little prior work on adapting interface generation systems to people's preferences, but there has been extensive prior work in the general area of preference elicitation.

Our approach focuses mainly on the issue of adapting interfaces to user preferences and improving the same according to their requirements. Below we discuss some relevant work on interaction techniques for eliciting user preference responses.

While eliciting user preferences, there has to be distinction between a user's fundamental objectives and the means of achieving them. This is important because if the system attributes do not reflect user's fundamental objectives, users will be unlikely to estimate the values of those attributes. For example critiquing [1] (sometimes referred to as "tweaking" [9]) is an alternative interaction technique that allows users to provide their feedback by proposing (or choosing) incremental improvements to solutions generated by a system [1, 9]. Such customization mechanisms however have two limitations. Firstly, it may be hard for the user to provide meaningful critiques until system can generate interfaces close to desired. Secondly, as this interaction is entirely user-driven [1], it does not guarantee a complete coverage of the interface design space. In contrast to user-driven example critiquing, system-driven interactions, where the system chooses what concrete examples to present to the user to request their opinion, can be designed to avoid the shortcomings of the user-driven approaches. Recent research [21] suggests that pair wise comparisons of suggestions may be the most robust interaction for eliciting preferences. In that way we are providing the user with two outcomes and is asked which of the two he or she prefers. In the proposed work we adopt a system-driven complement to the user-driven critiquing interaction.

3   Personalized V & I Interface for Recommender Systems

A recommender system through its interface or e-face provides its access to the user. Also, user's trust and their persistence of using the system can be increased by incorporating visually attractive interfaces [3, 4]. This paper proposes a visual interactive interface for a recommender system that is driven by user's favorites in order to deliver more actual and convincing recommendations. These endorsements are presented to the users keeping in view their individual requirements and analogous product rating for every recommendation. Customer can revise his existing needs interactively in order to fetch the most relevant set of recommendations as per his interest.

We enhanced a prior recommendation algorithm [6, 7] by implicit attribute grade calculation based on user profile. The enhanced work considers only those attributes for book recommendation generation which are relevant for the user as per the preference list specified by him and his communication history with the RS. In the proposed system user is also provided with a facility to modify the attributes' grading of the book for recommendation generation using the V & I interface.

Recommendation generation in the proposed system consists of the following basic steps:

1. The RS, considering profile of the user, computes grade for all book attributes for a particular category of book. Any book B is characterized by n attributes $(a_1, a_2, a_3.......a_n)$. For each attribute a_i it performs the following tasks:
a. The maximum frequency of book titles for each and every attribute a_i is calculated by the RS.
b. The system then chooses the highest frequency feature/attribute as the default grade.
2. The system allows the user to change the default grade using interactive visual interface. The attributes that have grade greater than an onset value will be deliberated for recommendation as IFS (Intuitionist Fuzzy Set) [5] generation of recommended books.

3. Recommender performs the first cycle of recommendation generation using modified IFS by calculating the DOI (Degree of Importance) as per the user preference list.
4. The system takes the user's feedback on the recommendations by having an explicit input from the user. The user specifies whether he accepts the recommendation or needs an improvement.
a. In case user accepts the recommendation, RS adds the accepted recommendation to update user's preference list.
b. In case of user wants to improve, RS calls for the next cycle of (improved) recommendation generation for the cases which requires improvement.
(i) RS again calculates grades for book attributes implicitly as per the new preference list. Through its visual interface the RS suggests further changes that the user can make to one or more book attributes, to generate more desirable recommendations. These grades can be changed interactively by the user if required.
(ii) Recalculate the DOI as per IFS to generate an improved set of recommendations for user. Go back to step 4 or quit.

The main focus of this paper is on the interface design for recommendation engines that provide suggestions based on user preferences. A previously developed RS for book recommendation generation [3, 4] was using a textual interface only. The users were required to explicitly give a grading input for all the book attributes to get recommendation from the system. Therefore, the RS did not have any implicit rating facility; neither had it allowed users to change the grades interactively over several recommendation cycles. The RS could also not provide any suggestions to guide the users in giving appropriate attribute grades to get better recommendations from the system. Users could not improve upon the recommendations iteratively. A new recommendation process has to be started every time in case of a preference or requirement change. Hence, we designed the proposed system to overcome these shortcomings. It allows users to concentrate on the utilization of visualization, explanation and interaction as the feedback mechanism to improve upon recommendations iteratively.

The interface layout is composed of the four main elements: a grading panel, an explanation panel, a product recommendation and a feedback panel. In the grading panel, each attribute has an automatic grading by RS and is provided with two small buttons, which allow users to increase or decrease a grade value when numeric attributes are taken into consideration, and to make an alteration in value in the case of categorical attributes such as the author type or publisher type (Fig. 1(a)). Since icons are perceived as being closer in meaning to the textual representation, the attributes in this panel are represented visually using the icons. The user can get further book details corresponding to a chosen attribute grade value by clicking the related icon. We have added tokens to the right side of each icon: an up arrow, a down arrow or an equal sign, to further indicate if the grade value was respectively increasing, decreasing or equal to the current best match. The recommender's suggestions for improving recommendations are represented by highlighting the relevant token(s) of the corresponding book attribute(s) that requires change. The explanation panel gives details of the semantics of attribute grading by RS (Fig. 1(a)). The product recommendation panel (Fig. 1(b) and 1(c)) shows the current recommended products which best matches the user's preferences and recommender's rating database. The users' ratings are also shown in percentage against each book recommendation. The interested users can also view other details of the books except those shown in the recommendation list, by clicking on the desired book icon.

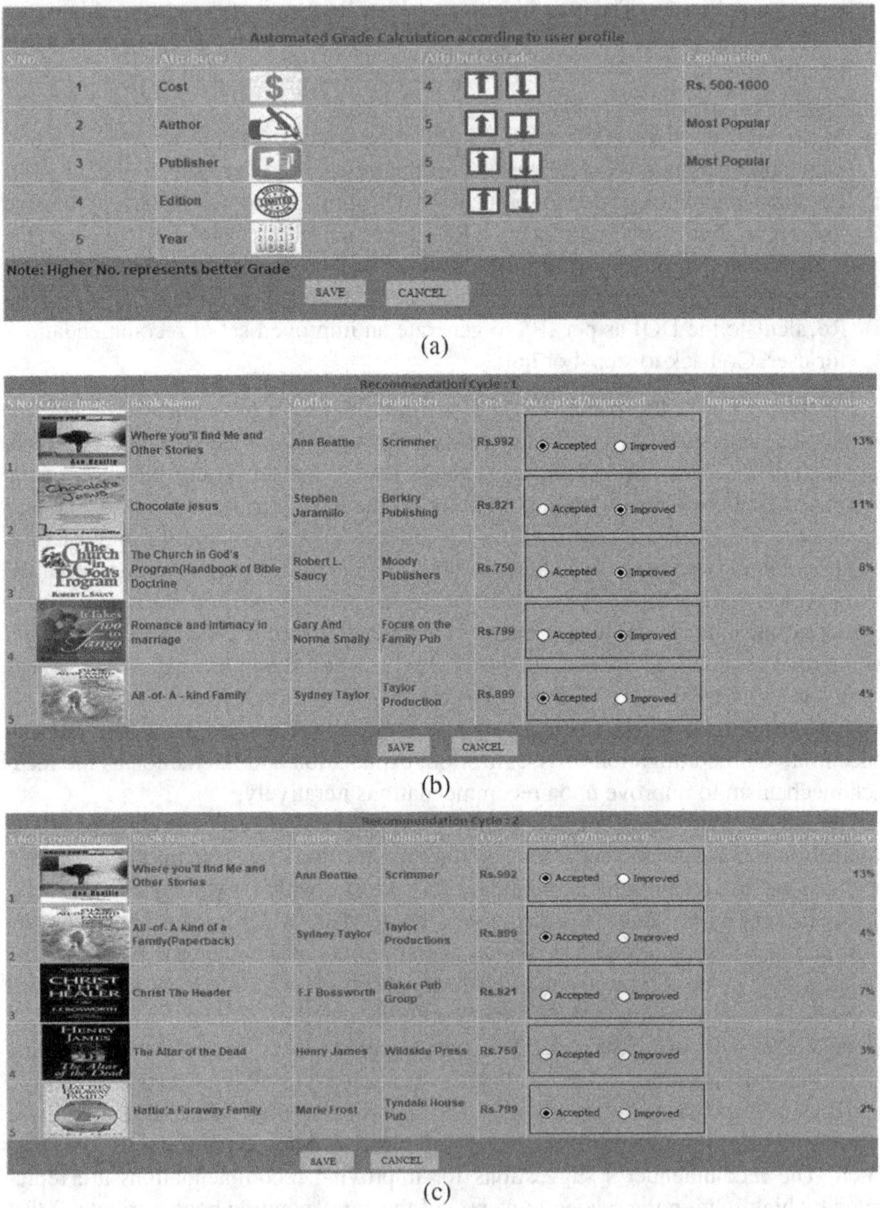

(a)

(b)

(c)

Fig. 1 **(a).** Snapshot of RS to show implicit grade calculation for relevant book attributes and its subsequent improvement. **(b).** Snapshot of RS to show initial recommendation cycle 1 and feedback as first iteration for a user's query. **(c).** Snapshot of RS to show improved recommendations in the recommendation cycle 2 as second iteration for the same user's query

This is done to hide the unnecessary details initially. The feedback panel is an augmentation to the list of recommendations shown as textual sentences. Users can provide a feedback by clicking the button "Accept" or "Improve" displayed on the right-hand side in the mentioned figures (see Fig. 1(b) and 1(c)). These four elements make up the main book RS interface and are always visible to end-users.

We are interested in getting a better perception of the role of the interface's design in the whole interaction process. We were in particular motivated by the frequent observation that people find the interfaces loaded with too many product attributes and admit to not actually reading all the information provided. In this context, we decided to create a visual representation of the most relevant product attributes adapted according to user's profile and hide others (details can be seen by the interested users by clicking icons). We then compare the proposed system with the traditional textual format through an experimental evaluation study as explained in the subsequent sections.

4   User Evaluation and Feedback: Experimental Results

The experimental set up for user evaluation was deliberately chosen to be extensive and exhaustive in order to put the system to a rigorous testing exercise. For this reason, the set up consisted of 638 target users who belonged to various walks of life like: authors/writers, research scholars, academicians, students, industry professionals and amateur users. Each user was made to use the RS based on previous textual interface and the proposed visual interface. Every user has performed a minimum of 25 recommendation iterations using each interface. Their experiences were recorded as explained below.

There are two types of evaluation criteria for measuring the recommender system's performance: the objective criteria measured using the precision, recall, F-measure and fall-out metrics and the subjective criteria based on users' opinions. Users' subjective opinions [17] include satisfaction, understandability, usability, intention to purchase, etc. They are obtained through several questions given below in Table 1.

Table 1. Post-stage assessment questionnaire

Questionnaire	
S. No.	Statement title
S1	It was simple to use the system
S2	The explanation provided by the system is clear
S3	It was easy to provide product preferences in the system
S4	The on-screen information is helpful to solve the task
S5	The feedback mechanism is good
S6	I am sure that this is the book I have been searching for
S7	I did not find the improved recommendations useful when searching for books
S8	Overall, it required too much effort to find my desired book
S9	The chosen product attributes were relevant to my preferences
S10	I am satisfied with the final book recommendation list
S11	Overall, I am satisfied with the system

The general evaluation procedure for both interfaces (textual and visual) consists of the following steps:

Step 1. The user inputs his/her background information.
Step 2. The user is able to input his/her initial preferences to start the recommendation process as given in the algorithm in Sect. 3.
Step 3. The user is asked to fill in a system assessment questionnaire to evaluate the system. He/she can indicate the level of agreement for each statement on a five-point scale, ranging from −2 to +2, where −2 means "strongly disagree" and +2 is "strongly agree".
Step 4. Recommendation accuracy is estimated by asking the user to compare his/her chosen book to the entire books' list in the relevant book category, to determine whether or not he/she prefers another book.
Step 5. The user will perform steps 2 to 4 to evaluate the textual interface as well.

To be efficacious, a recommender system must be able to efficiently lead a user through a product-space and, in general, higher precision is desirable. For evaluating, we found the number of products viewed by users before they agreed to the system's recommendation (precision) compared with the recall values (ratio of the relevant books suggested by the system and books choices of the user in the real recommendation list). Precision can be seen as a measure of exactness or quality, whereas recall is a measure of completeness or quantity. Though both precision and recall are important in estimating the performance of a system that generates top N recommendations; depending upon the requirements of an application, one needs to find an optimal trade-off between the two. A single-valued metric like the F_β measure [23] can be used to obtain an appropriate weighted combination of precision and recall (refer Eq. (1)).

$$F_\beta = \left(1 + \beta^2\right) \times \frac{Precision \times Recall}{\beta^2 \times Precision + Recall} \tag{1}$$

The parameter 'β' controls the trade-off between precision and recall. A special case of the F_β measure with $\beta = 1$ is the traditional F-measure or F_1, which places the same weight on both; precision and recall (refer Eq. (2)).

$$F - measure = \frac{2 \times Precision \times Recall}{Precision + Recall} \tag{2}$$

As F_1 places the same weight on both, it is sometimes also called a biased metric.

Further to support the notion of increasing the number of relevant items and subsequently decreasing irrelevant ones in the recommendation list of top N, the fall-out measure for three RS variants was evaluated. Fall-out is defined as the proportion of non-relevant items that are retrieved, out of all non-relevant items available (see Eq. (3)).

$$Fall - out = \frac{|non - relevant\ books\ recommended|}{|all\ non - relevant\ books\ retrieved\ and\ not\ retrieved|} \tag{3}$$

This measure can be looked at as the probability that a non-relevant item is retrieved by a query. Hence for obvious reasons it is desired to be the least.

Recommenders should also be measured by the quality of the recommendations over the course of a session. One factor for estimating recommendation quality is the recommendation relevance and accuracy, which can be measured by letting users to review their final selection with reference to the full set of books in the given book category. Here we also derive recommendation accuracy as the percentage of times that users choose to stick with their selected product (refer Q5 and Q6 in the System Assessment Questionnaire). If users consistently select a different product the recommender is judged to be not very accurate. The more people stick with their selected best-match product, the more accurate the recommender is considered to be. In addition to the above objective evaluation results we were also interested in understanding the quality of the user experience with the two interfaces. For this we used our post-stage system assessment questionnaire (Fig. 2). Summarizing, we wish to evaluate both interfaces (textual and visual) by measuring: recommendation accuracy, relevance and the user subjective opinion. The ratings given by the user for questionnaire were used for evaluation by measuring precision, recall, fall-out and F_β measure as shown in Table 2 for top N recommendations (where N = 3, 5, 10). The following observations were made from the results:

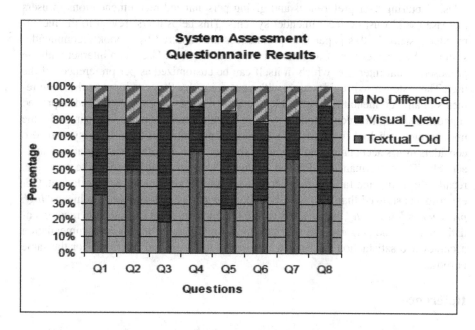

Fig. 2 Results of system assessment questionnaire

Table 2. Showing comparison of *Textual_old and Visual_new* systems using evaluation metrics for precision, recall, F_1 and fall-out.

Top N	3		5		10	
RS_type	Textual_old	Visual_new	Textual_old	Visual_new	Textual_old	Visual_new
Precision (P)	0.7504	0.9654	0.6634	0.8587	0.5444	0.7795
Recall (R)	0.2422	0.1884	0.3005	0.2381	0.3379	0.2912
F1	0.3662	0.3153	0.4136	0.3728	0.417	0.424
Fall-out	0.1116	0.0306	0.2	0.1012	0.2956	0.1285

The influence of integrating visual interfaces in our system on recommendations was observed. As shown in Table 2, with the enhancement of recommendation generation process, the precision is increased as one moves from Textual_old to Visual_new and Fall-out is decreased.

5   Conclusion

A competent method was developed for making recommendations, where both quantitative and qualitative analysis of user preferences and diverse opinions played important roles. Capturing user preferences and giving personalized recommendations to users increase users' trust on recommender systems. This helps users' revisit to the recommender system. In this paper user preferences are captured by a book recommender system which makes use of an interactive visual interface. Users can interact with the proposed visual interface, which in itself can be customized as per preferences of the user. The system also provides users with a provision that they can input further requirements in an incremental manner, which benefits them as they get better and improved suggestions from the recommender system. System becomes more transparent for the user as they can look beyond the suggestions presented to them. The system also considers user's acceptance and rejections for improvement of recommendations interactively. The performance of RS was evaluated using standard metrics like precision, recall, F-measure and fall-out for generating recommendations for a book dataset. Our experiments showed that the proposed recommender system is able to achieve *"high precision at low recall"*, hence users would find most relevant and accurate recommendations. Also, the personalized user interfaces significantly improve recommendation accuracy and satisfaction for users as compared to the textual interfaces for the same purpose.

References

1. Analytis, P., Schnabel, T., Herzog, S., Barkoczi, D., Joachims, T.: A preference elicitation interface for collecting dense recommender datasets with rich user information. In: Recsys 2017, Como, Italy (2017)
2. Armentano, M., Abalde, R., Schiaffino, S., Amandi, A.: User acceptance of recommender systems: influence of the preference elicitation algorithm. In: Proceedings of Semantic and Social Media Adaptation and Personalization (2014)

3. Bedi, P., Banati, H.: Trust aware usability. Spec. Issue Website Eval. J. Inf. Technol. Tourism **8**(3), 215–226 (2006)
4. Bedi, P., Banati, H.: Assessing user trust to improve web usability. J. Comput. Sci. **2**(3), 283–287 (2006)
5. Bedi, P., Sinha, A., Agarwal, S., Awasthi, A., Prasad, G., Saini, D.: Influence of Terrain on modern tactical combat: trust-based recommender system. Defense Sci. J. **60**(4), 405–411 (2010)
6. Bedi, P., Agarwal, S.: AORS: aspect-oriented recommender system. In: Proceedings CSNT 2011 - The International Conference on Communication Systems and Network Technologies, Jammu, India, 03–05 June, pp. 709–713. IEEE Computer Society, USA (2011a)
7. Bedi, P., Agarwal, S.: Preference learning in aspect oriented recommender system. In: CICN 2011 (2011b)
8. Berkovsky, S., Freyne, J., Oinas-Kukkonen, H.: Influencing individually: fusing personalization and persuasion. ACM Trans. Interact. Intell. Syst. (TiiS) **2**(2), article no. 9 (2012)
9. Burke, R.D., Hammond, K.J., Young, B.C.: The FindMe approach to assisted browsing. IEEE Expert Intell. Syst. Their Appl. **12**(4), 32–40 (1997)
10. Chen, L., Pu, P.: Critiquing-based recommenders: survey and emerging trends. User Model. User-Adap. Inter. **22**, 125–150 (2012)
11. Chesñevar, C., Maguitman, A.G., González, M.P.: Empowering recommendation technologies through argumentation. In: Simari, G., Rahwan, I. (eds.) Argumentation in Artificial Intelligence, pp. 403–422. Springer, Boston (2009). https://doi.org/10.1007/978-0-387-98197-0_20
12. Constantinides, M., Dowell, J.: User Interface Personalization in news apps. In: INRA Workshop, Halifax, Canada (2016)
13. Cremonesi, P., Garzotto, F., Turrin, R.: Investigating the persuasion potential of recommender systems from a quality perspective: an empirical study. ACM Trans. Interact. Intell. Syst. (TiiS), **2**(2), article no. 11 (2012)
14. He, C., Paara, D., Verbert, K.: Interactive recommender systems: a survey of the state of the art and future research challenges and opportunities. Expert Syst. Appl. **56**, 9–27 (2016)
15. Islam, M., Ding, C., Chi, C., Personalized recommender system on whom to follow in Twitter. In: Proceedings of Big Data and Cloud Computing, (IEEE Fourth International Conference) (2014)
16. Khribi, M.K., Jemni, M., Nasraoui, O.: Automatic Personalization in E-Learning Based on Recommendation Systems: An Overview (2011)
17. Pu, P., Chen, L.: A user-centric evaluation framework of recommender systems. In: Proceedings of the ACM RecSys 2010 Workshop on User-Centric Evaluation of Recommender Systems and Their Interfaces (UCERSTI), Barcelona, Spain, Published by CEUR-WS.org (2010). ISSN 1613-0073
18. Puerta, A.R.: A model-based interface development environment. IEEE Softw **14**(4), 40–47 (1997)
19. Ricci, F., Rokach, L., Shapira, B.: Introduction to recommender systems handbook. In: Ricci, F., Rokach, L., Shapira, B., Kantor, P. (eds.) Recommender Systems Handbook, pp. 1–35. Springer, Boston (2011)
20. Schafer, J.B., Konstan, J.A., Riedl, J.: E-commerce recommendation applications. In: Applications of Data Mining to Electronic Commerce, pp. 115–153. Springer US (2001)
21. Sharma, A., Yan, B.: Pairwise learning in recommendation: experiments with community recommendation on linkedin. In: Proceedings of the 7th ACM Conference on Recommender systems, pp. 193–200 (2013)

22. Sivapalan, S., Sadeghian, A., Rahnama, H.: Recommender systems in E-Commerce. In: Proceedings of the World Automation Congress (2014)
23. Van Rijsbergen, C.J.: Information Retrieval, 2nd edn. Butterworths, London (1979)
24. Vashisth, P., Bedi, P.: Interest-based personalized recommender system. In: Information and Communication Technologies (WICT), World Congress, pp. 245–250. IEEE, December 2011
25. Webb, G.I., Pazzani, M.J., Billsus, D.: Machine learning for user modeling. User Model. User-Adapt. Interact. 11(1–2), 19–29 (2001)
26. Yu, Y., He, J.: An analysis of users' cognitive factors towards icon in interactive interface. In: 2010 Second International Conference on Intelligent Human-Machine Systems and Cybernetics. IEEE, (2010). https://doi.org/10.1109/ihmsc.2010.105(2010)

Item-Based Collaborative Filtering Using Sentiment Analysis of User Reviews

Abhishek Dubey[✉], Ayush Gupta, Nitish Raturi, and Pranshu Saxena

Department of Computer Science and Engineering, Inderprastha Engineering College, Ghaziabad, India
abd6982@gmail.com, ayushgupta530@gmail.com,
raturinitish203@gmail.com, pranshusaxena@gmail.com

Abstract. Traditional Collaborative filtering algorithm works by using only the past experience of a user. To overcome the limitations of the traditional collaborative algorithm, an item based collaborative filtering system was introduced. In this paper, an improved recommender system is proposed. A dictionary of sentiment scores is created. These sentiment scores are calculated by finding the probability of the reviews to be positive. This sentiment score is used by an item based collaborative filtering system to improve the recommendations and filter out items with overall negative user opinion. The performance of the proposed system is compared with previous work done in this field.

Keywords: Collaborative filtering · Item based · Logistic regression
Recommender systems · Sentiment analysis

1 Introduction

The huge stock of data has given birth to the problem of determining which portion of information is exactly relevant to a particular recipient. Since it is virtually impossible to go through every bit of data to look for what is required, information filtering helps to make the process efficient [28]. A subclass of information filtering is Recommender System. Most noticeable application of recommender system these days can be found in e-commerce applications. Here, recommender system is a software that processes and analyses the available data and gives some products out of the complete set as suggestion to user. The data which is analysed can be choice patterns of other users who went through similar product choices as that of the current user, user's profile information and shopping history, demographic categories of the market and their trend or a combination of all these [2, 4]. Above data works as an input does the trick in most situations but lacks a humanitarian aspect of the choice prediction part. In some cases, products are recommended which do not have good customer feedback and review, making the process a machine logic generated instead of a particular to person experience. Also, for the recommendations, opinion of only a subset of users is considered ignoring the overall opinion of all the users.

The proposed recommender system aims to find out the overall sentiment about any product, which is suggested by any traditional recommender system, and present it to

G. C. Deka et al. (Eds.): ICACCT 2018, CCIS 899, pp. 77–87, 2018.
https://doi.org/10.1007/978-981-13-2035-4_8

user in product suggestions only if it qualifies its public reviews and opinions. Sentiment analysis has been used to judge the sentiment of any customer's comment using a Bag of words [6] model and supervised learning [18, 20] technique. An average customer's comment on any online platform is not well structured and does not follow language principles and grammar of the English language. Further, beautification of the language along with use of special features of language like idioms, proverbs, hyperbole and others, the meaning extraction becomes multifaceted and can easily mislead a machine to synthesize faulty predictions. For understanding and extracting the actual meaning of the text, natural language processing is used, which is a part of computational linguistics, studying interaction between computers and humans. The *first* part of system is sentiment analysis, performed using Supervised learning, which uses the Internet Movie Database (IMDb) review dataset [1]. The reviews labelled as '0' or '1' for denoting NEGATIVE and POSITIVE respectively forms the training dataset. These reviews contain irrelevant data such as HTML tags, digits, symbols, etc., which makes them unsuitable as training input. Pre-processing is applied to clean the data. The actual comments from e-commerce sites also need to be pre-processed. In pre-processing, HTML tags are removed, text is tokenized, words are reduced to their root form and those words are removed from the text which do not convey any useful meaning in deciding the sentiment. After cleaning the data, a Bag of Words model has been used to represent the text as a group of feature vectors containing term frequencies with tf-idf applied to it. Logistic regression has been used as the prediction algorithm. *Second* part of this system is the recommender system to which the derived sentiments are fed as an additional input along with user preferences. The recommender system is an item based collaborative filtering system which uses similarity as a measure. It finds the items which are most similar to the ones rated by the user and computes an average weighted sum of the ratings and similarity score. Including the sentiment score in the product improves the recommendations made by the system.

This paper is organized as follows: Sect. 2 presents a systematic review of sentiment analysis, recommender systems and different approaches for making recommendations followed by inference from review of literature. Section 3 presents the proposed model for making better recommendations using sentiment analysis in detail. Section 4 gives analysis of result of the presented model and future directions for research of considering limitations of the model, followed by conclusive remark is presented in Sect. 5.

2   Related Work

In recommender systems, collaborative filtering is used to build personalized recommendations to the users based on their behaviour. It uses the previous experiences of the users, their past ratings to predict ratings for the items they have not rated yet [22]. It uses the similarity between users to make better recommendations. The first paper on collaborative filtering was published in 1990s [38]. This required the users to manually give their opinions, but this system is not effective when the number of users become very large as each person cannot know about everything. Collaborative Filtering approaches can be categorised into 3 classes – Memory Based, Model Based and Hybrid.

A *memory based* collaborative filtering system consists of a matrix of user ratings for items. This matrix is used to find similarity between users and predict ratings for items which they have not experienced [17, 31, 33, 36]. They can be further sub-divided into user based and item based collaborative filtering systems. User based collaborative filtering is based on the idea that people having similar choices in the past may have similar choices in the future as well. This approach was first introducing by Group lens for recommending news articles [36] and was also used video [35] and movie [24] recommendations. However, user-based system is not appropriate when the number of users is very large as comparing a user to every other user for every recommendation can be very costly. To address this issue of scalability, Amazon invented the item based collaborative filtering system [26]. In this system Items are recommended based on the similarity with other items. When a user purchases an item, similar items are picked and recommended to the user. The similarity is computed between items based on how different users rated the items. For computing similarity, similarity measures like Pearson correlation [32, 33] can be used to find linear relationship between the user and item vectors. In *model-based* recommender systems [30, 32, 33], models of user ratings are built to give item recommendations. Model building is performed by various machine learning algorithms such as Bayesian Network [21], Clustering [10, 14], and Matrix Factorization [3]. *Hybrid* recommender systems are a combination of memory based and model based collaborative filtering systems. They are built to solve the issues of scalability and sparsity. However, none of these approaches put into consideration the opinions of users about the item. Textual reviews about various items can be found on different sites. These reviews tell a lot about the likability of an item. Even if an item may be similar to another item, but it may not be likable. Very little research has been carried out in this field.

In this section, some of the research related to sentiment analysis, recommender systems and collaborative filtering has been presented. Sentiment Analysis has been an idea of research since the 1950s. Various papers have shown different approaches towards sentiment classification and opinion mining [5, 11, 13, 16, 25, 37]. Sentiment Analysis can be performed by lexicon-based techniques [9, 12, 23] or by machine learning [15, 27, 28]. Lexicon based techniques aim to extract sentiments according to the words. However, since the amount of data available today to train the machine learning is enormous, these approaches outperform the lexicon-based approaches. Several studies have also been performed which show the comparison between these approaches [9, 12]. This paper focuses on the machine learning based approach for sentiment analysis. Leung et al. [19] proposed a rating inference approach to incorporate textual data into collaborative filtering systems. They proposed the idea of performing sentiment analysis on the reviews about a product to determine an overall sentiment. (i.e. recommended or not recommended). However, the model to incorporate the sentiments into collaborative filtering system was not specified. In this paper, this approach has been explained along with analysis of results. Krishna et al. [8] proposed a recommendation system using Learning Automata and Sentiment Analysis. The system optimizes the recommendation score produced by the proposed system using sentiment analysis and then recommends the places nearby the current location of the users by analysing the feedback from the places. However, the response time of the system increase with the increase in requests and issues a problem of scalability. This paper improves the recommendations without affecting the scalability of the recommender. Guimaraes et al. [5] presented a recommendation system based on sentiment analysis on textual data extracted from Social Networks. They used the polarity of the adverb in the sentences to classify them as positive or negative. But the recommendation model was not given which used the sentiments. The model proposed in this paper addresses the problems of low accuracy in sentiment analysis by using machine learning based sentiment analysis and the problem of scalability by using an item based collaborative filtering system. Further the results of the recommendation with and without the sentiment scores have been analysed which shows an improvement over the previous works.

3   Proposed Model

The proposed model consists of mainly two modules. The *first* module analyses the reviews and obtain overall sentiment about the products. The *second* module uses collaborative filtering for recommendations with the sentiment score as an input. Figure 1 shows our proposed framework.

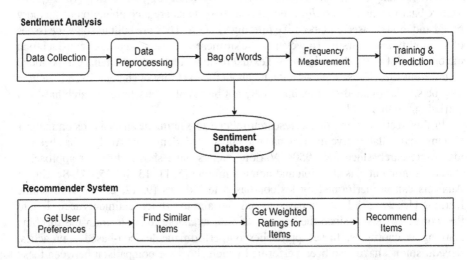

Fig. 1. Proposed framework for item based collaborative filtering using sentiment analysis

3.1   Sentiment Analysis

Sentiment analysis is the first component which has been divided into four major steps, data collection, followed by pre-processing, and construction of bag of words and finally, frequency measurement. These have been explained in further subsections.

3.1.1 Data Collection

Data collection is the process of collecting data from various sources. A huge amount of data is required for training the classifications algorithms. This data can be collected from various sources like crawling and scraping e-commerce websites, user forums, getting pre-built datasets or making own reviews for the dataset. For this research, the IMDb review dataset has been used [1]. It contains 25000 reviews labelled as '1' for positive and '0' for negative.

3.1.2 Pre-processing

After gathering data from various sources, it is made homogeneous. Different techniques are applied in the pre-processing of data. They are shown in Fig. 2.

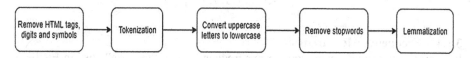

Fig. 2. Steps involved in data pre-processing

The data has to be cleaned. Reviews fetched from web contain html tags, which are removed. Symbols such as punctuation marks and digits which are irrelevant and do not give any information are also removed. Punctuation marks sometimes give an idea of the opinion expressed in a phrase or sentence. However, in the bag of words symbols are not useful in the bag of words representation. Tokenization involves splitting the sentences into words or 'tokens'. These tokens are later used in making the bag of words model. Uppercase text is converted to lowercase to avoid the differentiation between same words in different cases. Stop words are words in the corpus which give little or no information about the sentiment expressed and can reduce the accuracy of 'bag of words' since they have very high frequency. Lemmatization is the process of removing inflectional endings and to return the base or dictionary form of a word, known as 'lemma', by using a vocabulary and performing morphological analysis of words. So, words like trying, tried, etc. are all returned to the same base form 'try'.

3.1.3 Bag of Words

Textual data cannot be directly fed to the classification algorithms, as they require numerical feature vectors with a fixed size. The bag of words model is a method of representing textual data as a vector of numbers. In this model, text is represented as a set of words. This bag of words is used to generate term frequency. A subset of the terms is selected as features. The number of features selected is the size of vectors. These vectors represent the count of each word in the review. For e.g. consider two sentences (Table 1).

1. The quick brown fox jumps over the lazy dog
2. Never jump over the lazy dog quickly

Table 1. Bag of words model

	The	Quick	Brown	Fox	Jump	Over	Lazy	Dog	Never
The quick Brown Fox jumps over the lazy dog	2	1	1	1	1	1	1	1	0
Never jump over the lazy dog quickly	1	1	0	0	1	1	1	1	1

The aforementioned sentences can now be represented as vectors representing term counts. Each of them is a 9-element vector.

$$[2, 1, 1, 1, 1, 1, 1, 1, 0]$$

$$[1, 1, 0, 0, 1, 1, 1, 1, 1]$$

3.1.4 Frequency Measurement

In a large text corpus, some words occur frequently (e.g. "the", "a", "is" in English) hence carrying very little meaningful information about the actual contents of the document. If the count data is fed directly to a classifier, those very frequent terms will shadow the frequencies of rarer yet more interesting terms. In order to re-weight the count features into floating point values suitable for usage by a classifier, tf-idf transform is applied. tf means term-frequency while tf–idf means term-frequency times inverse document-frequency. The tf-idf is given by Eq. (1) and idf can be calculated using Eq. (2).

$$tf - idf(t, d) = tf(t, d) \times idf(t) \tag{1}$$

$$idf(t) = \log \frac{1 + n_d}{1 + df(d, t)} + 1 \tag{2}$$

Where n_d is the total number of documents, and $df(t, d)$ is the number of documents that contain term (t). The resulting tf-idf vectors are normalized by the Euclidean norm as shown in Eq. (3).

$$v_{norm} = \frac{v}{||v||} = \frac{v}{\sqrt{v_1^2 + v_2^2 + \dots + v_n^2}} \tag{3}$$

3.1.5 Training and Prediction

Now, the feature vectors are ready and can be fed to the classifier for training. A logistic regression classifier is trained using the 25000 training examples from the bag of words model. Then it is used to predict positive probability of the test reviews. Logistic Regression predicts a probability for a class in the range [0, 1] and then a threshold is applied to make the result binary (in case of binary classification). In this case, the probability of class being positive is taken.

3.2 Sentiment Database

In our database, we have calculated the overall sentiment of the users towards different movie based on the sentiments of their reviews towards the movie. Sample calculated rating for some movies are depicted in Table 2.

Table 2. Sample sentiment database

Sr. No.	Item name	Sentiment score
1.	Toy Story (1995)	0.96
2.	Golden Eye (1995)	0.83
3.	Four Rooms (1995)	0.64
4.	Get Shortly (1995)	0.94
5.	Copy Cat (1995)	0.96
6.	Babe (1995)	0.87
7.	Richard III (1995)	0.97

3.3 Recommender System

In our recommendation system, we are the *collaborative filtering* technique. It is one of the most widely used personalized recommendation technique. It processes and filters the information based on user ratings. To predict any product for a particular user, collaborative filtering compares the likeness and dis-likeness of other users towards that product.

This paper focuses on the Item based collaborative filtering system which uses similarity as a measure to recommend items. The Movielens dataset [7] by Grouplens research was used for testing the recommender system. The process is as follows: *First*, a model consisting of all items and their most similar items is built. Items in this data refers to movies. Pearson Correlation has been used as the means to find correlation among the items. High correlation suggests higher similarity and a higher chance that a person who liked one item may like the other one as well. Pearson Correlation can be calculated using Eq. (4).

$$r = \frac{n\left(\sum xy\right) - \left(\sum x\right)\left(\sum y\right)}{\sqrt{\left[n\sum x^2 - \left(\sum x\right)^2\right]\left[n\sum y^2 - \left(\sum y\right)^2\right]}} \tag{4}$$

Where 'x' and 'y' are vectors representing ratings of two items by different users and 'r' is the correlation coefficient. For prediction $P_{u,i}$ of an item i by a user u, a weighted sum of the ratings $R_{u,j}$, the similarity score $S_{i,j}$ and the sentiment score SS_i is computed for all the items similar to i rated by the user. Then the weighted sum is scaled by sum of similarities [36]. The prediction can be calculated using Eq. (5).

$$P_{u,i} = \frac{\sum_{j=1}^{n} \left(S_{i,j} \times R_{u,j} \times SS_i \right)}{\sum_{j=1}^{n} \left(\left| S_{i,j} \right| \right)} \tag{5}$$

Then the items are sorted in descending order of their prediction score and the topmost items are recommended to the user.

4   Result

The system needed a vast set of real user's sentiments and data for training the recommender system. For our experimental setup, we used the Movielens 100 k dataset. The dataset consists of 100,000 ratings from 1000 users on 1700 movies. The reviews for these movies were gathered using web scraping. The best practices for scraping were employed.

Having collected all the data we built sentiment database, which is an organized set of movie titles and their corresponding reviews. We used the IMDb review dataset [1] which consists of 25000 reviews classified as either positive or negative. The logistic regression classifier is trained on this dataset (all 25000 reviews). The title wise scraped reviews are then classified, and the final sentiment scores are calculated as the average of sentiment scores of all the reviews on any particular title. Thus, we get the recommendations without sentiment and with the calculated sentiments and then we compare the results. The logistic regression model was tested on the training data giving an accuracy of 92%. This model was used to predict positive sentiment probabilities on the reviews of the items from the movie lens dataset.

The recommender system initially predicted items which were similar based on the similarity score but had overall negative opinion by other users. After incorporating the sentiment scores in the weighted average for predicting rating of an item, the recommender showed improvement. The items which had overall negative opinion were either not recommended or had lower similarity score and were pushed backwards in the recommendation list. Table 3 shows the results of the recommender using sentiment vs not using sentiment. 10 results were taken for a test and the fraction has been computed as positive items per total recommendations and negative items per total recommendations.

Table 3. Comparison between previous and the improved recommender system.

S. No.	+ve per total recommendations (without sentiment)	−ve per total recommendations (without sentiment)	+ve per total recommendations (with sentiment)	−ve per total recommendations (with sentiment)
1	0.6	0.4	0.9	0.1
2	0.8	0.2	1.0	0.0
3	0.8	0.2	0.9	0.1
4	0.9	0.1	1.0	0.0
5	0.6	0.4	0.8	0.2
6	0.7	0.3	0.9	0.1
7	0.8	0.2	1.0	0.0

This approach increases the accuracy of the recommender while making a very little impact on the time required and performance as the opinions need to be computed only once for every item (or once in a while to incorporate the changes due to new reviews). Our work is in line with some of the other approaches on using the sentiment analysis with collaborative filtering, notably framework of Leung [19] to make sentiments representable to collaborative filtering using opinion dictionary. Our framework further provides scope of improving efficiency and making it calculable in addition to making sentiments representable to machines for the purpose of recommendations.

5 Conclusion

This paper presents an improved item-based recommendation using sentiment analysis of user reviews. Including sentiment score as one of the parameters for providing recommendations has changed the otherwise collected result. This system shows an improvement over traditional recommender system, improving the quality of predictions without major impact on performance. This supports the theory of overall user sentiments being helpful in determining quality of any item. All the recommendations would be ranked as the combination of both factors i.e. user's liking and item's quality. However, this system has its limitations like every other. Determining the sentiments cannot be always completely accurate. Sometimes positive comments are classified as negative and vice versa depending upon the usage of the language and its correctness. This is an initial work in the particular direction. With further research and adopting more efficient algorithms sentiment scores could be made more accurate.

References

1. Maas, A.L., Daly, R.E., Pham, P.T., Huang, D., Ng, A.Y., Potts, C.: Learning word vectors for sentiment analysis. In: The 49th Annual Meeting of the Association for Computational Linguistics (2018, updated)
2. Jena, K.C., Mishra, S., Sahoo, S., Mishra, B.K.: Principles, techniques and evaluation of recommendation systems. In: International Conference on Inventive Systems and Control, pp. 1–6 (2017)
3. Guo, G., Zhang, J., Yorke-Smith, N.: A novel recommendation model regularized with user trust and item ratings. IEEE Trans. Knowl. Data Eng. **28**, 1607–1620 (2016)
4. Beel, J., Gipp, B., Langer, S., Breitinger, C.: Research-paper recommender systems: a literature survey. Int. J. Digit. Libr. **17**(4), 305–338 (2016)
5. Guimarães, R., Rodríguez, D.Z., Rosa, R.L., Bressan, G.: Recommendation system using sentiment analysis considering the polarity of the adverb. In: IEEE International Symposium on Consumer Electronics, pp. 71–72 (2016)
6. Zhang, Y., Jin, R., Zhou, Z.-H.: Understanding bag-of-words model: a statistical framework. Int. J. Mach. Learn. Cybern. **1**(1–4), 43–52 (2010)
7. Harper, F.M., Konstan, J.A.: The MovieLens Datasets: History and Context. ACM Trans. Interact. Intell. Syst. (TiiS) **5**(4), 19:1–19:19 (2015). Regular Articles and Special issue on New Directions in Eye Gaze for Interactive Intelligent Systems (Part 1 of 2)

8. Krishna, P.V., Misra, S., Joshi, D., Obaidat, M.S.: Learning automata based sentiment analysis for recommender system on cloud. In: 2013 International Conference on Computer, Information and Telecommunication Systems, pp. 1–5 (2014)

9. Hailong, Z., Wenyan, G., Bo, J.: Machine learning and Lexicon based methods for sentiment classification: a survey. In: WISA 2014 Proceeding 11th Web Information System and Application Conference, pp. 262–265 (2014)

10. Zhang, D., Hsu, C.H., Chen, M., Chen, Q., Xiong, N., Lloret, J.: Cold-start recommendation using bi-clustering and fusion for large-scale social recommender systems. IEEE Trans. Emerg. Top. Comput. **2**(2), 239–250 (2013)

11. Neethu, M.S., Rajasree, R.: Sentiment analysis in twitter using machine learning techniques. In: 2013 Fourth International Conference on Computing, Communications and Networking Technologies (ICCCNT), pp. 1–5 (2013)

12. Feldman, R.: Techniques and applications for sentiment analysis. Commun. ACM **56**(4), 82–89 (2013)

13. Faridani, S.: Using canonical correlation analysis for generalized sentiment analysis, product recommendation and search. In: Proceedings of the Fifth ACM Conference on Recommender Systems, pp. 355–358 (2011)

14. Chakraborty, P.S.: A scalable collaborative filtering-based recommender system using incremental clustering. In: IEEE International Conference on Advance Computing, pp. 1526–1529 (2009)

15. Ye, Q., Law, R., Gu, B.: The impact of online user reviews on hotel room sales. Int. J. Hosp. Manag. **28**(1), 180–182 (2009)

16. Pang, B., Lee, L.: Opinion mining and sentiment analysis. Found. Trends Inf. Retr. **2**(1–2), 1–135 (2008)

17. Wan, X., Ninomiya, T., Okamoto, T.: A learner's role-based multi-dimensional collaborative recommendation (LRMDCR) for group learning support. In: IEEE International Joint Conference on Neural Networks (IEEE World Congress on Computational Intelligence), pp. 3912–3917 (2008)

18. Kotsiantis, S.B.: Supervised machine learning: a review of classification techniques. In: Proceedings of the 2007 Conference on Emerging Artificial Intelligence Applications in Computer Engineering: Real Word AI Systems with Applications in eHealth, HCI, Information Retrieval and Pervasive Technologies, pp. 3–24 (2007)

19. Leung, C.W., Chan, S.C., Chung, F.: Integrating collaborative filtering and sentiment analysis: a rating inference approach. In: ECAI 2006 Workshop on Recommender Systems, pp. 62–66 (2006)

20. Caruana, R., Niculescu-Mizil, A.: An empirical comparison of supervised learning algorithms. In: ICML 2006 Proceedings of the 23rd International Conference on Machine Learning, pp. 161–168 (2006)

21. Su, X., Khoshgoftaar, T.M.: Collaborative filtering for multi-class data using belief nets algorithms. In: ICTAI 2006 Proceedings of the 18th IEEE International Conference on Tools with Artificial Intelligence, pp. 497–504 (2006)

22. Adomavicius, G., Tuzhilin, A.: Toward the next generation of recommender systems: a survey of the state-of-the-art and possible extensions. IEEE Trans. Knowl. Data Eng. **17**(6), 734–749 (2005)

23. Hu, M., Liu, B.: Mining opinion features in customer reviews. In: AAAI 2004 Proceedings of the 19th National Conference on Artificial Intelligence, pp. 755–760 (2004)

24. Miller, B.N., Albert, I., Lam, S.K., Konstan, J.A., Riedl, J.: MovieLens unplugged: experiences with an occasionally connected recommender system. In: IUI 2003 Proceedings of the 8th International Conference on Intelligent User Interfaces, pp. 263–266 (2003)

25. Nasukawa, T., Yi, J.: Sentiment analysis: capturing favorability using natural language processing. In: K-CAP 2003 Proceedings of the 2nd International Conference on Knowledge Capture, pp. 70–77 (2003)
26. Linden, G., Smith, B., York, J.: Amazon.com recommendations: item-to-item collaborative filtering. IEEE Internet Comput. 7(1), 76–80 (2003)
27. Pang, B., Lee, L., Vaithyanathan, S.: Thumbs up? sentiment classification using machine learning techniques. In: Proceedings of the Conference on Empirical Methods in Natural Language Processing, pp. 79–86 (2002)
28. Turney, P.D.: Thumbs up or thumbs down? semantic orientation applied to unsupervised classification of reviews. In: Proceedings of the 40th Annual Meeting of the Association for Computational Linguistics, pp. 417–424 (2002)
29. Hanani, U., Shapira, B., Shoval, P.: Information filtering: overview of issues, research and systems. User Modeling User-Adapt. Interact. 11(3), 203–259 (2001)
30. Getoor, L., Sahami, M.: Using probabilistic relational models for collaborative filtering. In: Proceedings of the Workshop Web Usage Analysis and User Profiling (WEBKDD 1999) (1999)
31. Nakamura, A., Abe, N.: Collaborative filtering using weighted majority prediction algorithms. In: ICML 1998 Proceedings of the Fifteenth International Conference on Machine Learning, pp. 395–403 (1998)
32. Billsus, D., Pazzani, M.J.: Learning collaborative information filters. In: ICML 1998 Proceedings of the Fifteenth International Conference on Machine Learning, pp. 46–54 (1998)
33. Breese, J.S., Heckerman, D., Kadie, C.: Empirical analysis of predictive algorithms for collaborative filtering. In: UAI 1998 Proceedings of the Fourteenth Conference on Uncertainty in Artificial Intelligence, pp. 43–52 (1998)
34. Shardanand, U., Maes, P.: Social information filtering: algorithms for automating "word of mouth". In: CHI 1995 Proceedings of the SIGCHI Conference on Human Factors in Computing Systems, pp. 210–217 (1995)
35. Hill, W., Stead, L., Rosenstein, M., Furnas, G.: Recommending and evaluating choices in a virtual community of use. In: CHI 1995 Proceedings of the SIGCHI Conference on Human Factors in Computing Systems, pp. 194–201 (1995)
36. Resnick, P., Lacovou, N., Suchak, M., Bergstrom, P., Riedl, J.: GroupLens: an open architecture for collaborative filtering of netnews. In: CSCW 1994 Proceedings of the 1994 ACM Conference on Computer Supported Cooperative Work, pp. 175–186 (1994)
37. Cavnar, W.B., Trenkle, J.M.: N-gram-based text categorization. In: Proceedings of SDAIR-94, 3rd Annual Symposium on Document Analysis and Information Retrieval, pp. 161–175 (1994)
38. Goldberg, D., Nichols, D., Oki, B.M., Terry, D.: Using collaborative filtering to weave an information tapestry. Commun. ACM – Spec. Issue Inf. Filter. 35(12), 61–70 (1992)

Emotion Analysis of Twitter Data Using Hashtag Emotions

Prerna Goel[✉] and Reema Thareja

Department of Computer Science, Shyama Prasad Mukherjee College,
University of Delhi, Punjabi Bagh, New Delhi, India
angelprernagoel@gmail.com, reemathareja@gmail.com

Abstract. Twitter, being a social networking service used by millions of people to express their opinions, emotions on number of topics in form of short messages, makes it rich source of data for sentiment and emotion analysis. This paper analyses the various emotions expressed by twitter users and finds the most and least expressed emotion on twitter using sentiment analysis. Because of the recent trend of using hashtags with tweets, task of extracting tweets using specific hashtag keyword has simplified. These hashtags are utilized in this paper to extract tweets specifying particular emotions.

Keywords: Twitter mining · Sentiment analysis · Comparison cloud

1 Introduction

Today microblogging has become a very popular communication tool among Internet users. Twitter, being a microblogging tool, allow individuals to express their opinions, feelings, and thoughts on a variety of topics in the form of short text messages commonly known as tweets. These tweets may also include the emotions of individuals such as happiness, anger, anxiety, sadness [1]. For example, the tweet "dm me, I'm bored" shows that the person is getting bored and the tweet "I ordered pizza #happy" is expressing happy mood.

Here second example shows the use of twitter hashtags. A tweet may include one or more words immediately preceded with a hash symbol (#). Such words are called hashtags [12]. A hashtag is a way of categorizing tweets, making tweet part of a narrowed conversation. If hashtag is included in a tweet, people who search for that hashtag will be able to see that tweet. This put tweeter's thoughts into context and lets followers and those browsing search results know the specific topic to which tweet is associated. Thus, hashtags organize tweets so they are easier to find in Twitter search [2]. Hashtags can also indicate the tone of the message or the tweeter's emotions. For example, #happy is used for expressing happy emotion and #tired for expressing tiredness.

As of 2016, Twitter had more than 319 million monthly active users [3]. Due to its large audience, Twitter can be considered a rich repository of emotions, sentiments and moods. Also, Twitter limits tweet length to specific number of characters which is 140 characters currently [10]. This is very different from other microblogging sites, which allow individual's opinion and reviews to be consisted of multiple sentences. With the

© Springer Nature Singapore Pte Ltd. 2018
G. C. Deka et al. (Eds.): ICACCT 2018, CCIS 899, pp. 88–98, 2018.
https://doi.org/10.1007/978-981-13-2035-4_9

Twitter API and other tools, it is much easier to collect millions of tweets. Therefore, data from twitter can be suitably used in tasks like opinion mining, sentiment and emotion analysis [4].

2 Related Work

Social media alternatives such as Twitter allow the people to share their experiences and impressions about almost every facet of their lives. Millions of people use twitter to share their opinions, express emotions [13]. Being a rich source of data, it is widely used for sentiment analysis by researchers. Sentiment analysis, also called opinion mining, focuses on identifying and categorizing patterns expressed in a piece of text. It helps in determining one's attitude towards a particular topic, product etc. [5]. Classifying tweets based on their emotion or sentiment has been a growing area of research [1]. Several researchers have relied on emotion symbols like emoticons and emoji ideograms to classify Twitter messages [4, 11, 22, 23]. There are few examples in which researchers have used hashtag tweets for classification. In [1], Hasan, Rundensteiner and Agu proposed an approach for automatically classifying text messages of individuals to infer their emotional states. Davidov, Tsur and Rappoport in [14] utilized 50 Twitter tags and 15 smileys as sentiment labels for sentiment classification and showed identification of sentiment types of untagged sentences. Mohammad and Kiritchenko [12], have gone beyond the classification to investigate the relationship between emotions and personality using the Hashtag Emotion Lexicon.

There are few works employing Twitter hashtags to perform sentiment analysis and then using its result to perform sentiment analysis again, in order to obtain a wide range of emotion lexicons and find the least and most expressed emotion on twitter.

3 Proposed Work

3.1 Tweets Extraction for Emotion Analysis

The main problem is how to extract the rich information that is available on Twitter and how to use it to draw meaningful insight. Twitter messages, usually called tweets, are extracted with the help of twitter mining using R. The 'twitteR' package can be used to extract tweets from specific user or retrieve recent tweets containing particular search term [15]. Twitter has numerous regulations and rate limits imposed on its API, and for this reason it requires that all users must register an account and provide authentication details when they query the API [4]. We can't use the Search API to get tweets from a specific date range because it returns tweets created before the given date. Date should be formatted as YYYY-MM-DD. The search index has a 7-day limit. In other words, no tweets will be found for a date older than one week [16]. If Search API had worked properly for the date range then there was no need of finding emotion lexicons to determine the least and most expressed emotion on twitter. We could have relied on number of tweets extracted per emotion word within that specific date range.

We have used only hashtag tweets for our research work because it is easy to analyse the emotion expression expressed by tweeter using these emotion-word hashtag. For example, the tweet "Feeling left out... #bored" clearly shows that tweeter is feeling bored. But, there also exist tweets where reading just the message before the hashtag does not convey the emotions of the tweeter. For example the tweet "Mika used my poem for her assignment #angry". Here, the hashtag is providing information not present in the rest of the message. Also there are some tweets such as "It's raining:/ #joy" where tweet do not seem to express the emotions stated in the hashtags [12].

In [4], author was relied on assumption that "the emoticon in the tweet represents the overall emotion contained in that tweet" for successful classification of emotions. In our paper, we can't make this assumption because in some of the cases, we can't say that emotion expressed by the tweet is same as that of emotion-word hashtaged. For example, the tweet "first-ever Angry Birds World to open at DFC #angry#birds" has angry as the emotion-word hashtags while tweet itself do not seem to express angry emotion.

Due to the challenges outlined above, we cannot rely only on emotion-word hashtags to determine emotion, we have to make list of emotion lexicons using sentiment analysis of these emotion-word hashtag tweets and then further use these lexicon lists to perform emotion analysis on tweets. Therefore, Emotion analysis is done as an additional layer on top of the simpler sentiment classification [4]. So, finding least and most expressed emotion on twitter is the two-step process:

(1) Extracting emotion lexicons depicting various emotions using sentiment analysis
(2) Using extracted lists of various emotion lexicons to perform emotion analysis on twitter data

Although tweets extracted for this paper are specifically in English, as language can be specified while searching for tweets, the informal language that is used in tweets make sentiment analysis in Twitter a very different task [4]. Tweets often have spelling mistakes, short forms, and various other properties that make such text difficult to process by natural language systems [12].

3.2 Extracting Emotion Lexicons Using Hashtaged Tweets

Emotions can be defined as subjective feelings and Thoughts. Therefore they can be said to be closely related to sentiments [4]. People's emotions can be categorized into four distinct classes:

Happy-active
Happy-inactive
Unhappy-active
Unhappy-inactive [1]

To get the emotion lexicons, we need tweets with emotion-word hashtaged that depict different kind of emotions. For this purpose, 1000 tweets of each emotion-word hashtag are extracted with the help of twitter mining (Table 1).

Tweets extracted include only hashtag tweets. For example, to extract tweets expressing happy emotion, '#happy' keyword is used and '#tired' for tweets expressing tiredness.

Table 1. List of hashtags we have used from each emotion class

Class	Hash-Tags
Happy-active	#happy, #excited **example: might get a wii u for my birthday yessssss!#excited**
Happy-inactive	#relaxed, #sleepy **example: #sad A poor girl trying to earn some pennies in extreme cold**
Unhappy-active	#angry, #afraid **example: Do not be #afraid**
Unhappy-inactive	#tired, #bored, #sad **example: Buzzing for a day off #Tired**

Extracted tweets need to be processed in order to convert them in the form suitable for sentiment analysis:

Corpus of extracted tweets is created.

Preprocessing is done to obtain proper data set with accurate features. Text preprocessing include steps like removing English stop words, removing punctuations and urls, converting all text to lower case, removing numbers and words of single length and stripping off extra white spaces [6].

Splitting of processed tweets into individual words so they can be easily compared for sentiment analysis.

Splitted individual words are compared with list of already proposed positive and negative opinion words [7] to extract distinct words used for various emotions. This list of positive and negative opinion words contains many misspelled words. They are not mistakes but included because these misspelled words appear frequently in social media content. Also, the appearance of an opinion word in a sentence does not necessarily mean that the sentence expresses a positive or negative opinion [8]. For example, the tweet "I break her record #happy". Here, 'break' is a negative opinion word but used to express positive opinion. This problem is solved by using both positive and negative opinion words list while finding emotion lexicons.

Our splitted individual words are compared with list of both positive and negative opinion words. Because of this, in our previous example, 'break' will be included in the list of happy emotion words and while performing sentiment analysis in future tasks will give correct result. So, we can say that, even though appearance of an opinion word in a tweet does not express any opinion, presence of hashtag emotion in that tweet is enough to reveal the opinion expressed by that opinion word.

Positive and negative opinion words found after sentiment analysis of tweets with "#happy" keyword are named as happywords and those words found after sentiment analysis of tweets with "#sad" keyword are named as sadwords. Same is done for other emotions.

Some opinion words can be present in more than one emotion words list. For instance, "I'm so #excited right now because I ordered my Cockles Photo-op for my 1st Supernatural Con!!! #cantwait #happy", here, positive and negative opinion words present in this tweet will be included in both excitedwords and happywords list. Same holds for the tweet "3 more hours of a 12 h shift to go #coffee #tired #sleepy #bored", opinion words present will be included in all tiredwords, sleepywords and boredwords list.

[12289]	884	1844	NA	NA	NA	NA	NA	NA	778	NA	NA	NA	NA	927	NA	NA	NA	NA	NA	NA	NA	NA
[12321]	NA	NA	884	NA	1533	NA	NA	NA	NA	NA	NA	NA	NA	NA	NA	NA	NA	NA	NA	NA	NA	NA
[12353]	NA	NA	NA	NA	NA	884	NA	NA	NA	NA	NA	NA	NA	NA	1088	NA	NA	NA	1088	NA	NA	
[12385]	NA	NA	NA	NA	927	NA	NA	NA	NA	NA	NA	NA	NA	1160	1392	NA	884	NA	NA	NA	NA	
[12417]	NA	NA	NA	NA	830	NA	NA	NA	NA	1098	NA	NA	NA	NA	NA	NA	NA	NA	NA	NA	NA	
[12449]	NA	NA	NA	NA	NA	NA	NA	1098	NA	NA	NA	NA	NA	200	NA	NA	NA	NA	NA	NA	NA	
[12481]	NA	884	NA	NA	NA	NA	NA	NA	200	NA	NA	NA	NA	NA	NA	884	NA	NA	NA	NA	NA	
[12513]	NA	NA	NA	NA	NA	NA	NA	NA	NA	NA	NA	NA	NA	NA	1098	NA	NA	NA	NA	NA	NA	
[12545]	NA	NA	NA	NA	NA	NA	NA	NA	NA	NA	NA	NA	NA	NA	NA	884	NA	NA	NA	NA		
[12577]	NA	NA	NA	NA	NA	NA	NA	1098	884	NA	NA	NA	NA	NA	NA	200	NA	NA	NA	NA		
[12609]	NA	NA	NA	NA	NA	NA	884	NA	NA	NA	NA	NA	NA	NA	NA	NA	NA	884	NA	NA		
[12641]	NA	NA	NA	NA	NA	NA	NA	NA	NA	884	NA	1098	NA	NA	NA	NA	NA	NA	NA	NA		
[12673]	NA	NA	NA	NA	1987	NA	NA	297	NA	NA	NA	NA	NA	NA	NA	NA	884	NA	NA	NA	NA	
[12705]	NA	NA	NA	NA	NA	NA	NA	NA	NA	NA	NA	NA	NA	1723	NA	NA	NA	NA	NA	NA		
[12737]	1088	NA	NA	NA	NA	NA	884	NA	NA	89	778	1625	178	NA	387	NA	NA	NA	NA	NA	NA	1098
[12769]	NA	832	NA	260	884	NA	NA	NA	NA	NA	NA	NA	NA	NA	NA	NA	NA	NA	89	NA	778	NA
[12801]	NA	NA	NA	NA	NA	NA	NA	NA	1533	NA	NA	NA	NA	NA	NA	NA	NA	NA	89	NA	NA	
[12833]	NA	NA	NA	NA	NA	NA	NA	884	NA	NA	NA	NA	NA	NA	NA	NA	NA	165	NA	NA	1792	
[12865]	NA	NA	NA	NA	NA	NA	NA	NA	NA	NA	NA	1098	884	NA	NA	NA	NA	NA	NA	NA	NA	
[12897]	NA	NA	NA	NA	NA	NA	NA	NA	NA	NA	NA	NA	NA	NA	NA	NA	NA	NA	NA	NA	NA	
[12929]	NA	NA	NA	NA	NA	NA	NA	NA	NA	NA	NA	NA	NA	NA	NA	NA	NA	NA	NA	NA	NA	

Fig. 1. Happy hashtaged tweets after being compared with positive opinion words

Other than above mentioned challenges, one of the most difficult tasks is matching, which has to be done manually. As can be seen from numbering mentioned in Fig. 1, there are around 13000 words for 1000 tweets, obtained after removing punctuations, stopwords and splitting tweets into individual words. Figure 1 shows the result after comparing splitted words with positive opinion words. It gives NA when there is no match and whenever there is a match, number denotes the positive word. Matching these numbers with numbers in positive opinion list, gives us that positive word. Same is done for negative words. These numbers has to be matched manually with numbered positive words present in positive opinion words list to get the positive opinion represented by that number. This comparison is necessary, as only numbers are meaningless. They can only help in determining number of distinct opinion words that appear.

3.3 Emotion Analysis from Sentiment Analysis

Usually sentiment analysis is done using positive and negative opinion words to track attitudes and feelings of the individuals towards particular topic, service or product. In our paper, we have used it to track emotions of individuals which include extracting of emotion lexicons by categorizing positive and negative opinion words into emotion words. It resulted in 9 lists of emotion words obtained from tweets of 9 emotion hashtags: happy, excited, angry, sad, sleepy, relaxed, tired, bored, and afraid.

Emotion analysis is done as an additional layer on top of the sentiment classification. It will use these lists of emotion lexicons to perform sentiment analysis on varied amount of tweets extracted using twitter mining which is called emotion analysis. Tweets extracted for this purpose are not extracted using any particular keyword or hashtag. They are the recent general tweets which can include opinions, discussion and emotion about any topic.

Table 2 shows the result of emotion analysis when performed with 2000,5000, 10000 and 20000 tweets.

Table 2. Result of Emotion Analysis

Emotion words	Number of tweets			
	2000 tweets	5000 tweets	10000 tweets	20000 tweets
Happy	641	1780	3363	6279
Sad	820	2305	4211	7962
Angry	761	2126	4026	7511
Tired	732	2127	3825	7262
Afraid	353	1052	1850	3620
Sleepy	651	1868	3410	6390
Relaxed	577	1595	3011	5543
Bored	640	1992	3459	6401
Excited	617	1702	3235	5936

4   Result Representation

4.1   Line Graph Representation of Emotion Analysis

Line graph is showing the variation of emotions with varied number of tweets. We can say that for 2000 tweets, there is not much difference between sad, angry and tired words but as the number of tweets are increasing, difference can be seen clearly between these three (Fig. 2).

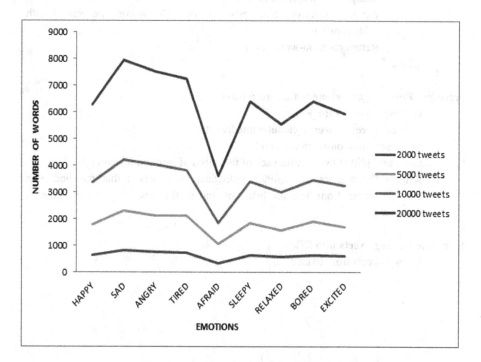

Fig. 2. Line graph for emotion analysis

Both line graph and table are sufficient to analyze that sadwords, which include the emotion lexicons used to express sadness, are the most used words while afraidwords, lexicons used to express afraid, are the least used words on twitter. So we can say that afraid is the least expressed and sadness is the most expressed emotion on twitter.

4.2   Algorithm and Code for Emotion Analysis

Algorithm EmotionAnalysis()
Create twitter account
Create twitter application
Obtain Consumer key, Consumer secret, Access Token, Access token secret
Setting up authorization
Extracting _emotion_lexicons();
Emotion_analysis(emotion-word lists);

Procedure **Extracting _emotion_lexicons()**
       Setting up authorization
       For each of the 9 emotions
              Getting_tweets_into_R() ;//hashtagged tweets are extracted
              Splitted_tweets=**Tweets_clean**(splitted tweets);
              Scan positive and negative opinion words into R
              Compare with splitted tweets
              Extract negative and positive opinion words matching with splitted tweets
              Return emotion-word list
    endfor

Procedure **Emotion_analysis**(emotion-word lists)
       Getting_tweets_into_R();
       Splitted_tweets=**Tweets_clean**(splittedtweets);
       Scan each emotion-word list into R
       Compare splitted tweets with each of the 9 lists of emotion lexicon
       Returns the number of splitted individual tweet words that matched with emotion-words from lexicon lists determines the amount of each emotion expressed

Procedure **Getting tweets into R()**
       Extract tweets from twitter

Mention number of tweets to be extracted, language, keyword to be used for searching tweets, result type
Import tweets in R

Procedure **Tweets_clean**(tweets)
Create corpus
Lowercase everything in corpus
Remove numbers and punctuations, cutout stop words, strip off whitespace
Split into individual words
Return splitted tweets

Above algorithm describes how emotion analysis is performed step by step using sentiment analysis [17–20].

Code for Emotion Analysis Written in R

```
//setting up authorization
setup_twitter_oauth(consumer_key,consumer_secret,access_toke
n,access_secret)

//tweets extraction from twitter
tweets<-searchTwitter("
",n=20000,lang='en',resultType="recent")

//creating corpus
tweets_text<-sapply(tweets,function(x) x$getText())
tweets_corpus<-Corpus(VectorSource(tweets_text))

//text prepocessing
tweets_clean<-tm_map(tweets_corpus,removePunctuation)
tweets_clean<-
tm_map(tweets_clean,content_transformer(tolower))
tweets_clean<-
tm_map(tweets_clean,removeWords,stopwords("english"))
tweets_clean<-tm_map(tweets_clean,removeNumbers)
tweets_clean<-tm_map(tweets_clean,stripWhitespace)
```

```
//splitting tweets into individual words
splitweets<-str_split(tweets_clean,pattern="\\s+")
//scanning emotion-word lists into R. (Shown only for happywords and sadwords lists)
happywords<-
scan('happywords.txt',what='character',comment.char=";")
sadwords<-
scan('sadwords.txt',what='character',comment.char=";")
```

```
// Compares and returns the number of splitted individual tweet words that matched with
emotion-words from lexicon lists(Shown only for happywords and sadwords lists)
sum(!is.na( match(splitweets,happywords)))
sum(!is.na( match(splitweets,sadwords)))
```

4.3   Comparison Cloud Representation

Wordcloud gives greater prominence to words that appear more frequently in the source text [9]. It adds simplicity and clarity and is easy to understand. A comparison cloud works on the same principles as a word cloud. It allows us to study the differences or similarities between two or more documents by simply plotting the word cloud of each against the other.

Figure 3 shows the comparison cloud [21] drawn after the emotion analysis of 2000 tweets. We can see the word clouds for nine emotions, together forming comparison cloud. Each word cloud is represented using a different colour. Cloud contains the various emotion-words obtained after performing emotion analysis on 2000 recent tweets. Emotion-words for same emotion are depicted using same colour. More highlighted the word, more is the frequency of its occurrence. For example, 'like' is the most used word for relaxed emotion while 'blessing' for afraid and 'burden' for bored. There are some emotion-words which are not present in comparison cloud, which means, that emotion-word has not been used in any of those 2000 tweets that were extracted for our purpose of emotion analysis. In this way, comparison cloud help in comparing the words used for different emotion and within each single emotion, helps in knowing frequency of words occurrence.

Fig. 3. Comparison cloud for emotion analysis

5 Conclusion

In this paper, Emotion analysis is performed over twitter data. To achieve the desired result sentiment analysis is done on twitter data to obtain words that are used to express different kinds of emotions. For this, hashtag tweets for different emotions are extracted from twitter using twitter mining. Emotion analysis is done on twitter data by performing sentiment analysis using various emotions. As a result, we found that afraid is the least expressed and sadness is the most expressed emotion on twitter. Obtained result is shown using line graph, to show variation of various emotions and through comparison cloud, to show frequency of occurrence of various words within each emotion.

References

1. Hasan, M., Rundensteiner, E., Agu, E.: EMOTEX: Detecting emotions in Twitter messages. In: ASE BigData/SocialCom/CyberSecurity Conference (2014)
2. Dugan, L.: Twitter 101: why use hashtags? (2011). http://www.adweek.com/digital/twitter-101-why-use-hashtags/. Accessed 31 Jan 2018
3. Twitter (2018). https://en.wikipedia.org/wiki/Twitter. Accessed 25 Jan 2018
4. Wolny, W.: Emotion analysis of Twitter data that use emoticons and emoji ideograms. In: 25th International Conference on Information Systems Development (2016)
5. Sentiment Analysis (2018). https://en.wikipedia.org/wiki/Sentiment_analysis. Accessed 3 Jan 2018
6. Sharma, P., Agrawal, A., Alai, L., Garg, A.: Challenges and techniques in preprocessing for Twitter data. Int. J. Eng. Sci. Comput. **7**(4), 6611–6613 (2017)
7. Hu, M., Liu, B.: Mining and summarizing customer reviews. In: Proceedings of the ACM SIGKDD International Conference on Knowledge Discovery and Data Mining (KDD-2004) (2004)
8. Liu, B.: Sentiment analysis and subjectivity. In: Handbook of Natural Language Processing, 2nd edn. (2010)
9. Wordle - Beautiful Word Clouds. http://www.wordle.net/. Accessed 15 Jan 2018
10. Counting Characters - Twitter Developers. https://developer.twitter.com/en/docs/basics/counting-characters. Accessed 18 Mar 2018
11. Ortony, A., Turner, T.J.: What's basic about basic emotions? Psychol. Rev. **97**(3), 315 (1990)
12. Mohamma, S.M., Kiritchenko, S.: Using hashtags to capture fine emotion categories from tweets. Comput. Intell. **31**(2), 301–326 (2015)
13. Gama, J., Rambocas, M.: Marketing research: the role of sentiment analysis (2013)
14. Davidov, D., Tsur, O., Rappoport, A.: Enhanced sentiment learning using Twitter hashtags and smileys. In: Proceedings of the 23rd International Conference on Computational Linguistics, pp. 241–249 (2010)
15. Cherian, P.: Extract tweets from within R (2016). http://rstatistics.net/extracting-tweets-with-r/. Accessed 18 Jan 2018
16. Standard search API - Twitter Developers. https://developer.twitter.com/en/docs/tweets/search/api-reference/get-search-tweets. Accessed 18 Jan 2018
17. Jalayer Academy: R - Twitter mining with R (part 1) [Video File] (2015). https://www.youtube.com/watch?v=lT4Kosc_ers&t=336s
18. Jalayer Academy: Text mining (part 4) - positive and negative terms for sentiment analysis in R [Video File] (2017). https://www.youtube.com/watch?v=WfoVINuxIJA
19. Jalayer Academy: Text mining (part 5) - import a Corpus in R [Video File] (2017). https://www.youtube.com/watch?v=pFinlXYLZ-A
20. Jalayer Academy: Text mining (part 6) - cleaning Corpus text in R [Video File] (2017). https://www.youtube.com/watch?v=jCrQYOsAcv4
21. Jalayer Academy: Text mining (part 7) - comparison Wordcloud in R [Video File] (2017). https://www.youtube.com/watch?v=pvjhm5TTd2A
22. Saif, H., He, Y., Alani, H.: Semantic sentiment analysis of Twitter. In: Cudré-Mauroux, P., et al. (eds.) ISWC 2012. LNCS, vol. 7649, pp. 508–524. Springer, Heidelberg (2012). https://doi.org/10.1007/978-3-642-35176-1_32
23. Pak, A., Paroubek, P.: Twitter as a Corpus for sentiment analysis and opinion mining. In: Proceedings of the Seventh Conference on International Language Resources and Evaluation (2010)

Secure Data Exchange and Data Leakage Detection in an Untrusted Cloud

Denis Ulybyshev[⊠], Bharat Bhargava, and Aala Oqab-Alsalem

Computer Science Department, CERIAS, Purdue University,
West Lafayette 47907, USA
{dulybysh, bbshail, alsalema}@purdue.edu

Abstract. In service-oriented architecture, services can communicate and share data amongst themselves. It is necessary to provide role-based access control for data. In addition, data leakages made by authorized insiders to unauthorized services should be detected and reported back to the data owner. In this paper, we propose a solution that uses role- and attribute-based access control for data exchange among services, including services hosted by untrusted environments. Our approach provides data leakage prevention and detection for multiple leakage scenarios. We also propose a damage assessment model for data leakages. The implemented prototype supports a privacy-preserving exchange of Electronic Health Records that can be hosted by untrusted cloud providers, as well as detecting leakages made by insiders.

Keywords: Data leakage detection · Access control · Privacy
Cloud security

1 Introduction

Services in Service-Oriented Architecture (SOA) can communicate and share data amongst themselves. A methodology for privacy-preserving data exchange among services in SOA, in which each service can access only those data items the service is authorized for, was presented in [3, 14]. In this paper, we extend that approach with data leakage detection capabilities and a damage assessment model for data leakages. Each service can have a database associated with it. Our solution handles non-relational databases stored as key-value pairs. The methodology employs Active Bundles (AB) [2, 3, 14], that contain key-value pairs with values in encrypted form; metadata; access control policies and a policy enforcement engine (virtual machine) [3]. Each subset of data (e.g. contact, medical or billing information of a patient) is encrypted with its own symmetric key, using an AES encryption scheme. Our solution supports both centralized and decentralized data exchanges. The Active Bundle can be hosted by the server or cloud provider that serve data requests. We also support fully decentralized architecture, when services in a peer-to-peer network exchange data by sending Active Bundle amongst themselves. Default implementation of Active Bundles used in the 'WAXEDPRUNE' project [1, 5] provides privacy-preserving data dissemination among services, but does not protect against data leakages made by insiders to unauthorized entities. In this paper, we address two scenarios of data leakages: leakage

© Springer Nature Singapore Pte Ltd. 2018
G. C. Deka et al. (Eds.): ICACCT 2018, CCIS 899, pp. 99–113, 2018.
https://doi.org/10.1007/978-981-13-2035-4_10

of the whole Active Bundle and leakage of the plaintext data to unauthorized services. In the first scenario, leakage is prevented by an Active Bundle kernel, which prohibits unauthorized data accesses and, in addition, contains digital watermark. The second scenario is more challenging since protection provided by the Active Bundle is removed in this case. As a solution, we employ digital and visual watermarks, as well as monitoring network traffic between web services in SOA. A web crawler with built-in classifier detects digital watermark, embedded into RGB images, if the leaked image is located in public network directory. Digital watermarks for RGB images are based on a pixel transformation function. Monitoring network messages and validating data packets with a specific pattern allows detecting data leakage for cases when data pattern can be validated. For instance, credit card number always follows the specific pattern that can be validated using regular expressions [18]. We embed visual watermarks on a web page when data retrieved from an Active Bundle are displayed in a client's browser. Zoomed visual watermarks can be used as evidence of data ownership. Our approach helps to investigate data leakages and do forensics based on provenance records that are made each time a data request is served by the Active Bundle. Provenance [8] records contain information regarding who is trying to access what class of data, when, and the origin of the Active Bundle.

The rest of the paper is organized as follows: Sect. 2 contains a brief overview of related work. Section 3 describes the core design. Section 4 presents the evaluation. Section 5 concludes the paper.

2 Related Work

There are variety of Digital Rights Management (DRM) protection tools [11] that provide role-based access control. These tools are supposed to protect against data leakages. Microsoft has DRM-service, called Windows Media DRM [12]. It is designed to provide dissemination of audio and video content over an IP network. The "MediaSnap©" DRM solution [24] was proposed to protect PDF documents. Most of its principles are applicable to other digital media content. The core component of the "MediaSnap©" system is a pdf-plugin. Our data exchange model considers the context and client's attributes, such as the trust level, which is constantly recalculated, cryptographic capabilities of a browser and authentication method. A Digital Cosine Transformation [9] can be used to create watermarks for images.

The hardware-based DRM approach provides a trusted hardware space for executing only permitted applications. "DRM services such as content decryption, authentication and rights rendering take place only in this trusted space" [11]. Advantages of hardware-based DRM are that it is resistant to security breaches in used operating systems, it is infeasible to bypass security features and it provides memory space protection. The main disadvantages are higher costs, limited flexibility and less interoperability [13].

Ranchal et al. [10] proposed a Framework for Enforcing Security Policies in Composite Web Services (EPICS), which protects data privacy throughout the service interaction lifecycle. The framework uses the Active Bundle concept [3, 14] for SOA. The solution ensures that the data are distributed along with the access control policies and with an execution monitor that controls data disclosures. The framework provides cross-domain privacy-preserving data dissemination in untrusted environments and reduces the risk of unauthorized access. We extend that approach with capabilities of detecting data leakages made by authorized insiders to unauthorized entities. We also consider wider set of attributes in attribute-based access control model.

Nevase et al. [19] proposed a steganography-based approach to detect leakages of images, text, video and audio content. Steganography provides covert communication channel between data entity and data owner by hiding the message in the sensitive content, e.g. in the image or text. The existence of sensitive message in the content is hidden for everyone except the data owner, who is able to decipher it. Steganography-based "forensic readiness model" [20] identifies and prevents emails, which attempt to leak data. Kaur et al. [21] also addressed prevention of data leakages that can be made by malicious insiders via emails. Email is protected via gateway during data transfer. The algorithm matches the email pattern with the stored keywords in order to detect leakage and take the action to prevent it.

Gupta and Singh [22] presented an approach for detecting intentional and inadvertent data leakages using a probabilistic model. Detecting a data leaking malicious entity is based on the allocation and distribution of data items among the agents using Bigraph.

3 Core Design

3.1 Data Leakage Detection

In our solution web services exchange data by means of *Active Bundles* [2, 3, 14]. Active Bundle is the core component that provides data leakage prevention in our system. Active Bundle is a self-protected structure that includes key-value pairs with encrypted values, access control policies, metadata and policy enforcement engine (virtual machine) [2, 3, 14]. Each subset of data (e.g. contact information of a patient, billing or medical information such as medical history, test results, diagnosis, prescriptions, etc.) is encrypted with its own symmetric key, using an AES encryption scheme. The key is generated on-the-fly using unique information produced in the execution control flow of an Active Bundle [3], depending on the subject's (service's) role, extracted from X.509 certificate of the subject (e.g. doctor, insurance agent or researcher), set of access control policies and on Active Bundle code, including authentication and authorization code. Details of the on-the-fly key derivation procedure are covered in [3]. One of the novelties offered by Active Bundle concept is that the symmetric keys used to encrypt/decrypt sensitive data are not stored neither on a cloud provider nor inside an Active Bundle nor on any Trusted Third Party (TTP). Firstly, the identity of service requesting data from an Active Bundle is verified. Services present their X.509 certificates signed by a trusted Certificate Authority (CA) to the Active Bundle [3]. Then, if authentication is granted, the client's attributes, such as browser's cryptographic capabilities, are evaluated. Then, access control policies stored in the Active Bundle are evaluated. Based on the evaluations made by the Active Bundle kernel, symmetric decryption keys are created to decrypt the accessible data items. Access control policies are enforced by the open-source policy enforcement engine "Balana" [4]. Based on derived decryption keys, the values from corresponding key-value pairs belonging to accessible data subsets are decrypted and sent back to the client by means of an https protocol. If a doctor requests for medical data, contact and billing information, the data will be extracted from Active Bundle, decrypted and sent back to the doctor. However, if the doctor sends a data request from an outdated and insecure browser, then a lesser portion of the medical data will be retrieved from the Electronic Health Record (EHR) of a patient. Each EHR is stored as an Active Bundle, one per patient. One of the key-value pairs (with encrypted value) from our Active Bundle is given below:

```
{ "ab.patientID" : "Enc(001122)" }
```

A Javascript object notation (JSON) [7] is used to store key-value pairs, where value is encrypted with a symmetric key generated for each data class. An Active Bundle has a built-in tamper-resistance mechanism, which is based on the digest of the Active Bundle components and their resources. This digest is calculated when an Active Bundle is created. Modification of any of the components' resources will lead to a different digest and to incorrect decryption key generation. It protects from an attacker that tries to:

(a) modify an Active Bundle code in order to bypass authentication phase or evaluation of access control policies and a client's attributes;
(b) modify access control policies in order to get access to unauthorized data;
(c) impersonate service identity by using the wrong certificate in order to get access to unauthorized data.

Instead of data, Active Bundles can store software modules in encrypted form. For instance, different departments within an organization may have different permission levels for software access and updates. Our approach guarantees that each software module can only be accessed by authorized entities.

Our methodology for data exchange in SOA supports both centralized and decentralized architectures. An Active Bundle can be hosted by a server or cloud provider that serves data requests for the Active Bundle. We also support fully decentralized architecture, when services in peer-to-peer network can exchange data by sending Active Bundle amongst each other. That is why all data that can be shared among services are included in encrypted form into an Active Bundle, but unauthorized data requests are denied, based on client's role and attributes, such as the cryptographic capabilities of the browser [15, 16] and trust level. To demonstrate the core design of our approach, we consider a hybrid architecture when both centralized and decentralized data exchanges among services are supported (see Fig. 1). A demo video of the implemented prototype for an EHR management system is available [17]. There is a Hospital Information System (IS), hosted by the cloud provider. It hosts EHRs of patients as Active Bundles, one Active Bundle per patient. The EHR of a patient consists of 3 types of data: contact, medical and billing information. There are three services (subjects): Doctor, Insurance Agent and Researcher, who can send data requests to the Hospital Information System, i.e. to Active Bundles (see Fig. 1). The access control matrix is given in Table 1.

Adversary Model:

1. Cloud provider or server may have curious or malicious administrator that tries to access confidential data or modify them.
2. Client can be malicious in terms of:
   a. leaking data, for which client is authorized, to unauthorized parties;
   b. modifying the Active Bundle code to extract the confidential data for which the client is unauthorized.

Table 1. Access control matrix for EHR

Role/Data class	Medical data	Contact information	Billing information
Doctor	Allow	Allow	Allow
Insurance agent	Deny	Allow	Allow
Researcher	Allow	Deny	Allow

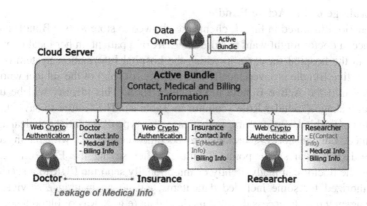

Fig. 1. Hospital information system (proposed by Dr. Leon Li, NGC)

Assumptions:

1. The entity that hosts/executes Active Bundle has trusted hardware, a trusted operating system and a trusted Java Virtual Machine.
2. Http(s) protocol is used for data exchanges amongst all the web services.
3. Leaked data is attempted to be used by the adversary that has it, i.e. the adversary tries to decrypt data from a leaked Active Bundle or uploads the leaked Active Bundle to a publicly available network directory. The analogy is that someone, who is using an unlicensed copy of the Microsoft Windows XP operating system, tries to update it from an official Microsoft repository.

4. Leaked data is accessible on the adversary's side. In case of investigating leakage incident by using visual watermarks, the investigator needs permission to search for leaked data, e.g. having a police order to examine a suspicious hard drive.

Default implementation of Active Bundles used in [1], does not protect against malicious insiders that leak data to unauthorized entities. We address two leakage scenarios in our extended solution below: leakage of the whole EHR in the form of Active Bundle and leakage of decrypted plaintext data without the Active Bundle. The following implemented features provide leakage detection/prevention:

(a) Active Bundle that stores data in encrypted form and access control policies.
(b) Digital watermark, embedded into Active Bundle.
(c) Digital watermark, embedded into RGB images, stored in Active Bundle.
(d) Visible and nearly invisible visual watermarks, used to display data.
(e) Monitoring network messages and validating data packets with a specific pattern, e.g. credit card number pattern, using regular expressions [18].

The limitation of digital/visual watermarking approach, used in methods (b), (c) and (d), is that it does not work once watermark is removed from the data. Ways to mitigate and prevent data leakages in this case are proposed in Sect. 3.1.3 below.

3.1.1   Leakage of the Active Bundle

In our scenario, illustrated in Fig. 1, clients are allowed to store Active Bundles locally. For instance, a doctor might want to store the EHR of a patient on her local department computer in the hospital for cases in which the hospital Information System is down. When an Active Bundle is saved locally, the identity (or role) of the subject who saved it is written into the Active Bundle in encrypted form. This identity will be used to detect data leakage ("Sender Role" column in Table 2). The feature to save the EHR locally can be disabled, if necessary. In that case, this type of potential data leakage will be prevented, but the network architecture becomes centralized with having central storage of EHRs as a single point of failure. After saving the EHR on her local repository, the doctor can inadvertently or intentionally send the EHR to a service that is not authorized for some included data items, e.g. to an insurance service. If the insurance agency tries to access detailed medical data (e.g. X-Ray or blood test results), this access will be denied by the Active Bundle, since access control policies embedded into the Active Bundle don't permit insurers to read the medical data of a patient; they only allow them to read contact and billing information. An attempt to decrypt data made by an unauthorized service will be recorded by a trusted Central Monitor (CM). Every Active Bundle transaction in the data exchange network is monitored by the CM, who is notified each time a client tries to decrypt a data subset from an Active Bundle. The notification message contains information on what service attempts to decrypt what type of data, when, who is the origin/sender of the Active Bundle. The Central Monitor queries its local database of access control policies, called *data obligations*, in order to check whether the service that tries to decrypt data is authorized for that class of data. Without obtaining permission from the trusted Central Monitor, the data decryption process will not continue. Figure 2 illustrates the process. An Active Bundle contains encrypted data **Enc [Data(D)]** = $\{\mathbf{Enc_{k1}}\ (\mathbf{d_1}),\ ...,\ \mathbf{Enc_{kn}}\ (\mathbf{d_n})\}$ and access control policies **(P)** = $\{\mathbf{p_1},\ ...\ ,\ \mathbf{p_k}\}$. Service M is authorized to read d_i and it may leak decrypted d_i (addressed in the Sect. 3.1.2) or the entire Active Bundle to service N, who is unauthorized to access d_i. If N attempts to decrypt d_i, the Active Bundle kernel sends a message to CM to verify whether d_i is supposed to be at N. In addition, service N might be asked to get an activation code from the authentication server, which is under our control, and which will again notify the Central Monitor that data of type d_i has arrived from service M to service N. If d_i is not supposed to be at N then:

(a) trust level of services M and N is decreased;
(b) data d_i is marked as compromised and all other services are notified about that;
(c) Active Bundle is re-created with stricter access control policies to make it stronger against similar leakages:
    (c1) separate compromised role (of service M) into *Role* and *Trustworthy_Role*;
    (c2) send new certificates with *Trustworthy_Role* to all trustworthy entities;
    (c3) create a new Active Bundle with modified policies to prohibit data access for *Role*;
    (c4) disable the "Save As" functionality to prohibit storing sensitive data locally;
    (c5) raise the sensitivity level for leaked data types to prevent leakage repetition.

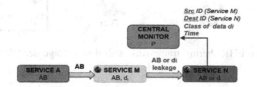

Fig. 2. Data leakage detection by central monitor

Table 2. Data obligations (access control policies)

Recipient role	Sender role	Data type	Access result
Doctor	Doctor	All	Allow
Doctor	Insurance	All	Allow
Doctor	Researcher	All	Allow
Insurance	Doctor	All	Deny
Insurance	Researcher	All	Deny
Researcher	Doctor	All	Deny
...	...	...	...
Insurance	Doctor	Medical	Deny
Insurance	Doctor	Contact	Allow
Researcher	Doctor	Contact	Deny
...	...	...	...
Researcher	Insurance	Contact	Deny
Doctor	Researcher	Contact	Deny
Insurance	Researcher	Contact	Deny

Service trust level is calculated by CM, based on the following parameters: (a) number of sent/received data requests, (b) number of rejected data requests, (c) number of communication errors, (d) CPU/Memory usage.

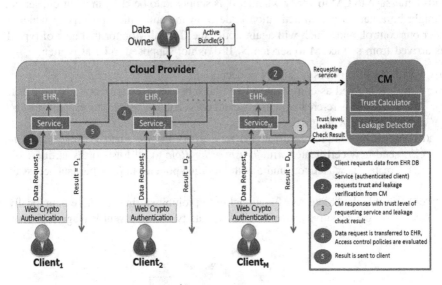

Fig. 3. Secure EHR sharing framework with data leakage detection capability

If the trust level goes below the specified threshold, future data requests coming from that service to the Active Bundle will be denied, even if access control policies allow that service to access a certain data item. Figure 3 illustrates the control flow for data request with added data leakage detection capability. As shown above, a data request is processed by the Leakage Detector and Trust Calculator. If a leakage is detected or the trust level is not sufficient, the data request is denied; otherwise, the data request will be transferred from the Central Monitor service to the Active Bundle (EHR), where a client's attributes and access control policies are evaluated. The Central Monitor hosts the relational database of obligations, i.e. of access control policies. To make a data leakage check, the Central Monitor issues a SQL query to this database. An example of the database used in our scenario with EHR sharing is given in Table 2.

In addition to the data obligations enforced by trusted Central Monitor, we implemented a web crawler to verify digital watermarks that are embedded into the Active Bundles. If an Active Bundle is uploaded to a publicly available directory in the network, the crawler verifies the digital watermark to check whether Active Bundle is supposed to be at that network node. We assume that it is possible to determine the identity of the node that hosts public directory (e.g. in the Hospital Intranet). Network nodes, participating in data exchanges, use X.509 certificates that identify their roles (e.g. doctor or insurance agent or researcher). Also, identity can be based on node's IP address or other attributes.

3.1.2   Leakage of Plaintext Data

A second, more challenging data leakage scenario that we address in this work, is when the service that is authorized for data di can get it from an Active Bundle (see Fig. 2), store it locally in plaintext form and then send it behind the scene as a plaintext to an unauthorized service without the Active Bundle. Even if local storage functionality is prohibited, an authorized client (malicious insider) can still take a picture of a displayed di on a mobile phone's camera when di is displayed on the screen.

Fig. 4. Retrieved medical information on a web page with visual watermarks

Protection provided by Active Bundle is gone in this case, and we cannot prevent plaintext di leakage. We aim to help investigating the leakage and do forensics based on provenance records that are stored on the trusted Central Monitor each time a data request is served by the Active Bundle. Provenance [8] records contain information on who is trying to access what class of data, when, and who is the origin/sender of that Active Bundle. To mitigate a leakage problem, we embed visual watermarks on a web page when data retrieved by client from an Active Bundle is displayed in the client's browser. Zoomed visual watermarks can be used as an evidence of data owner-ship. There are two types of visual watermarks that we use to display data: clearly visible (see text "Secure Dissemination of EHR" on Fig. 4) and very small ones that are only visible if zoomed. These watermarks will remain on the image if picture of a screen is taken by a malicious client. For some types of data, e.g. on Fig. 4, it is easy to reproduce the screen's content and write it down e.g. on a piece of paper. It removes the visual watermark. But for some types of medical data, e.g. X-Ray images, it is hard to reproduce them on a piece of paper and easier to take picture of a screen, which will contain both our visual watermarks: large visible and small invisible.

Additionally, we embed digital watermarks into RGB images. The conversion function F (r, g, b) is applied to every pixel. It changes the RGB image in such a way that it is indistinguishable by the human eye from the original RGB image. If we add +1 to the RGB values of every pixel, if the value is less than 255, it will not be distinguishable to human eye. However, our web crawler, which has a built-in classifier, is able to determine whether the RGB image has the embedded watermark or not. We assume an RGB values range from 0 to 255. This watermarking method works only if the RGB image is stored in a publicly available folder. The simple way to modify an RGB image is to change the RGB values for every pixel by adding or subtracting 1 in such a way that the sum of RGB values is always odd for every pixel. Initial values should be less than 255 for adding and greater than zero for subtracting. If all pixels of the RGB image follow this rule of odd sum of RGB values, our classifier considers this image to have a watermark. Once it is detected, the Central Monitor is notified, and it checks whether the given RGB image is supposed to be at that network node. We assume that it is possible to determine the identity of the node that hosts a public directory. Network nodes, participating in data exchanges, use X.509 certificates, that identify their roles (e.g. Doctor or Insurance Agent or Researcher). Also, identity can be based on node's IP address or other attributes. For instance, if a data obligations database (see Table 2) has no record that an 'Unknown' recipient is allowed to access a patient's medical data, a leakage alert will be raised. Instead of applying such a simple conversion function F (r, g, b) to every pixel such that the sum $r + g + b$ is odd, more secure conversion functions F can be used.

3.1.3   Proposed Work
The following additional data leakage detection/prevention methods [23] are proposed:

- **Partial data disclosure**
  - (a) Authorized client after the first data request is only given a portion of accessible data;
  - (b) Monitoring the client's trust level, which is constantly re-computed by the Central Monitor using the following metrics: (a) number of sent/received data requests, (b) number of rejected data requests, (c) number of communication errors, (d) CPU/Memory usage;
  - (c) Disclose the next accessible chunk of data, provided trust level is satisfactory.

- **"Fake" leakage**
  In case of detected data leakage, e.g. if the exam questions got leaked, several other "fake" versions of data, i.e. other exam questions, might be intentionally leaked to lower the value of leaked data.
- **Data classification level elevation**
  The idea is to raise the classification level for leaked data class to prevent leakage repetition.

3.2   Data Leakage Damage Evaluation

Data leakage damage is evaluated using the following information [23]:

- How malicious is the recipient of unauthorized data;
- Sensitivity of data that got leaked;

- Leakage timing
- Inference threat, which indicates whether other data can be inferred from the data that got leaked

$$\text{Damage} = \text{Kds(Data Sensitivity)} * \text{Ksm(Service Maliciousness)} * \text{F(t)} \quad (1)$$

Kds denotes data sensitivity coefficient, Ksm is service maliciousness coefficient, F(t) is data sensitivity function.

Figure 5 illustrates different data sensitivity functions. The data event (e.g. final exam) happens at time t_0. Damage from data being leaked before t_0 is high. Damage from data being leaked after t_0 either immediately drops to zero (e.g. final exam got leaked after the exam is over) or decreases linearly (e.g. newly invented cryptographic hash function, which is examined by users and attackers) or remains high (e.g. export-sensitive technology).

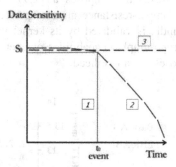

Fig. 5. Data sensitivity functions

4 Evaluation

We measured performance for clients sending data requests to EHR, represented as an Active Bundle, one per patient. Data request round-trip time (RTT) is measured between times of sending a data request and data retrieval from an Active Bundle. RTT is a sum of times spent for authentication, evaluation of access control policies and client's attributes, data leakage checks (if the data leakage detection feature is enabled), key generation and data retrieval. *ApacheBench* utility (version 2.3), as well as browser developer consoles (for Firefox browser) are used for RTT evaluation. Details of framework implementation are covered in [6].

Experiment 1
In this experiment, we aim to measure the latency of a data request sent to EHR, which is hosted by the Hospital Server, located in the same network as the requesting client. The Hospital Server that hosts EHR has the following characteristics:

Hardware: MacBook Pro, Intel Core i7 CPU @ 2.2 GHz, 16 GB memory
OS: macOS Sierra 10.12.6.

The client sends a request for Patient ID to the EHR, represented as an extended Active Bundle, and to the basic Active Bundle, which supports neither attribute-based access control nor tamper-resistance. In contrast, EHR supports tamper-resistance and extended attribute-based access control with checking cryptographic capabilities of the client's browser [1]. The Basic Active Bundle, as well as EHR, contains four access control policies. The access control matrix for EHR is shown in Table 1. Basic Active Bundle and EHR are running on a Hospital Server, located in the same network as the client. We measure RTT for data request processing at the server side, and do not consider network delays between client and server in this experiment. Results in Fig. 6 represent latency when a first initial data request is sent to EHR. We consider it to be a special case, since the very first request to the basic AB and to EHR (which is an extended AB) takes significantly longer to be executed due to the initial authentication phase and initial evaluation of attributes. The EHR with embedded attribute-based access control and tamper resistance imposes a 12.9% performance overhead as compared with basic AB. Tamper-resistance imposes performance overhead because the digest of an Active Bundle is validated by its kernel whenever the data request arrives. Detection of the cryptographic capabilities of client's browser and checking whether it is sufficient imposes extra overhead.

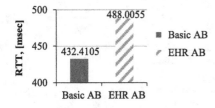

Fig. 6. EHR performance (initial request)   **Fig. 7.** EHR performance

In the next experiment, we run 50 similar data requests for Patient ID in a row. As shown in Fig. 7, mean RTT has been decreased 33.5 times for basic AB and 35.9 times for EHR. Having embedded attribute-based access control and tamper resistance in EHR imposes a 5.2% performance overhead as compared with basic AB.

Experiment 2

In this experiment, we aim to measure the latency of a data request sent to EHR which is hosted by Google Cloud Provider and has the following characteristics:

Hardware: Intel(R) Xeon(R) CPU 2.30 GHz
OS: Linux Debian 4.9.65-3 + deb9u2 (2018-01-04) x86 64, kernel 4.9.0-5-amd64
Ephemeral IP: 35.192.160.136

The procedure is same as in experiment 1, but now the client queries basic AB and EHR, running on a Google cloud instance. For the data request, we measure the overall RTT that includes network delays between client and cloud server in this experiment.

Results in Fig. 8 represent latency when the first initial data request is sent to EHR. As pointed in the previous experiment 1, we consider it to be a special case. EHR with embedded attribute-based access control and tamper resistance imposes a 2.6% performance overhead as compared with basic AB.

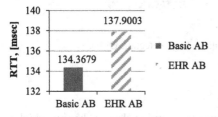

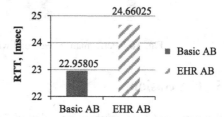

Fig. 8. Cloud EHR performance (initial request)   **Fig. 9.** Cloud EHR performance

In the next experiment, we run 50 similar data requests for Patient ID in a row. As shown in Fig. 9, mean RTT has been decreased 5.85 times for basic AB and 5.59 times for EHR. Having embedded attribute-based access control and tamper resistance in EHR imposes a 7.4% performance overhead as compared with basic AB.

Experiment 3

In this experiment, we measure performance overhead imposed by a *data leakage detection* feature added to the framework. There are four services (Hospital, Doctor, Researcher and Insurance), that are running as NodeJS servers at http://www. waxedprune.cs.purdue.edu:3000. Local data requests from a client with the role 'Doctor' are sent from the browser to the Active Bundle, hosted by the Hospital Information System at localhost: 3000. Network delays do not affect RTT measurements. The hospital server has the following specification:

> *Hardware: Intel Core i7, CPU 860 @2.8 GHz x8, 8 GB memory*
> *OS: Linux Ubuntu 14.04.5, kernel 3.13.0-107-generic, 64 bit*

The client sends a request to EHR, hosted by the server, from *Mozilla Firefox*, version 50.1.0, browser. In our experiment, the doctor requests all available information of a patient. Active Bundles, used in Data Leakage OFF/ON scenarios, contain the same data and access control policies. The tamper-resistance mechanism and the client's browser cryptographic capabilities detection are the same and are used in both scenarios. The only difference is the data leakage detection feature. If it is enabled, it requires the Central Monitor to examine every data access before accessible data can be retrieved from the EHR, if a leakage is not detected. As shown in Fig. 10, data leakage detection support adds a 60.8% performance overhead. Before approving or denying a data request, the Central Monitor issues a SQL query to the relational database of obligations (see Table 2) in order to check whether requested data is accessible by the requesting client. Then either data request is denied or approved, and the accessible data decryption process starts. Active Bundle also contains metadata of its origin and who currently hosts the Active Bundle. In the case of a leakage alert, the hosting site will be marked as potentially malicious.

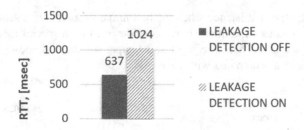

Fig. 10. Performance overhead with data leakage detection OFF/ON

5 Conclusion

We presented a comprehensive solution for privacy-preserving data exchange, which supports data leakage detection/prevention for several types of leakage scenarios. Data exchange mechanism does not need the data owner to be available since data, access control policies and policy enforcement engine are incorporated into a self-protected structure, called an "Active Bundle". The Active Bundle mechanism provides data integrity and confidentiality, protecting data from malicious/curious cloud administrators. Active Bundle supports role-and attribute-based access control. A client's attributes used by the data exchange model include level of cryptographic capabilities of a browser, authentication method and trust level of a client, which is constantly recomputed by a trusted Central Monitor. Data exchange also considers the context, e.g. normal vs. emergency. Data can be updated on-the-fly by multiple parties. Implemented data leakage detection mechanism imposes a 60.8% performance overhead. We also came up with a damage assessment model for data leakages. A demo video of the implemented EHR management system is available.

Acknowledgments. This work was funded by the Northrop Grumman Cybersecurity Research Consortium. The prototype was implemented in collaboration with Northrop Grumman and W3C/MIT and presented internally to Northrop Grumman in April 2017. We would like to thank Prof. Leszek Lilien (Purdue University, Western Michigan University) and Harry Halpin (MIT) for their collaboration and valuable feedback. We are also thankful to Miguel Villarreal-Vasquez, Ganapathy Mani, Rohit Ranchal and Savvas Savvides for their help and valuable feedback.

References

1. Ulybyshev, D., et al.: Privacy-preserving data dissemination in untrusted cloud. In: IEEE CLOUD, pp. 770–773 (2017)
2. Othmane, L.B., Lilien, L.: Protecting privacy in sensitive data dissemination with active bundles. In: 7th Annual Conference on Privacy, Security and Trust (PST 2009), Saint John, New Brunswick, Canada, pp. 202–213, August 2009
3. Ranchal, R.: Cross-domain data dissemination and policy enforcement. Ph.D. thesis, Purdue University (2015)
4. WSO2 Balana Implementation. https://github.com/wso2/balana. Accessed Mar 2018

5. 'WAXEDPRUNE' prototype demo video, part 1, https://www.dropbox.com/s/
   30scw1srqsmyq6d/BhargavaTeam_DemoVideo_Spring16.wmv?dl=0. Accessed Mar 2018
6. Ulybyshev, D., et al.: Secure dissemination of EHR in untrusted cloud, Project Tutorial.
   Purdue University (2016)
7. Lightweight data-interchange format JSON. http://json.org/. Accessed Mar 2018
8. Simmhan, Y.L., Plale, B., Gannon, D.A.: A survey of data provenance in e-science.
   SIGMOD Rec. **34**(3), 31–36 (2005)
9. Xu, Z.J., Wang, Z.Z., Lu, Q.: Research on image watermarking algorithm based on DCT.
   J. Procedia Environ. Sci. **10**, 1129–1135 (2011)
10. Ranchal, R., Bhargava, B., Angin, P., Othmane, L.B.: Epics: a framework for enforcing
    security policies in composite web services. IEEE Trans. Serv. Comput., 1 (2018)
11. Liu, Q., Safavi-Naini, R., Sheppard, N.: Digital rights management for content distribution.
    In: Proceedings of Australasian Information Security Workshop, pp. 49–58 (2003)
12. Windows media DRM. https://en.wikipedia.org/wiki/Windows_Media_DRM. Accessed
    Mar 2018
13. Nickolova, M., Nickolov, E.: Hardware-based and software-based security in digital rights
    management solutions. Int. J. Inf. Technol. Knowl. **2**, 163–168 (2008)
14. Othmane, L.B.: Active bundles for protecting confidentiality of sensitive data throughout
    their lifecycle. Ph. D. thesis, Western Michigan University, Kalamazoo, MI, USA,
    December 2010
15. W3C Web Cryptography API. https://www.w3.org/TR/WebCryptoAPI/. Accessed Mar
    2018
16. Web authentication: an API for accessing scoped credentials. http://www.w3.org/TR/
    webauthn. Accessed Mar 2018
17. 'WAXEDPRUNE' prototype demo video, part 2. https://www.dropbox.com/s/
    4wg3vuv52j4s16v/NGCRC-2017-Bhargava-Demo1.wmv?dl=0. Accessed Mar 2018
18. Finding or verifying credit card numbers. http://www.regular-expressions.info/creditcard.
    html. Accessed Mar 2018
19. Nevase, J., Chougale, P., Shewale, S., Bhosale, P.: Data leakage detection. Imperial J. Inter-
    disc. Res. **3**(5), 1232–1236 (2017). http://www.imperialjournals.com/index.php/IJIR/article/
    view/4923/4733
20. Stamati-Koromina, V., Ilioudis, C., Overill, R., Georgiadis, C.K., Stamatis, D.: Insider
    threats in corporate environments: a case study for data leakage prevention. In: Proceeding of
    5th Balkan Conference in Informatics, pp. 271–274 (2012)
21. Kaur, K., Gupta, I., AK, Singh: Data leakage prevention: e-mail protection via gateway.
    J. Phys: Conf. Ser. **933**(1), 012013 (2018)
22. Gupta, I., Singh, A.K.: A probability based model for data leakage detection using bigraph.
    In: 2007 Proceedings of the 7th International Conference on Communication and Network
    Security, pp. 1–5. ACM (2017)
23. Bhargava, B.: Secure/resilient systems and data dissemination/provenance. NGCRC Project
    Technology Final Report. CERIAS, Purdue University, September 2017
24. Sabadra, P., Stamp, M.: The MediaSnap© digital rights management system. In:
    Proceedings of Conference on Computer Science and its Applications, San-Diego, California
    (2003)

Computing and Network Technologies

Call Admission Control Scheme for Cellular Wireless Network Using Queueing Model

Jitendra Kumar[1(✉)], Vikas Shinde[1], and Punit Johari[2]

[1] Department of Applied Mathematics, Madhav Institute of Technology
and Science, Gwalior, M. P, India
jkmuthele@gmail.com, v_p_shinde@rediffmail.com
[2] Department of Computer Science Engineering and Information Technology,
Madhav Institute of Technology and Science, Gwalior, M. P, India
punitbhopal2006@gmail.com

Abstract. In this paper, we study a mathematical model for new and handoff calls with blocking under queueing system. The aim of this paper is to assign the available channel effectively to call admission control scheme, which is classified in three categories priority, non-priority and sub-rating. We apply an algorithm for evaluating the blocking probability for new and handoff calls. The proposed algorithm is analyzed the effectiveness of call admission control policy. Numerical illustrations have been validated our results.

Keywords: Queueing system · Cellular networks · Channel allocation scheme
Blocking & handoff probability

1 Introduction

Cellular mobile communication technology has greatly enhanced in last two decades. This technology provides users mobility, which makes it more popular. The cellular communication system has to provide an effective and efficient communication between user and system. Such a cellular communication system will be dedicated by handoff. There are various issues of wireless communication system in different dimension for efficient traffic management, channel allocation, tuning of frequency spectrum etc. Handoff is a quite common phenomenon of changing channels while the call is in progress for which mobile industry has to develop new infrastructure to accommodate more users. The users require quality of service (QoS) which includes messages, audio, video etc., and are ascending exponentially. Effective and efficient utilization of bandwidth is more important to meet up the better quality of service. Quality of service is more important to determine predictable service from available resources in communication system. Which are as follows:

- Blocking probability in which a new and handoff calls are blocked.
- Dropping probability in which a call is either blocked or admitted under the life cycle of call and the occurrence of immature call is terminated.

Generally a mobile consumer moves to and fro during the call then call may be transmitted to the new base station. On the other hand, the link with the existing base

G. C. Deka et al. (Eds.): ICACCT 2018, CCIS 899, pp. 117–129, 2018.
https://doi.org/10.1007/978-981-13-2035-4_11

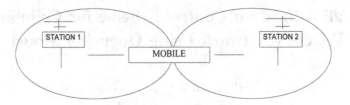

Fig. 1. Structure of handoff call

station occurs too poor as the distance is more. When the call will be dropped, then handoff will shift the mobile network.

In Fig. 1, we have shown the mobile users are served by BS in cell. The BS (Base Station) establishes the call between two users in the network. To establish a call or connection, user must specify its traffic characteristics and quality of service. Such issue developed the need of new and tangible analytical technology to examine the QoS. In order to handle the huge consumers of multimedia applications with immediate requirement of new call admission control (CAC). In communication networks, CAC can ensure a few level of quality for improvement in bandwidth. CAC algorithm runs by provision of the total consumed bandwidth, the entire number of calls routing the special node (Fig. 2).

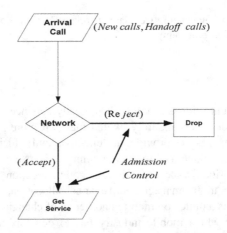

Fig. 2. Control system for call admission process

The channel allocation of cellular network is done by using queueing model to allocate the cell. Queueing model is an effective tool to resolve these issues.

2 Literature Review

Recent development of next generation of cellular mobile network and its related technology is being enhanced. Service area of cellular wireless network cells are served by channels and channels accept new and handoff calls. Calls of network are heavily loaded because of too much multimedia applications are simultaneously performed by consumers. Therefore call is not able to establish every time. This is cause of call blocking and dropping. These issues attract the attention of researchers to enhance the performance of handoff calls. Hong and Rappaopt [1] proposed various priority schemes for handoff calls. Katzeal and Naghshineh [2] established new channel assignment schemes which treat the handoff calls. Sidi and Starobinski [3] complexity of non-priority scheme of handoff call were analyzed and elaborated. Haring et al. [4] considered cell duration time and service time distribution which is followed by arbitrary distribution. Rajaratnam and Takawira [5] observed that Poisson process may not sufficient to handle the handoff traffic because handoff calls crossed a large number of boundaries. They also employed blocking of handoff calls. Rajaratnam and Takawira [6] extended earlier work for analyzing the performance of cellular networks with general arrival of handoff and channel reservation. Xie and Kuck [7] described a traffic model for one and two dimensions with identical density of mobile consumers which is equally fit for moving in any direction. Zeng et al. [8] established traffic model of any dimension in which effective termination probability and blocking probability of calls are in small amount. Zeng and Agrawal [9, 10] discussed the handoff in different dimension assumed to be occurring at cell boundary and including handoff limitations as well as quality of services. Jain [11] developed allocation policy for voice and data traffic for wireless communication systems with the regulation of subdivision of rating. Samanta et al. [12] evaluated dropping probabilities of cellular wireless networks by queueing handoff; in place of guard channels with gamma inter arrival and general service time distribution. Saini and Gupta [13] for improving the avidity of the soft handoff calls in mobile communication were studied. Jain and Mittal [14] presented allocation scheme for admission control policies by exploiting the soft handoff coverage area of soft handoff calls. Shen and Hou [16] compared the first model and second model engaging handoff calls by using the sub division policy. Kim [15], Shen and Hou [17] dealt with the heavy network traffic of handoff calls under the sub division policy support to step down for blocking the incoming calls.

3 Assumption and Mathematical Description of Model

We assume the following nomenclature
λ_N = average arrival rate for new calls
λ_H = average arrival rate for handoff calls
λ_{hd} = average arrival rate for handoff data calls
σ_{nv} = average arrival rate for new voice calls
CBP = Call blocking probability according new calls in the cell
CHP = Call handoff probability according handoff calls in the cell
N = Number of channels
N_C = Number of remaining channels
N_R = Number of assigned channels
r = Number of extra channels.

Integrated wireless and mobile network of a single cell is discussed. We focus on the traffic of new and handoff calls due to high mobility. Traffic under different channel allocation scheme have been analyzed in three category such as Priority Scheme (PS), Non-Priority Scheme (NPS) and Sub-Rating Scheme (SRS).

A. Priority Scheme

Priority of handoff requests by assigning N_R channels exclusively for handoff calls among the N channels in a cell. The remaining N_C (=$N - N_R$) channels are shared by both originating calls and handoff requests. An originating call is blocked if the number of available channels in the cell is less than or equal to N_R (=$N - N_C$). A handoff request is blocked if no channel is available in the target cell. The system model is shown in Fig. 3.

We define the state i ($i = 0, 1, \cdots, N$) of a cell as the number of calls in progress for the BS of that cell. Let $P(i)$ represent the steady-state probability that the BS is in state i. The probabilities $P(i)$ can be determined in the usual way for birth–death processes. The pertinent state transition diagram is shown in Fig. 6, the state balance equations are

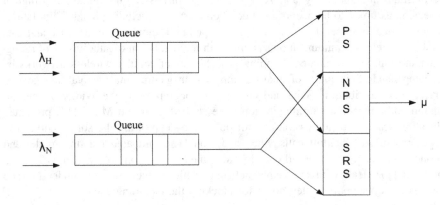

Fig. 3. System model with priority for handoff call

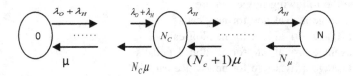

Fig. 4. State transition diagrams

$$\begin{cases} i\mu P_i = (\lambda_O + \lambda_H)P_{i-1}, & 0 < i < N_C \\ i\mu P_i = (\lambda_H)P_{i-1}, & N_C < i < N \end{cases} \tag{1}$$

Using normalize condition, we have

$$\sum_{i=0}^{N} P_i = 1 \tag{2}$$

Apply steady-state condition, we get

$$P_i = \begin{cases} \dfrac{(\lambda_O + \lambda_H)^i}{i!\mu} P_0, & 0 < i < N_C \\[2mm] \dfrac{(\lambda_O + \lambda_H)^{N_C} (\lambda_H)^{i-N_C}}{i!\mu} P_0, & N_C < i < N \end{cases} \tag{3}$$

where

$$P_0 = \left\{ \sum_{i=0}^{N_C} \frac{(\lambda_O + \lambda_H)^i}{i!\mu} + \sum_{i=N_C+1}^{N} \frac{(\lambda_O + \lambda_H)^{N_C} (\lambda_H)^{i-N_C}}{i!\mu} \right\}^{-1} \tag{4}$$

B. Non-priority Scheme

All N channels are shared by both originating and handoff request calls. The BS handles a handoff request exactly in the same way as an originating call. Both kind of request are blocked if no free channel is available. The system model is shown in Fig. 5.

With the blocking call cleared (BCC) policy, we can describe the behavior of a cell as a $(N + 1)$ states Markov process.

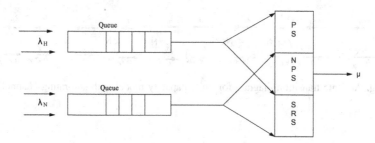

Fig. 5. System model with non-priority for handoff

The state transition diagram is shown in Fig. 4. The system model is modeled by a typical $M/M/N/N$ queueing model.

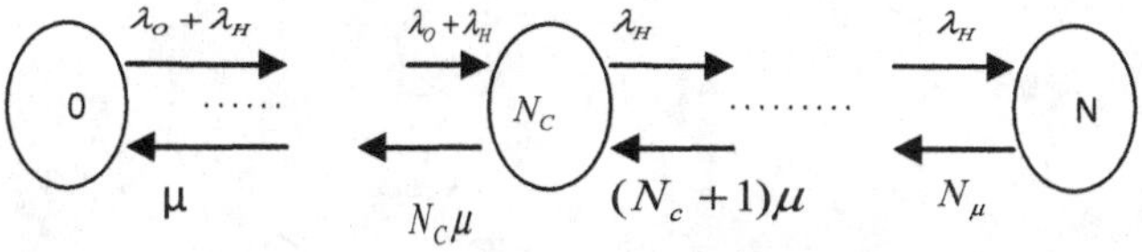

Fig. 6. State transition diagrams

Let $P(i)$ be the probability that the system is in state i. The probabilities $P(i)$ can be determined in the usual way for birth–death processes. From Fig. 6, the state equilibrium equation is

$$P_i = \frac{(\lambda_O + \lambda_H)}{i\mu} P_{i-1}, \quad 0 \leq i \leq N \tag{5}$$

Using the above equation recursively, along with the normalization condition

$$\sum_{i=0}^{N} P_i = 1 \tag{6}$$

The steady-state probability $P(i)$ is easily found as follows:

$$P_i = \frac{(\lambda_O + \lambda_H)^i}{i!\mu} P_0, \quad 0 \leq i \leq N \quad \text{where } P_0 = \frac{1}{\sum_{i=0}^{N} \frac{(\lambda_O + \lambda_H)^i}{i!\mu}} \tag{7}$$

C. Sub-Rating Scheme

Sub-Rating Scheme is capable to increase system's capacity to serve more handoff voice attempts. For this purpose, sub-rating scheme is used for reserve channels which are split into two half rate channels to serve more handoff voice attempts. The state transition diagram for this model is shown in Fig. 7. The steady state probabilities for this model can be obtained using the product type solution and is given by

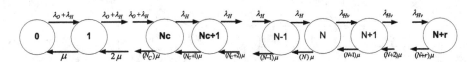

Fig. 7. State transition diagram for finite capacity model with sub-rating channel

$$P_i = \begin{cases} \frac{1}{i} \frac{(\lambda_O + \lambda_H)^i}{\mu} P_0, & 1 \leq i \leq N - r \\ (\lambda_O + \lambda_H)^r \frac{(\lambda_H)^{i-(N-r)}}{i!\mu^r} P_0, & N - r + 1 \leq i \leq N \\ (\lambda_O + \lambda_H)^r \frac{(\lambda_H)^{(N-r)}(\lambda_{Hv})^{(i-N)}}{i!\mu^r} P_0, & N + 1 \leq i \leq N + r \end{cases} \tag{8}$$

Where

$$P_0 = \left\{ \sum_{i=0}^{N-r} \frac{(\lambda_O + \lambda_H)^i}{i!\mu} + \sum_{i=N-r+1}^{N} (\lambda_O + \lambda_H)^r \frac{(\lambda_H)^{i-(N-r)}}{i!\mu^r} + \sum_{i=N+1}^{N+r} (\lambda_O + \lambda_H)^r \frac{(\lambda_H)^{(N-r)}(\lambda_{Hv})^{(i-N)}}{i!\mu^r} \right\}^{-1}$$

(9)

D. Estimation of Blocking probabilities for New and Handoff calls with priority scheme:

The call blocking probability P_B for new call is described as

$$BP(P_B) = \sum_{i=r}^{N} P_i$$

(10)

The call blocking probability P_H for a handoff request is

$$HP(P_H) = \frac{(\lambda_O + \lambda_H)^r \lambda_H^{(N-r)}}{N!\,\mu^N} P_0$$

(11)

E. Estimation of Blocking Probabilities for New and Handoff calls with non-priority scheme:

The call blocking probability P_B for new call is

$$BP(P_B) = \frac{(\lambda_O + \lambda_H)^N}{N!\,\mu^i} P_0$$

(12)

The blocking probability P_H of a handoff request is

$$BP(P_B) = HP(P_H)$$

(13)

Equation (13) is known as the Erlang-B formula.

F. Estimation of Blocking Probabilities for New and Handoff calls with sub-rating scheme:

The average blocking probability B_P for new call is

$$BP(P_B) = \sum_{i=N-r}^{N+r} P_i$$

(14)

The blocking probability P_H handoff data calls is

$$HP(P_H) = \sum_{i=N}^{N+r} P_i$$

(15)

4 Proposed Algorithm

In the proposed algorithm is capable to handle the call admission control policy. We consider the different incoming calls which are assigned respective categories viz priority, non priority and sub-rating by using Boolean value. Depending on the category of the incoming call, the channel is allotted to process it. All the priorities calls are treated straightforwardly. However the other categories of calls (non priority and sub-ratting) are further filtered through mean and deviation method. They are sorted on the basis of frequency. This is conversion of non priority and sub rating calls into high frequency range/call. Low frequency range of this category is discarded. The call queues are indexed according to the respective frequency assigned to them (high frequency and low frequency) and they have been allotted channels on the basis of index to process it. Remaining calls have been discarded.

Initialize

- Call queue $(C_1, C_2, \ldots, C_n)$ //A queue that hold all incoming call
- Boolean priority (C_i) //Returns the boolean value (1: priority call, 0: non-priority call)
- Boolean non-priority (C_i) //Return the frequency level of call C_i in boolean value where 0: high frequency and 1: low frequency.
- Boolean sub rating (C_i) //Return the boolean value 1: if call is sub rating call otherwise 0.

Initialize i=1;
   Step 1: Process call queue $(C_1, C_2, \ldots, C_n)$ in FIFO basis.
   Step 2: **If (Priority $(C_i) == 1$)**
         {
             Assign channel to call (C_i)
         }
         Else
         {
             If (sub-ratting $((C_i) == 1$)
             {
         Calculate mean and deviation of frequency assigned to call sub-ratting competitive calls & sort calls on the basis of frequency
             }
             Else
             {
         Calculate mean & deviation of frequency assigned to all non-priority call.
             }
         }
   Step 3: Merge & sort both sub-rating & non-priority calls.
   Step 4: Assigned channel based on indexing and remaining calls has been straight forward discarded.
   Step 5: if (i <n) then goto step 1 else goto step 6.
   Step 6: Stop

5   Sensitivity Analysis

We have fixed some parameter to evaluate the performance measures to consider that priority calls have no barricades (Tables 1, 2 and 3).

Table 1. Performance measures

Parameters	Descriptions	Value
N	Number of channels (N) per BS	20
r	Number of extra channels ®	05
λ_N	Average arrival rate for new calls	0.5 call/sec
λ_H	Average arrival rate for handoff calls	30 s
$1/\mu$	Mean cell residence time	40 s

Table 2. Analytical evaluation for new and handoff call arrival rate.

S. No.	New call arrival rate	Handoff call arrival rate	Sub-ratting calls		Non- priority calls	
			Blocking probability	Handoff probability	Blocking probability	Handoff probability
1	0.02	0.001	0.94	0.90	0.90	0.88
2	0.04	0.003	0.62	0.60	0.54	0.59
3	0.06	0.005	0.49	0.48	0.45	0.45
4	0.08	0.007	0.35	0.33	0.32	0.32
5	0.1	0.009	0.3	0.29	0.29	0.25
6	0.12	0.011	0.24	0.23	0.21	0.20
7	0.14	0.012	0.20	0.19	0.19	0.18
8	0.16	0.013	0.18	0.17	0.17	0.16
9	0.18	0.015	0.15	0.14	0.145	0.13
10	0.2	0.017	0.123	0.12	0.121	0.11
11	0.22	0.018	0.122	0.123	0.12	0.115
12	0.24	0.019	0.121	0.112	0.12	0.110
13	0.26	0.021	0.121	0.111	0.11	0.109
14	0.28	0.023	0.120	0.110	0.115	0.108
15	0.3	0.025	0.119	0.109	0.112	0.106
16	0.32	0.025	0.118	0.108	0.111	0.105
17	0.34	0.027	0.117	0.106	0.110	0.104
18	0.36	0.029	0.116	0.105	0.109	0.103
19	0.38	0.031	0.115	0.103	0.108	0.102
20	0.4	0.033	0.114	0.102	0.105	0.101
21	0.42	0.035	0.113	0.101	0.104	0.100
22	0.44	0.037	0.112	0.101	0.103	0.090
23	0.46	0.039	0.110	0.09	0.102	0.089
24	0.48	0.041	0.109	0.08	0.1025	0.088
25	0.50	0.043	0.107	0.05	0.10	0.085

Table 3. Implementation of suggested algorithm for new and handoff call arrival rate.

S. No.	New call arrival rate	Handoff call arrival rate	Sub-ratting calls		Non- priority calls	
			Blocking probability	Handoff probability	Blocking probability	Handoff probability
1	0.02	0.001	0.01	0.01	0.10	0.02
2	0.04	0.003	0.05	0.04	0.20	0.04
3	0.06	0.005	0.12	0.09	0.30	0.06
4	0.08	0.007	0.21	0.19	0.40	0.08
5	0.1	0.009	0.32	0.25	0.50	0.16
6	0.12	0.011	0.42	0.36	0.60	0.20
7	0.14	0.012	0.51	0.40	0.70	0.34
8	0.16	0.013	0.70	0.55	0.75	0.42
9	0.18	0.015	0.76	0.59	0.78	0.54
10	0.2	0.017	0.80	0.60	0.80	0.58
11	0.22	0.018	0.86	0.69	0.83	0.64
12	0.24	0.019	0.87	0.75	0.86	0.70
13	0.26	0.021	0.88	0.82	0.87	0.76
14	0.28	0.023	0.89	0.84	0.88	0.80
15	0.3	0.025	0.90	0.86	0.89	0.83
16	0.32	0.025	0.91	0.88	0.90	0.84
17	0.34	0.027	0.92	0.89	0.91	0.87
18	0.36	0.029	0.93	0.90	0.92	0.88
19	0.38	0.031	0.94	0.92	0.93	0.89
20	0.4	0.033	0.95	0.93	0.94	0.91
21	0.42	0.035	0.959	0.94	0.95	0.92
22	0.44	0.037	0.96	0.949	0.959	0.93
23	0.46	0.039	0.96	0.95	096	0.94
24	0.48	0.041	0.97	0.96	0. 96	0.95
25	0.50	0.043	0.978	0.98	0.97	0.96

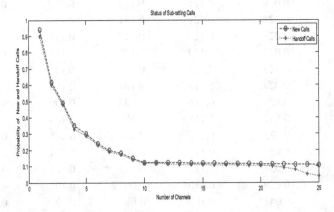

Fig. 8. Number of channel vs prob. of new and handoff calls for sub-ratting call

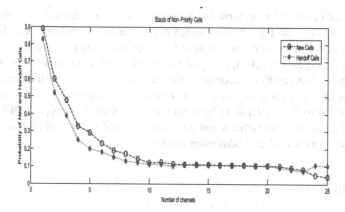

Fig. 9. Number of channel vs prob. of new and handoff calls for non- priority call

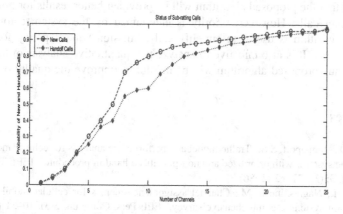

Fig. 10. Number of channel vs prob. of new and handoff calls for sub-ratting call

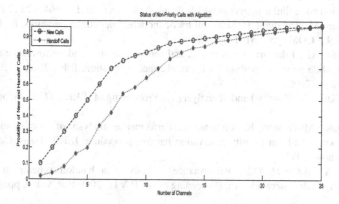

Fig. 11. Number of channel vs prob. of new and handoff calls for non- priority call

Numerical values have been plotted between numbers of channel vs probability of new and handoff calls in Figs. 8 and 9 which depict that the probability of calls is going down with respect to the increasing assigned number of channels. Some time it is found that the calls are being blocked, dropped and overlapped. After employing this algorithm we have observed that the dropout rate of calls is minimize which indicate that the proposed algorithm is being capable to enhance the efficiency of the cellular system which described in Figs. 10 and 11 between numbers of channel vs probability of new and handoff calls. We also noticed that the more assigned number of channels provide the better performance of call admission control scheme.

6 Conclusion

Mobile customers require more effective service from cellular network system. Call admission control scheme provides better quality of service (QoS) to the mobile users. In this paper, cellular mobile network for new and handoff calls have been analyzed. It is observed that the proposed algorithm will be provided better results for non-priority and sub-rating calls. However, priority is entertained by the system automatically. Described algorithm is useful to simplify call admission control policy for cellular mobile networks. It is also effective to analyze the quantitative analysis of the system behavior. Thus proposed algorithm will be helpful to improve the quality of service.

References

1. Hong, D., Rappaport, S.S.: Traffic model and performance analysis for cellular mobile radio telephone systems with prioritized and non-prioritized handoff procedures. IEEE Trans. Veh. Technol. **35**(3), 77–92 (1986)
2. Katzela, I., Naghishinesh, M.: Channel assignment schemes for cellular mobile telecommunication system, a comprehensive survey. IEEE Pers. Commun. **3**(3), 10–31 (1996)
3. Sidi, M., Starobinki, D.: New call blocking vs handoff blocking in cellular networks. ACM J. Wirel. Netw. **3**(1), 17–27 (1997)
4. Haring, G., Maric, R., Puigjaner, R., Trivedi, K.S.: Loss formula and their application to optimization for cellular networks. IEEE Trans. Veh. Technol. **50**, 664–673 (2001)
5. Rajaratnam, M., Takawira, F.: Hand-off traffic modeling in cellular networks. In: Proceeding of the Globe COM, pp. 131–137 (1997)
6. Rajaratnam, M., Takawira, F.: Non-classical traffic modeling and performance analysis of cellular mobile networks with and without channel reservation. IEEE Trans. Veh. Technol. **49**, 817–834 (2000)
7. Xie, H., Kuek, S.: Priority handoff analysis. In: Proceeding of IEEE VTC 1993, pp. 855–858 (1993)
8. Zeng, Q.A., Mukumoto, K., Fukuda, A.: Performance analysis of mobile cellular radio systems with two-level priority reservation handoff procedure. IEICE Trans. Commun. **80** (4), 598–604 (1997)
9. Zeng, Q.A., Agrawal, D.P.: Performance analysis of a handoff scheme in integrated voice/data wireless networks. In: Proceeding of IEEE VTC 2000 Fall, vol. 4, pp. 1986–1992 (2000)

10. Zeng, Q.A., Agrawal, D.P.: An analytical modeling of handoff for integrated voice/data wireless networks with priority reservation and preemptive priority procedures. In: Proceeding ICPP 2000 Workshop on Wireless Networks and Mobile Computing, pp. 523–529 (2000)
11. Jain, M.: Channel allocation policy in cellular radio network. Appl. Math. Model. **29**, 65–83 (2005)
12. Samanta, R.K., Bhattacharjee, P., Sanyal, G.: Performance analysis of cellular wireless network by queueing priority handoff calls. Int. J. Electr. Electron. Eng. **3**(8), 472–477 (2009)
13. Saini, V.K., Gupta, S.C.: Improving capacity of soft handoff performance in wireless mobile communication using macro diversity. Int. J. Comput. Sci. Eng. **3**(6), 2217–2223 (2011)
14. Jain, M., Mittal, R.: Call admission control for handoff coverage in CDMA Cellular System. Int. J. Wirel. Inf. Netw. **22**, 53–66 (2015)
15. Kim, D.K., Sung, D.K.: Traffic management in a multi code CDMA system supporting soft handoffs. IEEE Trans. Veh. Technol. **51**, 52–62 (2002)
16. Sheu, T.L., Hou, T.L.: An analytical model of cell coverage for soft handoffs in cellular CDMA systems. GESTS Int. Trans. Comput. Sci. Eng. **18**(1), 209–223 (2005)
17. Sheu, T.L., Hou, T.L.: On the influences of enlarging or shrinking the soft handoff coverage for a cellular CDMA system. J. Inf. Sci. Eng. **23**, 1453–1467 (2007)

On Scalability of Interconnection Network Topologies

Nibedita Adhikari[(⊠)] and C. R. Tripathy

Biju Patnaik University of Technology Odisha, Rourkela, India
drnibeditaadhikari@gmail.com, crtvssut@gmail.com

Abstract. An in depth study in the field of advanced computer architecture reveals that the quest for faster processing has resulted in different architectural innovations. The current work attempts to compare different networks proposed earlier. All the interconnection networks are compared on a common platform with fixed node degree. The various parameters that are taken into consideration are network size, diameter, cost, message traffic density and reliability. The main objective is to find the best network among all on the basis of cost optimality and scalability.

Keywords: Isoefficiency · FCC · FMC · SCC · ECC · MCC

1 Introduction

The reliable performance of the interconnection network topologies is an important issue in the design of parallel computer systems. The scalability of a parallel system is a measure of its capacity to increase speedup in proportion to the number of Processing Elements (PE) [1, 2]. It also reflects a parallel system's ability to utilize increasing processing resources effectively. The Efficiency is a measure of the fraction of time for which the PE is usefully employed [3, 4]. For a given problem size, if the number of processing elements is increased, then the overhead of the system or the idle time of the PE also increases. The scalability and the efficiency both depend on the problem size which is also termed as the input size. For the sequential algorithms the time complexity is expressed as a function of input size.

The cost of solving a problem on a parallel system is the product of parallel runtime and number of processing elements. A parallel system is said to be cost optimal if the cost of solving a problem on a parallel computer has the same asymptotic growth as a function of input size similar to complexity of serial runtime. In parallel systems, the number of processors, the input size, the problem size and the maximum number of parallel computations etc should be taken into consideration equally. The network's packing density also plays a very important role in design of parallel interconnection topology [5]. If the network's packing density matches with the desired input size, the system is regarded as cost optimal [6].

While studying the scalability of the parallel systems, the Isoefficiency function needs to be determined. The Isoefficiency is defined as the ratio of speedup to the total number of processors in the system. It determines the ease with which the parallel

© Springer Nature Singapore Pte Ltd. 2018
G. C. Deka et al. (Eds.): ICACCT 2018, CCIS 899, pp. 130–138, 2018.
https://doi.org/10.1007/978-981-13-2035-4_12

system can maintain the constant efficiency and hence can achieve scalability [3–5]. The parallel systems efficiency can be maintained at any value between 0 and 1 depending upon the network size. Due to architectural innovations there are several modifications suggested to improve the interconnection networks. To achieve faster processing the alternatives suggested are – folding technique, cross linking, extension, load balancing, hierarchical connection, replacement of nodes etc.

The current paper attempts to compare the performance of all the networks which are proposed in [7–15]. A common platform is used to measure and compare the performance of these networks. The networks taken for comparison are: Folded crossed cube [7], Meta crossed cube [8], Balanced varietal hypercube [9], Folded meta cube [10, 11], Star crossed cube [12], Extended crossed cube [13], Extended star [14] and the Meta star [15]. In Sect. 2 the different performance metrics of all the above said networks are evaluated and compared. The *Isoefficiency* metric of scalability is defined in Sect. 3. For some specified problem size the suitability of these networks is evaluated in Sect. 4. Basing on the comparisons, cost optimality of the proposed systems are discussed. The Sect. 5 concludes the paper.

2 Comparison of Topological Properties of the Various Networks

Some new classes of parallel interconnection networks namely Folded crossed cube (FCC), Folded dual cube (FDC), Folded meta cube (FMC), Extended crossed cube (ECC), Extended star (ES), Star crossed cube (SCC), Meta crossed cube (MCC), Meta star (M-star) and the Balanced varietal hypercube (BVH) are proposed earlier. The different topological properties of the above said networks are also derived. The most suitable way for evaluating the networks is to conduct a comparative study among the topological properties. The comparison of the topological properties such as degree, diameter, cost, the total number of nodes and edges of the proposed networks is done and presented in Table 1. The various performance parameters for them are presented in Tables 2 and 3. As listed in the table, all of them have different parameters. The parameter used for FCC network is n similar to that of Hypercube [6]. The FMC and MCC networks have two distinct parameters k and m. Similarly, the SCC has m and n as its parameters to describe its dimension and other properties. Next, the ECC and the ES network have a couple of parameters namely (k, l) and (n, k). The M-star network contains two variables specifically k and m to describe the topological structure. Due to the existence of a variety of parameters, a common platform is needed to compare these networks. Hence the link complexity is chosen as the common platform. At first, the network size is computed for different values of node degree to observe the scalability of these networks. The computed values are shown in Table 4.

In Table 4, the total number of nodes of different networks is listed for the node degrees varying from 3 to 6 respectively. The growth rate of the FCC is the least among all whereas all other networks grow comparatively at a high rate. This is because they are all having two layered structures with two parameters. The ES, M-star and MCC networks show their existence at node degree 3 and the M-star possesses the highest value. With degree 4, the highest value of total nodes is observed to be found in case of

M-star whereas least value is seen in case of ECC. Same number of nodes in FDC and FMC are found for node degree 4.

For degree 5, higher values are obtained in case of M-star and significantly higher values for MCC and FMC. The smaller values are found for FCC, SCC and ECC. Evaluating for degree 6, FMC value can be regarded for getting highest value where as M-Star value can supersede in specific conditions. However, values in increasing order

Table 1. Comparison of topological properties of the networks

Proposed networks	Nodes	Degree	Diameter	Edges
FCC(n)	2^n	$(n + 1)$	$\lceil \frac{n}{2} \rceil$	$(n+1)2^{2n-2}$
FDC(1, m) $(r = 1 + m)$	2^{2m+1}	$(r + 1)$	$(2r - 2)$	$(r + 1) \, 2^{\,2r-2}$
FMC(k, m) $(r = k + m)$	$2^{2^k m + k}$	$(r + 1)$	$(2r - 2)$	$(r + 1) \, 2^{\,mh+k-1}$
ECC(k, l)	$2^{kl} + \frac{2^{kl}-1}{2^k-1}$	$(k + 1)$	$\lceil \frac{k+1}{2} \rceil + 2(l - 1)$	$2^k \left(\frac{k}{2} + 1 \right) \times 2^{k(l-1)} \left(\frac{1-2^{-kl}}{1-2^{-k}} \right)$
ES(n, k)	$n!^k + \frac{n!^k-1}{n!-1}$	(n)	$\lfloor \frac{3}{2}(n - 1) \rfloor + 2(k - 1)$	$\frac{1}{2}(n+1)! \times \frac{(n!)^k-1}{n!-1}$
SCC(m, n)	$n! \times 2^m$	$(m + n - 1)$	$\lceil \frac{m+1}{2} \rceil + \lfloor \frac{3(n-1)}{2} \rfloor$.	$n! \times 2^{m-1}(m+n-1)$.
MCC(k,m)	$2^{m2^k + k}$	$(k + m)$	$\left(\lceil \frac{m+1}{2} \rceil + 1 \right) 2^k$	$2^{mh+k} \left(\frac{m+k}{2} \right)$
M-star(k, m)	$2^k m! m!$	$(k + m - 1)$	$\left(\lfloor \frac{3(m-1)}{2} \rfloor + 1 \right) 2^k$	$(2^k m! m!) \times (k+m-1)/2$
BVH(2n)	2^{2n}	$2n$	$\lceil n + \frac{n}{2} \rceil$	$n \times 2^{2n}$

Table 2. Comparison of cost factor

Proposed networks	Cost
FCC(n)	$\lceil \frac{n}{2} \rceil (n+1)$
FDC(1, m) $(r = 1 + m)$	$(r + 1)(2r - 2)$
FMC(k, m) $(r = k + m)$	$(r + 1)(2r - 2)$
ECC(k, l)	$\dfrac{\left(\lceil \frac{k+1}{2} \rceil + 2(l-1) \right) \left((k+1)2^{kl} + (2^k + k + 1) \left(\frac{2^{kl}-1}{2^k-1} \right) \right)}{2^{kl} + (2^k + k + 1)(2^{kl}-1)}$
ES(n, k)	$\left(\lfloor \frac{3}{2}(n - 1) \rfloor + 2(k - 1) \right) \times \dfrac{n(n!)^k + (n! + n) \left(\frac{(n!)^k - 1}{(n!-1)} \right)}{(n!)^k + (n! + n)((n!)^k - 1))}$
SCC(m, n)	$(m + n - 1) \left(\lfloor \frac{3(n-1)}{2} \rfloor + \lceil \frac{m+1}{2} \rceil \right)$
MCC(k, m)	$(m + k) \left(\lceil \frac{m+1}{2} \rceil + 1 \right) 2^k$
M-star(k, m)	$\left(\lfloor \frac{3(m-1)}{2} \rfloor + 1 \right) 2^k (k + m - 1)$
BVH(2n)	$2n \times \lceil n + \frac{n}{2} \rceil$

Table 3. Comparison of performance parameters of the proposed networks

Proposed networks	CEF	TCEF
FCC(n)	$\dfrac{1}{1+\rho\left(\frac{n+1}{2}\right)}$	$\dfrac{1+\sigma}{1+\rho\left(\frac{n+1}{2}\right)+\frac{\sigma}{2^n}}$
FDC(1, m) (r = 1 + m)	$\dfrac{1}{1+\rho\left(\frac{m+2}{2}\right)}$	$\dfrac{1+\sigma}{1+\rho\left(\frac{m+2}{2}\right)+\left(\frac{\sigma}{2^{mh+k}}\right)}$
FMC(k, m) (r = k + m)	$\dfrac{1}{1+\rho\left(\frac{m+k+1}{2}\right)}$	$\dfrac{1+\sigma}{1+\rho\left(\frac{m+k+1}{2}\right)+\left(\frac{\sigma}{2^{mh+k}}\right)}$
ECC(k, l)	$\dfrac{1}{1+\rho\left(1-\frac{1}{p}\right)\left(\frac{k}{2}+1\right)}$	$\dfrac{1+\sigma}{1+\rho\left(1-\frac{1}{p}\right)\left(\frac{k}{2}+1\right)+\frac{\sigma}{p}}$
ES(n, k)	$\dfrac{1}{1+\rho\times\frac{(n+1)!}{2}\times\left(1-\frac{(n!)^k}{p}\right)}$	$\dfrac{1+\sigma}{1+\rho\frac{(n+1)!}{2}\times\left(1-\frac{(n!)^k}{p}\right)+\frac{(n!-1)\sigma}{(n!)^{k+1}-1}}$
SCC(m,n)	$\dfrac{1}{1+\rho\frac{m+n-1}{2}}$	$\dfrac{1+\sigma}{1+\rho\left(\frac{m+n-1}{2}\right)+\left(\frac{\sigma}{2^m n!}\right)}$
MCC(k, m)	$\dfrac{1}{1+\rho\left(\frac{m+k}{2}\right)}$	$\dfrac{1+\sigma}{1+\rho\left(\frac{m+k}{2}\right)+\frac{\sigma}{p}}$
M-star(k, m)	$\dfrac{2}{2+\rho(k+m-1)}$	$\dfrac{(1+\sigma)2p}{2+2p+\rho p(k+m-1)}$
BVH(2n)	$\dfrac{1}{1+\rho n}$	$\dfrac{1+\sigma}{1+\rho n+\frac{\sigma}{2^{2n}}}$

Table 4. Comparison of network size with links per node in proposed networks

Links/node	FCC	FDC	FMC	ECC	ES	SCC	M-star	MCC	BVH
3	-	-	-	-	7	-	72	32	-
4	8	32	32	9	25,43	24	1152	128, 1024	16
5	16	128	128, 1024	73	121,259, 601	48	2304,28800	512, 16384	-
6	32	512	16384	273,585	14,000	96, 192	4608, 57600	2048, 26,000	64

for this node degree is observed in the order FCC, BVH, SCC and ECC. However the BVH have its existence at even values only.

The packing density of an interconnection network is defined as the ratio of total number of nodes to the cost of the network. For VLSI layout design smaller chip area is preferred for which higher packing density is required, hence the comparison of packing density of the proposed network topologies is done with respect to link complexity. The comparison of packing density is shown in Fig. 1. The M-star has the highest value requiring lowest chip area. The Figure depicts that the MCC comes next followed by the FMC network. The other networks namely the SCC, ES, FCC and the BVH all lie in the lowest density level.

The comparison of various topological properties with link complexity is essential as it establishes the superiority of a network over other networks. A network of fixed size of node degree is preferred and for that value of node degree all the topological properties namely network size, diameter, cost, total number of edges, average distance are evaluated. Also the performance parameters namely the cost effectiveness, time cost

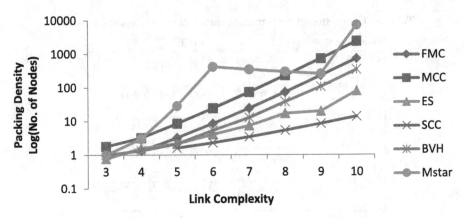

Fig. 1. Comparison of packing density of the proposed networks

effectiveness and reliability are evaluated and shown in the Tables 5 and 6. In Table 5, the results are shown for an odd degree that is 5. The Table 6 shows values for an even node degree that is 6. The comparison in the Tables clearly shows that the M-star can build sufficiently large scale parallel system with having very small links per node. The MCC contains 16384 numbers of nodes with 40960 numbers of edges which comes next in the comparison.

Table 5. Comparison of parameters of proposed networks at even node degree ($d_g = 5$)

Links/per node(5)	FCC	FMC	ECC	ES	SCC	MCC	Mstar	BVH
Nodes	16	128 1024	17	121	48	512, 16384	2304, 28800	16
Diameter	3	8, 8	3	6	6	12, 20	20,14	3
Cost	15	40, 40	15	30	30	60, 100	100,70	12
Edges	40	320, 2560	48	360	210	1280 40960	5706, 72000	32
Average distance	2.06	2.25	1.9	2.29	2.87	5.8	11.56	3.52
CEF	0.769	0.769	0.456	0.626	0.800	0.80	0.88	0.9
TCEF	1.502	1.536	1.720	1.247	1.573	1.59	1.599	1.74
Reliability	0.827	0.905	0.650	0.600	0.842	0.60	0.55	0.99

Other parameters are well compared for different networks and can be suitably adopted for prioritizing the parameters in preference. So far as links per node odd or even is concerned, M-star is found to be more suitable in both the cases. However, the TCEF was found to be decreasing with increase in node degree as the TCEF will attain its maximum for a fixed node size. The ECC, ES and MCC have higher TCEF values. The reliability of all the networks decreases with respect to increase in network size. The BVH network is found to have highest reliability.

Table 6. Comparison of parameters of proposed networks at odd node degree ($d_g = 6$)

Links/per node(6)	FCC	FMC		ECC	ES	SCC	MCC	M-star	BVH
		(1, 4)	(2, 3)						
Nodes	32	512	16384	33	721	96	2048, 262144	57600	64
Diameter	3	10,10		3	7, 6	6	14, 24	28	5
Cost	18	60, 60		18	35, 30	30	84, 144	168	30
Edges	96	320, 49152		112,3696	516	210	6144, 786432	34500	192
Average distance	2.406	3.25		6.26	3.23	3.87	6.3,11.6	18.73	5.69
CEF	0.740	0.769		0.445	0.588	0.769	0.76	0.869	0.76
TCEF	1.464	1.481		1.73	1.76	1.526	1.768	1.53	1.76
Reliability	0.829	0.891		0.650	0.600	0.813	0.495	0.469	0.983

3   Comparison of *Isoefficiency* for the Proposed Networks

For Interconnection networks's scalability study, the *Isoefficiency* (f_e) is defined as follows:

Generally the parallel run time (T_p) for 'p' processing elements and input size 'w' is defined as [3]

$$T_p = \frac{w + T_o(w,p)}{p} \tag{1}$$

where T_o is the overhead of the system due to idling of the processor.

The speedup (S) is defined as

$$S = \frac{W}{T_p} \tag{2}$$

The *Isoefficiency* $f_e(p)$ is defined as

$$f_e(p) = \frac{S}{p} = \frac{1}{1 + T_o(w,p)/w} \tag{3}$$

If a system can maintain constant *Isoefficiency* for different problem sizes then it is said to be scalable. Using Eq. 3, the *Isoefficiency* metric for all the proposed networks is evaluated. For evaluation the input size 'w' need to be specified. For the present work the problem size specification is stated as follows:

For all these networks the efficiency is evaluated using Eq. 3 for different desired problem sizes as discussed in Table 7. The computed values and there comparison for the proposed networks are shown below in Figs. 2, 3, 4, 5 and 6. In the figures the horizontal axis denotes the problem size and the vertical axis denotes the computed *Isoefficiency* values.

As depicted in the comparative graphs it is found that the FCC, SCC, M-star and MCC networks have continuous curves showing their existence at all values of network size as shown in Figs. 2 and 6. The discontinuity in the curves of FDC, FMC, ECC, ES

Table 7. Problem size specification

Size(w)	Scale
50–100	Small scale
100–500	Medium scale
500–1000	Big scale
1000–10000	Large scale

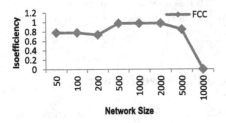

Fig. 2. *Isoefficiency* of FCC network

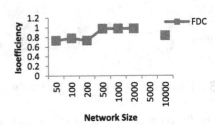

Fig. 3. *Isoefficiency* of FDC network

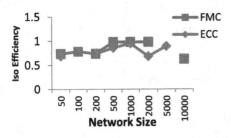

Fig. 4. *Isoefficiency* of FMC and ECC network

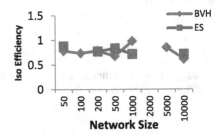

Fig. 5. *Isoefficiency* of ES and BVH network

and BVH reveal that they lack to fit in the network size band as shown in Figs. 3, 4 and 5. The up and down nature of the curves indicate that the *Isoefficiency* is not maintained at a constant value. However the FCC network found to maintain a constant value in the range of 50 to 200 and 500 to 2000. Similarly in case of FDC and FMC constancy was observed from 50 to 200 and 500 to 2000 (Figs. 3 and 4). In case of ECC the efficiency level is maintained at an increasing level from 200 to 1000 indicating suitability for medium scale problems. The value of efficiency does not exceed 0.9 for higher network size. The ECC network is also fit for problems of size 2000 to 5000 for its increasing trend as shown in Fig. 4. The *Isoefficiency* of BVH network ranges within 0.8 to 0.9 for small and large scale problems as shown in Fig. 5. For ES network the efficiency label is around 8 but the discontinuity indicates inferior usability.

The SCC network maintains a throughout continuity at 0.96 for network size starting from 50 to 5000 as depicted in Fig. 6. Beyond that the value decreases. Hence

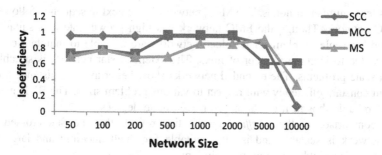

Fig. 6. Comparison of *Isoefficiency* of SCC, MCC and Meta star network

the SCC network is observed to be suitable for small scale, medium scale and large scale problem sizes yielding a cost optimal solution.

The MCC network has the least efficiency that is around 0.6 for very large scale problems, *Isoefficiency* level of 0.8 for small scale and 0.9 for medium to large scale problem size. Beyond 5000 also MCC network exhibits comparatively better efficiency. Lastly for the Meta star network *Isoefficiency* range fluctuates from 0.6 to 0.85 for problem size of small to very large scale.

4 Results

The new networks discussed are of various categories namely multi level, hierarchical network, hybrid network, and load balanced. The FCC is a modified network with additional links in pure network. The FDC and FMC are two level structures. The ECC and ES are hierarchical in nature. But the SCC, MCC and M-star are hybrid networks while the BVH is load balanced. The growth rate of FCC network is least while for others it is very high. The Meta star network possesses highest network size resulting in highest packing density. Though M-star is scalable, but is highly unreliable due to increase in total number of edges. The MCC network also exhibits similar phenomena. The ECC network is suitable for small as well as medium scale problems with comparatively better reliability and higher cost effectiveness. The extended star network has shown similar properties only for medium scale problems with still improved cost effectiveness. For FMC network growth rate is high but it is suitable for small and big scale problems with better reliability. It fails to help in very large scale problem. Due to load balancing BVH is highly reliable but it is suitable for small and medium scale problems. The star crossed cube network is scalable while maintaining high end reliability like MCC with better cost effectiveness and with a good packing density.

5 Conclusions

The current work attempts to compare different types of interconnection networks on the basis of a single parameter that is the link complexity. The comparison of packing density revel that the M-star contains highest number of nodes. The FCC network contains least number of nodes. The MCC network is the next in sequence followed by the FMC network. Though the FMC network has high growth rate it is suitable for small and big scale problems. The folded networks are not able to maintain constant efficiency due to increase number of links. The extended star network is suitable for medium scale problems. The extended networks show better average distance but fail to exhibit constant efficiency with respect to various problem sizes. The BVH network is highly reliable though it exists only for even node degrees.

The comparison of the *Isoefficiency* function reveals that the Star crossed cube (SCC) network is scalable and is most suitable for small, medium and large scale problems. It also yields cost optimal solutions.

References

1. Bhuyan, L.N., Agrawal, D.P.: Performance of multiprocessor interconnection network. IEEE Comput. **22**, 25–37 (1989)
2. Feng, T.: A survey of interconnection networks. IEEE Comput. **1**(4), 12–27 (1981)
3. Gram, A., Gupta, A., Kumar, V.: Isoefficiency: measuring the scalability of parallel algorithms and architectures. IEEE Parallel Distrib. Technol. **12**(9), 12–21 (1993)
4. Decker, T., Krandick, W.: Isoefficiency and the parallel descartes method. In: Alefeld, G., Rohn, J., Rump, S., Yamamoto, T. (eds.) Symbolic Algebraic Methods and Verification Methods. Springer, Vienna (2001). https://doi.org/10.1007/978-3-7091-6280-4_6
5. Grama, A., Gupta, A., Karypis, G., Kumar, V.: Introduction to Parallel Computing. Pearson Education, London (2003)
6. Saad, Y., Schultz, M.H.: Topological properties of hypercubes. IEEE Trans. Comput. **37**(7), 867–872 (1988)
7. Adhikari, N., Tripathy, C.R.: The folded crossed cube: a new interconnection network for parallel systems. Int. J. Comput. Appl. **4**(3), 42–50 (2010)
8. Adhikari, N., Tripathy, C.R.: Metacrossedcube: a new interconnection topology for large scale parallel systems. Int. J. Comput. Eng. Comput. Appl. **7**(1), 15–22 (2011)
9. Adhikari, N., Tripathy, C.R.: On a new multicomputer interconnection topology for massively parallel systems. Int. J. Distrib. Parallel Syst. (IJDPS) **2**(4), 162–180 (2011)
10. Adhikari, N., Tripathy, C.R.: On a new interconnection network for large scale parallel systems. Int. J. Comput. Appl. **23**(1), 39–46 (2011)
11. Adhikari, N., Tripathy, C.R.: Folded metacube: an efficient large scale parallel interconnection network. In: IEEE International Advance Computing Conference, 6–7 March, pp. 1281–1285 (2009)
12. Adhikari, N., Tripathy, C.R.: Star crossed cube: an alternative to star graph. Turk. J. Electr. Eng. Comput. Sci. **22**, 719–734 (2014)
13. Adhikari, N.: Extended crossed cube: a new fault tolerant interconnection network. Int. J. Eng. Sci. Inven. **6**(9), 60–70 (2017)
14. Adhikari, N., Nag, B.: On topological properties of a star based large scale parallel system. In: Proceedings of ETNCC2011, International Conference on Emerging Trends in Networks and Computer Communications, 22–24 April. IEI Udaipur Section (2011)
15. Adhikari, N., Tripathy, C.R.: Mstar : a new two level interconnection network. In: Ramanujam, R., Ramaswamy, S. (eds.) ICDCIT 2012. LNCS, vol. 7154, pp. 50–61. Springer, Heidelberg (2012). https://doi.org/10.1007/978-3-642-28073-3_5

Minimizing Route Coupling Effect in Multipath Video Streaming Over Vehicular Network

Ahmed Aliyu[1,2(✉)], Abdul Hanan Abdullah[1], Ajay Sikandar[3], Usman M. Joda[1,2], Fatai I. Sadiq[1], and Abubakar Ado[4]

[1] Faculty of Computing, Universiti Teknologi Malaysia, Johor Bahru, Malaysia
ahmedaliyu8513@gmail.com, hanan@utm.my, umjoda@gmail.com
[2] Bauchi State University, Gadau, Nigeria
[3] Department of Information Technology, GL Bajaj Institute of Technology and Management,
Greater Noida 201306, India
ajay.sikandar@gmail.com
[4] Northwest Univerity Kano, Kano, Nigeria
adamrogo@yahoo.com

Abstract. Multipath video streaming is one of the most commonly used strategies for high data rate transmission. It is employed to achieve lower delay, load balancing, and path diversity. However, multipath strategy experiences the problem of route coupling due to concurrent transmission via multiple paths. This problem leads to data collision and wireless contention. Therefore, in this paper, estimation of the angle between multiple paths to minimize route coupling effect and the use of Packet Error Rate (PER) as a link quality parameter for multipath video streaming has been considered in order to achieve qualitative video delivery, by minimizing interference due to route coupling effect. Firstly, mathematical formulations of the path selection and PER parameters based on the angle of forwarding are presented. Further, the numerical formulations are implemented using Matlab. The numerical results are presented showing the probability of the presence of a vehicle in an angle area. The PER is analyzed considering both shadowing and non-shadowing settings. The results based on the PER demonstrate its impact on the angle of path selection, which in turn improve the quality of the video streaming.

Keywords: Video streaming · Multipath · Vehicular network · Route coupling
Forward error correction · VANETs

1 Introduction

The advancement in vehicular communication improves on-road safety and infotainment services. The Intelligent Transportation Systems (ITS) are designed systems that minimize on-road accident and enhances mechanisms for emergency response. This had lead to several contributions by both industries and researchers to improve on protocols and mechanism that enhance on-road safety and infotainment services. In most of the recent contributions, text message-based and signal message-based data are mostly considered. However, the nature of the data does not provide a more realistic information

© Springer Nature Singapore Pte Ltd. 2018
G. C. Deka et al. (Eds.): ICACCT 2018, CCIS 899, pp. 139–151, 2018.
https://doi.org/10.1007/978-981-13-2035-4_13

on on-road accident and infotainment [1]. The VANETs has also been applied in cloud computing for better infotainment [2–5]. Therefore, streaming of video for on-road safety and infotainment has been considered in some research work. Video data provides information that is more appealing, comprehensive, interactive and understanding to vehicle users [6]. Most of the research works which are based on FEC techniques generates duplicate packets during transmission, this lead to redundant packets and large bandwidth consumption [7]. Protocols including forwarding Error Correction (FEC) and multipath solutions have been employed in several research studies. Both the FEC and multipath solutions are often cross-layer based approach. Multipath approach has been employed in several research studies to reduce high data rate and minimize delay in video streaming transmission.

In this paper, we proposed a route coupling effect minimization mechanism for multipath video streaming. The mechanism considers route coupling effect between nodes of multiple paths during video transmission. Further, the link quality parameters are considered for selection of next forwarding vehicle. The remaining parts of the paper are structured as follows; In Sect. 2, the related works have been discussed. In Sect. 3, we suggest our proposed mathematical formulations. Section 4, presents the numerical results and their analysis, and finally, Sect. 5 concludes the paper.

2 The Related Work

In this section, related literature are discussed considering their relationship with the aforementioned problem and proposed solution. The literature is divided into two, namely multipath video streaming solutions and geographical routing for vehicular communication. These are discussed in Subsects. 2.1 and 2.2 respectively.

2.1 Multipath Video Streaming Solution

In recent research works, which are based on multipath video streaming [6, 8, 9]. It is believed that the approach is based on video frames partitioning in order to transmit the frames through multiple paths (see Fig. 1). This approach minimizes the high data rate issues in video transmission. However, in the multipath formation, the signal coverage of the nodes in different paths are not considered. Hence, this may lead to contention, collision, and congestion of video packets, which in turn causes video packet loss. The loss of the video packets affects the quality of the video streaming. Therefore, in order to have a quality video streaming, the signal coverage of nodes in the multipath and the most suitable routing protocol must be taken into consideration during paths formation. Thus, the interference in multiple paths can be minimized. Video streaming in vehicular environment encounters several challenges due to the high data rate of the video stream, the dynamic topology of VANETs and constrained resources (see Fig. 2).

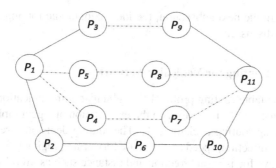

Fig. 1. Multipath video streaming scenario

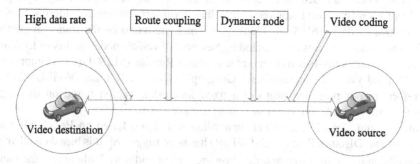

Fig. 2. Constraints of video streaming in vehicular communication

In Xie *et al.* [6], video streaming solution for VANETs using multipath transmission has been suggested. The multipath transmission considers node and link disjoint strategy in order to minimize interference, which leads higher delay and transmission rate, and wireless contention in the network. Further, the I-frame of the video packet is transmitted via TCP protocol, while other frames including P and B frames are transmitted through UDP protocol. Moreover, A TCP-ETX metric is employed to enhance the delay encountered when utilizing TCP transmission. However, the node and link disjoint strategy did not adequately handle the problem of route coupling effect, because separation distance between the nodes of the multipath is not considered hence contention might persist. To achieve node separation of the multipath solution, the degree of closeness of the nodes has been employed in order to minimize route coupling effect in [18]. The scheme employs location information in order to select nodes that are short and far apart for multipath formation. The multipath is based on receiver based video data forwarding concept. However, due to high dynamicity of the VANETs nodes the position estimation alone may not be very feasible. In addition, the same author tries to improve the aforementioned studies by considering three paths for the multipath transmission. Because in the aforementioned studies only two paths were considered. However, the findings in the study reveal that the more the number of paths the higher the route coupling effect. Thus, the suitable number of multiple paths is two [19]. Therefore, in the proposed solution, the use of angle and PER as the link quality parameters for video streaming has been considered. The entire idea is based on geographical routing using geocast and location concept. In the next subsection, the ideal geographic routing in the vehicular network has been discussed.

2.2   Geographic Routing for Vehicular Network

One of the most suitable routing protocol for vehicular communication is geographic-based routing protocol [10]. It is based on the exploitation of a geographical position of a vehicle for making routing decision [11]. The routing decisions are often based on parameters such as direction, speed and/or static forwarding region [12, 13, 33]. Several research studies have focused on direction and distance such as Mobility-Aware which is an improvement on Greedy Forwarding protocol (MAGF) in Brahmi *et al.* [14], forwarding decision based on Directional Greedy Routing (DGR) in Gong *et al.* [15] and data forwarding based on Greedy Stateless Perimeter Routing considering Motion Vector (GSPR-MV) [16]. Some techniques which are based on the static geographic region have also been suggested including Segment of vehicle node, quality of Link and Degree of connectivity-based Geographic DIstance Routing (SLDGDIR) in Omprakash *et al.* [13] and Voronoi Diagram-based Geographic Distance Routing (V-GEDIR) [12]. Therefore, in our proposed protocol a fixed forwarding region based on the angle between multiple paths for video streaming is considered.

In Raw and Das [25], a packet forwarding techniques based on Peripheral node GEographical DIstance Routing (P-GEDIR) has been suggested. It is based on all vehicles available inside the circular strip coverage area of width $R/2$ where R is the transmission range of a vehicle which is in the direction of destination vehicle. The vehicles in the circular strip coverage area are called the peripheral vehicle as shown in Fig. 3. However, this protocol might not be very suitable for large number of vehicles due to it node selection criteria.

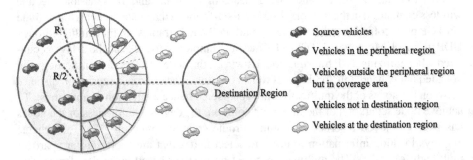

Fig. 3.   Forwarding region using peripheral zone

Further, a scheme based on the selection of next hop vehicle has been proposed in [13]. The segment region is an estimated small area at the boundary of the signal coverage area, which is based on sector angle as depicted in Fig. 4. The scheme further employs link quality metrics with distance for estimating the quality of next hop vehicle in the segment area. The link quality considers packet error rate and degree of connectivity for connectivity assurance. In another hand, a highway traffic setting considering

Free standing Position-Based Routing (FPBR) has been suggested in [26]. The FPBR protocol has various modules that handle different highway settings issues for example propagation condition and high-speed vehicle. Meanwhile, the protocol is limited to the only highway traffic situation.

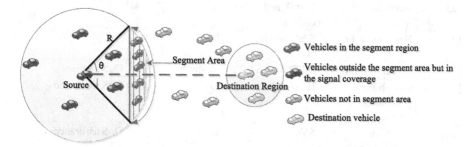

Fig. 4. Next forwarding vehicle selection based on segment region

Interestingly, a routing algorithm that predicts vehicle next future position based on Grid Predictive Geographical Routing (GPGR) has been proposed to minimize the link breakage during packet forwarding [27]. The protocol minimizes the breakage of the link, which occurs during packet forwarding by estimating the future position of the next hop vehicle. However, due to the present structure of roads, the grid packet forwarding concept might not perform efficiently. Further, Soares *et al.* [28] proposed a geographical routing scheme for delay tolerant network named GeoSpray. The scheme is the integration of two forwarding techniques including single-copy and multiple-copy forwarding techniques. The scheme considers the multiple-copy technique to spread some number of the packet in the network. Then, it employs a forwarding technique that guarantees the delivery of the packet to the vehicle that is close to the destination vehicle based on inter-vehicle contact. Nevertheless, the waiting period during packet forwarding has not been considered in this study. Conversely, an approach that is centered on Relative Position-Based Message Dissemination (RPB-MD) protocol for the vehicular network has been suggested [29]. The protocol predicts the destination by employing anonymous addressing scheme considering the relative position of vehicles. Greedy broadcast forwarding based on direction is employed once the destination is identified. The messages are forwarded to a selected set of upstream vehicles for holding messaged and enhancing forwarding reliability. However, all the aforementioned geographical routing approaches have not considered high data rate situations and have not employed the multipath routing approaches considering video streaming. Meanwhile, some research studies have considered multipath packet forwarding using geographical routing approaches, for example in [30–32].

However, the summary of multipath video streaming considering interference and reliability standard has been presented in Table 1. The table entails the reference, approaches interference-aware schemes and reliability standards.

Table 1. Comparison of Multi-path Video Streaming Based on Reliability Standard and Interference

Author	Approaches		Interference-aware scheme	Reliability standard
	Routing	Encoding		
[7]	Network proxy	MPEG-4 AVC	Low	Nil
[23]	Network coding	Distributed video coding	Low	Nil
[24]	Network coding	Scalable video coding (SVC)	Low	Nil
[18]	Location-aware	MPEG-4 AVC	Medium	QoS assurance
[21]	Probability generation function	H.264 AVC	Low	QoS assurance
[22]	Adaptive provisioning	SVC	Low	QoS assurance
[19]	Location-aware	Erasure coding	Medium	Nil
[9]	Field-based anycast routing	MPEG-4 AVC	Low	Nil
[20]	Distributed beaconles video dissemination	MPEG-4 AVC	Low	QoE Assurance
[6]	AOMDV with TCP-ETX	H.264/MPEG-4 AVC	Medium	TCP & UDP

3   The Proposed Work

In this section, the main contributions of this study have been presented, which is based on minimization of route coupling effect in multipath video streaming. It includes the angle of multipath and its probabilistic analysis considering shadowing and non-shadowing settings. Followed by the mathematical formulation of the PER as the link quality parameter.

3.1   Angle of Multipath

The interference level of nodes in a multipath setup can be symmetrically reduced if the angle between the source node and the corresponding two forwarding nodes are widened such that the signal coverage of each node does not overlap with one another. In order to mathematically model the concept of the angle. We consider a line with a distinct endpoint $\overline{P_1 P_2}$ where P_1 serve as a Source Vehicle Node SVN and P_2 is the intermediary node (relay node). Since we are considering two paths transmission, we consider another line P_3 connecting from P_1 that is $\overrightarrow{P_1 P_3}$, hence, an angle is formed between two paths with the same starting point, which is calculated in degree and is named angle of the multipath, that is $\angle P_2 P_1 P_3$ (see Fig. 5). In multipath video transmission, the angle between the SVN and the two relay nodes from the corresponding two paths need to be considered. The angle between the SVN and the two relay nodes of the selected paths is proportional to the interference coverage area of each node in the two paths. The suitable separation angle from P_1 between P_2, P_3 is an obtuse angle, since $\angle P_2 P_1 P_3 > 90°$ and $\angle P_2 P_1 P_3 < 180°$ which has the ability of reducing interference in the multipath communication.

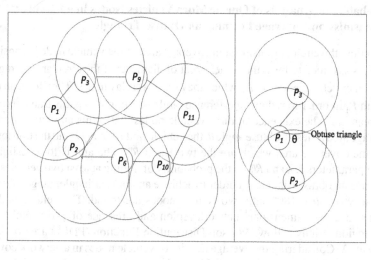

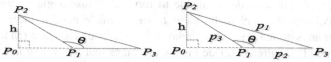

Fig. 5. Vehicular communication scenario forms an obtuse triangle

First of all, we relate the area of the obtuse triangle considering $\overrightarrow{P_1 P_3}$ as the base of the triangle (see Eq. 1).

$$\text{Area of } P_1 P_2 P_3 = [P_0 P_2 P_3] - [P_0 P_2 P_1]. \tag{1}$$

Where breadth of the obtuse triangle area (O_{area}) is $P_1 P_3 = b$. Therefore, we deduced that area of triangle is expressed as in Eq. 2:

$$O_{area} = P_1 P_2 P_3 = 1/2\, h \times b. \tag{2}$$

To estimate an angle of the multipath video packet forwarding, we need to calculate the obtuse angle where $90° > \theta < 180°$. Using cosine rule, an obtuse triangle with side dimensions $p_1 p_2 p_3$ can be used to calculate the multipath suitable angle, we consider θ for angle P_1, which is opposite side p_1 as follows:

$$\cos \theta = \frac{p_2^2 + p_3^2 - p_1^2}{2 p_2 p_3}. \tag{3}$$

An angle is said to be obtuse, if and only if $\cos\theta < 0$. Hence, an obtuse triangle fulfils $p_2^2 + p_3^2 < p_1, p_3^2 + p_1^2 < p_2,$ and $p_1^2 + p_2^2 < p_3$. In the next subsection, the probability analysis of finding one or more vehicles in an obtuse triangle area is presented.

3.2 Probabilistic Analysis of One or More Vehicles Nodes in a Circular Transmission Coverage Forming an Obtuse Triangle

In this section, the circular transmission coverage area of the vehicle node is considered. A SVN P_1 is assumed to be at the center point of diameter of the circular coverage area with two other vehicle nodes P_2P_3, which they serve as relay nodes. They form an obtuse angle with P_1 in order to reduce interference while creating two paths transmission for video streaming. The existence of three vehicle nodes that forms an obtuse triangle in the coverage area relies on obtuse angle θ, the vehicle node density λ and the transmission paths in the coverage area which are the two Radii $R_{P_2}^{p_3}$. The aim is to investigate the impact of parameters θ, λ and $R_{P_2}^{p_3}$ on the probability of finding at least two vehicles nodes which forms an obtuse triangle. In order to achieve an obtuse triangle, range of θ values is given as $90° > \theta < 180°$ until two vehicle nodes are found. The vehicle nodes are navigating in a two dimensional network region and presence of two vehicles in the network region strictly follows Poisson Distribution Function (PDF) based on vehicle node density λ. Considering the average density of vehicle nodes in a network coverage, the frequency of vehicle nodes available to form an obtuse angle is calculated by employing Poisson distribution. In addition, each vehicle node is independent and vehicle nodes are selected to serve as a relay node, which are chosen at random considering obtuse angle requirement. Due to lack of studies that focuses on interference in the routing process. Hence, we use angle estimation for minimizing interference in a multipath video streaming transmission. The investigation deduced that large dispersion of angle θ that is $90° > \theta < 180°$ connected to the two paths reduces multipath route coupling effect. Also, if the density of vehicles is high, there is need for smaller transmission coverage in order to do away with interference, because it lead to video data collision. Hence, we consider a value of radius (200 m) for the coverage area in this study. Let assume Y represents the random variable which is the frequency of vehicle nodes that can form an obtuse triangle, then the probability of the availability of g vehicle nodes that forms an obtuse triangle area in a Non-Shadowing Setting (NSS) $P_{O_{area}}^{NSS}(Y = g)$ is calculated as shown in Eq. (4):

$$P_{O_{area}}^{NSS}(Y = g) = \frac{(\lambda \times O_{area})^g \times e^{-(\lambda \times O_{area})}}{g!}. \tag{4}$$

By substituting O_{area} given in Eq. (2), then we have Eq. (4):

The probability $P_{O_{area}}^{NSS}(Y = 1)$ of the presence of at least one vehicle node in the obtuse triangle area considering NSS is presented as follows in Eq. (5):

$$P_{O_{area}}^{NSS}(Y = 1) = 1 - e^{-\lambda\left(\frac{1}{2}h(b)\right)}. \tag{5}$$

3.3 Impact of Shadowing on the Probabilistic Analysis of the Presence of One or More Vehicles in an Obtuse Triangle Area

To achieve a more realistic probabilistic analysis of the presence of one or more vehicles in an obtuse triangle area, a Shadowing Settings (SS) must be considered. Shadowing is caused due to obstruction of huge vehicles, buildings, and other physical objects. These lead to non-circular transmission coverage. Therefore, non-circular transmission coverage is employed for integrating shadowing model considering obtuse triangle area. Transmission coverage is usually varied in terms of direction due to the impact of shadowing on the received signal power [17]. The received signal power is expressed as in Eq. (6):

$$PS_r = PS_t \left\{ 10 \log_{10} K - 10 \omega \log_{10} \frac{d}{d_0} - \tau \right\}. \tag{6}$$

The received signal power is PS_r and the transmission signal power is PS_t. Constant K represents channel attenuation and antenna characteristics, path loss exponent is represented as ω. Distance between nodes and reference distance for nodes' antenna are denoted as d and d_0 respectively. Where τ is the Gaussian non-centralized random variable. In other to estimate the impact of shadowing in a circular transmission coverage, a small additional area sa at a certain distance r can be used to find the UnBlocked area (UB_{area}) between circular transmission area and the unblocked coverage area. In UB_{area}, the received signal power PS_r often maintains greatness above the minimum required signal power PS_{min} to interpret a signal. Thus, UB_{area} is mathematically represented in Eq. (7) and further derived Eq. (8)

$$UB_{area} = \frac{1}{\pi R^2} \int_0^{2\pi} \int_0^R P\left(PS_r(r) \geq PS_{min}\right) r dr \, d\theta. \tag{7}$$

$$P_{Oarea}^{SS}(Y \geq 1) = 1 - e^{-\lambda \left(\frac{1}{2}h(b)\right)} \times \left(\frac{UB_{area}}{\pi R^2}\right). \tag{8}$$

Link Quality: In order to evaluate the impact of packet error rate on link quality, we assume the following mathematical formulations for packet error rate on the proposed multipath angle of forwarding considering shadowing and non-shadowing settings. Packet Error Rate PER_l^n of a multiple path with n retransmission in a link l, which is made up of k number of nodes is expressed as in Eq. (9):

$$PER_{path}^n = 1 - \left(1 - PER_l^n\right)^k. \tag{9}$$

For the two paths is mathematically formulated as presented in Eq. (10)

$$PER_{Mpath}^n = 1 - \left(\left(1 - PER_l^n\right)^k\right)^2. \tag{10}$$

4 Analytical Results

In this section, the numerical results have been generated using MATLAB to examine the effect of parameter variations on the mathematical formulations. The effect of parameter variations on the probability of availability of one or more vehicle nodes in an obtuse triangle area considering non-shadowing settings ($P_{Oarea}^{NSS}(Y \geq 1)$) and shadowing settings ($P_{Oarea}^{SS}(Y \geq 1)$) are depicted in Fig. 6(a). Considering the results shown in Fig. 6(a), it demonstrates the effect of shadowing on the probability of availability of

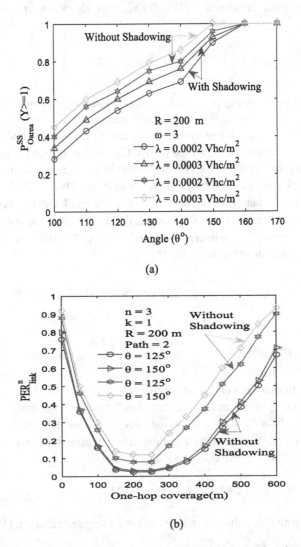

(a)

(b)

Fig. 6. The probability of availability of one or more vehicle in the obtuse triangle area considering two paths with NSS and SS, (a) and (b) represents vehicle availability versus angle and PER of different one-hop coverage respectively.

one or more vehicles in the obtuse triangle area. The result demonstrates that, shadowing has great effect on a smaller obtuse triangle angle. For example, when $\theta < 120°$, but with the rise in obtuse triangle angle $\theta > 130°$ the effect is minimized significantly. Further, Fig. 6(b) depict the probability of two paths PER in one hop coverage considering NSS and SS.

The results of the probability of PER based on multipath PER^n_{Mpath} with n retransmission are shown in Fig. 6(b). The result shows that the effect of shadowing on packet error rate is lower for the multipath one-hop coverage. It shows that the effect of shadowing rises significantly as the one-hop coverage becomes greater than 250 m. From closer observation, whenever the link path coverage becomes larger than 250 m, then the PER^n_{path} increases due to high probability of blockage and interference by other vehicles.

However, due to consideration of interference using larger angle θ of connectivity greater than 90° and less 180° with path diversity for selection of multiple paths in video streaming. Hence, the PER has been minimized which in turn improve the quality video streaming.

5 Conclusion

In this study, minimizing route coupling effect in multipath video streaming over a vehicular network based on the multipath angle of packet forwarding and link quality parameter have been proposed. The aim is to achieve high-quality video streaming in multipath vehicular communication. The results demonstrate that the assumption of angle in the coverage area of vehicle node is feasible, hence route coupling effect can be minimized. The transmission quality is evaluated based on PER considering both SS and NSS. It also shows that the PER parameter can express the route coupling effect and improve the quality of video transmission. Therefore, the results obtained has proven that our proposed work has the ability to minimize route coupling effect and improve the quality of the video streaming.

Acknowledgements. The research is supported by Ministry of Education Malaysia (MOE) and conducted in collaboration with Research Management Center (RMC) at University Teknologi Malaysia (UTM) under VOT NUMBER: RJ130000.7828.4F708.

References

1. Hartenstein, H., Laberteaux, K. (eds.): VANET: Vehicular Applications and Inter-networking Technologies, vol. 1. Wiley, Chichester (2009)
2. Aliyu, A., Abdullah, A.H., Kaiwartya, O., Ullah, F., Joda, U.M., Hassan, A.N.: Multi-path video streaming in vehicular communication: approaches and challenges. In: 2017 6th ICT International Student Project Conference (ICT-ISPC), pp. 1–4. IEEE, May 2017
3. Aliyu, A., et al.: Towards video streaming in IoT Environments: vehicular communication perspective. Comput. Commun. **118**, 93–119 (2017)

4. Ahmed, A., Hanan, A.A., Omprakash, K., Usman, M.J., Syed, O.: Mobile Cloud Computing Energy-aware Task Offloading (MCC: ETO). In: Proceedings of the International Conference on Communication and Computing Systems (ICCCS 2016), Gurgaon, India, 9–11 September 2016, p. 359. CRC Press, February 2017
5. Aliyu, A., et al.: Cloud computing in VANETs: architecture, taxonomy, and challenges. IETE Tech. Rev., 1–25, August 2017
6. Xie, H., Boukerche, A., Loureiro, A.A.: A multipath video streaming solution for vehicular networks with link disjoint and node-disjoint. IEEE Trans. Parallel Distrib. Syst. **26**, 3223–3235 (2015)
7. Tsai, M.F., Shieh, C.K., Huang, T.C., Deng, D.J.: Forward-looking forward error correction mechanism for video streaming over wireless networks. IEEE Syst. J. **5**, 460–473 (2011)
8. Rezende, C., Boukerche, A., Ramos, H.S., Loureiro, A.A.: A reactive and scalable unicast solution for video streaming over VANETs. IEEE Trans. Comput. **64**, 614–626 (2015)
9. Kserawi, M., Jung, S., Lee, D., Sung, J., Rhee, J.K.K.: Multipath video real-time streaming by field-based anycast routing. IEEE Trans. Multimed. **16**, 533–540 (2014)
10. Rao, A., Ratnasamy, S., Papadimitriou, C., Shenker, S., Stoica, I.: Geographic routing without location information. In: Proceedings of the 9th Annual International Conference on Mobile Computing and Networking, pp. 96–108. ACM, September 2003
11. Kaiwartya, O., Kumar, S.: Guaranteed geocast routing protocol for vehicular adhoc networks in highway traffic environment. Wirel. Pers. Commun. **83**, 2657–2682 (2015)
12. Stojmenovic, I., Ruhil, A.P., Lobiyal, D.K.: Voronoi diagram and convex hull based geocasting and routing in wireless networks. Wirel. Commun. Mob. Comput. **6**, 247–258 (2006)
13. Kaiwartya, O., Kumar, S., Lobiyal, D.K., Abdullah, A.H., Hassan, A.N.: Performance improvement in geographic routing for vehicular Ad Hoc networks. Sensors **14**, 22342–22371 (2014)
14. Brahmi, N., Boussedjra, M., Mouzna, J., Bayart, M.: Adaptative movement aware routing for vehicular ad hoc networks. In: Proceedings of the 2009 International Conference on Wireless Communications and Mobile Computing: Connecting the World Wirelessly, pp. 1310–1315. ACM, June 2009
15. Gong, J., Xu, C.Z., Holle, J.: Predictive directional greedy routing in vehicular ad hoc networks. In: 2007 27th International Conference IEEE on Distributed Computing Systems Workshops, ICDCSW 2007, p. 2, June 2007
16. Tu, H., Peng, L., Li, H., Liu, F.: GSPR-MV: a routing protocol based on motion vector for VANET. In: 2014 12th International Conference IEEE on Signal Processing (ICSP), pp. 2354–2359, October 2014
17. Goldsmith, A.: Wireless Communications. Cambridge University Press, New York (2005)
18. Wang, R., Rezende, C., Ramos, H.S., Pazzi, R.W., Boukerche, A., Loureiro, A.A.: LIAITHON: a location-aware multipath video streaming scheme for urban vehicular networks. In: IEEE Symposium on Computers and Communications (ISCC), pp. 436–441. IEEE, July 2012
19. Wang, R., Almulla, M., Rezende, C., Boukerche, A.: Video streaming over vehicular networks by a multiple path solution with error correction. In: IEEE International Conference on Communications (ICC), pp. 580–585. IEEE, June 2014
20. De Felice, M., Cerqueira, E., Melo, A., Gerla, M., Cuomo, F., Baiocchi, A.: A distributed beaconless routing protocol for real-time video dissemination in multimedia VANETs. Comput. Commun. **58**, 40–52 (2015)

21. Song, W., Zhuang, W.: Performance analysis of probabilistic multipath transmission of video streaming traffic over multi-radio wireless devices. IEEE Trans. Wirel. Commun. **11**(4), 1554–1564 (2012)

22. Zhu, Z., Li, S., Chen, X.: Design QoS-aware multi-path provisioning strategies for efficient cloud-assisted SVC video streaming to heterogeneous clients. IEEE Trans. Multimed. **15**(4), 758–768 (2013)

23. Li, M., Yang, Z., Lou, W.: Codeon: cooperative popular content distribution for vehicular networks using symbol level network coding. IEEE J. Sel. Areas Commun. **29**(1), 223–235 (2011)

24. Zou, J., Xiong, H., Li, C., Song, L., He, Z., Chen, T.: Prioritized flow optimization with multipath and network coding based routing for scalable multirate multicasting. IEEE Trans. Circuits Syst. Video Technol. **21**(3), 259–273 (2011)

25. Raw, R.S., Das, S.: Performance analysis of P-GEDIR protocol for vehicular ad hoc network in urban traffic environments. Wirel. Pers. Commun. **68**(1), 65–78 (2013)

26. Galaviz-Mosqueda, G.A., Aquino-Santos, R., Villarreal-Reyes, S., Rivera-Rodríguez, R., Villaseñor-González, L., Edwards, A.: Reliable freestanding position-based routing in highway scenarios. Sensors **12**(11), 14262–14291 (2012)

27. Cha, S.H., Lee, K.W., Cho, H.S.: Grid-based predictive geographical routing for inter-vehicle communication in urban areas. Int. J. Distrib. Sens. Netw. **8**(3), 819497 (2012)

28. Soares, V.N., Rodrigues, J.J., Farahmand, F.: GeoSpray: a geographic routing protocol for vehicular delay-tolerant networks. Inf. Fusion **15**, 102–113 (2014)

29. Liu, C., Chigan, C.: RPB-MD: Providing robust message dissemination for vehicular ad hoc networks. Ad Hoc Netw. **10**(3), 497–511 (2012)

30. Sermpezis, P., Koltsidas, G., Pavlidou, F.N.: Investigating a junction-based multipath source routing algorithm for VANETs. IEEE Commun. Lett. **17**(3), 600–603 (2013)

31. Chen, Y., Bell, M.G., Bogenberger, K.: Reliable pretrip multipath planning and dynamic adaptation for a centralized road navigation system. IEEE Trans. Intell. Transp. Syst. **8**(1), 14–20 (2007)

32. Huang, X., Fang, Y.: Performance study of node-disjoint multipath routing in vehicular ad hoc networks. IEEE Trans. Veh. Technol. **58**(4), 1942–1950 (2009)

33. Hassan, A.N., Abdullah, A.H., Kaiwartya, O., Sheet, D.K., Aliyu, A.: Geographic forwarding techniques: limitations and future challenges in IVC. In: 2017 6th ICT International Student Project Conference (ICT-ISPC), pp. 1–5. IEEE, 23 May 2017

Wireless EEG Signal Transmission Using Visible Light Optical Camera Communication

Geetika Aggarwal[1]([⊠]), Xuewu Dai[1], Richard Binns[1], Reza Saatchi[2], Krishna Busawon[1], and Edward Bentley[1]

[1] Department of Mathematics, Physics and Electrical Engineering, Northumbria University, Newcastle Upon Tyne NE1 8ST, UK
geetika.aggarwal@northumbria.ac.uk
[2] Department of Engineering and Mathematics, Sheffield University, Sheffield S1 1WB, UK

Abstract. Electroencephalogram (EEG) has been widely adopted for the brain monitoring. The transmission of the EEG signals captured from the scalp using electrodes to a displayed screen is often performed through wires utilizing Radio Frequency (RF) communication technology. The wired EEG transmission restricts the patient movement during the entire EEG recordings. However, patient movement is necessary during EEG recordings in certain medical scenario. Towards this end, wireless transmission of the EEG signals enables patient movements during the recordings. In this context, this paper proposes a Visible Light Optical Camera Communication (VL-OCC) system for wireless transmission of EEG signal. The signal transmission under the LOS, line of sight is conducted modulation scheme namely On-Off-Keying (OOK), Non-Return-to-Zero (NRZ). Specifically, organic light emitting diode, and optical camera are used as sender and receiver in the system, respectively. The performance of VL-OCC system is evaluated by developing an experimental prototype under realistic medical scenario.

Keywords: EEG · Biomedical data · Visible Light Communication Organic Light Emitting Diode · Optical Camera Communication

1 Introduction

Monitoring the brain electrical activity has great possibility to perceive the brain functionality and to diagnose the brain abnormalities. The traditional Electroencephalogram (EEG) monitoring systems deploy several scalp electrodes, physically connected to the EEG recording machine however recently the wearable EEG devices have gained wide popularity due to lesser number of electrodes, ease and comfort [1]. Some of the EEG machines deploy wireless Radio Frequency communication protocols alike Bluetooth and ZigBee to transmit signal information wirelessly; however, both Bluetooth and ZigBee dependent EEG machines emit radio frequency signal that may interfere to other medical equipment. Radio Frequency (RF) communication plays an important role in daily life such as TV, radio, Wi-Fi and so on. Furthermore, the RF signal transmitted is susceptible to contamination by other RF signals in the neighboring environment [2].

© Springer Nature Singapore Pte Ltd. 2018
G. C. Deka et al. (Eds.): ICACCT 2018, CCIS 899, pp. 152–161, 2018.
https://doi.org/10.1007/978-981-13-2035-4_14

As RF spectrum is immensely crowded, therefore to meet the requirements of the increasing bandwidth is possibly one of the biggest challenges or drawbacks of RF. In healthcare, the RF radiation may cause interference with the operation of some equipment to hospital equipment, therefore owing to shortcomings of RF, the Visible Light Communications (VLC) technology is an alternative solution since VLC uses the license free light spectrum (380–780 nm) and free from electromagnetic interference with enhanced security [3]. Recent reports showed that VLC communication systems employing Light Emitting Diodes (LEDs) have been widely adopted and have reached gigabit transmission speed [4], however the Organic Light Emitting Diode (OLED) is promising area for research due to easy integration and fabrication, wide beam angle, rich colors and flexibility. As the latest development of VLC, Optical Camera Communication (OCC) has shown its existence in several applications [5], hence due to advances in imaging technology and an extension of IEEE 802.15.7 standard for VLC, OCC presents a promising vision of optical communications [6]. The eruption in the usage of smart and advancement in technology over the decade unfolds the capacity of VLC implementation for the smart devices or camera with no hardware modifications [7], hence the proposed research in this paper comprises of visible light and optical camera communication between the OLED screen and image sensor of the camera.

Over the years, there has been an increase in improvement in healthcare quality at several hospitals and nursing homes thereby bringing the wireless technology due to high mobility and flexibility [8]. However, the most important thing for the wireless technology to be adapted and used in hospitals is that it should be free from invisible Electromagnetic Interference (EMI) which tends to affect the medical equipment's and their functionality thus posing a threat to both patient's health and medical equipment. Hence, the Optical wireless communication such as Visible Light Communication (VLC) is most suited for the environment such as hospitals as VLC is free from electromagnetic inference, highly reliable and low cost [9]. In [10], it has been stated that the usage of communication technology such as RF in medical applications, mainly EEG is flustered because of EMI hence affecting the reliability and accuracy of the transmitted data.

This paper proposes a new optical/electrical front-end and experimental system for VLC-OCC system thus achieving data rate of 2 kbps over free space at camera frame rate of 30 frames per second. Organic Light Emitting diode, OLED screen acting as transmitter converts the EEG signal into two dimensional images by displaying the images. The camera operates as the receiver and detects the images shown on the OLED screen and thereafter a computer to demodulate the EEG signal from image further processes the image received by the camera. This paper suggests a novel scheme for wireless transmission of EEG signals deploying OOK_NRZ modulation scheme employing OLED screen at the transmitter and camera at the receiver. The paper is divides into four different sections. Section 2 presents the proposed system for EEG use case. Section 3 discusses experiments and analysis of results followed by conclusion presented in Sect. 4.

2 Visible Light Optical Camera Communication (VL-OCC) System

This section illustrates the system modelling of the optical wireless communication link as shown in Fig. 1. In this system, the transmitted bits in the form of OOK-NRZ is represented by b_n. The system has three major operational components including EEG data processing, microcontroller, and offline processing module. The EEG signal module is responsible for generating raw data from the signal. The microcontroller takes raw EEG data as input and perform Serial-to-Parallel (S/P) operation on data. The offline processing module is responsible for generating final EEG output focusing on image processing, decision processing, and parallel to serial operation. The OLED screen is divided into rows and columns. The number of bits transmitted simultaneously in parallel using OOK-NRZ modulation scheme in each frame can be computed by $N = R_1 \times C_1$. Thereafter, following serial to parallel conversion the signal is transmitted in dimensional form and can be written as $s^{(t)} = [n_1, n_2]$, with n_1 and n_2 representing the discrete spatial coordinates of the OLED Display pixels and t denotes t^{th} frame.

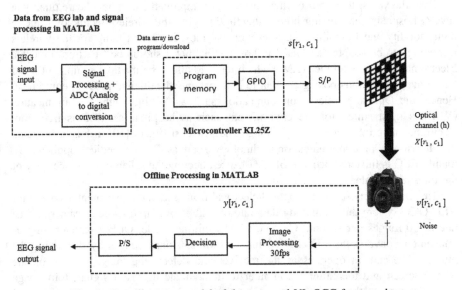

Fig. 1. Overall system model of the proposed VL-OCC framework

The information bits consist of square of pixels of size D. Hence, the number of bits effectively transmitted per frame changes with the value of D, thus number of transmitted bits per frame N given by Eq. (1).

$$(S_{z_{row}}/D) \times (S_{z_{column}}/D) = R_1 \times C_1 \qquad (1)$$

Where, $S_{z_{row}}$ and $S_{z_{column}}$ is number of rows and number of columns respectively. Following the transit from the optical, channel the signal can be computed as given by Eq. (2).

$$x^{(t)}[r_1, c_1] = (s * h)^{(t)}[r_1, c_1] \tag{2}$$

Where, h is impulse response. Hence, at receiver the signal can be represented by Eq. (3).

$$y^{(t)}[r_1, c_1] = (x)^{(t)}[r_1, c_1] + (v)^{(t)}[r_1, c_1] \tag{3}$$

Representing the signal received at the camera in the form of pixels of matrix. Also, $(v)^{(t)}[r_1, c_1]$ is a realization of White Gaussian Noise (WGN) with mean value equal to zero, variance σ_v^2 and is independent of the pixels. Table 1 shown below provides the description of the symbols and notations used in system model.

Table 1. Nomenclature

Notation	Description
N	Number of bits transmitted by formation of rows and columns on OLED screen
D	Size of Pixel
R_1	Number of rows per frame
C_1	Number of columns per frame
b_n	Transmitted bits from Microcontroller before S/P
$s^{(t)}$	dimensional signal transmitted after S/P in t-the time frame
$y^{(t)}$	Received dimensional signal
$v^{(t)}$	Noise realization which is known by white noise
$x^{(t)}$	Signal at optical channel
S/P	Serial to Parallel
P/S	Parallel to Serial
fps	Frames per second

The EEG signal extracted from EEG lab toolbox is downloaded to MATLAB, thereafter signal processing and Analogue to Digital Conversion (ADC) is done before uploading the data to the program memory of microcontroller thus forming patterns on OLED screen which are captured by camera in the video form and finally the offline processing in MATLAB. The number of frames or the length of the video depends upon the pixel size and the data rate transmitted. For example: if the pixel size is 16 and the number of bits transmitted are 256 at a data rate of 256 bps then the number of frames needed to transmit 256 bits will be $256/16 = 16$.

3   Experiments and Results Analysis

3.1   Experimental Setup and Hardware

EEG signal is of low amplitude of the order of some micro volts and a mixture of different frequencies or EEG bands comprising of waves divided into category of delta (δ, 0.7 Hz–5 Hz), theta (θ,5 Hz–9 Hz,) alpha (α, 9 Hz–15 Hz) and beta (β,15 Hz –35 Hz) [11]. Table 2. Illustrates the equipment and the model used for experimental set-up.

Table 2. Experimental Equipment

Equipment	Model
OLED Display Module	DD-160128FC with EVK board with a resolution of 160RGB × 128 dots
Microprocessor	ARM Processor FRDM KL25Z
Thorlabs Camera	DCC 1645C
Language/Software used for coding	C, MATLAB
Power Supply	EL302D Dual Power Supply 13.3 V which is regulated to 3.3 V using Voltage regulator

In the experiment testbed, the EEG signal transmitted shown in Fig. 2(a) and (b) was obtained from EEG toolbox [12] using MATLAB.

The normalized EEG signal obtained is then amplified to a desirable voltage level with the help of amplifiers and filtered by making use of a low pass filter ranging between 0.5 Hz to 40 Hz to remove the noise and artifacts. For the analogue to digital conversion, a 16 bit ADC was chosen to allow for higher resolution and low quantization error. The selected microprocessor was FRDM-KL25Z, because of high speed and low power consumption.

DD-160128FC OLED [13] screen is preferred as the transmitter with an active area of 28.78 mm into 23.024 mm and a weight of 3.6 g. The evaluation board of OLED screen required a voltage of 2.8 V to switch on the OLED screen hence, switching board designed using KICAD software having resistors forming a potential divider thus reducing the voltage level of power of the microcontroller from 3.3 V to the voltage level of 2.8 V required to switch on the OLED screen. The optical camera is tested at the receiver section to capture the video of the OLED screen at several distances in Line of Sight (LOS). Figure 3 represents the experimental hardware where microprocessor connected to the OLED screen through the switching board and the 741 op-amp designed as voltage regulator in order to regulate the dual power supply.

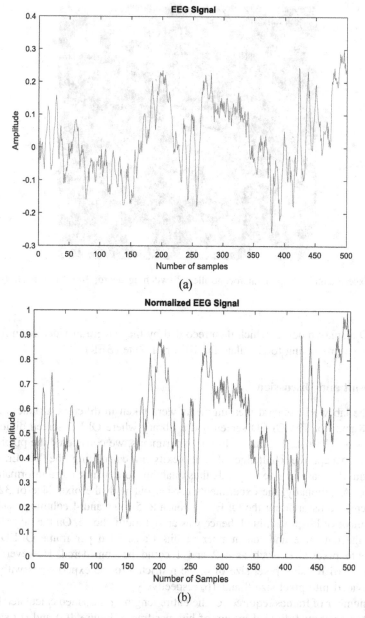

Fig. 2. (a) EEG signal from EEG tool box, (b) Normalized EEG signal for VLC-OCC

The OLED screen is a power efficient operating at 2.8 V hence switching board drops down the voltage coming from microcontroller to 2.8 V. The bits in the form of OOK_NRZ uploaded to the microcontroller through software written in the C language. With the help of switching board, the patterns based on transmitted bits formed

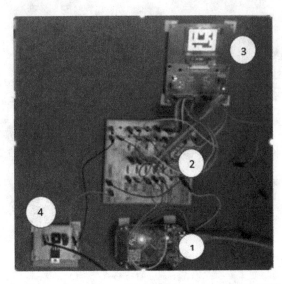

Fig. 3. Experimental set-up: 1-microcontroller, 2-switching board, 3-OLED screen, 4- voltage regulator

on OLED display module, which then recorded by the camera in video form followed up by image processing to calculate the Bit Error Rate (BER).

3.2   Result and Discussion

During the lab work, several measurements were taken in different distances at pixel sizes of 8 and 16. The OLED screen had a library where OLED screen divided into pixel sizes of 32, 16, 8, 4, 2 and 1. In our experiments, we considered the pixel sizes 8 and 16 to accept the challenge of complexity in calculating the Bit Error Rate (BER) with decrease in size of pixels thus enabling to transmit more information bits per frame. Additionally, the experiments carried out with the pixel size of 32 of the OLED screen thus dividing the OLED screen into 5 rows and 4 columns resulting in lesser number of bits transmitted, hence was an optimum choice. On the other hand, to increase the data rate and the number of bits transmitted per frame OLED screen divided into pixel sizes such as 4, 2 and 1 could be considered. However, due to reduction in BER using pixel size of 4, we restricted to the experiments with OLED screen divided into pixel size 8 and 16, respectively.

The number of frames required for the entire length of the video calculated by total no of bits transmitted divided by no. of bits per frame. Figure 4(a) and (b) show the image processing at pixel size 16 and 8, respectively. It illustrates the transmitted information per frame captured, and the gray image conversion after the border detection and then the cropped image taking the background off.

As shown in Fig. 3 the cropped image is identical to the transmitted information hence illustrating the successful optical transmission of electroencephalogram signals. After the video capture the image processing is performed for BER calculation by

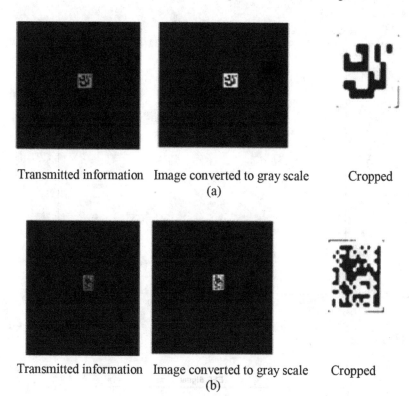

Transmitted information   Image converted to gray scale   Cropped
(a)

Transmitted information   Image converted to gray scale   Cropped
(b)

Fig. 4. Image Processing, (a) at pixel size 16, (b) at pixel size 8

comparing the bits obtained per frame and the entire video. The BER obtained at pixel size 16 was lower or better than BER obtained at pixel size as shown in Fig. 5. Though the number of bits transmitted using 8-pixel size are increased in comparison to number of bits transmitted using the pixel size 16. It is a trade-off between BER and symbol size. The increase in pixel size results in increase bit number possibly transmitted per frame hence, the information capacity or data rate improves significantly however, processing speed increases and possibly increases the BER too. After demodulation and digital to analogue converter the received original transmitted EEG signal in shown in Fig. 6. The received EEG signal is same as that of transmitted EEG signal, hence implicates the successful and error free optical transmission of EEG signal. Furthermore, the detection of transmitted bits is clearly possible for images and videos however, the BER changes with increase in distance.

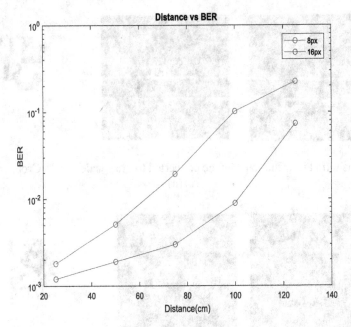

Fig. 5. BER vs Distance

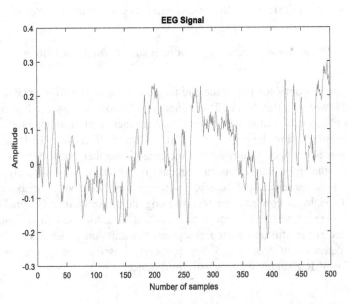

Fig. 6. Amplitude of received EEG signal Vs number of samples

4   Conclusion

This paper suggested a novel technique to transmit EEG signals using VL-OCC system. The system proposed deployed in healthcare without generating any RF radiation in the sensitive areas such as hospitals. Furthermore, we successfully proposed a technique that could replace current EEG systems deployed in clinical applications based on RF, which suffer from electromagnetic interference and signal loss. The BER obtained from the pixel sizes of 8 and 16 respectively at 25 cm is of the order of 10e-3. However, with the increase in distance, the BER for 8-pixel size drops considerably after 50 cm unlike 16-pixel size where the BER obtained is of the order of 10e-3 up to 75 cm and the data rate achieved was 2 kbps at a camera frame rate of 30 frames per second.

References

1. Ahmad, R.F., Malik, A.S., Kamel, N., Reza, F.: A proposed frame work for real time epileptic seizure prediction using scalp EEG. In: 2013 IEEE International Conference on Control System, Computing and Engineering (ICCSCE), pp. 284–289 (2013)
2. Dhatchayeny, D.R., Sewaiwar, A., Tiwari, S.V., Chung, Y.H.: Experimental biomedical EEG signal transmission using VLC. IEEE Sens. J. **15**, 5386–5387 (2015)
3. Jungnickel, V., Uysal, M., Ghassemlooy, Z.: A European view on the next generation optical wireless communication standard. In: IEEE Conference on Standards for Communications and Networking (2015)
4. Haigh, P.A., Bausi, F., et al.: A 10mb/s visible light communication system using a low bandwidth polymer light emitting diode. In: Proceedings of the IEEE CSNDSP, pp. 999–1004, July 2014
5. Boubezari, R., Minh, H.L., Ghassemlooy, Z., Bouridane, A.: Smartphone camera based visible light communication. IEEE J. Lightwave Technol. **34**(17), 4121–4127 (2016)
6. Deguchi, J., Yamagishi, T., Majima, H.: A 1.4 Mpixel CMOS image sensor with multiple row-rescan based data sampling for optical camera communication. In: Solid-State Circuits Conference (A-SSCC), 2014. IEEE Asian (2015)
7. Roberts, R.D.: Space-time forward error correction for dimmable undersampled frequency shift ON-OFF keying camera communications (CamCom). In: 2013 Fifth International Conference on Ubiquitous and Future Networks (ICUFN), pp. 459–464, 2–5 July 2013
8. Nezhad, M.H., Subari, K.S., Yahyavi, M.: Improvement of wireless transmission system performance for EEG signals based on development of scalar quantization. J. Electr. Bioimpedance **4**, 62–72 (2013)
9. Rachim, V.P., Jiang, Y., Lee, H.S., Chung, W.Y.: Demonstration of long-distance hazard - free wearable monitioring system using mobile phone visible light. Opt. Express **25**, 713–719 (2017)
10. Yu, Y.H., et al.: An inflatable and wearable wireless system for making 32-channel electroencephalogram measurements. IEEE Trans. Neural Syst. Rehabil. Eng. **24**, 806–813 (2016)
11. Chatterjee, S., Miller, A.: Biomedical Instrumentation Systems. Delmar, Cenage Learning (2010)
12. Etoolbox.: Bioelectromagnetism MATLAB Toolbox. http://eeg.sourceforge.net. Accessed 28 Mar 2017
13. DD-160128FC-1A DENSITRON, Graphic OLED, 160 × 128, RGB, 2.8 V, Parallel, Serial, 35.8 mm × 30.8 mm, −20 °C | Farnell UK

Aeronautical Assisted IoT Implementation: Route Lifetime and Load Capacity Perspective

Kirshna Kumar[✉], Pankaj Kumar Kashyap, and Sushil Kumar

Wireless Communication and Networking Research Lab, School of Computer
and Systems Sciences, Jawaharlal Nehru University, New Delhi 110067, India
kirshnakumar7@gmail.com, pankaj76_scs@jnu.ac.in,
skdohare@mail.jnu.ac.in

Abstract. Aeronautical ad hoc networks (AANET) support IoT while allowing communication between aircraft and the ground in flight systems. Current research is focused on aeronautical data-based IoT applications thus leaving the gap between benefits and services of IoT objects and aeronautical objects. In the present scenario, quality of service provisioning is the most prominent requirements in aeronautical flight communication systems. For this perspective, in this paper we propose QoS aware routing protocol (QSRP) to enhance network performance in Aeronautical ad hoc networks assisted IoT environment. The proposed QSRP includes two QoS metrics: route availability period and residual route load capacity for route finding process and describes a broadcast optimization technique to reduce traffic overhead. Finally, the performance of the proposed QSPR is compared with AODV and GPSR in terms of ground connectivity, packet delivery ratio and route load balancing. The simulation results prove that the performance of QSRP is better as compared to state of arts protocols.

Keywords: Internet of Things · Routing · Quality of service · AANET
Load balancing

1 Introduction

Internet of Things (IoT) is a system of interconnected computing devices, digital and mechanical machines, objects, animals or people having unique identities and the ability of transferring data across a network with or without human to human or human to device interaction [1]. The new domain including aircraft simulation, smart home, smart city, smart healthcare, forest fire detection, air pollution monitoring, inventory and Product management are few examples of revolution in IoT environment [2]. In aircraft applications, in order to transmit and view data immediately, Internet is used to connect sensors and actuators in the aircrafts. After completion of trip, tracking of flight data in real-time would be done with IoT in place of downloading data from sensors [3].

While including multi hop ad hoc networking between aircrafts, extension of network architecture is called aeronautical ad hoc network (AANET) [4]. While allowing communication from aircraft to ground, over the region with no communication infrastructure, AANET can be worked as a complementary communication

© Springer Nature Singapore Pte Ltd. 2018
G. C. Deka et al. (Eds.): ICACCT 2018, CCIS 899, pp. 162–172, 2018.
https://doi.org/10.1007/978-981-13-2035-4_15

system. AANET facilitates Internet access to these aircrafts traversing via these areas, with no use of high delay and costly satellite links [5]. In AANETs assisted flight communication systems, providing reliable and stable communication among aircraft and ground stations is a great challenge [4].

The demand of aeronautical networks having QoS provisioning motivates to design a QoS aware routing protocol in IoT. In this context, this paper proposes QoS aware routing protocol (QSRP) to enhance network performance in Aeronautical ad hoc networks assisted IoT environment. In this paper, first we use route availability period and residual route load capacity as the metric for QoS provisioning in route selection process respectively, which results stable and traffic balanced route between aircraft and ground stations. Second, we utilize broadcast optimization technique to minimize the overhead message generated during route selection process. Finally we evaluate and compare proposed QSRP protocol with greedy perimeter stateless routing (GPSR) [6] and ad hoc on demand distance vector (AODV) protocols.

The rest of the paper is structured as follows. Section 2 covers related literatures. In Sect. 3, proposed QSRP protocol is described. In Sect. 4, simulation results are discussed. Conclusion of the work and future research direction in IoT are presented in Sect. 5.

2 Related Literatures

In Ad hoc On Demand Vector Protocol (AODV) [7] minimal number of hops is the basis of root selection process. Routes are discovered on demand. AODV utilizes HELLO packets periodically for checking about active neighbors. It provides well defined structure, low complexity and low overhead because of on-demand routes. Failure of single route increases delay and failure rate of data delivery. More packet loss due to short route, lacking of energy efficiency mechanism and reliable data transmission results in energy holes. Ad hoc routing protocol for aeronautical mobile ad hoc networks [8] exploits the proactive functions and the geo-localization information to find the shortest and complete path. However, as route selection metric it only considers number of hops or distance and provides less route stability.

Geographic load share routing (GLSR) [9] utilizes the position information of aircraft and information of buffer size while exploiting the total air-2-ground (A to G) capacity. Unfortunately, GLSR consider only static topology. Link availability estimation-based routing [10] considers only the link availability parameter for selecting and updating route. Firstly, to imitate the airliners behavior, semi- Markov mobility model is proposed, then for selecting reliable path in terms of link availability period, expectation of link lifetime and pdf for the relative speed is utilized. It exploits the pdf of the link lifetime and relative speed to derive the parameter of link availability for selection of reliable route. Load balancing metric is not considered in it.

Delay aware routing protocol [11], is a reactive routing protocol in which route finding decisions are taken on the basis of expected node delay metric. The performance metrics such as network stability and traffic demand are used to analyze their scheme. Load balancing metric is also not considered in this protocol. Multipath Doppler routing protocol (MUDOR) [12] exploits Doppler frequency shift based relative velocity of nodes to establish stable routes. However, it does not consider quality of service (QoS) and load balancing issues. On the basis of MUDOR, QoS-MUDOR [13] has been proposed to provide better link stability, while provisioning QoS parameters. But only theoretical analysis has been considered and deeply details of specific QoS metrics have not been described. A geo-location assisted aeronautical routing protocol for highly dynamic telemetry environments (AeroRP) [14] has been proposed, while exploiting the broadcasting of wireless channel and location of node to mention necessity of airborne telemetry usage. But it does not reduce the network delay factor and causes network congestion. A novel geographical routing protocol for AANETs (A-GR) [15] eliminates beaconing of traditional routing while utilizing velocity and position of aircraft. For neighbor hop selection it uses metric based on velocity. In case of heavy data traffic, performance of this protocol is poor.

3 Proposed QSRP

In this section, network model for proposed QSRP protocol has been described. Then QoS metrics: route availability period and residual route load capacity are formulated. Thereafter, route selection process and broadcast optimization technique has been discussed. The network model has three main components: airports, aircraft and ground stations. Here ground stations works as Internet gateways (IGs). In this scenario, main focus is only on the aircraft and IGs communication, not aircraft-aircraft communication.

The following assumptions have been made for simplicity.

- All aircrafts are distributed in a plane.
- Physical layer, transmission power and transmission range are uniform for all aircrafts.
- ADS-B system is being equipped in all aircrafts for getting real-time state vector like position, velocity, ID and other information.

3.1 Route Availability Period

Route availability period between two nodes those are not neighbors, is defined as the minimum link availability period between intermediate nodes in this route. Let node i and j are two intermediate nodes and lie in the transmission range a of each other. The coordinate of node i and node j are (x^i, y^i) and (x^j, y^j) respectively. Let v^i and v^j are speeds, and θ^i and θ^j are moving directions of node i and node j respectively $(0 \leq \theta^i, \theta^j \leq 2\pi)$. If a link from node i and node j has link availability period l^p_{ij} [16]. Then l^p_{ij} is formulated as

$$l^p_{ij} = \frac{-(pq + rs) \pm \sqrt{(p^2 + r^2)a^2 - (ps - qr)^2}}{p^2 + r^2} \tag{1}$$

Where

$$p = v^i \cos \theta^i - v^j \cos \theta^j$$

$$r = v^i \sin \theta^i - v^j \sin \theta^j$$

$$q = x^i - x^j$$

$$s = y^i - y^j$$

Here, l_{ij}^p becomes ∞ when $\theta^i = \theta^j$ and $v^i = v^j$.

Let L^k is the route availability period of route k, then route availability period of route k is estimated as

$$L^k = \min\left\{ l_{ij}^p \right\} \tag{2}$$

3.2   Residual Route Load Capacity

In this section, residual route load capacity is defined as minimum residual load capacity among all node's residual load capacities in the route. Let c_i is the residual load capacity of node i. Then c^i is formulated as

$$c^i = \delta - \sum_{i=1}^{m} \omega_i l_i \tag{3}$$

Where, δ be the maximum load capacity of node i, and l_i and ω_i be the average packet size of traffic and average packet arrival rate from m sources, respectively. If C^k is residual load capacity of route k, then C^k is estimated as

$$C^k = \min\{c^i\} \tag{4}$$

In our scheme, during route selection process, route with maximum residual load capacity is considered.

3.3   Joint Metric

In QSRP protocol, both QoS metrics: route availability period and residual route load capacity are integrated to find the optimized route. If the joint metric of route k is P^k, then P^k is formulated as

$$P^k = \alpha.\left(\frac{L^k}{L^{max}}\right) + \beta.\left(\frac{C^k}{C^{max}}\right) \tag{5}$$

Where C^{max} and L^{max} are maximum residual route load capacity and maximum route availability period respectively. α and β are weight factors corresponding to both

QoS metrics in joint metric. Where $\alpha + \beta = 1$, and $\{0 \leq \alpha, \beta \leq 1\}$. α and β can be set for different values to prioritize any parameter on the basis of network preferences.

3.4   Optimal Route Selection

In QSRP, IGs send IG advertisements (IGADs) to advertise their QoS metrics periodically over the network. Then aircraft knows their information because of IGADs. Let IGAD interval for all IGs is same in this scheme. The format of IGAD message is presented in Fig. 1.

Packet. Type	Source. Address	Destination Address	X. Coordinates	Y. Coordinates	Velocity	L^{GAD}	C^{GAD}	Timestamp	Broadcast ID	Hop Count

Fig. 1. Format of IGAD message

Algorithm1: route finding process

Notations:

   X: Sender's X coordinate; Y: Sender's Y coordinate; V: Sender's velocity;
   L^{GAD}: route availability period; C^{GAD}: route available capacity;
   TS: Timestamp or Time at which packet is sent; BcID: Broadcast ID

Input: IGAD(X, Y, V, $L^{GAD} = 0$, C^{GAD}, TS, BcID)
Process:
1.   IG send IGADs periodically
2.   Aircraft node k receive IGAD packet
3.   **if** received packet based on BADF scheme condition **then**
4.   Compute L^k and C^k according to Eq. (1) and (3)
5.   **If** $L^{GAD} = 0$ or $L^k < L^{GAD}$ **then**
6. $L^{GAD} = L^k$
7.   **end if**
8.   **if** $C^k < C^{GAD}$ **then**
9. $C^{GAD} = C^k$
10. **end if**
11. Update IGAD packet while replacing, X, Y and V with X_k, Y_k and V_k, and updating TS.
12. Update route QoS metrics ($L. C$) in routing table of node k
13. Forward IGAD packet based on BADF scheme
14. **else** discard IGAD packet

When IGAD is received by aircraft node, then L^k and C^k are computed according to Eqs. (1) and (3). If L^k or/and C^k are less than L^{GAD} or/and C^{GAD}, then parameters are updated in routing table of aircraft node and in IGAD also. Otherwise existing L^{GAD} or/and C^{GAD} are used. Algorithm 1 presents the basic algorithm for route finding process.

Route update message is unicasted to source node by intermediate node, if new link is established or existing link breaks on the route. On the basis of updated parameters of route, source node chooses a potential route. The aircraft node maintains QoS parameters of every route to IGs in its routing table. According to Algorithm 2, the joint metric for every route is calculated by aircraft node and route with maximum joint metric is selected. Then after establishing forward route, IG in this route is selected as IG for the aircraft node.

Algorithm2: optimal route and IG selection

Input: Set of routes with QoS metrics $(L. C)$
  Process:
  15. Compute P^k for each route k according to Eq. 5 from routing table of aircraft node
  16. $P^r = \max\{P^k\}$
  17. Select the route with P^r
  18. Select the IG with P^r
Output: Optimized route and IG

3.5 BADF Broadcasting Optimization Scheme

In this section, Best advertisement forwarding (BADF) scheme is presented, while involving three aspects to control the overhead of advertisement flooding. First, aircraft discards the duplicate IGADs, while checking originator IP address and broadcast ID of newly received IGADs and already received IGADs. Second, the aircrafts already landed or not yet taken off (with velocity 0) discard the received IGADs and not be considered for computing routing table. Finally, an aircraft only rebroadcasts the advertisements having route availability period and residual route load capacity less than setting threshold. Hop count from node to IG should be lesser than maximum hop count set in advanced. Therefore, traffic overhead in term of broadcasting advertisement is minimized.

4 Experimental Results and Discussion

4.1 Simulation Environment

The simulation experiments for the evaluation of the performance of QSRP protocol have been conducted in ns2. Here, the weight factors for both metrics have been assigned equally: $\alpha = \beta = 0.5$ (Table 1).

4.2 Experimental Results (with Same Weight Factors)

Packet delivery ratio (PDR) is described as the ratio of the number of successfully transmitted packets to the total number of transmitted packets. Figure 2 illustrates that

Table 1. Simulation parameters.

Parameters	Values
Area	200 km × 200 km
Propagation model	Free space
Simulation time	150 min
Trans/Receiv antenna	Omnidirectional
IGAD interval	Uniform (3.5, 4.5) seconds
A to A trans range	40 km
A to G trans range	40 km

how PDR vary in case of all three routing protocols as interval of aircraft departure increases (aircraft density decreases). As shown in Fig. 2, from starting to threshold value (40 min) PDR increases (aircraft density decreases) for all three routing protocols. As aircraft density decreases (interval of aircraft departure increases), then overhead reduces and PDR increases. PDR for QSRP is lesser than GPSR in case of small interval of aircraft departure, but better in case of higher interval of departure (more than 30 min).

Figure 3 shows impact of traffic load on PDR, while keeping interval of departure 20 min. As the traffic load increases, QSRP performs better in terms of PDR as compared to GPSR and AODV, because path load balancing factor has been considered in QSRP but not considered in GPSR and AODV protocol.

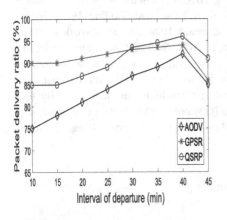

Fig. 2. PDR vs Interval of departure

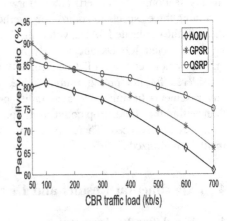

Fig. 3. PDR vs Traffic load

Overhead is defined as the amount of excess packets generated by routing protocols for the successful delivery of actual packets from the source to destination. Figure 4 shows the overhead incurred in case of all three routing protocols. The overhead for QSRP is far lower than AODV, because it utilizes BADF scheme for overhead minimization. But GPSR incur less overhead rather than QSRP and AODV, because periodic hello packet sent in neighbor discovery scheme utilized in GPSR is smaller than IGAD packet of QSRP.

Stability is defined in terms of number of the handoffs. It is inversely, proportional to the number of handoffs. Figure 5 shows that how Average handoffs per hour vary in case of all three routing protocols as interval of aircraft departure increases (aircraft density decreases). QSRP performs better with less number of handoffs (higher stability) as compared to GPSR and AODV, because of consideration of better path duration for the selection of new route. But GPSR and AODV protocols do not consider any path stability metric.

Ground Connectivity is described as the fraction of directly connected aircrafts or aircrafts having at least one multiple route to an IG at a particular time. Figure 6 illustrates that how ground connectivity vary according to the variation in interval of aircraft departure. According to Fig. 6, as the interval of aircraft departure decreases, ground connectivity enhances in case of all three protocols. When interval of departure is 20 min or lower, ground connectivity of all the protocols reaches to almost 100%. In case of interval of departure lower than 40 min, QSRP performs better than other protocols, but in case of more than 40 min, ground connectivity of QSRP is relatively weak, because building up of routes becomes relatively difficult due to strict IGADs forwarding conditions in QSRP.

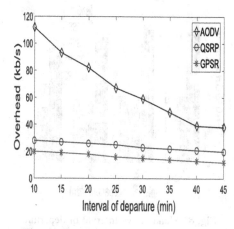

Fig. 4. Overhead vs Interval of departure

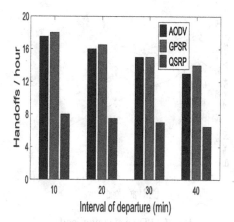

Fig. 5. Handoffs vs Interval of departure

4.3 Experimental Results (with Different Weight Factors)

Simulation has also been performed for the proposed QSRP protocol while considering various weight factors corresponds to route metrics to enhance the performance of QSRP. Two different scenarios have been described in simulation. In first scenario, route availability period has been preferred by considering weight factors: $\alpha = 0.7$ and $\beta = 0.3$ and in this scenario, QSRP is denoted as QSRP1. In second scenario, residual route load capacity has been preferred, while taking weight factors: $\alpha = 0.3$ and $\beta = 0.7$ and denoted as QSRP2. Then performance of QSRP1 and QSRP2 have been compared with QSRP0 (without weights), GPSR and AODV protocols.

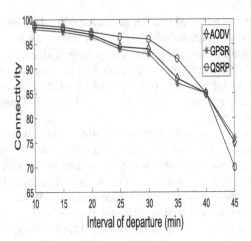

Fig. 6. Connectivity vs Interval of departure

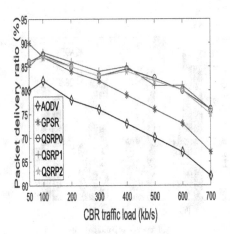

Fig. 7. PDR vs Traffic load

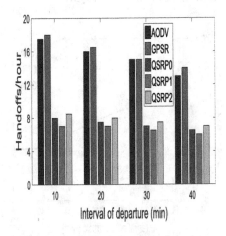

Fig. 8. Handoffs vs Interval of departure

Figure 7 shows the variation of PDR with respect to various traffic load in all scenarios. PDR in all scenarios is almost same, but is better than GPSR and AODV protocols. It illustrates that for improving PDR, more interest in route load balancing and stability should be taken in case of heavy traffic. Figure 8 shows that number of handoffs in case of QSRP1 are slightly reduced as compared to QSRP0, but for QSRP these are slightly more than QSRP0. But number of handoffs in all scenarios are far lesser than AODV and GPSR protocols. These results with different weight factors show that route stability and network PDR can be enhanced in some scenarios.

5 Conclusion and Future Work

In this paper, we propose QoS aware routing protocol (QSRP) to enhance network performance in Aeronautical ad hoc networks assisted IoT environment. The proposed QSRP includes two QoS metrics: path availability period and residual path load capacity for route finding process and describes a BADF technique to reduce flooding. Through simulation experiments, we analyzed and compared the performance of the proposed QSRP with respect to GPSR and AODV protocol, in terms of ground connectivity, packet delivery ratio and path load balancing. The simulation results show that the performance of QSRP is better as compared to state of arts protocols. In future, we will enhance the proposed work while considering delay, energy consumption as performance metric by modifying the design. We will also explore our work in diverse scenarios and applications in future.

References

1. Islam, S.M.R., Kwak, D., Kabir, M.H., Hossain, M., Kwak, S.K.: The Internet of Things for health care: a comprehensive survey. IEEE Access **3**, 678–708 (2015)
2. Gubbi, J., Buyya, R., Marusic, S., Palaniswami, M.: Internet of Things (IoT): a vision, architectural elements and future directions. Future Gener. Comput. Syst. **29**(7), 1645–1660 (2013)
3. Schnell, M., Scalise, S.: NEWSKY-Concept for networking the SKY for civil aeronautical communications. IEEE Aerosp. Electron. Syst. Mag. **22**(5), 25–29 (2007)
4. Vey, Q., Pirovano, A., Radzik, J., Garcia, F.: Aeronautical ad hoc network for civil aviation. In: Communication Technologies for Vehicles, pp. 81–93. Springer, Cham (2014)
5. Garcia, F., Pirovano, A., Royer, M., Vey, Q.: Aeronautical air-ground data communication: current and future trends. Clean Mobility Intell. Transp. Syst., 40–416 (2015). IET Digit. Libr., UK
6. Karp, B., Kung, H.T.: GPSR: Greedy perimeter stateless routing for wireless networks. In: Proceedings of the 6th ACM International Conference on Mobile Computing Network, Boston, MA, USA, pp. 243–254 (2000)
7. Perkins, C., Belding-Royer, E., Das, S.: Ad hoc on Demand Distance Vector (AODV) Routing (RFC3561). http://www.ietf.org/rfc/rfc3561.txt. Accessed 30 Jan 2013
8. Iordanakis, M., et al.: Ad-hoc routing protocol for aeronautical mobile ad-hoc networks. In: Proceedings of the 5th International Symposium on Communication System Network. Digital Signal Processing (CSNDSP), Patras, Greece, pp. 543–547 (2006)
9. Medina, D., Hoffmann, F., Rossetto, F., Rokitansky, C.H.: A geographic routing strategy for North Atlantic in-flight Internet access via airborne mesh networking. ACM Trans. Netw. **20**(4), 1231–1244 (2012)
10. Lei, L., Wang, D., Zhou, L., Chen, X., Cai, S.: Link availability estimation based reliable routing for aeronautical ad hoc networks. Ad Hoc Netw. **20**, 53–63 (2014)
11. Gu, W., Li, J., He, F., Cai, F., Yang, F.: Delay-aware stable routing protocol for aeronautical ad hoc networks. J. Inf. Comput. Sci. **9**(2), 347–360 (2012)
12. Sakhaee, E., Jamalipour, A.: The global in-flight Internet. IEEE J. Sel. Areas Commun. **24**(9), 1748–1757 (2006)

13. Sakhaee, E., Jamalipour, A., Kato, N.: Multipath Doppler routing with QoS support in pseudo-linear highly mobile ad hoc networks. In: Proceedings of the IEEE International Conference on Communications, Istanbul, Turkey, vol. 8, pp. 3566–3571 (2006)
14. Jabbar, A., Sterbenz, J.P.G.: AeroRP: A geolocation assisted aeronautical routing protocol for highly dynamic telemetry environments. In: Proceedings of the International Telemetering Conference (ITC), Las Vegas, October 2009
15. Wang, S., et al.: A-GR: A novel geographical routing protocol for AANETs. J. Sys. Archit. **59**(10), 931–937 (2013)
16. Su, W., Lee, S.J., Gerla, M.: Mobility prediction and routing in ad hoc wireless networks. Int. J. Netw. Manag. **11**(1), 3–30 (2001)

An Efficient Best Fit Channel Switching (BFCS) Scheme for Cognitive Radio Networks

Anisha Grover[1]([✉]) and Vikram Bali[2]

[1] Department of Computer Science and Engineering,
PIET Samalkha, Panipat, India
anishagrover.91@gmail.com
[2] Department of Computer Science and Engineering,
JSS Academy Of Technical Education, Noida, India
vikramgcet@gmail.com

Abstract. This paper represents a scheme for solving the problem that is faced by the Secondary Users for channel switching in Cognitive Radio networks. In this work, an efficient proactive channel selection and switching framework called Best Fit Channel Switching (BFCS) is proposed to minimize the amount of channel switching overhead for SUs between different channels. Based on channel usage information of PU and application specific parameters, One State Transition Probability (OSTP) and Two State Transition Probability (TSTP) are calculated. Then with the help of OSTP and TSTP a list of best channels for switching is obtained. Thus the proposed scheme enables the SUs to proactively predict the future spectrum availability status and switch to the best channel for communication when any PU arrives amidst of its current transmission. The proposed method is compared with the existing methods to evaluate its performance for parameters like channel switching cost.

Keywords: Cognitive Radio · Cognitive Radio Network · Secondary users
Primary users

1 Introduction

Cognitive Radio operates with the help of its underlying SDR Technology. Furthermore, the CR can also be programmed to transmit and receive on a range of frequencies and utilize various transmission access technologies are supported by its hardware [1, 2]. Cognitive Radio Network (CRN) also known as secondary network or unlicensed network comprises of collection of nodes equipped with CR [3]. CR enables the CRNs to utilize the temporally unused spectrum referred to as spectrum hole or white space [4]. In case this band is utilized by the licensed user, SU node moves to another white space or alter its transmission powers level while staying in the same spectrum band. This avoids the interference to the PU. Thus CRNs can be said to dynamically access the spectrum bands opportunistically with the help of CR [3]. Generally in CRN, a channel selection algorithm selects the most appropriate spectrum band or channel for the radio interface of the SU based on parameters like throughput, spectrum utilization etc.

In this paper, our research works focuses on reducing the switching overhead by reducing the channel switching cost for the secondary user. An algorithm called Best

© Springer Nature Singapore Pte Ltd. 2018
G. C. Deka et al. (Eds.): ICACCT 2018, CCIS 899, pp. 173–186, 2018.
https://doi.org/10.1007/978-981-13-2035-4_16

Fit Channel switching (BFCS) has been developed for this which mainly calculates two probabilities-OSTP and TSTP for short listing the number of channels with their ranking in decreasing order from n number of channels. The main advantage of the algorithm is that it gives the less number of channels to be selected for the switching. One needs not to consider all the channels for switching which in turn reduces the chances of delaying the decision for channel switching for the Secondary User and improves the network performance by reducing the switching cost and increasing the throughput.

The rest of the paper is divided into the following parts. Section 2 of the paper provides the Literature Review. Section 3 consists of Proposed methodology. Section 4 includes the Results and Analysis, Sect. 5 focuses on comparative study of the proposed scheme Best Fit Channel Switching (BFCS). Section 6 consists of Conclusion and Future Scope.

2   Literature Review

This section focuses on the various research works done in this filed so far. In general the existing schemes for channel selection can be categorized in three categories [5] as follows in Fig. 1:

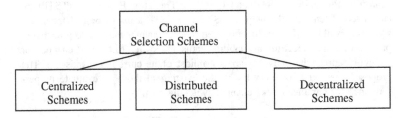

Fig. 1. Categories of channel selection schemes

In Centralized schemes of channel selection [6], a central entity (supervising node) obtains the link and local spectrum information from all other nodes to perform mapping for all the nodes and links in the network. The result of this mapping is then passed on to the nodes with the help of which all the nodes efficiently configure their interfaces. In the distributed channel selection schemes [7], each and every node in the network evaluates the potential free channels for its links by local observation. Distributed channel selection schemes are prone to channel oscillation and ripple effect problems since the local information does not guarantee the optimal channel selection. Finally, the decentralized channel selection schemes [8] clubs the merits of both distributed and centralized schemes implemented in cluster based class of wireless networks. In this, a supervising node (called cluster head) within each cluster helps in configuring the interfaces of all other nodes in that cluster by using the local information of the cluster. After that all the cluster heads collaborate and share information to determine the inter cluster channel selection.

Furthermore, the shifting of SU from one spectrum band to other spectrum band on arrival of PU is called Channel Switching. There are mainly two types of spectrum switching techniques: Reactive channel switching and Proactive Channel Switching [9]. Reactive channel switching is a passive switching wherein SUs communicate via one channel until any PU is detected. When a PU appears, SU switches from that channel by sequentially sensing all licensed channels until it finds some idle channel.

In proactive channel switching technique, SUs periodically monitor the spectrum bands or channels and utilize the past channel observations to estimate future availability of free channel in the spectrum. Then, on arrival of any PU, the SUs can switch channel smartly and quickly while avoiding any collision with the PU [9]. In this paper, a channel switching scheme is proposed in which the SUs estimate channel usage pattern and determine the most desirable channel whenever it needs to locate an idle channel for switching.

In [10] authors have proposed a stochastic channel selection algorithm based on the learning automata techniques to avoid costly channel switches. Kannan et al. [11] have proposed the movement and channel availability prediction scheme (MCAP), a new channel selection scheme for CRNs that take into account both future location of SU and prediction about the channel availability. The objective of their work is to improve the channel switching decision by reducing the number of unnecessary SU switches as well as the number of disconnections. Feng et al. [9] have proposed a new channel switching algorithm, which considers the drastic cost of channel switching. In their algorithm, the SUs decide whether to switch or not based on the channel information prediction. Devnarayana et al. [12] have discussed a channel set selection scheme to perform channel switching. Their algorithm is based on Markov process where each SU calculates the reward of using each channel and then selects the channel set with the highest reward.

Husari et al. [13] have proposed a handoff scheme which employs the markov model to predict the activity of the PU's future locations in order to make better hand off decisions. Meghanathan et al. [14] have proposed new local spectrum knowledge based minimum channel switching routing (MCSR) for CRNs. MCSR models the weight of an SU-SU edge as 0 if the two end nodes of the edge have the same preferred PU channel or as 1 otherwise. Finally it chooses the SU-SU path that has least sum of weights of edges. Ashtiani et al. [15] have given a probabilistic approach in determining the initial and the target channel for the handoff procedure in a single SU network. To characterize the network, a queuing theoretical framework has been introduced. Both stay and change handoff policies are addressed. Gabriel et al. [16] have investigated the interference among the cognitive emergency wireless networks and define a fractional service area, or a metric for evaluating service provisioning capabilities in coexisting networks that share the same TV white space.

Ferrus et al. [17] specifies the importance of sharing the spectrum band in improving the capability of public safety networks in the regions that are affected by any natural disasters and therefore relieving conditions are organized. Mishra et al. [18] categorize the channel allocation algorithms which depend on the ways to assign the channels and the platform to execute them. But, the differentiation of algorithms of allocating channels are dependent on distribution of the traffic, the expense to implement that algorithm, awareness for the wireless network, scalability of the network, the extend of efficiency of algorithm, the extent of robust behavior etc.

Chieochan et al. [19] have surveyed existing methods of channel assignment for infrastructure-based 802.11 WLANs. [20] have presented the most fundamental methods to solve the problem of assigning spectrum and the state-of-the art spectrum assignment algorithms in the Cognitive Radio Networks. Salem et al. [21] have researched on Cooperating spectrum sensing in CRN. They concluded that the issue of identification of PU activity onset is not completely tackled by cooperative spectrum sensing. Hence they have proposed a new channel selection scheme ICSSSS (Intelligent Channel Selection Scheme for cognitive radio ad hoc network using Self organized map followed by simple Segregation) to deal with the above issue. They have coupled segregation with mapping technique to locate the best channel for selection along with reducing the chance of false detection of PUs. Misra et al. [22] have proposed a new clustering based technique called k-hop knowledge algorithm. Their algorithm has $O(n^2m)$ complexity where n signifies the number of secondary users and m denotes the number of clusters. Their simulation results have outperformed existing schemes in terms of both inner and outer channel indices.

3   Proposed Methodology

Motivated with the challenges of channel switching in Cognitive Radio Networks (CRNs), we propose an Best Fit Channel Switching (BFCS) scheme to minimize the switching overhead and improve network performance.

3.1   Assumptions

A network environment is considered where both primary and secondary users coexist while operation of the network. The operational frequency band of the spectrum is divided into n number of non overlapping homogenous channels. Each of the above channels is divided into number of slots T1, T2, T3....Tm. Each slot is further divided into two sub slots: sensing slot (Ts) and transmission slot (Tt). Therefore any slot can be represented as: $Ti = Ts + Tt$, where $i = 1$ to m. We also considered that the channels are modelled as alternative exponential ON/OFF model where ON means a busy state and OFF means idle state [9]. ON/OFF periods are assumed to be independent and identically distributed as shown in following Fig. 2.

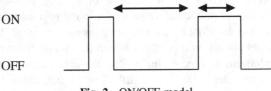

Fig. 2. ON/OFF model

Each slot is represented either by 0 or 1 where 0 means idle slot and 1 means busy slot as shown in following Table 1:

Table 1. PU channel usage matrix

C1	0	1	0	0	1	..	1
C2	0	0	0	1	0	..	1
C3	1	0	0	0	1	..	0
.	.	.	.	.	.	..	.
Cn	0	0	1	1	0	..	0

The above channel usage history of the PU is gathered from the ON-OFF model.

3.2 Proposed Best Fit Channel Switching (BFCS)

BFCS scheme is primarily a proactive channel handoff framework that works for minimizing the number of channel switching between different channels for SUs. From the PU channel usage matrix, SU can predict the reappearance of PU. Some channels are heavily utilized by PU and some channels always remain idle. In the proposed BFCS scheme, all the available channels are arranged as a list of best or maximum idle channels (Bc1, Bc2...BcN). Thus using the proposed scheme, the SU will select the channels which have the highest probability of being in the idle state. SU sense the channel from the list of best channels, if the channel is idle then SU transmits data. Furthermore the proposed scheme can be represented as comprising of following modules:

I One State Transition Probability (OSTP)

In this step, SU calculates the one state transition probability (OSTP) for all channels. OSTP means the probability of two consecutive slots being in idle state. Suppose C1, C2, C3.....Cn are the channels and T1, T2, T3....Tm are the slots for each channel. Then OSTP means if slot Ti of channel Cj is idle then what is probability that slot Ti + 1 will be idle in the same channel. OSTP is calculated with the help of functions F1 and Count1 defined as follows:

```
F1 (Ti, Ti+1) = 1 if slots Ti, Ti+1 are idle;
0 otherwise
Where i = 1 to m
Also, Count1 (Ti, Ti+1) = m-1∑ i =1 F1 (Ti, Ti+1)
OSTP = P1 (Ti, Ti+1) = Count1 (Ti, Ti+1)
```

II Two State Transition Probability (TSTP)

In this step, once the OSTP is calculated, SU calculates the two state transition probability (TSTP) for the channels whose OSTP is greater than or equal to the Threshold. TSTP means the probability of three consecutive slots being in idle state. Suppose out of C1, C2, C3.....Cn channels, k channels are shortlisted and T1, T2, T3....Tm are the slots for each channel. Then TSTP means if slot Ti of channel Cj is idle then what is probability that slot Ti + 1, Ti + 2 will be idle in the same channel. TSTP is calculated with the help of functions F2 and Count2 defined as follows:

```
F2 (Ti, Ti+1,Ti+2) = 1 if slots Ti, Ti+1,  Ti+2 are idle;
0 otherwise
Where i = 1  to m

  Also,   Count2   (Ti,    Ti+1,Ti+2)   =   m-1∑  i   =1
  F1(Ti,Ti+1,Ti+2)
  TSTP = P2 (Ti,  Ti+1,Ti+2) = Count2 (Ti, Ti+1,Ti+2)
```

III Channel Ranking

TSTP as explained above is calculated for all channels whose OSTP is greater than or equal to threshold. Other channels with OSTP less than threshold are considered busy. On the basis of TSTP probability, channels are arranged in descending order. The channel which has highest TSTP values will be considered as rank 1 and will be the first in the list and so on.

IV Selection of Best Channel and Communication

From the above channel ranking step, the channel ranking list is obtained with decreasing TSTP values. The channel with rank 1 is considered to be the best idle channel among all channels with lesser appearance of primary users. Hence secondary users select the channel which has the highest rank for communication and starts sensing a slot, if the slot is idle then the SU transmits the data and go on sensing and transmitting until the slots are free. If any slot is found to be busy then the SU will switch to the channel with next rank. This way, process continues until secondary users have some data to transfer.

3.3 Algorithm

The algorithm consists of two parts-one is the main algorithm called Best Fit Channel. Switching and other is the sub algorithm called Channel Ranking Algorithm.

When the main algorithm begins, the sub algorithm is called in which firstly we update the channel usage matrix i.e. we will check whether the Primary User is using its channel or not. If not, then we will update the threshold for the application, and then we will check if OSTP $\geq$ Threshold. The channels for which this condition is satisfied then we will calculated the TSTP for those channels. So we will get a list of channels with their ranking in descending order.

Then we will return to main algorithm, in which the initial switch count is zero, loop will be initialize and we will sense if the slot j of channel i is empty, if yes then we will transmit the data. If no more data is left, then the algorithm will end. But if more data is to be transmitted then we will sense the another slot of the same channel and transmit the data if it is empty. But if the data is still remaining but the slot of the channel is not empty, then we will switch to another channel and increment the switch count to 1 and again the loop will be executed until the data is transferred. This switch count tells the actual cost of algorithm.

Main Algorithm: Best Fit Channel Switching (BFCS)

```
STEP1.Begin

STEP2.Call    the    Sub    Algorithm    CRA

STEP3.Get Ranked Channel List from CRA

STEP4.Initialize Switch Count = 0, i=1, j=1

STEP5.Select channel Rᵢ with the highest rank in the Channel
List with k channels

STEP6.Sense Slotⱼ of channel Rᵢ

STEP7.If (Slotⱼ = = 0) Then

STEP8.Transmit the Data in the Current slot

STEP9.Update Channel Usage Matrix

STEP10.If Data == Empty    Then

STEP11.Go To Step 20

STEP12.Else Increment j and Go To Step 6

STEP13.End If

STEP14.Else If i <= k Then

STEP15.Increment Switch Count and i

STEP16.Set j = 1 and Go To Step 6

STEP17.Else Go To Step 20

STEP18.End If

STEP19.Return Switch Count

STEP20.End
```

Sub Algorithm: Channel Ranking Algorithm (CRA)

```
STEP1.Begin

STEP2.Update the PU channel usage matrix

STEP3.Update Threshold value(β)

STEP4.For each channel Ci ( where i= 1 to N)

STEP5.Calculate the OSTP for every channel with the
given PU channel history

STEP6.If (OSTP≥ Threshold) Then

STEP7.Calculate the TSTP of   the channel

STEP8.End If

STEP9.End For

STEP10.Sort and Rank the Channel List according to
TSTP in descending order

Return Channel List with Ranking
```

3.4   Flow Chart

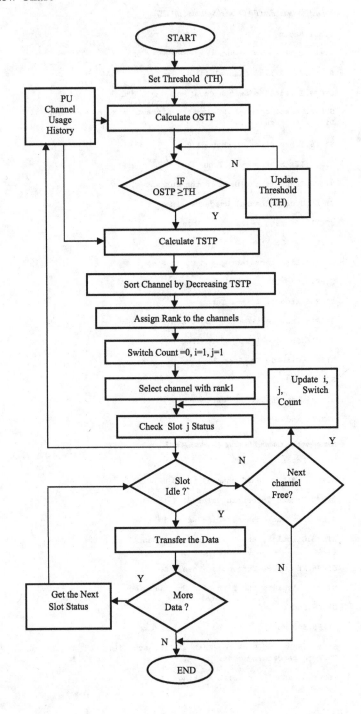

4 Results and Analysis

This section shows the simulation results for the comparison of performance of our proposed approach BFCS with other schemes like Sequential channel Switching (SCS) and Random Channel Switching (RCS) in MATLAB. In SCS, SUs select the channel sequentially from the given list of channel for communication while in RCS SUs select channel for switching randomly among the available channels.

4.1 List of Parameters

The following Table 2 shows the list of parameters used along with their range values during simulations:

Table 2. List of parameters for simulation

Parameter	Value
No. of Channels	3, 5, 7, 8, 9, 11
No. of SU	1 (with varying load)
Packet length	200
No. of slots	10
β (Threshold for TSTP)	0.2

4.2 Results

The results shown below reflect the number of channel switches while the number of channels in the spectrum or the SU load increases. In the first scenario, spectrum handoff with varying number of channels and a constant SU load is depicted. Following Table 3 shows the number of channel switches for SCS, RCS and BFCS respectively with increasing number of spectrum channels and fixed SU load (4000 bytes).

Table 3. Number of switches versus number of channel

No. of channels	Switches in SCS	Switches in RCS	Switches in BFCS
5	4	4	2
10	9	9	7
15	13	10	4

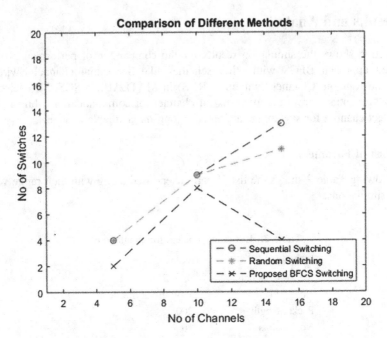

Fig. 3. Number of switches versus number of channels

The above Fig. 3 shows that channel switches for the proposed scheme BFCS are lower than both SCS and RCS scheme. Hence switching overhead had reduced and overall performance of the network had improved.

In second scenario, we vary the load of SU while keeping the number of channels to be fixed. Tables 4, 5 and 6 shows the variation of number of channel switches with respect to varying SU data load when the number of channels is kept fixed at 7, 9 and 11.

Table 4. Number of switches versus SU data load when number of channels is 7

SU data load (Bytes)	Switches in SCS	Switches in RCS	Switches in BFCS
1600	5	4	3
1800	5	5	4
2000	5	2	4
2200	5	4	4
2400	6	6	4

Table 5. Number of switches versus SU data load when number of channels is 9

SU data load (Bytes)	Switches in SCS	Switches in RCS	Switches in BFCS
1600	4	2	2
1800	6	4	2
2000	7	7	2
2200	8	8	2
2400	8	8	2

Table 6. Number of Switches versus SU data load when number of Channels is 11

SU data load (Bytes)	Switches in SCS	Switches in RCS	Switches in BFCS
1600	6	9	2
1800	6	5	2
2000	6	5	3
2200	6	9	4
2400	9	10	4

Figures 3, 4 and 5 shows the comparison graphs of SCS, RCS and BFCS schemes with varying SU load and fixed number of spectrum channels.

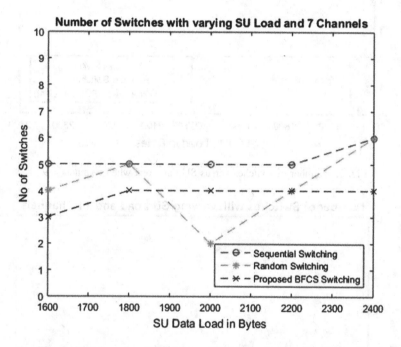

Fig. 4. Number of switches versus SU data load when channels = 7

It is clearly observed from the above Figs. 4, 5 and 6 that BFCS incur lesser number of channel switches and hence lesser switching cost as compared to SCS and RCS Thus the proposed channel selection and switching scheme BFCS proves better than the existing SCS and RCS schemes in overall performance of the network.

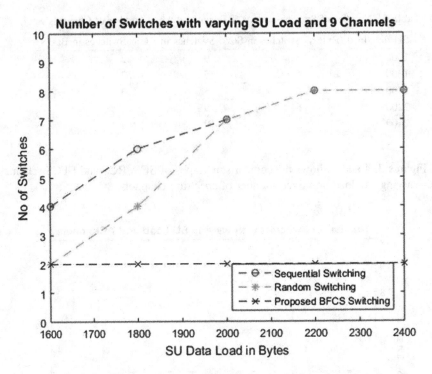

Fig. 5. Number of switches versus SU data load when channels = 9

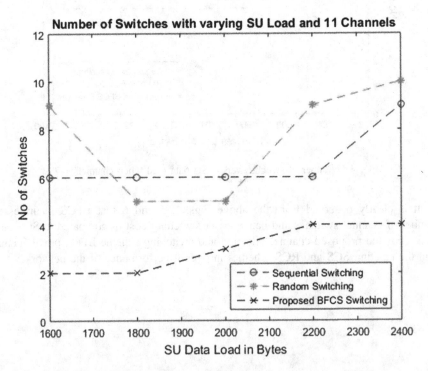

Fig. 6. Number of switches versus SU data load when channels = 11

5 Comparative Study of BFCS, SCS and RCS

The following table summarizes the comparison between the three schemes i.e. Sequential Channel switching (SCS), Random Channel Switching (RCS) and proposed scheme Best Fit Channel switching (BFCS).

S. No.	Performance factor	No of switches in SCS	No of switches in RCS	No of switches in BFCS
1	When Load of SU is fixed and channels are increasing	Max 13	Max 10	Max 7
2	When channel is fixed (no. 7) but load of SU is varying	Max 6	Max 6	Max 4
3	When channel is fixed (no. 9) but load of SU is varying	Max 8	Max 8	Max 2
4	When channel is fixed (no. 11) but load of SU is varying	Max 9	Max 10	Max 4

So from the above table it can be clearly mentioned that the proposed scheme (BFCS) is better than the other two Schemes (SCS) and (RCS) in every respect which is taken.

6 Conclusion

In this paper a Best Fit Channel Switching (BFCS) scheme has been proposed to minimize switching overhead in cognitive radio networks. The proposed BFCS scheme provides an efficient way for SUs to select the best channel among all idle channels of the licensed spectrum which minimizes the amount of channel switching and hence the total network overhead. The experimental and graphical results show that the proposed channel switching scheme BFCS performs better than SCS and RCS by reducing the number of channel switches. Channel switching cost eventually decreases when number of switches decrease.

References

1. Facilitating opportunities for flexible, efficient and reliable spectrum use employing cognitive radio technologies, Notice of proposed rulemaking and order. FCC, ET Docket No. 03-108, December 2003
2. Jondral, F.K.: Software defined radio – basic and evolution to cognitive radio. EURASIP J. Wirel. Commun. Netw. **3**, 275–283 (2005)
3. Akyildiz, I., Lee, W., Mohanty, S., Vuran, M.: Next generation/dynamic spectrum access/cognitive radio wireless networks: a survey. Comput. Netw. **50**, 2127–2159 (2006)
4. Haykin, S.: Cognitive radio: brain-empowered wireless communications. IEEE J. Sel. Areas Commun. **23**(2), 201–220 (2005)
5. Ahmed, E., et al.: Channel assignment algorithms in CRN. IEEE (2016)

6. Sarasvathi, V., Iyengar, N.C.S.N.: Centralized rank based channel assignment for multi-radio multi-channel wireless mesh networks. Procedia Technol. **4**(1), 182–186 (2012)

7. Conti, M., Das, S., Lenzini, L., Skalli, H.: Channel assignment strategies for wireless mesh networks. In: Hossain, E., Leung, K. (eds.) Wireless Mesh Networks, pp. 113–142. Springer, Boston (2007). https://doi.org/10.1007/978-0-387-68839-8_5

8. Saffre, F., Tateson, R., Ghanea-Hercock, R.: Reliable sensor networks using decentralised channel selection. Comput. Netw. **46**(5), 651–663 (2004)

9. Feng, X., Daiming, Q.: Smart channel switching in cognitive radio networks. In: Proceedings of the 2nd International CISP, China, pp. 1–5 (2009)

10. Yang, S., Fang, Y., Zhang, Y.: Stochastic channel selection in cognitive radio networks. In: Global Telecommunications Conference, GLOBECOM 2007. IEEE (2007)

11. Kanan, E., et al.: Towards improving channel switching in cognitive radio networks. In: International Conference on Information and Communication Systems (ICICS) (2015)

12. Devnarayan, C., et al.: Proactive channel access in CRN based on user statistics. In: International Workshop (2014)

13. Husari, G., et al.: Improving vertical handoffs using mobility prediction. IJACSA **7**, 413–419 (2016)

14. Meghanthan, N.: A minimum channel switch routing protocol for CRAHNs. IEEE (2015)

15. Ashtiani, F., et al.: Optimal probabilistic initial and target channel selection for spectrum handoff in CRN. IEEE Trans. Wirel. Commun. **14**, 570–584 (2015)

16. Villardi, G.P., Thadeu Freitas de Abreu, G., Harada, H.: TV white space technology: interference in portable cognitive emergency network. IEEE Veh. Technol. Mag. **7**(2), 47–53 (2012)

17. Ferrus, R., Sallent, O., Baldini, G., Goratti, L.: Public safety communications: Enhancement through cognitive radio and spectrum sharing principles. IEEE Veh. Technol. Mag. **7**(2), 54–61 (2012)

18. Mishra, M., Saxena, P.: Survey of channel allocation algorithms research for cellular systems. Int. J. Netw. Commun. **2**(5), 75–104 (2012)

19. Chieochan, S., Hossain, E., Diamond, J.: Channel assignment schemes for infrastructure-based 802.11 WLANs: a survey. IEEE Commun. Surv. Tutor. **12**(1), 124–136 (2010)

20. Tragos, E., Zeadally, S., Fragkiadakis, A., Siris, V.: Spectrum assignment in cognitive radio networks: A comprehensive survey. IEEE Commun. Surv. Tutor. **15**(3), 1108–1135 (2013)

21. Salem, T.M., Abdel, S.: ICSSSS: an intelligent channel selection scheme for cognitive radio ad hoc networks using a self organized map followed by simple segregation. Pervasive Mob. Comput. **39**, 195–213 (2017)

22. Misra, R., Yadav, R.N.: k-hop neighbour knowledge-based clustering in CRN under opportunistic channel access. Int. J. Commun. Netw. Distrib. Syst. **19**(4), 369–393 (2017)

Coarse-Grain Localization in Underwater Acoustic Wireless Sensor Networks

Archana Toky[1](✉), Rishi Pal Singh[1], and Sanjoy Das[2]

[1] Department of Computer Science and Engineering, GJUS&T, Hisar, Haryana, India
archanatoky@gmail.com, pal_rishi@yahoo.com
[2] Department of Computer Science, IGNTU, Regional Campus Manipur,
Manipur 795136, India
sdas.jnu@gmail.com

Abstract. Underwater Acoustic Wireless Sensor Networks (UASNs) is the way to connect underwater environment with the rest of the world. The existence of the huge number of applications which need to monitor the underwater environment, it is gaining popularity. The collected data from these networks are meaningless without the physical location of the sensor nodes. Localization schemes relate the data with its spatial information. In this paper, we have developed a localization scheme for Underwater Sensor Networks which gives a Coarse-Grain location information of the sensor nodes. The simulation results show that with a less energy consumption more than 90% of underwater sensor nodes can be localized by the proposed scheme.

Keywords: Underwater Acoustic Sensor Networks (UASNs)
Coarse-grain localization · Autonomous Underwater Vehicles (AUVs)

1 Introduction

Underwater Acoustic Sensor Networks (UASNs) is a way to connect the underwater environment with the rest of the world. The existence of the huge number of applications makes it popular among the researchers, these applications include underwater military tactical surveillance, mining, pollution monitoring and natural disaster prevention etc. [1,2]. The existence of some applications requiring the sensor's location information encourage the development of scheme to find the underwater position of sensor nodes for UASNs. Localization is a way to relate gathered information from underwater with its spatial information [3]. The underwater networks are a group of sensor nodes, Autonomous Underwater Vehicles (AUVs) which work together and collaborate to monitor the application area [4]. AUVs are used in localization scheme because it follows a predefined trajectory and can be controlled easily.

The underwater sensor networks are different from the terrestrial sensor networks as there is a need for sparse deployment of the sensor network for better coverage. Secondly, The acoustic communication channel is used for inter-node communication which is much costlier as compared to radio communication

© Springer Nature Singapore Pte Ltd. 2018
G. C. Deka et al. (Eds.): ICACCT 2018, CCIS 899, pp. 187–196, 2018.
https://doi.org/10.1007/978-981-13-2035-4_17

channel of the terrestrial sensor networks [5]. Acoustic communication channels also suffer from low bandwidth, high error rate, high propagation delay, and limited battery power [8]. Due to the differences between these two networks, The localization schemes developed for terrestrial sensor networks do not work for underwater acoustic sensor networks [10]. Another challenge in developing localization scheme for UASNs is the unavailability of the Global Positing System (GPS) because of high attenuation of Radio Frequency waves (RF) under water [6].

We are motivated to develop a localization scheme for underwater sensor network which can provide a coarse-grain localization with less amount of energy consumption. We have also observed a few facts are as follows firstly, the sensor nodes can get their depth information through the pressure sensor attached to it we need to calculate only the two-dimensional coordinates of the sensor node. Secondly, the availability of mobile AUVs to assist the localization process. The proposed scheme reduces the energy consumption by reducing the inter-sensor node communication.

In this paper, a localization scheme has been developed for Underwater Acoustic Wireless Sensor Networks. A coarse-grain estimation is provided by the proposed scheme instead of the accurate location of the sensor nodes. The aim of the localization scheme is to reduce the energy consumption and the computational complexity of the localization scheme.

It is anchor-free localization scheme using an Autonomous Underwater Vehicles (AUV). AUV dives into the water, after reaching to a predefined depth it starts moving horizontally at slow speed among the sensor networks. While wandering in the network, AUV broadcast its location periodically at multiple power levels from each broadcasting positions. The sensor nodes after hearing the broadcast messages record the power level and the position of AUV from where the message was sent and forward it to an underwater sink node. Due to a better storage capacity and powerful battery life, the sink node takes the initiative to estimate the location of the sensor nodes. The rest of the paper is organized as follows: Sect. 2 gives a brief introduction of localization scheme developed for UASNs. Section 3 describes the proposed localization scheme. Section 4 presents the performance analysis of the proposed scheme. Section 5 concludes the paper.

2   Releted Work

For underwater acoustic sensor networks, on the bases of communication method, there are two broad categories of localization schemes namely range-based and range-free localization scheme. To estimate the location of the sensor nodes range-based schemes relies on the distance or angle measurement form some reference point in the network. To estimate the distance and angle one of the following techniques used: TDoA (Time Difference of Arrival), ToA (Time-of-Arrival), RSSI (Received Signal Strength Indicator), and AoA (Angle-of-Arrival) [9]. Then, the position of the sensor node is computed using trilateration or multilateration techniques. Range-free localization schemes do not depend on any calculation about the range or angle information of the sensor node rather they use network topology and position of the nearby anchor nodes. A range-free localization scheme gives a coarse-grain estimation of the location. In [7], A survey on the architecture and the localization schemes for underwater acoustic sensor networks is presented.

SLMP (Scalable Localization with Mobility Prediction) localization scheme for large-scale underwater sensor network to attain better accuracy and network coverage is proposed in [11]. Each node calculates its location based on the mobility prediction and its past known position information. The major drawback of the SLMP is the need of a large number of anchor nodes although it increases the localization accuracy it also increases the communication overhead.

The localization schemes using projection technique is proposed in [12–14]. In the projection based localization schemes, the anchor nodes are projected to a horizontal virtual plane at the depth of the sensor node. The sensor nodes get their location by at least three anchor nodes using trilateration or triangulation technique. UPS (Underwater Positioning Scheme) proposed in [15,16], is a localization scheme without time synchronization. In UPS sensor nodes first calculates its range from at least four anchor nodes using TDoA than convert it into the position information using trilateration method. The scheme assumes that the whole application area can be covered by only four reference node which reduces the application area of the network and also the sensor nodes cannot be localized uniquely. A localization scheme proposed in [17], Wide Coverage Positioning (WPS) scheme generalized the UPS with N nodes. The scheme introduces the fifth anchor node if the node cannot be localized by four anchor nodes. Although WPS increases the localization area, it also increases the communication overhead but it guarantees the unique localization. An Area-based Localization Scheme which estimates the area where the sensor node lies in the network was intially developed for terrestrial sensor network [18] with the inspiration of which a localization scheme for UASNs was developed in [19]. Instead of providing the actual location of the sensor node it gives an estimation of the area where the node lies in. The whole domain area is divided into different regions by the anchor nodes using multiple power levels of beacon messages. The range of the power levels covered by the power levels divides the network into different sections. The sensor node after hearing the beacon messages records two information. First is the ID of the reference node from where the signal is being received and second is the power level at which the beacon was sent. Sensor nodes forward this information to an underwater sink node where the estimation of the position is performed. DNR localization scheme proposed in [20] uses a mobile anchor node instead of stationary anchor node. The anchor moves vertically in the network into the water and sends the beacon message in the network after regular intervals. The sensor nodes remain silent and estimate the distance between the mobile anchor node using ToA of the message.

The Advantages of Area Localization scheme and DNR localization schemes are combined in 3D-MALS (3-dimensional multi-power area localization scheme) proposed in [21]. Instead of using stationary anchor nodes of ALS, anchor nodes dive and rise into the water and sends the beacon message at multiple power levels. The major drawback of the scheme is high energy consumption due to the large number of message exchange. The contribution our paper is to reduce the energy consumption by using a single AUV in place of multiple DNRs of 3D-MALS scheme.

3   Proposed Scheme

The structure of the network for proposed scheme is shown in Fig. 1. The types of nodes in the networks are Autonomous Underwater Vehicle (AUV), sensor node, and the underwater sink node.

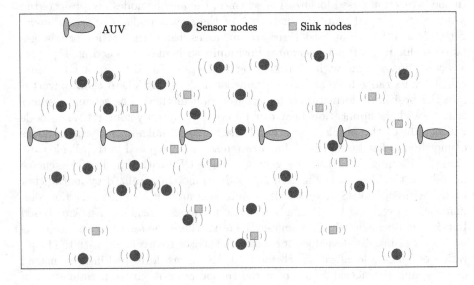

Fig. 1. Structure of the network model

AUVs are the important part of underwater wireless networks, due to the rich battery life it has the capability to work underwater continuously for a longer period of time. The battery can be solar-powered and can be recharged from solar energy while floating on the surface of the sea or it can be recharged from the sub-sea docking stations [22]. An AUV named REMUS 600 can operate underwater for at least 24 h up to the depths 600 m and it can be configured for 1500 m operations. The AUV consumes 110 W propulsion power to move at the speed 2.9 m/s, and 15 W propulsion power to move at the speed of 1.5 m/s [23]. Deployment of the sensor nodes underwater is random which keep moving in the network due to the effect of fluid dynamics. A pressure sensor is attached to all sensor nodes from where we can get the depth of the sensors which reduces our three-dimensional problem in Two-dimensional. All computations are performed by underwater sink nodes which have better computational and storage capacity.

Figure 2 represents the movement of the AUV in the network. AUV dives underwater to reach a predefined depth and starts moving horizontally in the network among the sensor nodes.

pos_1 pos_2 pos_k

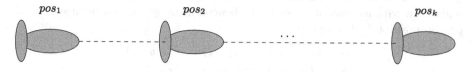

Fig. 2. Movement of AUV

While wandering in the network, it broadcast a beacon messages at multiple power levels after a regular time interval. The packet format of the beacon message is shown in Fig. 3. The beacon message informs the sensor nodes about the position of the AUV and the power level of the beacon message. The sensor nodes adds its ID to the packet received from the AUV and send it to the sink node as shon in Fig. 4. The sink node then estimates the position of the sensor node. To reduce the length of the packet a number corresponding to each power level is used eg. $i = [1...n]$ where 1 indicates the smallest power level and n shows the highest power level. The sink nodes stores these numbers with corresponding power levels.

X-coordinate of AUV	Y-coordinate of AUV	Power Level

Fig. 3. Packet format of messages send by AUV

Sensor's ID	X-coordinate of AUV	Y-coordinate of AUV	First-heard PL	Last-heard PL

Fig. 4. Packet format of messages send by sensor nodes

During the localization process, the AUV will broadcast the beacon messages at different power levels after a fixed time interval while moving in the network. For example the AUV at position pos_i will broadcast the beacon messages at power levels $PL_1, PL_2, ..., PL_n$. The set $PS = PL_1, PL_2, ..., PL_n$ contains all power levels in increasing order. n indicates the number of power levels in the set PS i.e. PL_i, $i = [1, n]$. The distances covered by each power level from set PS is indicated by the set $SD = S_1, S_2, ..., S_n$ where, S_i, $i = [1, n]$ represents the distance covered by the power level PL_i when a sensor node $S(x, y, z)$ receives a AUV's beacon message from position (x_j, y_j, z_j) at power level PL_m, $m \in [1, n]$ than the following equations are attained

$$(x - x_j)^2 + (y - y_j)^2 + (z - z_j)^2 <= S_m$$
$$(x - x_j)^2 + (y - y_j)^2 + (z - z_j)^2 > S_{m-1} \tag{1}$$

3.1 Location Estimation

Suppose there are total k positions $pos_1, pos_2, ..., pos_k$ from where AUV broadcasts the beacon message, and the coordinates of the positions are (x_j, y_j, c), for $j = [1, k]$ as shown in Fig. 2. Since the depth of the AUV is predefined we have replaced it with a constant value c. The beacon message correspondence to each beacon position is denoted by:

$$pos_1 : (x_1, y_1, 1), (x_1, y_1, 2), ..., (x_1, y_1, n)$$
$$pos_2 : (x_2, y_2, 1), (x_2, y_2, 2), ..., (x_2, y_2, n)$$

$$\vdots$$

$$pos_k : (x_k, y_k, 1), (x_k, y_k, 2), ..., (x_k, y_k, n)$$

The set of power levels is $PS\{1, 2, ..., n\}$ which is indicated by the elements $\{N_1, N_2, ..., N_n\}$ such that $N_{n-1} = N_n - 1$.

We are calculating the location of one sensor node similar procedure can be followed to find the location of the other nodes. We are assuming that the underwater node say A at position (x_a, y_a, z_a) can receive the beacon signal from all k positions of the AUV and the lowest power level received from these positions are represented by a set $PLS\{PL_{(1,N_a)}, PL_{(2,N_b)}, ..., PL_{(k,N_x)}\}$ and the corresponding distance covered is denoted by the set SDS $\{SD_{(1,N_a)}, SD_{(2,N_b)}, ..., SD_{(k,N_x)}\}$. where $N_a, N_b, ..., N_x \in PS$ and $PL_{(1,N_a)}$ represents that N_a is the lowest power level received from position pos_1 and the distance covered by the power level is $SD_{(1,N_a)}$ that is S_a. From the Eq. 3 we can say that A can't receive the power level from these positions are $\{PL_{(1,N_a-1)}, PL_{(2,N_b-1)}, ..., PL_{(k,N_x-1)}\}$ and $\{SD_{(1,N_a-1)}, SD_{(2,N_b-1)}, ..., SD_{(k,N_x-1)}\}$ are their corresponding spreading distances which gives us the relations:

$$\begin{cases} (x_1 - x_a)^2 + (y_1 - y_a)^2 <= SD_{(1,N_a)}^2 - c^2 = C_1 \\ (x_2 - x_b)^2 + (y_2 - y_b)^2 <= SD_{(1,N_b)}^2 - c^2 = C_2 \\ \vdots \\ (x_k - x_x)^2 + (y_k - y_x)^2 <= SD_{(1,N_x)}^2 - c^2 = C_k \end{cases} \tag{2}$$

and

$$\begin{cases} (x_1 - x_a)^2 + (y_1 - y_a)^2 > SD_{(1,N_a-1)}^2 - c^2 = C_1 \\ (x_2 - x_b)^2 + (y_2 - y_b)^2 > SD_{(1,N_b-1)}^2 - c^2 = C_2 \\ \vdots \\ (x_k - x_x)^2 + (y_k - y_x)^2 > SD_{(1,N_x-1)}^2 - c^2 = C_k \end{cases} \tag{3}$$

The bounded region covered by all these circles are assumed as the location area of the sensor. Center of the area covered by these circles is estimated as the coordinates of the sensor node. Figure 5 illustrates the localization scheme with k positions of AUV and four power levels at which beacon messages are sent from all positions.

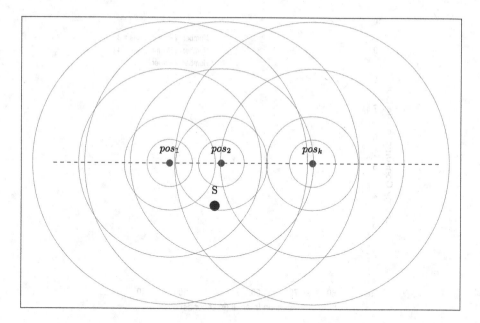

Fig. 5. Example of area estimation with four power levels from k beacon positions

4   Performance Evaluation

Performance analysis of the presented scheme is evaluated using MATLAB simulation. The localization area is considered as 1500 m × 1500 m with a maximum depth of 1000m. The speed of acoustic sound is set to 1500m. The number of sensor nodes deployed in the network is 500 and the beacon interval is set to 50 s which increases up to 120 s. The packet size is taken as 80 bits. The power level required to send and receive a packet is set to 35 w and 0.3 w respectively. The performance is evaluated for the parameters Localization success and energy consumption of the scheme. Localization success indicates the percentage of nodes localized by the presented scheme. Energy consumption indicates the energy consumed by the inter-node communication during the localization period.

Figure 6 indicates the impact of the beacon interval on energy consumption with the different number of power levels. The beacon interval is initially set to 50 s and increases with the step of 10 s up to 120 s. The number of different power levels at which the AUV sends the beacon messages is set to 3, 4, and 5. The graph clearly shows that energy consumption of the proposed scheme decreases with the increasing beacon interval the fact behind it is when we increase the beacon interval the number of positions from where AUV sends the beacon decrease which results in the decrease of the total number of beacon messages. The graph also shows that the energy consumption increases with the number of power levels of the AUV's beacon messages.

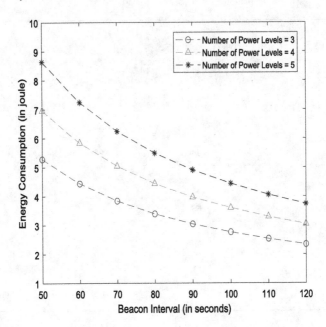

Fig. 6. Energy Consumption when the number of power levels are 3,4, and 5

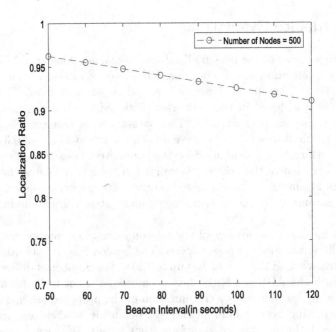

Fig. 7. Localization Ratio

Figure 7 shows the localization ratio with respect to the beacon interval. Initially, the beacon interval is taken as 50 s and increases regularly at the interval of 10 s and reaches upto 120 s. Localization ratio is above 95% when the beacon interval is 50 s. The number of nodes deployed in the network is 500. The localization ratio decreases when we increase the beacon interval. The reason behind it is, some of the nodes may not receive the beacon messages from all positions of the AUV. The overall localization ratio of the proposed scheme is above 90%

5   Conclusion

In this paper, we have presented a localization scheme for underwater acoustic wireless sensor networks which gives a coarse-grain location information of the sensor node underwater. The new scheme has three kind of nodes namely: AUV, sensor nodes, and the underwater sink node. AUV act as an anchor node which moves in the network and broadcast the beacon messages from different positions at multiple power levels. The sensor nodes are deployed underwater and listen to the beacon messages silently and sends the information about the position of AUV and the power level received to the sink node for location estimation. As the underwater sensor networks are very complex and expensive as compare to terrestrial sensor networks. We have develop a localization scheme which has very low computational complexity. The localization scheme has very low energy consumption due to the silent nature of the sensor nodes in the network. The simulation of the proposed scheme results in high localization success with less energy consumption.

References

1. Akyildiz, I.F., Pompili, D., Melodia, T.: Underwater acoustic sensor networks: research challenges. Ad Hoc Netw. **3**, 257–279 (2005)
2. Heidemann, J., Ye, W., Wills, J., Syed, A., Li, Y.: Research challenges and applications for underwater sensor networking. In: Wireless Communications and Networking Conference, pp. 228–235. WCNC IEEE (2006)
3. Erol-Kantarci, M., Mouftah, H.T., Oktug, S.: Localization techniques for underwater acoustic sensor networks. IEEE Commun. Mag. **48**(12), 152–158 (2010)
4. Yick, J., Mukherjee, B., Ghosal, D.: Wireless sensor network survey. Comput. Netw. **52**(12), 2292–330 (2008)
5. Vuran, M.C., Akan, Ö.B., Akyildiz, F.: Spatio-temporal correlation: theory and applications for wireless sensor networks. Comput. Netw. **45**(3), 245–259 (2004)
6. Lanbo, L., Shengli, Z., Jun-Hong, C.: Prospects and problems of wireless communication for underwater sensor networks. Wireless Commun. Mobile Comput. **8**(8), 977–994 (2008)
7. Erol-Kantarci, M., Mouftah, H.T., Oktug, S.: A survey of architectures and localization techniques for underwater acoustic sensor networks. IEEE Commun. Surv. Tutor. **13**(3), 487–502 (2011)
8. Partan, J., Kurose, J., Levine, B.N.: A survey of practical issues in underwater networks. ACM SIGMOBILE Mobile Comput. Commun. Rev. **11**(4), 23–33 (2007)

9. Ko, J.H., Shin, J., Kim, C.: Localization of sensor nodes in underwater acoustic sensor networks using two reference points. In: International Conference on Information Networking, pp. 1–5. IEEE ICOIN (2008)

10. Chandrasekhar, V., Seah, W.K., Choo, Y.S., Ee, H.V.: Localization in underwater sensor networks: survey and challenges. In: Proceedings of the 1st ACM International Workshop on Underwater Networks, pp. 33–40. ACM (2006)

11. Zhou, Z., Peng, Z., Cui, J.H., Shi, Z., Bagtzoglou, A.: Scalable localization with mobility prediction for underwater sensor networks. IEEE Trans. Mobile Comput. **10**(3), 335–348 (2011)

12. Isik, M.T., Akan, O.B.: A three dimensional localization algorithm for underwater acoustic sensor networks. IEEE Trans. Wireless Commun. **8**(9) (2009)

13. Cheng, W., Thaeler, A., Cheng, X., Liu, F., Lu, X., Lu, Z.: Time-synchronization free localization in large scale underwater acoustic sensor networks. In: 29th IEEE International Conference on Distributed Computing Systems Workshops, ICDCS Workshops 2009, pp. 80–87 (2009)

14. Teymorian, A.Y., Cheng, W., Ma, L., Cheng, X., Lu, X., Lu, Z.: 3D underwater sensor network localization. IEEE Trans. Mobile Comput. **8** (2009)

15. Cheng, X., Shu, H., Liang, Q., Du, D.H.C.: Silent positioning in underwater acoustic sensor networks. IEEE Trans. Veh. Technol. **57**, 1756–1766 (2008)

16. Cheng, X., Shu, H.S.H., Liang, Q.: A range-difference based self-positioning scheme for underwater acoustic sensor networks. In: International Conference on Wireless Algorithms, Systems and Applications, WASA 2007, pp. 38–43. IEEE (2007)

17. Tan, H.P., Gabor, A.F., Eu, Z.A., Seah, W.K.G.: A wide coverage positioning system (WPS) for underwater localization. In: 2010 IEEE International Conference on Communications (ICC), pp. 1–5. IEEE (2010)

18. Yao, Q., Tan, S.K., Ge, Y., Yeo, B.S., Yin, Q.: An area localization scheme for large wireless sensor networks. In: IEEE 61st Vehicular Technology Conference VTC 2005-Spring, pp. 2835–2839 (2005)

19. Chandrasekhar, V., Seah, W.: An area localization scheme for underwater sensor networks. In: OCEANS 2006-Asia Pacific, pp. 1–8. IEEE (2006)

20. Erol, M., Vieira, L.F., Gerla, M.: Localization with Dive'N'Rise (DNR) beacons for underwater acoustic sensor networks. In: Proceedings of the Second Workshop on Underwater Networks, pp. 97–100. ACM (2007)

21. Zhou, Y., Gu, B.J., Chen, K., Chen, J.B., Guan, H.B.: An range-free localization scheme for large scale underwater wireless sensor networks. J. Shanghai Jiaotong Univ. (Sci.) **14**(5), 562 (2009)

22. Allen, B., Austin, T., Forrester, N., Goldsborough, R., Kukulya, A., Packard, G., Purcell, M., Stokey, R.: Autonomous docking demonstrations with enhanced REMUS technology. In: OCEANS 2006, pp. 1–6. IEEE (2006)

23. Stokey, R.P., Roup, A., von Alt, C., Allen, B., Forrester, N., Austin, T., Goldsborough, R., Purcell, M., Jaffre, F., Packard, G., Kukulya, A.: Development of the REMUS 600 autonomous underwater vehicle. In: Proceedings of MTS/IEEE OCEANS, pp. 1301–1304. IEEE (2005)

Content Credibility Check on Twitter

Priya Gupta$^{(\boxtimes)}$, Vihaan Pathak, Naman Goyal, Jaskirat Singh,
Vibhu Varshney, and Sunil Kumar

Maharaja Agrasen College, University of Delhi, Delhi, India
pgupta1902@gmail.com, vihaan_pathak@yahoo.com,
namangoyal.official@gmail.com, jaskirat965@gmail.com,
varshney.vibhu.50@gmail.com, suniljmijnu@gmail.com

Abstract. During large-scale events, a large volume of content is posted on Twitter, but not all of this content is trustworthy. The presence of spam, advertisements, rumours and fake images reduces the value of information collected from Twitter. In this research work, various facets of assessing the credibility of user–generated content on Twitter are described, and a novel real-time system to assess the integrity of tweets has been proposed. The system has been proposed to achieve this by assigning a score or rating to content on Twitter to indicate its trustworthiness.

Keywords: Fact-checking · Knowledge graph · String matching

1 Introduction

Twitter is a micro-blogging web service with 319 million average monthly active users all across the globe. Twitter has gained reputation over the years as a prominent news media, disseminating information faster than conventional media. Researchers have shown how Twitter plays a role in aiding crisis management teams by providing on the ground information, helping in reaching out to people in need, and helping in the coordination of relief efforts [8]. On the other hand, Twitter's role in spreading rumours and fake news has also been a major cause of concern. Due to the dynamic nature of Twitter, fake news or rumours spread quickly on Twitter and this can adversely affect thousands of people. The current methods to filter out false content rely mostly on human monitoring. With this proposed model we aim to automate the process to a great extent. In this research work, various facets of assessing the credibility of user gen-erated content on Twitter are described, and a three-pronged system to assess its veracity has been proposed. Our model is named "CCC" (for Content Credibility Check) - a model to impede the flow of false news. In the following sections, we talk about the literature review in which we discuss the previous work which has been done in this field. We take our inspiration for the work of well renowned researchers and build our concept on the basis of success and failure of the researchers who worked before us. We also present the results of a survey conducted by us to understand the thinking process of a wide variety of our society. Then we give a brief about the technical concepts and API's we have employed in our model and finally present our model. The description of the working helps us understand the breakdown of the model

© Springer Nature Singapore Pte Ltd. 2018
G. C. Deka et al. (Eds.): ICACCT 2018, CCIS 899, pp. 197–212, 2018.
https://doi.org/10.1007/978-981-13-2035-4_18

and it will help us distinguish credible tweets from fake news. Finally, we talk about the limitations of our program and what future work can be done in order to improve upon the model.

2 Literature Review

The work that has been done in this field so far has been focussed on both, the theoretical understanding of the phenomenon that is fake news and the practical creation and deployment of a viable system to filter out fake news. One of the major driving factors behind carrying out this research work was the realisation that this field requires greater awareness, especially in today's times. The effects of propagating non-verified information on Twitter and in other OSM (Online Social Media) have been studied by researchers before. Carvalho et al. [2] analyzed the effects of what they termed as a false news shock. They took up an episode from September 2008 wherein a six-year-old article about the 2002 bankruptcy of United Airlines' parent company had resurfaced on the Internet and was mistakenly believed to be reporting a new bankruptcy filing by the company. This episode caused the company's stock price to drop by as much as 76% in just a few minutes, before NASDAQ halted trading. After the "news" had been identified as false, the stock price rebounded, but still ended the day 11.2% below the previous close. They also found out that it had a persistent effect on the stock prices of other major airline companies too.

Supervised classification has been applied by researchers to detect credible and incredible content in OSM. Castillo et al. [3] showed that automated classification techniques can be used to detect news topics from conversational topics and assessed their credibility based on various Twitter features. They achieved a precision and recall of 70–80% using decision-tree based algorithm. They evaluated their results with respect to data annotated by humans as ground truth. Wang [20] proposed a spam detection prototype system to identify suspicious users on Twitter. He found out that the Bayesian classifier had the best overall performance in terms of F-measure, achieving 89% precision. Some researchers focused their study of trustworthy or credible information during particular events which had high impact. Donovan et al. [18] focused their work on finding indicators of credibility during different situations (8 separate event tweets were considered). Their results showed that the best indicators of credibility were URLs, mentions, retweets and tweet length. Also, they observed that the presence and effectiveness of these features increased a lot during emergency events. Location-based Social Networks (LBSNs) like Twitter are designed as platforms allowing the creation, storage and retrieval of vast amounts of georeferenced and user-generated contents. De Longueville et al. [6] explored as to how LBSN can be used as a reliable source of spatio-temporal information, by analysing the temporal, spatial and social dynamics of Twitter activity during a major forest fire event in the Marseille, France in July 2009. Oh et al. [19] analyzed the content of Twitter postings of the 2008 Mumbai terror attack and based on that they suggested a conceptual framework for analyzing information control in the context of terrorism.

Some of the research work done to assess, characterize, analyze and compute trust and credibility of content on online social media is mentioned here. Truthy was a live web service developed by Ratkiewicz et al. [20] to study information diffusion on Twitter and compute a trustworthiness score for a public stream of microblogging updates related to an event to detect political smears, astroturfing, misinformation, and other forms of social pollution. Gupta et al. [8] created TweetCred, a practical system to assess credibility of tweets, based on training data obtained from six high-impact crisis events of 2013. They developed a semi-supervised ranking model using SVM-rank to rank the tweets. The way our proposed model differs here is that it adds a bit of granularity in terms of user verification. Finn et al. [7] introduced a tool called TRAILS which made use of propagation, timeline, retweet and co-retweeted network visualizations to make it easier to investigate a suspicious story. By inputting a single tweet into the system, and selecting keywords relevant to the story being investigated, the system gathered a dataset of tweets through which the user could trace the story origin.

Researchers have sought varied routes to frame this problem of filtering fake news. Ciampaglia et al. [4] framed fact-checking as a network problem. They showed that by finding the shortest path between concept nodes under properly defined semantic proximity metrics on knowledge graphs, this approach is feasible with efficient computational techniques. Liben-Nowell et al. [14] proposed a random link predictor for social networks and also examined other approaches to link prediction based on measures for analysing the "proximity" of nodes in a social network. But they concluded that all methods so far lack accuracy, even the best proving to be correct on just 16% of its predictions. Wu et al. [22] proposed a framework that viewed claims based on structured data as parameterized queries. A key insight was that a lot could be learned about a claim by perturbing its parameters and seeing how its conclusion changes. They formulated practical fact-checking tasks–reverse-engineering (often intentionally) vague claims, and countering questionable claims–as computational problems. Our research work, while drawing upon some of the feature sets employed in previous papers, seeks to add new layers of verification in the overall fact-checking process.

3 Survey Results and Employed Concepts

'False news' has rapidly become a catch-all term to discredit all kinds of stories. In its purest form, false news is completely made up, manipulated to resemble credible journalism and attract maximum attention and, with it, advertising revenue. It includes news articles that are intentionally and verifiably false, and could mislead readers.

Analysis by BuzzFeed found that fake news stories drew more shares and engagement during the final three months of the US presidential campaign than reports from (for example) the New York Times, the Washington Post and CNN [1].

There are various motivations to spread false news. One is pecuniary: news articles that go viral on social media can draw significant advertising revenue when users click to the original site. Another is ideological: fake news providers seek to advance candidates they favour.

We need to be smarter at recognizing and combating such outright fabrication.

3.1 Survey

A survey was conducted to analyse how most of us get notified about the news and how vulnerable we are to fake news. Here are the key findings (Figs. 1, 2, 3, 4, 5, 6, 7 and 8):

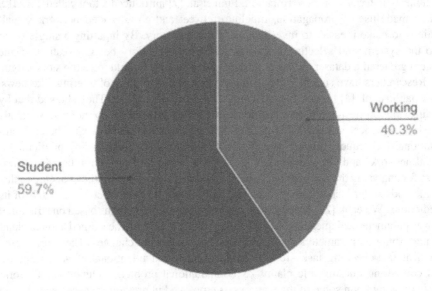

Fig. 1. Occupation of sample surveyed

In this survey both, the working class people and college students, were covered to ensure wide variety of view-points are obtained. Social media, which is the most unreliable source of news as nobody cross-checks it, came out to be the topmost source as expected. In that, approximately more than 80% of the people believe the news they come across. Softwares made to check validity of social media news are unheard of by roughly 67% of the respondents. A strong majority of the respondents feel this area requires more awareness, motivating us to continue with this project.

This survey shows us how people from across the spectrum view the phenomenon that is false news. It pushes us to delve further into this area and work together to produce a reliable solution.

3.2 Concepts Employed

The concepts of knowledge graph, string matching and Twitter's Streaming API have been used to work on the project. A detailed course of action is given below.

Count of What is your topmost source of news consumption?

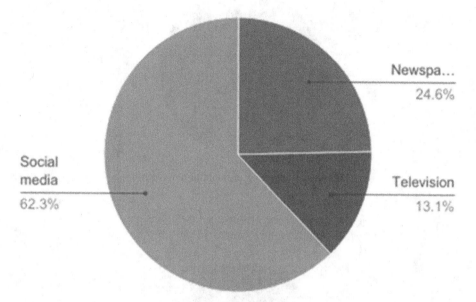

Fig. 2. Sources of news consumption

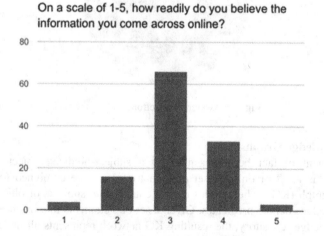

1-never, 2-rarely, 3-sometimes, 4-most of the times, 5-always

Fig. 3. Respondents' readiness to believe

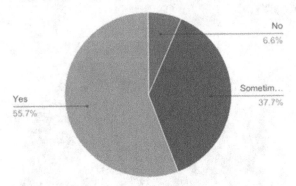

Fig. 4. Self-checking of doubtful news items

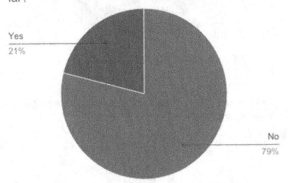

Fig. 5. Awareness of efforts in this area

3.2.1 Knowledge Graphs

Let a statement of fact be represented by a subject-predicate-object triple, e.g., ("Socrates," "is a," "person"). A set of such triples can be combined to produce a knowledge graph (KG), where nodes denote entities (i.e. subjects or objects of statements), and edges denote predicates. Given a set of statements that has been extracted from a knowledge repository, the resulting KG network represents all factual relations among entities mentioned in those statements. Given a new statement, it is expected to be true if it exists as an edge of the KG, or if there is a short path linking its subject to its object within the KG. If, however, the statement is untrue, there should be neither edges nor short paths that connect subject and object.

In a KG distinct paths between the same subject and object typically provide different factual support for the statement those nodes represent, even if the paths

Count of Have you heard about TweetCred, Project
FiB, Snopes, Check4Spam etc. ?

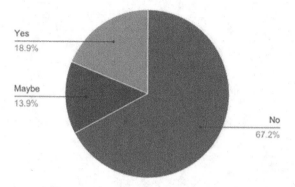

Fig. 6. Awareness of current initiatives

Count of Do you feel this is an important issue that
requires more awareness?

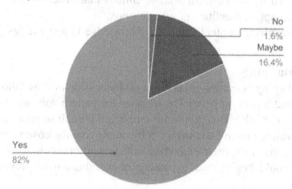

Fig. 7. Perception of the issue's importance

contain the same number of intermediate nodes. For example, paths that contain generic entities, such as "United States" or "Male," provide weaker support because these nodes link to many entities and thus yield little specific information. Conversely, paths comprised of very specific entities, such as "positronic flux capacitor" or "terminal deoxynucleotidyl transferase," provide stronger support [4]. A fundamental insight that underpins our approach is that the definition of path length used for fact checking should account for such information-theoretic considerations.

It is proposed to use Google's Knowledge Graph Search API to match the tweets with the relevant news articles. Google's knowledge base compares subjects and objects as nodes and predicates as edges and gives the required comparison result. The API uses standard schema.org types and is compliant with the JSON-LD specification [11].

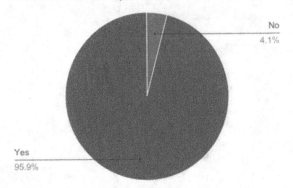

Count of If there is a tool to help you fact check
issues online, would you be interested to use it?

No
4.1%

Yes
95.9%

Fig. 8. Respondents' interest for fact-checking tools

Some examples of how the Knowledge Graph Search API can be used include:

- Getting a ranked list of the most notable entities that match certain criteria.
- Predictively completing entities in a search box.
- Annotating/organizing content using the Knowledge Graph entities.

3.2.2   String Matching

The fundamental string searching (matching) problem is defined as follows: given two strings – a text and a pattern, determine whether the pattern appears in the text.

Knuth-Morris-Pratt (KMP) algorithm is employed here. It searches for occurrences of a "word" W within a main "text string" S by employing the observation that when a mismatch occurs, the word itself embodies sufficient information to determine where the next match could begin, thus bypassing re-examination of previously matched characters.

3.2.3   Streaming API

The Streaming APIs give developers low latency access to Twitter's global stream of Tweet data. A streaming client will be pushed messages indicating Tweets and other events have occurred, without any of the overhead associated with polling a REST endpoint.

The streaming process gets the input Tweets and performs any parsing, filtering, and/or aggregation needed before storing the result to a data store. The HTTP handling process queries the data store for results in response to user requests. While this model is more complex than using the REST API, the benefits from having a real-time stream of Tweet data makes the integration worthwhile for many types of apps [13].

Twitter Firehose is another option that can be used to receive data. It is in fact very similar to Twitter's Streaming API as it pushes data to end users in near real-time, but the Twitter Firehose guarantees delivery of 100% of the tweets that match your criteria. The reason it has not been used here is because it proves to be very costly for an individual user, unlike Streaming API which is free of cost.

4 Features Used by the Credibility Model

The following features have been used in this model:

1. **Tweet Meta-data Features**: Number of seconds since the tweet, Source of tweet (mobile/web/etc.), Tweet contains geo-coordinates
2. **Tweet Content Features**: Number of characters, Number of words, Number of URLs, Number of hashtags, Number of unique characters, Presence of stock symbol, Presence of happy smiley, Presence of sad smiley, Tweet contains 'via', Presence of colon symbol
3. **User based Features**: Number of followers, friends, time since the user is on Twitter, etc.
4. **Network Features**: Number of retweets, Number of mentions, Tweet is a reply, Tweet is a retweet
5. **Linguistic Features**: Presence of swear words, Presence of negative emotion words, Presence of positive emotion words, Presence of pronouns, Mention of self-words in tweet (I, my, mine)
6. **External Resource Features**: WOT score for the URL, Ratio of likes/dislikes for a YouTube video

5 Proposed Model (CCC)

As shown so far, it is understandable that there is a clear need for trustworthy sources on the Internet.

For our proposed model (Fig. 9), we take Twitter as an example. It shall be a three dimensional model, the dimensions being:

1. News Authentication
2. Viewers Authentication
3. User Authentication

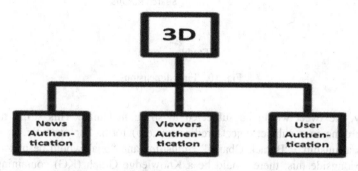

Fig. 9. Proposed three-dimensional model

The basic idea behind our model centres on matching the information present in a tweet to our database of authentic news websites. The top 5 sites would be chosen based on their traffic and general reputability. Alexa- a web traffic data analytics firm- continually shows the top ranking sites, by category and otherwise.

To adjudge the veracity of a tweet, a method of calculating a credibility score has been developed. The components of the score are as follows (Table 1):

Table 1. Breakup of the model

Component	Percentage share
News websites	60
Retweets	15
Tweeters	25

5.1 First Dimension

The first dimension (Fig. 10) of our model i.e. our news sites explained as follows:

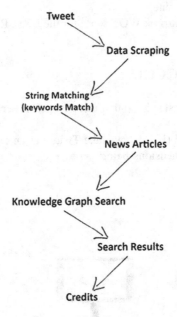

Fig. 10. First dimension

Firstly, the tweet would be subjected to string matching. This string matching would be done in a subject-object-predicate (s,o,p) form. For example, in "Barack Obama is a muslim", "Barack Obama", "muslim" and "is a" would be matched separately. Alongside this, there would be a Knowledge Graph (KG) containing nodes representing subjects and objects, and edges representing predicates joining these nodes. Upon a successful match, the model would tap into the KG to find out how strong the links actually are. Based on the links, a credibility score would be assigned to the tweets i.e. the higher the number of direct links or higher the number of shortest paths between subject and object, greater would be the credibility score.

The following screenshot shows one kind of request you can send to Google's Knowledge Graph Search API (Fig. 11).

```
https://kgsearch.googleapis.com/v1/entities:search?query=taylor+swift&key=API_KEY&limit=1&indent=True
```

The sample search above returns a JSON-LD result similar to the following:

```json
{
  "@context": {
    "@vocab": "http://schema.org/",
    "goog": "http://schema.googleapis.com/",
    "resultScore": "goog:resultScore",
    "detailedDescription": "goog:detailedDescription",
    "EntitySearchResult": "goog:EntitySearchResult",
    "kg": "http://g.co/kg"
  },
  "@type": "ItemList",
  "itemListElement": [
    {
      "@type": "EntitySearchResult",
      "result": {
        "@id": "kg:/m/0dl567",
        "name": "Taylor Swift",
        "@type": [
          "Thing",
          "Person"
        ],
        "description": "Singer-songwriter",
        "image": {
          "contentUrl": "https://t1.gstatic.com/images?q=tbn:ANd9GcQmVDAhjhWnN2OWys2ZMO3PGAhupp5tN2Lw
          "url": "https://en.wikipedia.org/wiki/Taylor_Swift",
          "license": "http://creativecommons.org/licenses/by-sa/2.0"
        },
        "detailedDescription": {
          "articleBody": "Taylor Alison Swift is an American singer-songwriter and actress. Raised in
          "url": "http://en.wikipedia.org/wiki/Taylor_Swift",
          "license": "https://en.wikipedia.org/wiki/Wikipedia:Text_of_Creative_Commons_Attribution-Sh
        },
        "url": "http://taylorswift.com/"
      },
      "resultScore": 896.576599
```

Fig. 11. Result obtained from Google knowledge graph search API

The following code sample (Fig. 12) shows how to perform a similar search in JavaScript. This search returns entries matching Taylor Swift.

```
<!DOCTYPE html>
<html>
<head>
    <script src="http://ajax.googleapis.com/ajax/libs/jquery/2.1.4/jquery.min.js"></script>
</head>
<body>
<script>
  var service_url = 'https://kgsearch.googleapis.com/v1/entities:search';
  var params = {
    'query': 'Taylor Swift',
    'limit': 10,
    'indent': true,
    'key' : '<put your api_key here>',
  };
  $.getJSON(service_url + '?callback=?', params, function(response) {
    $.each(response.itemListElement, function(i, element) {
      $('<div>', {text:element['result']['name']}).appendTo(document.body);
    });
  });
</script>
</body>
</html>
```

Fig. 12. Performing a search query

5.2   Second Dimension

Retweets play a crucial role in spreading stories and information. But there needs to be a check on the fact/story being spread, as a lot of propaganda thrives on these retweets.

For our model, a score of 0–15 is assigned to retweets (Fig. 13). This would be done in three slabs: a score of 0–5 for below average number of retweets, 5–10 for average and 10–15 for more than the average. This average is crucial to understand here. This average would be obtained by analysing the number of retweets experienced by previous hot topics on Twitter. This is not fool-proof but the reason average is taken as the deciding factor is because this is one way to make use of already available data about hot and consequently, verified topics.

5.3   Third Dimension

A tweeter is an entity who tweets. We say entity because it is not only humans who tweet. The spread of a lot of false information on Twitter is done through bots- programs that produce automated posts.

So, there are two things to be considered in this aspect.

- User verification- Is the user verified by Twitter?
- Past activity- How many positive credibility scores have the user's past tweets accumulated?

The 25% share assigned to this dimension would have three components as shown in the table below (Table 2).

The score for the number of followers would again be calculated by taking the average of some verified and authentic accounts (Fig. 14).

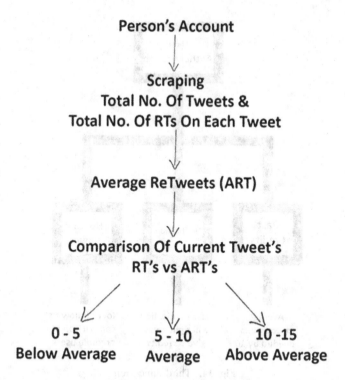

Fig. 13. Second dimension

Table 2. Share breakup for tweeters

Component	Percentage share
Past credits	10
Verification	8
Number of followers	7

6 Limitations of Proposed Model and Future Scope

The model despite its three-pronged approach has some limitations. Time complexity cannot be exactly determined as Google's Knowledge Graph API does not provide it. Twitter's Streaming API does not always guarantee delivery of 100% of the tweets. Even with the amount of tweets that are available to us, the precision to discern people-generated tweets from bot activity would still require a lot more effort. As user feed-back is crucial for improvement of proposed solution, first-hand awareness needs to be created that there exists a dangerous phenomenon online called fake news.

The generation of fake news cannot be completely abolished but the spread of fake news can surely be impeded by coming up with more accurate credibility check methods. The proposed model can be further employed to make a user level applica-tion, for fact-checking. This is the very next step to be done. For this, advanced

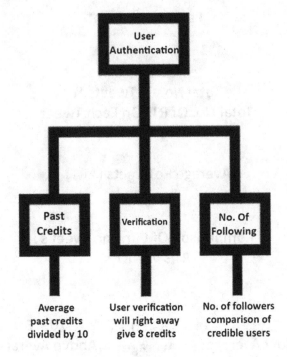

Fig. 14. Third dimension

regression analysis might need to be carried out to predict how false news spreads, at least during major events like disasters and big elections. The check on fake news can be implemented on other social networking and media sites as well, apart from Twitter.

7 Conclusion

The presence of false news presents a set of problems to deal with. Our model uses an algorithmic approach to assign credibility scores, rather than totally relying on human involvement. The 60% weightage given to authentic news websites in our model ensures very little deviation from truthful content. The remaining 40%, consisting of retweet traction and tweeter verifiability, would depend on the set of users trying out the system at that particular point in time. Before the proposed solution is converted to an end product, this would be carried out for different types of events and news stories. We have inferred that this part would require another check in the future to obtain greater transparency.

References

1. Allcott, H., Gentzkow, M.: Social media and fake news in the 2016 election (No. w23089). National Bureau of Economic Research (2017)
2. Carvalho, C., Klagge, N., Moench, E.: The persistent effects of a false news shock. J. Empir. Finance 18(4), 597–615 (2011)
3. Castillo, C., Mendoza, M., Poblete, B.: Information credibility on twitter. In: Proceedings of the 20th International Conference on World Wide Web, pp. 675–684. ACM, March 2011
4. Ciampaglia, G.L., Shiralkar, P., Rocha, L.M., Bollen, J., Menczer, F., Flammini, A.: Computational fact checking from knowledge networks. PLoS One 10(6), e0128193 (2015). https://doi.org/10.1371/journal.pone.0128193
5. DeDeo, S.: Collective phenomena and non-finite state computation in a human social system. PLoS One 8(10), e75818 (2013)
6. De Longueville, B., Smith, R.S., Luraschi, G.: Omg, from here, i can see the flames!: a use case of mining location based social networks to acquire spatio-temporal data on forest fires. In: Proceedings of the 2009 International Workshop on Location Based Social Networks, pp. 73–80. ACM, November 2009
7. Finn, S., Metaxas, P.T., Mustafaraj, E., O'Keefe, M., Tang, L., Tang, S., Zeng, L.: TRAILS: a system for monitoring the propagation of rumors on twitter. In: Computation and Journalism Symposium, NYC, NY (2014)
8. Gupta, A., Kumaraguru, P., Castillo, C., Meier, P.: TweetCred: real-time credibility assessment of content on Twitter. In: Aiello, L.M., McFarland, D. (eds.) SocInfo 2014. LNCS, vol. 8851, pp. 228–243. Springer, Cham (2014). https://doi.org/10.1007/978-3-319-13734-6_16
9. Gupta, A., Lamba, H., Kumaraguru, P., Joshi, A.: Faking sandy: characterizing and identifying fake images on twitter during hurricane sandy. In: Proceedings of the 22nd International Conference on World Wide Web, pp. 729–736. ACM, May 2013
10. Gupta, P., Kamra, A., Thakral, R., Aggarwal, M., Bhatti, S., Jain, V.: A proposed framework to analyze abusive tweets on the social networks. Int. J. Mod. Educ. Comput. Sci. 1, 46–56 (2018). https://doi.org/10.5815/ijmecs.2018.01.05. http://www.mecs-press.org/
11. (n.d.). https://developers.google.com/knowledge-graph/. Accessed 14 Jan 2017
12. FiB. (n.d.). https://devpost.com/software/fib. Accessed 14 Jan 2017
13. Docs - Twitter Developers. (n.d.). https://dev.twitter.com/streaming/overview. Accessed 20 Jan 2017
14. Liben-Nowell, D., Kleinberg, J.: The link-prediction problem for social networks. J. Assoc. Inf. Sci. Technol. 58(7), 1019–1031 (2007)
15. Maia, M., Almeida, J., Almeida, V.: Identifying user behavior in online social networks. In: Proceedings of the 1st Workshop on Social Network Systems, pp. 1–6. ACM, April 2008
16. Mendoza, M., Poblete, B., Castillo, C.: Twitter under crisis: can we trust what we RT?. In: Proceedings of the First Workshop on Social Media Analytics, pp. 71–79. ACM, July 2010
17. Morstatter, F., Pfeffer, J., Liu, H., Carley, K.M.: Is the sample good enough? comparing data from twitter's streaming api with twitter's firehose (2013). arXiv preprint, arXiv:1306.5204
18. O'Donovan, J., Kang, B., Meyer, G., Hllerer, T., Adali, S.: Credibility in context: an analysis of feature distributions in twitter. ASE. In: IEEE International Conference on Social Computing, SocialCom (2012)
19. Oh, O., Agrawal, M., Rao, H.R.: Information control and terrorism: tracking the Mumbai terrorist attack through twitter. Inf. Syst. Front. 13(1), 33–43 (2011)

20. Ratkiewicz, J., Conover, M., Meiss, M., Gonçalves, B., Patil, S., Flammini, A., Menczer, F.: Detecting and tracking the spread of astroturf memes in microblog streams (2010). arXiv preprint, arXiv:1011.3768
21. Wang, A.H.: Don't follow me: Spam detection in twitter. In: Proceedings of the 2010 International Conference on Security and Cryptography (SECRYPT), pp. 1–10. IEEE, July 2010
22. Wu, Y., Agarwal, P.K., Li, C., Yang, J., Yu, C.: Toward computational fact-checking. Proc. VLDB Endow. 7(7), 589–600 (2014)

Transmission Line Sag Calculation
with Ampacities of Different Conductors

Sandeep Gupta$^{(\boxtimes)}$ and Shashi Kant Vij

Department of Electrical Engineering,
JECRC University, Jaipur 303905, Rajasthan, India
jecsandeep@gmail.com, shashikantvij@yahoo.com

Abstract. Whenever a transmission line conductor is erected between two towers; due to action of gravity on conductor weight; transmission line is not a straight line joining the two points but it slackens which is termed as sag. It is the lowest point between the two towers and nearest to the ground. It is both the advantage and disadvantage due to the presence of sag in transmission line as on the one hand it maintains the safe tension level and on the other hand to maintain the greater ampacity and required ground clearance transmission lines are to be erected at towers on greater heights. In this paper, different factors are explained which affects the transmission line sag. This paper focuses on calculating the sag produced by transmission lines using different types of conductors such as ACSR, ACCC and ACSS under different conditions. There is also a comparison between various conductors in which sag develops. Effect of loading on the development of conductor sag will also be considered in this paper. This paper uses MATLAB programming for the calculating the results and graphical outputs and simulation results and modeling for the comparative study among various conductors. The importance of this paper is that it will help in deciding the kind of conductor which is to be used for any particular power system design especially for the transmission network with sag.

Keywords: Sag · Different conductors (ACSR, ACCC and ACSS)
Ampacities and transmission line

1 Introduction

Electrical design engineers always take care of the different electrical and mechanical parameters while designing a transmission line along with the topology of the earth for which civil engineers are also involved in discussion [1]. Based on the generation capacity of the power station the transmission lines are held responsible for transmitting the bulk power to greater distances with minimum power loss. Main talking point of the loss is the heat generated while transmitting the power. This heat generated is due as transmission line carries the required current. Since current is being carried by the conductors which itself have greater weight density; hence the need is felt to built mechanically strong towers and its cross arms. These towers should be capable enough to withstand weight as well as the natural parameters such as wind, ice etc. Care should also be taken that these towers do not require frequent maintenance as erection and

© Springer Nature Singapore Pte Ltd. 2018
G. C. Deka et al. (Eds.): ICACCT 2018, CCIS 899, pp. 213–224, 2018.
https://doi.org/10.1007/978-981-13-2035-4_19

maintenance at greater heights is a tedious task given the heavy weight of the conductors as well as tower metals [2]. While erecting the transmission conductor's care should be taken that tension is not exceeding the breaking load.

Due to excessive weight of transmission line conductors due to their high weight density (another reason of their higher weight between the conductors is due the hundreds of distance between the towers) it is quite natural to have a sag; as it cannot defy the gravitational pull [3–6]. The distance between the towers is a function of high voltage it is carrying, topology of the earth in the area under study and the right of way available in the area. Every country have ground clearance safety norms to safe guard its citizens which is directly based on the sags produced by transmission lines of different capacities. In general we talk of a single sag present on the planes which is the lowest point of the transmission line conductor but when the transmission line of hilly areas are being studied or designed we have two sags one each nearer to tower [1, 13].

The factors which affect the sag were taken; for example span or the distance between the towers (or line supports), tension in the line, line supports, weight of the conductor, various conductor configuration and its effects. Sag is directly proportional to weight per unit length of conductor [7]. A longer span causes more sag, simple logic behind is that as the span increases the weight of the conductor increases resulting in more sag [8]. Sag is inversely proportional to conductor tension [7]. Hence for sag compensation either conductor selection is such which produces least sag despite carrying the high currents or sag compensators are attached to the lines so that it can remove the sag as and when it appears. Generally a combination of both is used. Sag compensators are primarily used as a backup sag protection, secondly during short term over load condition; line can carry extra current without being overheating or sagging. Therefore correctness of sag is the important demand for the present power sector scenario.

This paper gives the important information about sag with respect to the choice of conductor and setting of ground clearance during the designing and erection of lines. This paper also discussed the factors on which the sag mainly depends. Section 2 is based on the different case studies and problem formulation with mathematical calculations. MATLAB graphical outputs of different cases are also shown in this section. It is followed by comparisons among different conductors are shown graphically. Finally, Sect. 4 concludes this paper.

2   Case Studies and Problem Formulation

In this section, there is sag calculation for different cases considering various arrangements i.e. supports at different levels. In this section, the ice and wind load is also considered for sag calculation. Effect of loading on the development of conductor sag will be shown here. In this section, the mathematical formulation responsible for sags of parabolic shape is presented and analyzed the difference of magnitude between them using results of MATLAB programming [9].

2.1   Case 1: Sag Calculation Without Any Load for Supports at the Different Level at Given Span

Many a times (especially in hilly areas) the two supports of a span may be at different levels. Such a section suspended between two supports which are at different levels. Let two supports are 'B' and 'C'. In such condition the curve is not complete parabola but a part of parabola.

Let 'L' be the actual span (horizontal distance between B and C), 'T' is the tension of conductor, 'W' is the weight of conductor and 'h' is the vertical difference in level between two supports. 'S_1' is the sag from level C (sag from low level) and 'S_2' is the sag from level B (sag from high level) as shown in Fig. 1. Then,

$$S_1 = [(WX_1^2)/(2T)]; \quad S_2 = [(WX_2^2)/(2T)]$$

where

X_1 = Horizontal distance of foot of level C from O.

and

X_2 = Horizontal distance of foot of level B from O.

thus

$$X_1 + X_2 = L \tag{1}$$

Now

$$S_2 - S_1 = [\{W(X_2^2 - X_1^2)\}/(2T)] = [\{W(X_2 + X_1) \times (X_2 - X_1)\}/(2T)]$$
$$= [\{WL(X_2 - X_1)\}/(2T)]$$

But

$$S_2 - S_1 = h$$

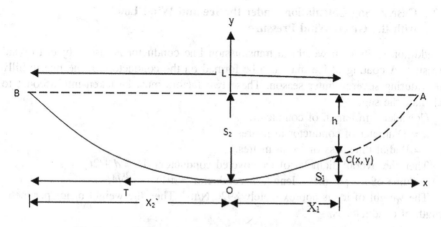

Fig. 1. Sag (without any load) for supports at different level.

so,

$$h = [\{WL(X_2 - X_1)\}/(2T)]$$

or

$$X_2 - X_1 = [(2Th)/(WL)] \tag{2}$$

Solving Eqs. 1 and 2, we get

$$X_1 = [(L/2) - \{(Th)/(WL)\}]; \quad X_2 = [(L/2) + \{(Th)/(WL)\}]$$

Data for sag calculation (without any load) for supports at different level is given in Table 1. Using these data, MATLAB output of the sags due to the weight of the conductor, supported at different levels is obtained in Fig. 2. These results are also given in Table 1.

Table 1. Data for Sag calculation (without any load) for supports at different level.

S.No.	Input		Output (in m)	
1.	Length of span between two different supports	600 m	The distance (X_1) of foot of support at lower level (or C) from O	270.0170
2.	Conductor tension	3520 kg	The distance (X_2) of foot of support at higher level (or B) from O	329.9830
3.	Conductor weight per unit length	2.935 kg/m	Minimum sag (S_1)	30.3961
4.	The difference in levels between two supports	15 m	Maximum sag (S_2)	45.3961

2.2 Case 2: Sag Calculation Under the Ice and Wind Load, with the Given Wind Pressure

In addition to its own weight, a transmission line conductor is also subject to wind pressure. A coating of ice may also be formed on the conductors of the line in hilly areas during severe winter season. These two factors must be taken into account to calculate the sag.

Consider ℓ m length of conductor.

d = Diameter of conductor in metres.

t = Radial thickness of ice in metres.

Then the overall diameter of ice covered conductors: $D = d + 2t$.

Volume of ice per metre length of conductor = $\pi(D^2 - d^2)/4$.

The weight of ice is approximately 8920 N/m^3. Then the weight of ice per metre length of conductor is:

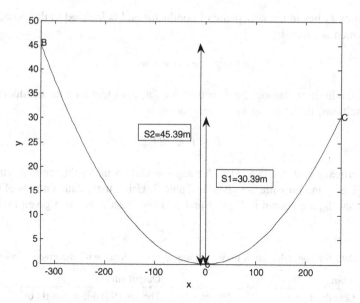

Fig. 2. MATLAB Output of the sags due to the weight of the conductor, supported at different levels.

$$w_i = 8920\,\pi\left(D^2 - d^2\right)/4 \ \text{N/m.}$$
$$w_i = 2.8 \times 10^4\,t(d + t) \ \text{N/m.}$$

The wind pressure is assumed to act horizontally on the projected area of the ice covered conductor with different forces as shown in Fig. 3. This projected area is D sq. m per metre length of conductor.

For a wind pressure of p Newton per sq. m of projected area, wind load F_w is:

$$F_w = pD \ \text{N/m.}$$

If the wind velocity is known, the wind pressure p is taken as $0.059v^2$ N/m, where v is wind velocity in km/h. The total force F_t acting on the conductor per metre length is:

$$F_t = \left[(w + w_i)^2 + F_w^2\right]^{1/2} \ \text{N/m.}$$

Fig. 3. Forces acting on the conductor.

The force F_t lies in the new plane of conductor and is inclined to the vertical at an angle γ which is given by:

$$\tan \gamma = F_w/(w + w_i).$$

If T is the limiting tension and F_t is the total force per metre on the conductor under worst conditions, then the sag in the new plane is:

$$S = F_t L^2 / 8T.$$

The vertical sag is S cos γ. Data for sag calculation under the ice and wind load, with the given wind pressure are given in Table 2. Using these data, outputs of the sags of S_w, S_v and S_n are shown in Figs. 4 and 5. These results are also given in Table 2.

Table 2. Data for Sag calculation under the ice and wind load, with the given wind pressure.

S.No.	Input		Output (in m)	
1.	Length of span	350 m	The sag (S_w) due to weight of	3.8969
2.	Conductor weight per unit length	8.5 N/m	the conductor alone	
3.	Internal diameter of conductor	0.0195 m		
4.	Radial thickness of ice on each side	0.0096 m	The sag (S_n) in the new plane	10.0983
5.	Limiting conductor tension	33400 N		
6.	Wind pressure on projected area	382 N/m²	The vertical sag (S_v)	7.4859
7.	Force per unit volume exhibited by ice	8920 N/m³		

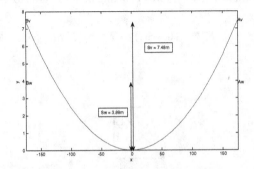

Fig. 4. MATLAB Output of the sags of S_w and S_v (in 2D).

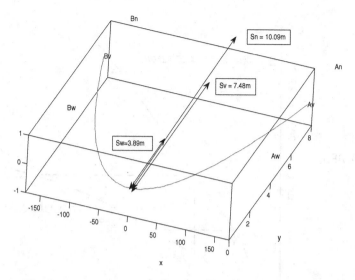

Fig. 5. MATLAB Output of the sags of S_w, S_v and S_n. (in 3D).

As of now, we have studied about the various factors which affect the sag and the parameters on which the sag is decided. Now, the next section will help in deciding the kind of conductor which is to be used for any particular power system design especially for the transmission network with sag.

3   Results Comparison Between Different Conductors

The main aim of the power system is to transmit the bulk power from one place to the other, with minimal requirement of material and money and the power system is designed for the voltage at which the transmission will take place. Now it is left to the ability of the conductors to carry large currents. As the conductors attempt to carry large currents their conductor temperature rise; their metal cores expand and the lines sag. So the conductor with high thermal capacity will transmit more power with less sag. This section focuses on calculating the sag produced by transmission lines (using different types of conductors for e.g., ACSR (Aluminium Conductor Steel Reinforced), ACCC (Aluminium Composite Core Cable), ACCR (Aluminium Conductor Composite Reinforced) and ACSS (Aluminium Conductor Steel Supported) etc.) [10].

3.1   Comparison Between ACCR and ACSR

The Fig. 6 clearly suggest the higher ampacities (current carrying capacities) of the ACCR conductor as they can with stand the higher conductor temperature of 210 °C. The ACCR 795 kcmil (Al area unit; 2 kcmil = 1 mm^2) conductor can carry the current which even an ACSR 1590 kcmil can't.

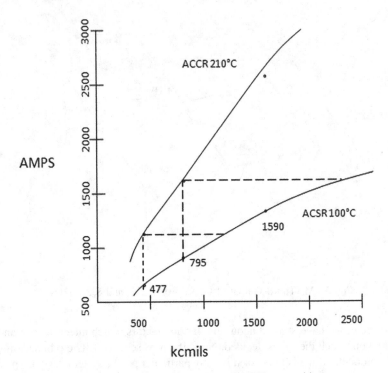

Fig. 6. Comparison of ACCR and ACSR ampacities.

Consider a power system which is designed for the conductor whose aluminium area is 795 kcmil (402.9 mm^2) as in the above case, from the Fig. 7. It is clear that for ACCR when the conductor temperature is 50 °C, sag is 8.6868 m (converted from the feet in the Fig. 7) but for the same temperature the sag produced by the ACSR conductor is 9.9669 m although the safe limit is 11.7957 m. The safe temperature limit of the aluminium is 75 °C although in few literatures we find it up to 100 °C. Therefore comparing on those lines for ACCR when the conductor temperature is 100 °C, sag is 9.6012 m but ACSR reach safe limit of 11.7957 m at this temperature. ACCR is found to work satisfactorily and continuously up to 210 °C (and up to 240 °C for short duration during emergency) for which the sag produced is only 10.9118 m.

3.2   Comparison Between ACSS and ACSR

Consider ACSS/TW 795 kcmil (402.9 mm^2) fully annealed aluminium wires formed into trapezoidal shape [3]. It creates a more compact conductor with same metal but smaller diameter; it results in smaller ice and wind loading on the conductor. Also consider a 795 kcmil 26/7 ACSR "Drake". Now if the ampacities are calculated assuming the ambient temperature of 40 °C, 0.61 m/s wind, sun, 0.5 coefficient of emissivity and absorptivity, then we get the following results as shown in Table 3.

Again we have observed that ACSS due to its higher thermal capacity can have high ampacities than ACSR of same area and will also have less sag generated.

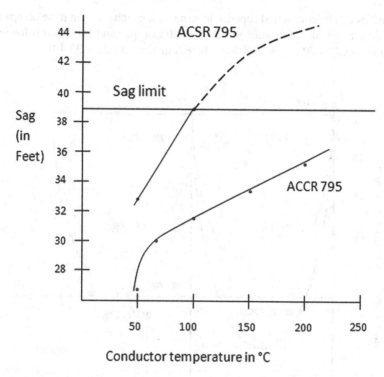

Fig. 7. Sag-temperature chart showing ACCR provides larger ampacity by operating at higher temperatures also exhibiting reduced sag.

Table 3. Comparison of Ampacities of ACSS/ TW and ACSR conductors.

Conductor temperature (in °C)	Standard 795 ACSR (Ampacities in Amps)	ACSS/TW equal area (Ampacities in Amps)
75	730	720
100	990	980
150	–	1320
200	–	1560
250	–	1740

3.3 Comparison Between ACSS and ACCR

The results of Fig. 8 shown in graphical manner assumes ACSS and ACCR at 1,300 feet (396 m) ruling span, initial tension: 6,557 lbs (2,974 kg) maximum loading at –1 °C), no ice, 5.4 kg wind load; 0.6 m/s wind speed, perpendicular wind direction, 0.5 emissivity and solar absorption. Based on the above figures and table we can compare the ACSS and ACCR conductors. If we take ACSS and ACCR conductors of equal area say 795 kcmil then it is found that the current carrying capacity of ACCR at 210 °C is 1692A while that of ACSS at same conductor temperature is approximately 1610 A, hence ACCR can be considered superior in terms of ampacity. Again if we compare the sags produced by both the conductors based on 305 m span and 150 °C; it is found that the sag produced by ACSS is 37.8 feet whereas that of ACCR is 33.4 ft.

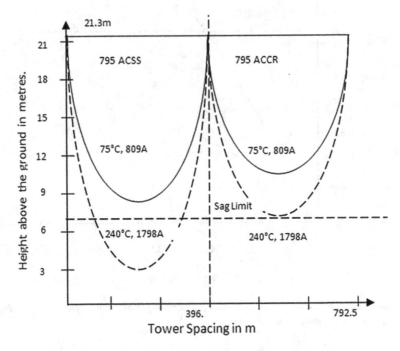

Fig. 8. Sag comparison of ACSS and ACCR conductors.

3.4   Comparison Between ACSR and Other Conductors

There are few other lesser known conductors [11, 12] which discussed here in brief:

(a) ZTACIR (Zirconium Alloy Aluminium Conductor Invar Steel Reinforced): It has high-temperature aluminium strands over a low-thermal elongation steel core. It can operate up to 210 °C satisfactorily.

(b) GTACSR (Gap Type heat resistant Aluminium alloy Conductor Steel Reinforced): It has high temperature aluminium, grease-filled gap between core/inner layer. It gives satisfactory operation till 150 °C. GZTACSR (Gap Type Super Heat Resistant Aluminium Alloy Conductor Steel Reinforced), it has inferior properties than GTACSR in terms of area of cross section used for similar ampacity but it is superior than ACSR for sag comparison.

(c) CRAC (Composite Reinforced Aluminium Conductor): It has annealed aluminium over fibreglass/thermoplastic composite segmented core. It has the probable satisfactory operation up to 150 °C.

(d) ACCFR (Aluminium Conductor Composite Carbon Fibre Reinforced) Annealed or high-temperature aluminium alloy over a core of strands with carbon fibre material in a matrix of aluminium. It has the probable satisfactory operation up to 210 °C.

From the Fig. 9 we can clearly observe that the ACSR conductors require less cross sectional area for the same current carrying capacity than GTACSR or GZTACSR. Figure 10 suggests that for the same conductor temperature the sag produced by the ACSR conductor is more than that of GZTACSR.

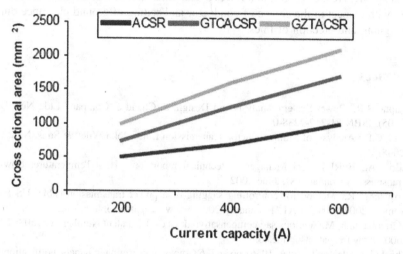

Fig. 9. Comparison of current carrying capacities of ACSR, GTACSR and GZTACSR.

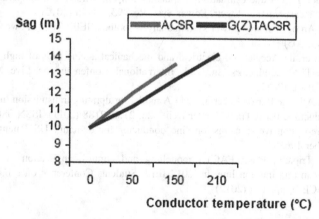

Fig. 10. Sag comparison between ACSR and GZTACSR.

4 Conclusions

This paper takes up various case studies in which the sag calculation is done using different conditions such as calculating sag with supports at different level. Sag calculation for the ice and wind Load, with the given wind pressure, with loading conditions are shown in this paper. From simulation results, it can be also said that the ampacity of the various conductors in increasing order is ACSR, ACCC, ACSS, and ACCR. Similarly the sag produced by various conductors of same size in decreasing order is ACSR, ACCC, ACSS, and ACCR. This information will have the crucial role to play with respect to the choice of conductor and setting of ground clearance during the designing and erection of lines.

References

1. Gupta, B.R.: Power System Analysis and Design. S. Chand & Company Ltd., New Delhi (2005). ISBN 81-219-2238-0
2. Paul, C.R.: Analysis of Multiconductor Transmission Lines. John Wiley & Sons, New York (2008)
3. Edris, A.: EPRI Project Manager of technical report on, "High-Temperature, Low-Sag Transmission Conductors", June 2002
4. Browning, R.: Method for controlling sagging of a power transmission cable. US Patent Number 2007/0009224 A1, 11 January 2007. www.freepatentsonline.com
5. Shirmohamadi, M.: Various sag compensative devices. US Patent Number 6057508, 2 May 2000. www.freepatentsonline.com
6. The Indian electricity rules 1956, pp. 63–68. www.powermin.nic.in/acts_notification/pdf/ier1956.pdfnotification/pdf/ier1956.pdf
7. Desai, Y.M., Yu, P., Popplewell, N., Shah, A.H.: Finite element modelling of transmission line galloping. Comput. Struct. **57**(3), 407–420 (1995)
8. Du, Y., Liao, Y.: On-line estimation of transmission line parameters, temperature and sag using PMU measurements. Electr. Power Syst. Res. **93**, 39–45 (2012)
9. Milano, F.: An open source power system analysis toolbox. IEEE Trans. Power Syst. **20**(3), 1199–1206 (2005)
10. Stengel, D., et al.: Accelerated electrical and mechanical ageing tests of high temperature low sag (HTLS) conductors. In: 12th International Conference on Live Maintenance (ICOLIM). IEEE (2017)
11. da Silva, A.A.P., de Barros Bezerra, J.M.: A model for uprating transmission lines by using HTLS conductors. IEEE Trans. Power Deliv. **26**, 2180–2188 (2011). ISSN 0885-8977
12. Temperature-responsive transmission line conductor for de-icing. US Patent 3,218,384, 16 November 1965
13. Gupta, S., Tripathi, R.K.: FACTS modelling and control: application of CSC based STATCOM in transmission line. In: 2012 IEEE Students Conference on Engineering and Systems (SCES), pp. 1–5 (2012)

Fuzzy-Kohonen Self-organizing Clustering Algorithm in Wireless Sensor Networks

Pankaj Kumar Kashyap[✉], Kirshna Kumar, and Sushil Kumar

Wireless Communication and Networking Research Lab, School of Computer and Systems Sciences, Jawaharlal Nehru University, New Delhi 110067, India
{Pankaj76_scs,kirshn44_scs}@jnu.ac.in,
skdohare@mail.jnu.ac.in

Abstract. Rapid development of smart device because of internet of thing it opens the door for configures the wireless sensor network by self-organization and force to use soft computing technique rather than mathematical tool. The most appealing issue in wireless sensor networks to produce self-organized network which balance the network load. In this paper we proposed self-organizing cluster technique based on Fuzzy C-Means and Kohonen clustering network (KCN). KCN is well known for cluster formation but it have some disadvantage such as termination is not converged, learning strategy does not optimized any model. So we use the feature of Fuzzy C-means algorithm of self-optimization and membership function for learning rate in Kohonen-model which significantly enhance the clustering formation process, better convergence rate and optimized self-organization by size of neighborhood updated. The simulations shows that our algorithm outperforms from other clustering based protocol with best convergence rate and formed evenly distributed clusters.

Keywords: Fuzzy C-Means · Kohonen self-organizing map · Learning rate Membership function

1 Introduction

The previous couple of years have been seen expanding use wireless sensor networks (WSNs) in various applications ranging from health-care, military (missile tracking), domestic services, industrial and scientific approach, active volcano and seismic detection, vehicle tracking and many more [1, 2]. Also the use of smart devices in the world of Internet of things (IoT) creates new domains in WSNs to increase the sensor requirement in vehicular telecommunication for navigation as well as fleet navigation, production and industrial management [3]. WSNs typically comprise of large number of tiny, compact sensors (hundred to ten thousands) deployed arbitrarily in the territory within specified area where these sensor nodes rarely attended. These sensor nodes powered by low-cost non-rechargeable battery (irreplaceable in nature) so energy conservation most valuable priority for enhancement of network lifetime, network coverage and for robust network [4].

Grouping the similar pattern into number of cluster is powerful way to enhance the network throughput. Within clustering, each cluster there is one representative known

© Springer Nature Singapore Pte Ltd. 2018
G. C. Deka et al. (Eds.): ICACCT 2018, CCIS 899, pp. 225–236, 2018.
https://doi.org/10.1007/978-981-13-2035-4_20

as cluster head, cluster head having responsibility of receiving the information from its member nodes and aggregate into single packet of fixed size thereafter aggregated packet forwarded to base station. This feature reduces the number of message exchange between base station and cluster head, so significantly it reduces the energy consumption and optimizes the bandwidth utilization [5]. Clustering in wireless sensing network generally carried out by two main approaches. First one is hard clustering or C-means Clustering where sensor nodes belong to one cluster only that is degree of membership for any node either one or zero as proposed by MacQueen [6]. Practically, Sensor node has membership value between zero and one (Node may belong to more than one cluster) as fuzzy logic so Fuzzy C-means clustering comes into the picture also known as soft clustering. Fuzzy C-Means (FCM) first proposed by Dunn in 1973 later it is improved by Bezdek in 1981 [7, 8]. The membership value (μ) for node lie in the range [1, N]. When membership parameter is at one it show crisp clustering point and when membership parameter more than one it shows decision space increases. How the cluster head chosen per cycle is the most difficult part and rotation of cluster head role through network for balance the network load is prominent question. To addressing these questions we integrate the feature of FCM and KCN.

Kohonen Clustering networks (KCN) are unsupervised learning approach which locates the best arrangement of weights for hard clustering in repetitive and consecutive way [9]. It has turned out to be popular in the recent years because of widespread use of in the field of neural network theory, structures and applications. However, KCN have several disadvantage such as termination is done by external force, there is often guarantee of convergence and learning strategy does not optimized any dataset of model. Fuzzy Kohonen Clustering Network (FKCN) which combines the feature of FCM model into the update strategy and learning rate of the KCN model was proposed by Bezdek [7]. FKCN integrate the advantage of FCM, use the membership function in learning rate and parallel processing of input parameters. Therefore it produces a kind of self-organized neural network with improved convergence rate and with updated learning rate. So we proposed Fuzzy Kohonen Self-Organizing Clustering Protocol (FKSOCP) based on integration of both FCM and KCN.

The remaining section of the paper organized as follow. In Sect. 2 brief discussion of related works is explained. System and Energy model describes into Sect. 3. In Sect. 4 our proposed algorithm FKSCOP is illustrated. In the next Sect. 5 simulation and result are shown and in the last Sect. 6 concluding remark of our work has been given.

2 Related Works

There are various clustering algorithm has been proposed in recent years. The most recognized classical one is LEACH, which select the cluster head in probabilistic manner and role of cluster head dynamically changes during each round [10]. However, in LEACH cluster distribution is not uniform, the next one is PEGASIS [11] extension of LEACH, where nodes are organized in a chain based on greedy approach and the nodes share data to their closet neighbor. These shared data moved from one node to another node, get aggregated and designated node transit data to base station, here also the role of cluster head changed by another node. Both above two protocols need strict time synchronization for cluster formation. Whereas HEED [12] clustering protocol took two parameters for the selection of cluster head, residual energy and node proximity (number of neighbor nodes) of each node. HEED terminates in O (1) iterations. HEED also have problems such as some nodes are not able to join any clusters that means unattended nodes create hotspot in network.

Recently Fuzzy Logic also applied in various clustering algorithm, in order to improve processing speed and reduce the computation. CHEF [13] protocol use two fuzzy parameters, residual energy and local distance. This protocol is localized in manner because base station does not involve in selection of cluster head, sensor nodes themselves the cluster head using fuzzy inference system. The cluster head selection procedure of CHEF similar as LEACH protocol. CHEF gave much improve performance than LEACH in terms of network lifetime and distribution of clusters. LEACH-FL is another improve version of LEACH based on fuzzy logic [14]. Base station is responsible for the selection of cluster head, it receive the information (energy level, node density, distance to base station) about the sensor nodes via acknowledgement and apply mamdani type fuzzy logic inference to select optimal number of cluster head. Since fuzzy logic is very intensive computation but they are lacking from self-organization and updating of learning rule.

Self-Organizing map (SOM) based on neural network cope up with learning rule strategy and better convergence rate enables us to use in variety of application such as remote sensing, time series estimation etc. Neural networks have special capability like as parallel processing of input, effective learning potentials. Therefore use of both fuzzy logic and neural networks turn out to be effective in WSNs. Teuvo Kohonen in 1980 proposed a method [15] where weight of winner neurons in competitive layer and neighborhood size are updated. This method is also known as Self-Organizing Map (SOM) based on unsupervised learning approach. SOM algorithm works in five steps, first step is Initialization: where random weight are assigned to connection, second steps chose one of the input member, third step declare the wining neuron which is closest to input vector neuron, weight of wining neuron and size of its neighborhood are updated in fourth step, in fifth step process is continue until procedure is converged or maximum iteration reached.

The proposed algorithm FKSCOP based on fuzzy c-Means (FCM) and Kohonen clustering network (KCN) to overcome each other limitations and get benefitted. The combined Fuzzy Kohonen Clustering Network (FKCN) counter several problems with the scope of include membership value of FCM in learning rate of KCN, Optimization and parallel processing feature of FCN into KCN, and update and structure rule of KCN into FCN. Above related works show that FKCN is most suitable approach in developing the self-organized, evenly distributions of clusters for improve the network lifetime and throughput.

3 System and Energy Model

Different constraint and architecture have been considered for various applications in WSNs. Some of the relevant parameters and architecture are listed below, which is used in our proposed algorithm.

- Sensor nodes are dispersed randomly in specified area by air scattering. These sensor nodes are remain static after deployment.
- All the sensor nodes are isomorphic in nature (having similar operation capability such as sensing, processing, broadcasting and communication power level).
- The communication link between the sensor nodes is symmetric (it consumed equal amount of energy in either direction) having flexible transmission power according to which they send data to their cluster head or directly to the base station.
- Sensor nodes are not equipped with GPS, base station broadcast beacon signal to all sensors and they calculate their position (co-ordinate) using received signal strength indicator (RSSI).

We directly applied the same first order radio hardware [10] for estimation of energy consumption in all sensor nodes as follow: Energy consumed in transmission (E_{trans}) of d-bit of data over distance r required summation of energy exhaust in transmission circuit (E_{tst}) and amplifying circuit (E_{amt}).

$$E_{trans}(u, v) = E_{tst}(u, v) + E_{amt}(u, v)$$
$$\begin{cases} v * E_{tst} + v * \mathcal{E}_{freep} * r^2, \text{if } v < v_o \\ v * E_{tst} + v * \mathcal{E}_{mulp} * r^2, \quad \text{if } v \geq v_o \end{cases} \tag{1}$$

And for energy consumed in receiving (E_{rece}) d-bit of packet is equal to energy spent in only transmission circuit of sensor node.

$$E_{rece} = E_{tst}(v) = v * E_{tst} \tag{2}$$

Where $\mathcal{E}_{freep}$ and $\mathcal{E}_{mulp}$ are amplifying energy consumed in free space and multipath fading models respectively. Where v_o is the threshold distance (calculated as $v_o = \sqrt{\mathcal{E}_{freep}/\mathcal{E}_{mulp}}$) is used to determine which energy consumption model is suitable for sensor node. If transmission distance v is underneath threshold distance v_o then free space path prototype is used for energy consumption otherwise multipath fading prototype is used.

4 Fuzzy Kohonen Self-organizing Clustering Protocol (FKSOCP)

In this section we proposed a hybrid approach of fuzzy c-means with Kohonen self-organizing clustering. This approach is first considered by Huntsberger and Ajji-marangsee [15] because of optimization feature of fuzzy c-Means (FCM) [6] which is not included in the KCN self-organizing model (heuristic approach).Which integrate the idea of fuzzy membership values for learning rate and update the neighborhood size parameter to make Kohonen self-organizing feature map as optimization procedure. The proposed FKSOCP works in two phases. In first phase cluster is formed based upon Fuzzy Kohonen feature map and cluster head is selected for each clusters thereafter in second phase cluster binding and data transmission takes place.

4.1   Cluster Formation Phase

In this phase, we are using residual energy and node density (number of neighbor nodes) of each sensor node as fuzzy input for the selection of cluster head. We are using same mamdani based fuzzy logic system for the membership value of the input parameter [16]. The linguistic variable for residual energy (RE) = {little, medium, enough} and node density = {sparse, medium, dense}. For little and enough value of residual energy, sparse and dense value of node density Trapezoidal nature of membership function is applied and for all the other remaining linguistic variable are operated with triangular membership function. The output variable function of sensor node has nine linguistic variables such as capability (CP) = {underflow, useless, powerless, dull, mean, average, enough, effective, powerful}. These rules are stored in fuzzy inference knowledge system shown in Table 1. Sensor nodes having little residual energy and sparse nature neighbor nodes are useless and cannot be cluster head in other hand sensor nodes having enough residual energy and dense number of neighbor nodes then it has powerful capability to become cluster head.

Table 1. Fuzzy logic rules

SL.No.	Residual energy	Node density	Capability
1.	little	sparse	underflow
2.	little	medium	useless
3.	little	dense	powerless
4.	medium	sparse	dull
5.	medium	medium	mean
6.	medium	dense	average
7.	enough	sparse	enough
8.	enough	medium	effective
9.	enough	dense	powerful

Fuzzy logic inference system has four components shown in Fig. 1, in the first component input parameters (residual energy and node density of sensor nodes) are fuzzied and membership function is plot against input parameter shown in Figs. 2 and 3. In second component fuzzy rule are fired according to given nine rules. Selection is done using minimum AND operator among various input parameter. In third component aggregation is done among different output to generate single fuzzy output set using maximum OR operator and thereafter in fourth component defuzzication is done by using center of area or centroid method [16]. The output (chance) of fuzzier is membership function depending upon the input parameters shown in Fig. 4. These chance membership functions of each sensor nodes are given to Kohonen self-organizing neural network to obtain clustering depending upon the parameters.

Cluster formation is done by Kohonen-self Organizing map (KSOM) and learning rate and neighborhood size is updated with the help of membership value of fuzzy c-means. KSOM is feed forwarded, competitive type neural network which used

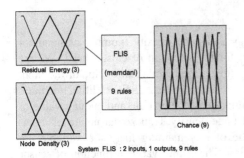

Fig. 1. Block Diagram of FLIS

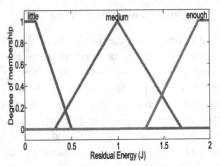

Fig. 2. Membership function of residual energy

unsupervised learning method, that means no expected output is presented or output is not known prior the start of learning process. In the learning process KSOM find the measurable similarities in its input space and consequently creates distinctive clusters or groups which represents various classes of input space. KSOM have two layers, first is input layer where number of neurons is equal to input parameters or patterns used and the output layer is known as competitive layer where in every repetition single neuron or node is winning amongst all other nodes. Competitive layer is generally organized as two-dimensional grids, where each input neuron is connected to output neuron. The typical example KSOM neural network is shown in Fig. 5. The competitive layer neurons discover the association of connection among input neurons, which are grouped by the competitive neurons and sort out a topological map from arbitrary beginning stage, and the relationship between the given patterns are shown in KSOM clustering map. Output layer consist number of neurons greater than two times the input neuron in form of grid with number of suitable neighborhood node value.

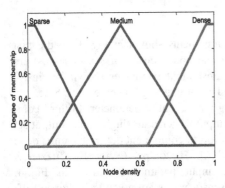

Fig. 3. Membership function for Node density

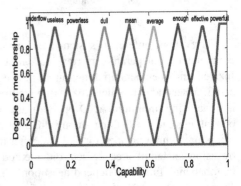

Fig. 4. Membership function of Capability

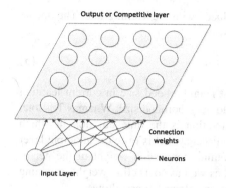

Fig. 5. Typical KSOM network

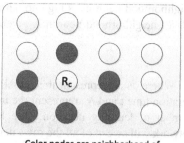

Color nodes are neighborhood of wining node R_c

Fig. 6. Grid pattern of wining node with neighbor nodes

4.2   Learning Algorithm

The KSOM neural network organized as with the set of training input neuron corresponding to each sensor. Let the input training patterns are: $S = \{s_1, s_2, s_3, \ldots \ldots, s_n\}$ where n is number of sensor nodes in the front layer (as input). The competitive layer or output layer has total p number of sensor nodes. Let R_j is the jth output neuron. So in total output layer neuron is represented as $R = \{R_1, R_2, R_3, \ldots \ldots, R_p\}$. For every output neuron R_j there are total n numbers of connection from each input neuron. Let the weight of each connection is represented as W, then any output layer neuron R_j is set incoming weight connection from each input neuron is $W_j = \{W_{j1}, W_{j2}, W_{j3}, W_{j4}, \ldots \ldots W_{jv}\}$. The Euclidean distance X_j is calculated for any arbitrary competitive layer neuron R_j whenever input training pattern S is given.

$$X_j = \sqrt{\sum_{i=1}^{n} (S_i - W_{ji})^2} \tag{3}$$

$$R_c = \min \{X_j\} \tag{4}$$

At this stage (competitive level), the output neurons compete among themselves and winner neuron R_c is announced with the minimum Euclidean distance (that means weight connection is nearest to input pattern) with respect to current input pattern. The next step is identified neighborhood neuron around the wining neuron (R_c). This is simply the set of neuron inside the square with wining neuron R_c as center shown in Fig. 6. This wining neuron is selected as cluster head and neighborhood neurons as member neurons of clusters.

In the next stage (Learning stage) update the size of neighborhood neurons around the wining neuron and also weight of wining neuron is updated. Initially the size of neighborhood neurons is big enough and it reduced with the learning rate. The update rule of neighborhood neuron is given as follow.

$$N_t = N_o(1 - t/T) \tag{5}$$

Where as N_t represent the actual or current neighborhood size in current learning iteration time t and N_o represent the initial or old neighborhood size. Whereas T is total number of learning iteration. One learning iteration is the time duration in which network will sweep of all the rows neurons of adjacency matrix once (as in output layer neuron are represents as grid form). The incoming connection weight of the neighboring neuron of the wining neuron is updated as well as connection weight of wining neuron is also updated according to fuzzy c-means algorithm as follows.

$$W_{j,t+1} = W_{j,t} + \frac{\sum_{k=1}^{n} \beta_{jk,t+1}(S_k - W_{j,t})}{\sum_{j=1}^{v} \beta_{jk,t+1}} \tag{6}$$

Where $W_{j,t+1}$ updated weight of jth neuron at current iteration t + 1, $W_{j,t}$ is old weight of the neuron and S_k represent the Kth input pattern. The learning parameter is represented as β_{jk}. Huntsberger defined the learning parameter β_{jk} as follow:

$$\beta_{jk,t} = (\delta_{jk,t})^{m_t} \tag{7}$$

Where m_t fuzzification index is defined in fuzzy c-means algorithm and $\delta_{jk,t}$ is membership function of the input pattern S_k being the part of jth cluster. Both of these two parameters vary with iteration t according to given equation as follow.

$$\delta_{jk,t} = \frac{1}{\sum_{j=1}^{v} \left(\|X_k - R_{i,t+1}/X_k - R_{j,t+1}\|\right)^{2/m-1}}, \quad \begin{matrix} 1 \leq k \leq n \\ 1 \leq j \leq v \end{matrix} \tag{8}$$

$$X_{jk} = (R_k - W_j)^T (R_k - W_j) \tag{9}$$

$$m_t = (m_0 - tm_\Delta) \tag{10}$$

$$m_\Delta = (m_0 - 1)/t_d \tag{11}$$

Where as X_{jk} is Euclidean distance and m_0 is some positive integer more prominent than one and $m_\infty = 1$. In practice t cannot be infinity so we can use Eq. (8) and t_d define the maximum number of iteration in fuzzy Kohonen c-means. The final value of fuzzification parameter m_f should not less than one keep in mind to divide by zero in Eq. (5).

Algorithm 1- Fuzzy Kohonen Self- organizing Cluster formation

---

1. **Begin**
2. **Input:** Given input pattern $S = \{s_1, s_2, s_3, \ldots \ldots, s_n\}$, $S_i \in R^f$, where f is dimension of pattern or grid; Euclidian distance X_j; learning rate $\beta_{jk,t}$; total number of cluster head p and small positive error threshold constant $\varepsilon > 0$.
3. **Initialization:** Output vector of cluster head or center (unknown) $R = \{R_1, R_2, R_3, \ldots \ldots, R_p\}$, choose any random value $m_0 > 1$ and set maximum iteration limit to t_{max}.
4. **For** t=1 to t_{max}.
   a. Calculate X_j for all nodes k=1,2,3,..v by using equation (4).
   b. Select the winner output neuron R_c using equation (4).
   c. Compute learning rate $\beta_{jk,t}$ for all cluster head or neuron by using equation (7) and equation (8).
   d. Update all the weight connection of wining neuron by using equation (6).
   e. Update the size of neighborhood neuron N_t.
   f. Compute error rate for the current iteration $E_t = \|R_{t+1} - R_t\|^2 = \sum_i \|R_{j,t+1} - R_{j,t}\|^2$.
   g. **If** $E_t \leq \varepsilon$ then stop
      Else go to step 4.
5. **END**

4.3   Cluster Binding and Transmission Phase

Initially base station starts the process of clustering. Base station broadcast a beacon message in network for requesting residual energy and node density, respond to beacon message each sensor node forward their residual energy and location related particulars to base station. Each sensor node calculates their location using Received Signal Strength meter (RSSI) as follow:

$$RSSI = -(10n \, log_{10} \, l + A) \qquad (11)$$

Where n is the signal propagation parameter, l is the distance between base station to node and A is the no- obstacle received signal strength in one meter. Cluster is formed according to Fuzzy Kohoen self-organizing map and Wining node of cluster is selected as cluster head. This process of selection of cluster head is repeated in every round to balance the load of cluster head, so all the sensor nodes get benefitted (position of cluster head rotated through all sensor nodes), as a consequence network lifetime would be enhanced.

After cluster formation and selection of cluster head, the next stage of data gathering from member nodes of each clusters to their respective cluster head stated according to TDMA schedule (to reduce inter-cluster inference) created by each cluster head for their member nodes. Member nodes in each cluster head sends their data to cluster head according to TDMA schedule in only wake up (only in their slotted time) mode after that these member nodes goes onto sleep mode to prevent energy consumption. Now, cluster head applies data aggregation on these receive data to convert multiple packet in single packet of fixed size, the data aggregation feature to bring down the number of message exchange between cluster head and base station. Now each cluster head send their packet to base station directly and after that energy of each sensor node including cluster head is updated and the start the FKSOCP process for the next round.

5   Experimental Results and Discussion

The simulation tool used in our work is Matlab 2013b and parameters shown in Table 2. Figure 7 shows that the node death percentage over rounds. In LEACH initially at the start of algorithm sensor nodes dies slowly but after 2000 rounds sensor nodes dies rapidly and almost all the nods are died up to 2500 rounds. Whereas CHEF and FCM perform better than LEACH, about 10% less death recorded than LEACH. Death percentage rate of node in our proposed algorithm FKSCOP is very steady and up to 3500 rounds 20% node are still alive, so results show that FKSCOP perform 12% to 15% better than FCM and about 45% better than LEACH. Figure 8 show that LEACH perform worst and in CHEF and FCM nodes losses their energy comparative slower than LEACH about 25%. Whereas FKSOCP shows that energy consumption in each round is very low and sensor nodes have still some energy after reached maximum number of rounds, it is because of FKSCOP produce better cluster classification.

Table 2. Simulation Metrics

Metrics	Values
Area	250×250
No. of nodes	300
Location of BS	(50,60)
Initial energy	2 J
E_{tst}	50nJ/bit
ε_{freep}	10pJ/bit/m^2
ε_{mulp}	0.0013pJ/bit/m^4
t_d	70
Cycle time	60 μs

Figure 9 shows that LEACH perform poorest than all other after 1500 rounds number of alive nodes sharply down and almost 2500 rounds it reaches up to zero. CHEF and FCM have 15% improvement over LEACH. The result shows that FKSOCP perform better than all other algorithm and it have 20%, 10% and 13% enhancement over LEACH, CHEF and FCM respectively. In Fig. 10 LEACH sows that there is

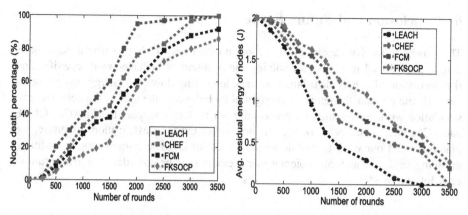

Fig. 7. Node death percentage

Fig. 8. Avg. residual energy over rounds

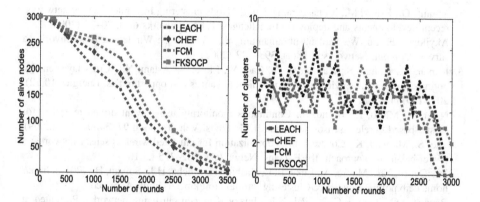

Fig. 9. No. of alive nodes over rounds

Fig. 10. No. of clusters over rounds

uneven number of cluster formed as round varies, at 1250 rounds number of cluster is 9 and at 1500 round it is 4 and up to 2700 rounds number of cluster is zero because of all the sensor nodes are died. CHEF produce cluster on average 4 as rounds varies but it also produce no cluster at all at 2800 rounds, whereas FCM shows much improvement over both LEACH and CHEF and produce even number of clusters. But FKSCOP give optimal number of clusters as round number of rounds increase on average number of cluster is 5. Table 3 shows the comparative study among LEACH, CHEF, FCM and FKSCOP.

Table 3. Comparative study of various algorithms with different parameter

Parameter (up to 3000 rounds)	LEACH	CHEF	FCM	FKSCOP
Node death percentage	98.99	96.78	82.42	77.54
Avg. residual energy of nodes	0.002 J	0.44 J	0.58 J	0.72 J
Number of alive nodes	12	26	34	58
Avg. number of cluster formed	6	4	5	5

6 Conclusion and Future Scope

This works show that capability of self-organized Fuzzy Kohonen neural network as computational tool in WSNs for solving the problem of better network classification (i.e. formation of evenly distributed cluster), also bring down the energy dissipation in network and escalate the network throughput by balancing the load in the network. The simulation work proves that our proposed work performs surpass the LEACH, CHEF and FCM with better network lifetime and better cluster classification. In future, we plan to extend our work to mobile sensor nodes for large scale-networks. In addition, grouping resilience and fault-tolerant management may be considered in near future in both Iot and WSNs.

References

1. Younis, O., Krunz, M., Ramasubramanian, S.: Node clustering in wireless sensor networks: recent developments and deployment challenges. IEEE Networks 6(5), 20–25 (2006)
2. Akyildiz, I.F., Su, W., Sankarasubramanium, Y., Cayirrci, E.: Wireless sensor networks: a survey. Comput. Networks J. 38(4), 393–422 (2002)
3. Kumar, K., Kumar, S., Kaiwartya, O., Cao, Y., Lloret, J., Aslam, N.: "Cross-layer energy optimization for IoT environments": technical advances and opportunities. Energies 10(12), 2073 (2017)
4. Nizar, v., Mario, E., Bruno, S.: Continuous monitoring using event driven reporting for cluster-based wireless sensor networks. IEEE Trans. Veh. Technol. 97, 3460–3497 (2009)
5. Tao, S., Marwan, K.: Coverage-time optimization for clustered wireless sensor networks: a power-balancing approach. IEEE Trans. Netw. 2(1), 202–215 (2010)
6. MacQueen, J.B., Moore, A., Luke, B.T., Rashid, T., Mucha, H.J., Sofyan, H.: (2017). http://home.deib.polimi.it/matteucc/Clustering/tutorial.html/kmeans.html. Accessed
7. Bezdek, J.C., Tsao, E.C.-K., Pal, N.R.: Fuzzy Kohonen clustering networks. Presented at IEEE International Conference on Fuzzy Systems (1992)
8. Bezdek, J.C.: Pattern Recognition with Fuzzy Objective Function Algorithms. Plenum Press, New York (1981)
9. Kohonen, T.: The Self-organizing map. Proc. IEEE 78, 1464–1480 (1990)
10. Heinzelman, W.R., Chandrakasan, A., Balakrishnan, H.: Energy efficient communication protocol for wireless micro sensor networks. In: Proceeding of the IEEE Annual Hawaii International Conference on System Sciences, pp. 3005–3014 (2000)
11. Lindsey, S., Raghavendra, C.S.: PEGASIS: "Power efficient gathering in sensor information systems". In: Proceedings of the IEEE Aerospace Conference, vol. 3, pp. 1125–1130 (2003)
12. Younis, O., Fahmy, S.: HEED: A Hybrid Energy Efficient Distributed Clustering approach for Adhoc sensor networks. IEEE Trans. Mob. Comput. 3, 366–379 (2004)
13. Kim, J., Park, S., Han, Y., Chung, T.: CHEF: cluster head election mechanism using fuzzy logic in wireless sensor networks. In: Proceeding International Conference Advance Communication Technology, pp. 654–659, February 2008
14. Ran, G., Zhang, H., Gong, S.: Improving on LEACH protocol of wireless sensor networks using fuzzy logic. J. Inf. Comput. Sci. 7, 767–775 (2010)
15. Huntsberger, T., Ajjimarangsee, P.: Parallel self-organizing feature maps for unsupervised pattern recognition. Int. J. Gen Syst 16, 357–372 (1989)
16. Zadeh, L.A.: Fuzzy sets. Inf. Control 8, 338–353 (1965)

IEEE 802.11 Based Heterogeneous Networking: An Experimental Study

Piyush Dhawankar[1](✉) and Rupak Kharel[2]

[1] Department of Mathematics, Physics and Electrical Engineering,
Northumbria University, Newcastle upon Tyne, UK
piyush.s.dhawankar@northumbria.ac.uk
[2] School of Engineering, Manchester Metropolitan University, Manchester, UK
r.kharel@mmu.ac.uk

Abstract. This paper analyses the results from an experimental study on the performance of the heterogeneous wireless networks based on IEEE 802.11a, 802.11n and 802.11ac standards in an indoor environment considering the key features of PHY layers mainly, Multiple Input Multiple Output (MIMO), Multi-User Multiple Input Multiple Output (MU-MIMO), Channel Bonding and Short-Guard Interval (SGI). The experiment is conducted for the IEEE 802.11ac standard along with the legacy protocols 802.11a/n in a heterogeneous environment. It calculates the maximum throughput of IEEE 802.11 standard amendments, compares the theoretical and experimental throughput over TCP and UDP and their efficiency. To achieve this desired goal, different tests are proposed. The result of these tests will determine the capability of each protocol and their efficiency in a heterogeneous environment.

Keywords: Local Area Network (LAN)
Wireless Local Area Network (WLAN)
Quality of Service (QoS) and AP (Access Point)

1 Introduction

The Wireless LAN (WLAN) technology have seen tremendous growth and benefits due to major changes in the world of Local Area Network (LANs), as the WLAN technology has matured and it is now the core of internet communication. In IEEE 802.11, 802.11a specifications provide up to 54 Mbps data rates [1]. However, the practical and theoretical throughput of IEEE 802.11a are 25 Mb/s and physical-layer (PHY) data rate are 54 Mb/s respectively [2]. The IEEE 802.11n standard introduced the MIMO by implementing spatial diversity, which enables it to achieve at least four times more throughput than legacy protocols [3].

The wireless network standards IEEE 802.11a/n works reliably. However, their speed does not satisfy users' demand and the throughput may not support large data files under various condition, hence, the latest amendment of IEEE 802.11ac is invented to improve transmission performance [4]. The 802.11ac is the latest WLAN standard that is rapidly being adapted due to the potential of delivering very high throughput. The throughput increase in 802.11ac are due to larger channel width

© Springer Nature Singapore Pte Ltd. 2018
G. C. Deka et al. (Eds.): ICACCT 2018, CCIS 899, pp. 237–246, 2018.
https://doi.org/10.1007/978-981-13-2035-4_21

(80/160 MHz) which support for denser modulation (256 QAM) with increased number of spatial streams for MIMO and MU-MIMO [5]. The 802.11ac is a faster, improved and more scalable version of the 802.11n with the capabilities of Gigabit Ethernet with a wider bandwidth [6].

The deployment of wireless network in 2.4 GHz frequency band over the years has started to show limitations due to number of interference issues between neighboring devices which affects the performance of entire wireless network [7]. The emerging wireless technologies which operates in 5 GHz frequency spectrum has number of advantages over 2.4 GHz in terms of non-overlapping channels with wider channel bandwidth for gaining higher throughput. However, 5 GHz wireless network technology suffers the signal attenuation at higher frequencies which results in lower range compared to 2.4 GHz network technology. The IEEE 802.11 protocols operate in multiple frequency spectrum band, some of them operate in both bands (2.4 and 5 GHz) like, 802.11n and others 802.11a/ac operates in single band (5 GHz). The 802.11 WLAN efficiency is severely compromised due to interference of other Wireless LAN technology operating in same environment and this affects the data throughput and efficiency of Wireless Network. The performance evaluation of IEEE 802.11ac has been widely explored over simulation platform, although there is not much experimental evaluation done in practical scenarios [8, 9].

The objective of this research is to test 802.11ac experimentally with legacy protocol 802.11a/n for throughput and efficiency operating in heterogeneous environment. The rest of the paper is organised as follows. Section 2, provides a brief discussion on details and problems of the IEEE 802.11 and their amendments in heterogeneous environment. Section 3, describes the design and arrangement of the experiment. It includes the network diagram, list of equipment's used and test cases for testing the throughput and efficiency. The results are discussed in Sect. 4. We conclude the presented work in Sect. 5.

2   Related Work

According to [10] if there are two access points placed in an indoor environment, one is an 802.11n and the other is an 802.11ac, then the signals transmitted by the 802.11ac will overlap with the signal of legacy protocol 802.11n resulting narrower channel width and hence decrementing the network throughput. Another issue stated by [11] when an 802.11n and 802.11ac are deployed in an indoor environment the Time Difference of Arrival (TDOA) of signal of 802.11ac compared to 802.11n decreases because of interference with 802.11n signal, also use of wider bandwidth with 802.11ac, thus can improve the accuracy and stability of TDOA at lower sound to noise ratio (SNR). Another interoperability issue stated by [12], that 802.11ac works only on a 5 GHz band and the 802.11n works on 2.4/5 GHz band and there is no 80 and 160 MHz channel in 802.11n. Moreover, 802.11n only works on 20 and 40 MHz, hence the backward compatibility should be checked with existing 802.11a/n devices.

The problem can be elaborated with the help of the following examples. In a heterogeneous environment consisting of two access points namely AP-1 and AP-2 working on different protocols, when the clients boot up, it sees the signal from AP-1 stronger than AP-2 and gets connected. But in another case, the AP-1 offers 54 Mbps of data rate at −35 dBm and AP-2 offers 64 Mbps at −45 dBm. In this case the client has to make a decision whether it should connect to the access point which offers higher data rate or connect to a slower network with stronger signal. In both of these cases, the clients have to spend more power since the slower network would transmit the data with lower data rate and it has to send more number of frames to transfer particular data, which would consume more power. On the other hand, if the clients connect to the other access point, which offer higher data rate but with lower signal strength, it again has to spend more power, in such case the decision has to be made by the clients' algorithm whether to spend more power to connect the weak but fast network or strong but slow network.

This paper intends to study the problem stated above and to check the behaviour of TCP and UDP protocols in terms of their theoretical data rate, practical data rate and efficiency while connecting to a particular heterogeneous wireless network. Thus, our contribution is to build a test bed and set of tests to determine the capability of each protocol (IEEE 802.11a/n/ac) and their efficiency in a heterogeneous environment with off-the-shelf equipment and indoor heterogeneous environment. The results obtained by the tests performed will be useful in understanding protocols in wireless networks.

3 Design of Experiment

The test-bed is described in Fig. 1, followed by the details of equipment used for test-bed. In order to investigate the performance in terms of data throughput of wired and wireless hosts against the advertised data rates by implementing test cases provided in Table 1.

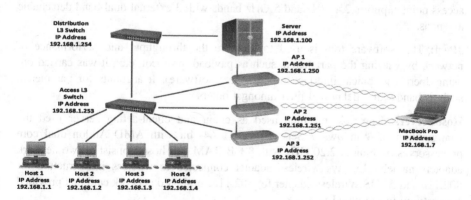

Fig. 1. Network diagram for experiment

Distribution Layer Switch: The distribution switch (Cisco 3560) consists of 12 fibre gigabit Ethernet and 2 copper gigabit ports. The IP traffic generator used on a server which acts as a host connected to the gigabit port on distribution switch. Fibre optic port are providing the downlink connection from the distribution switch to access the layer switch. Both 802.11n and 802.11ac supports the data rates up to 600 Mbps and 867 Mbps.

Table 1. Test cases used for experiment.

Test	Test cases
1	Wired
2	802.11a 5 GHz 20 MHz
3	802.11n 5 GHz 20 MHz, 1 Stream and SGI=ON
4	802.11n 5 GHz 20 MHz, 2 Stream and SGI=ON
5	802.11n 5 GHz 40 MHz, 1 Stream and SGI=ON
6	802.11n 5 GHz 40 MHz, 2 Stream and SGI=ON
7	802.11ac 5 GHz 20 MHz, 3 Stream and SGI=ON
8	802.11ac 5 GHz 40 MHz, 3 Stream and SGI=ON
9	802.11ac 5 GHz 80 MHz, 3 Stream and SGI=ON

Access Layer Switch: Cisco 3560 switch used as an access layer switch consists of 12 copper gigabit Ethernet ports. This switch is used to terminate all access points and host connections.

Access Point 1: The AIR-AP-1242AG-E-K9 access point was used to test 802.11a. It supports the 802.11a/b/g/n. In this experiment to measure the throughput for 802.11a, the other data rates 802.11b/g/n were disabled to make sure that the client should stay connected to the 802.11a.

Access Point 2: The AIR-AP126N-E-K9 access point was used to test 802.11n. This access point supports 2.4 GHz and 5 GHz bands.

Access Point 3: The Asus RT-AC66U access point was used to test 802.11ac. This access point supports 2.4 GHz and 5 GHz bands with 3 external dual-band detachable antennas.

JPerf: This software tool is used to measure the throughput and performance of network by varying the parameters such as payload, protocol, etc., it was carried out using Jperf's graphical interface (open source software). It accounts for parameters such as bandwidth, delay and jitter amongst others.

Host/Servers: The host machine used as client and client-acting server used the configuration of Windows 7 Service Pack 1 64- bit with AMD Athlon dual core processors is running at 2.20 GHz with 8 GB RAM. All hosts consist of two network adapters namely, Linksys wireless adapter connected to wireless infrastructure for 802.11n and ASUS Wireless adapter for 802.11ac on-board network card that provided connectivity to the wired network.

USB Wireless Adaptor: The external USB wireless adapters used for wireless connectivity are Cisco-Linksys WUSB600N and ASUS dual band USB-AC56.

Mac Book: A Mac Book Pro with 2.5 GHz Intel i5 processor with 4 GB of RAM used for the range test.

Wi-Fi Scanner: It is a convenient tool for gathering information like signal strength, noise, SNR and data rates.

4 Results

The throughput test is designed to test the throughput of all the protocols (IEEE 802.11a/n/ac) as mentioned in the earlier section. This results in a large number of outcomes but only the necessary number of outcomes are considered in this paper. The omitted outcomes are mainly with the protocols tested with the setting Short-Guard Interval (SGI=OFF), because this setting in the access points only affect the throughput results by 10%.

4.1 Averages

All the outcomes obtained from the experiment are summarised in Table 2. The wired test also called Ethernet, which shows the maximum throughput with the increased number of hosts and found much higher value than any wireless protocols tested in this experiment. The TCP is found to perform better than UDP on wired network while UDP outruns TCP on wireless network. The reason behind this is TCP negotiate the connection between source and destination and it adjusts the contention window or buffer size according to the capacity of the media, while UDP does not have any such property and sends the data across the link without knowing the capacity of the media which connects the source and destination [13, 14].

Table 2. Comparison of average against number of hosts for TCP and UDP.

Protocol/Host	TCP				UDP			
	1 Host	2 Host	3 Host	4 Host	1 Host	2 Host	3 Host	4 Host
Wired	687.8	850.8	855	837	131.5	244.5	421.9	532.1
a 5G 20M 1 Stream ON	23.25	20.7	19.59	18.17	25.83	26.33	26.61	22.81
n 5G 20M 1 Stream ON	44.23	50.05	52.64	44.00	59.22	61.33	61.39	60.73
n 5G 20M 2 Stream ON	67.75	75.14	90.96	91.79	113.9	114.5	114.8	113.6
n 5G 40M 1 Stream ON	74.46	91.44	94.09	94.41	116.5	117.5	117.5	117.19
n 5G 40M 2 Stream ON	114.7	122.8	134.9	144.2	180.6	196.7	192.8	188.5
ac 5G 20M 3 Stream ON	76.15	93.45	104.2	96.27	108.2	111.9	114.6	108.08
ac 5G 40M 3 Stream ON	106.8	145.5	160.8	170.1	125.5	201.5	209.1	215.5
ac 5G 80M 3 Stream ON	110.4	175.2	189.3	217.3	117.6	199.2	215.9	223.5

In the case of 802.11a the performance decreases as the number of host increases. The main reason behind this is a collision, as every host looks for a free channel to transmit. If the channel is free for the DIFS interval it can transmit, otherwise the transmission is interrupted by a random back off timer. The method of identifying the collision and to avoid it, causes the drop in the throughput of 802.11a with a number of host increases. The maximum throughput recorded by 802.11a on TCP is 23.25 Mbps and on UDP is 26.61 Mbps but as the number of hosts increasing the throughput drop can be seen in the Table 2. This affects the performance of the network. While designing the network the number of hosts connected to a given access point must be considered.

The 5 GHz spectrum has very little interference during the test which helps 802.11n to achieve the higher throughput in 5 GHz frequency spectrum. The 802.11n is tested with 20 MHz and 40 MHz channel bandwidth with 1 and 2 streams. The maximum throughput achieved on 802.11n 20 MHz single stream is 52.64 Mbps, while with multiple stream it is 91.79 Mbps. This denotes that the multiple stream performs better and gives the maximum throughput. On the other hand, the throughput achieved on 802.11n 40 MHz channel bandwidth is almost double the throughput of 802.11n with 20 MHz channel bandwidth; the maximum throughput achieved on 802.11n 40 MHz single stream and multiple stream is 94.41 Mbps and 144.2 Mbps respectively. The same results are observed with 802.11n 5 GHz frequency with 20/40 MHz channel bandwidth using UDP. It can be safely concluded that the channel bonding feature in 802.11n increases the performance.

The recent amendment of IEEE is 802.11ac and it works on 5 GHz frequency with 20/40/80 MHz channel bandwidths. The access point used for this test supports 866 Mbps data rate with three spatial streams and due to limited number of external network adapter (i.e., 4) test results are constrained. The 802.11ac test on a 20 MHz channel bandwidth shows the throughput drop after 4 hosts transmitting simultaneously. However, with the channel bonding (i.e., 40 MHz and 80 MHz) the throughput increases as the new hosts are connected and this nature is observed on both TCP and UDP. The maximum throughput achieved with 4 hosts transmitting simultaneously using 80 MHz channel bandwidth on TCP is 217.38 Mbps and on UDP is 223.54 Mbps. It can also be seen that with 40 MHz channel bandwidth the 802.11ac with 4 hosts transmitting simultaneously generate the throughput of 170.1 Mbps on TCP, while 802.11ac with 80 MHz bandwidth with 4 hosts transmitting simultaneously and generate the throughput of 217.38 Mbps. The Figs. (2, 3, 4 and 5) below shows the graphical representation of the results with various test case scenarios.

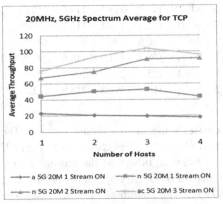

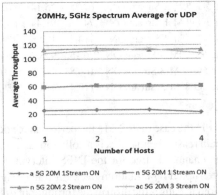

Fig. 2. 5 GHz, 20 MHz, Average for TCP   **Fig. 3.** 5 GHz, 20 MHz, Average for UDP

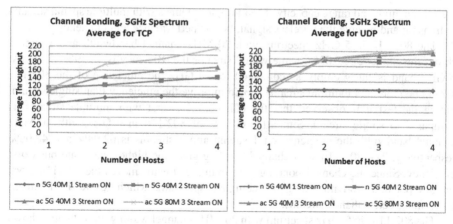

Fig. 4. 5 GHz, Channel Bonding for TCP   **Fig. 5.** 5 GHz, Channel Bonding for UDP

4.2 Efficiency of Protocols

This section analyses the results from the previous sections and the efficiency of protocols are tested. Every protocol offers different data rates, hence to compare all the protocols data rate, throughput and efficiency on the same scale, we calculate Efficiency (E) as follows:

$$E = \left(\frac{Average\ throughput\ obtained\ from\ 10\ runs}{Maximum\ data\ rate\ offered\ by\ that\ protocol} \right) \times 100 \qquad (1)$$

4.2.1 TCP and UDP Efficiency

The graph below shows that the efficiency of TCP on the protocols tested. The highest efficiency achieved by wired network is about 85%. The efficiency is tested by simultaneously transmitting 3 streams of data from the host to the server. We found that after connecting 3 hosts this efficiency and throughput drops. In a wired network, the throughput and efficiency increases as new hosts are added till a certain limit. When comparing the wired network with the wireless network the efficiency drops are seen in wireless network as new hosts are connected. In case of 802.11a, the first host connecting gives the highest throughput but as soon as new hosts are added, the throughput drops. The wired network is full duplex and the wireless network is half-duplex. However, the wireless network also has to handle collision detection; hence, the efficiency of the wireless network decreases as new hosts are connected. 802.11a with one host shows the efficiency of 43.055% and as the number of hosts increases, it drops to 33.648% at 4 hosts. But in case of 802.11n and 802.11ac, the throughput increases as new hosts are added till certain limit. Thus, it is safely concluded that the 802.11n and 802.11ac are better than 802.11a. The 802.11n and 802.11ac behaves like wired network in terms of throughput and efficiency because it has a feature called MIMO and MU-MIMO respectively. This new feature introduced in wireless network protocols has improved their throughput and range capacity. The multiple antennas with multiple spatial streams to transmit and receive the wireless signal, boosts performance and efficiency.

The 802.11n in 5 GHz spectrum with 20 MHz channel bandwidth and 1 stream shows the efficiency 35.09%, while with 2 streams the efficiency is 30.59%. Since the 5 GHz band is fairly empty as compared to 2.4 GHz the efficiency of the 802.11n should be more and multiple streams should improve the efficiency than single stream, but in the test it is observed that the efficiency is worst with multiple streams as compared to single stream. Similarly, in case of 802.11n in 5 GHz with 40 MHz channel bandwidth the efficiency on 1 stream and 2 streams is 62.94% and 48.06% respectively. The 802.11n with channel bonding gives the highest data rate but worst efficiency. Since the channel bonding with multiple streams makes the 802.11n work on full potential and not using the complete spectrum, which results in 1 stream performing better than 2 streams.

The 802.11ac in 5 GHz spectrum with 20 MHz channel width with 3 streams shows the efficiency 12.03%, while other variants 40 MHz and 80 MHz show 19.64% and 25.10% efficiency respectively. Due to the limited resources in terms of equipment, further tests are not being performed. The 802.11ac with all variants shows the similar characteristics; as new hosts are added the throughput and efficiency increases. In the case of 802.11ac with 20 MHz, the 1 host efficiency is 8.79% and increasing linearly till the 3 hosts delivering 12.03%. The data rates achieved by the 802.11ac and all their variants are better than 802.11n but in terms of efficiency the 802.11ac fails to keep up with 802.11n protocol. The Fig. 6 shows the graphical representation of TCP protocol efficiency.

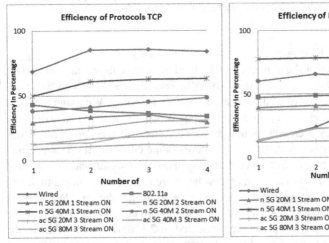

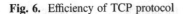

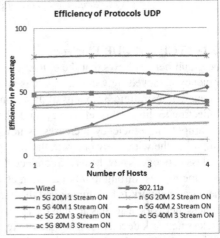

Fig. 6. Efficiency of TCP protocol   **Fig. 7.** Efficiency of UDP protocol

The Fig. 7 above shows the graphical representation of UDP protocol efficiency. The UDP efficiency of the 802.11a is 49.27%. The throughput and efficiency increases till a certain host, then it drops down. With UDP all wireless protocols and their variations show better efficiency than TCP. The reason behind this is that UDP operates without overhead for setting up the connection and acknowledgement and UDP is a best effort delivery protocol, which makes it faster than TCP. The all variants of 802.11n shows similar behavior as TCP, increasing throughput till certain point and then decreases with a constant rate. The wired network on a UDP performs poorer than TCP and the peak value of UDP is not even close to the value with one host on the TCP; for a wired network on a UDP efficiency of 1 host is 13.11%, while the maximum efficiency noted is 53.2%.

The 802.11n in 5 GHz spectrum with 20 MHz channel width with 1 stream, shows the maximum efficiency of 40.48% and with 2 streams it shows 37.96%. It can be seen here that 1 stream performs better than 2 streams. The same phenomenon is observed with 802.11n with channel bonding the maximum efficiency with 1 stream is 78.38%, while with 2 streams it is 65.52%. The main cause of that the 802.11n gives best throughput with channel bonding and multiple spatial streams but not utilizing the spectrum completely.

The 802.11ac in 5 GHz spectrum with 20 MHz channel bandwidth with 3 streams shows the maximum efficiency of 13.24%, while the other variants 40 MHz and 80 MHz shows 24.88% and 25.81% respectively. The efficiency increases as the number of hosts increases till a certain limit but it drops after that. The 802.11ac with 20 MHz channel starts with 1 host at 12.50% and reaches peak value at 13.24% at host 3. In case of 802.11ac with channel bonding, the throughput and efficiency increases till the last host. The 802.11ac and all variants give maximum throughput but they show less efficiency than any variant of the 802.11n.

UDP outruns TCP in terms of throughput and efficiency but it is not as reliable as TCP. The single stream performs better than the multiple streams but multiple streams give a better throughput. The 802.11n with channel bonding has a better efficiency than all the variants of the 802.11ac.

5   Conclusion

This paper included test scenarios which are designed for the 802.11ac to compare throughput performance and their efficiency with the legacy protocols (802.11a/n) in 2.4 and 5 GHz frequency spectrum. The throughput test outcomes show that the theoretical throughputs are never achieved during this experiment. On the platform of TCP and UDP the advertised throughputs of protocols are never reached; TCP shows 50% and UDP shows 65% of the actual advertised data rate of the protocol. The short guard interval (i.e.400 ns), boosts the data rate by 8–12%. It can be clearly concluded that wired network are still better than the wireless network in terms of data rate and efficiency. The increment in the throughput of the 802.11n and the 802.11ac with new features like, short guard interval, channel bonding, MIMO and MU-MIMO helps the wireless networks to achieve data rate and throughput close to the wired networks. The validation of this paper could serve as proof of content, of newer approaches or tests that could be designed to prove either one to be better.

References

1. Yang, X., Rosdahl, J.: Throughput and delay limits of IEEE 802.11. IEEE Commun. Lett. **6**(8), 355–357 (2002)
2. Abdullah, A.N.M., Moinudeen, H., Al-Khateeb, W.: Scalability and performance analysis of IEEE 802.11a. In: Canadian Conference on Electrical and Computer Engineering, pp. 1626–1629 (2005)
3. Zhuo, C., Hajime, S.: Performance of 802.11n WLAN with transmit antenna selection in measured indoor channels. In: 2008 Australian Communications Theory Workshop, pp. 139–143 (2008)
4. Kaewkiriya, T.: Performance comparison of Wi-Fi IEEE 802.11ac and Wi-Fi IEEE 802.11n. In: 2017 2nd International Conference on Communication Systems, Computing and IT Applications (CSCITA), pp. 235–240 (2017)
5. Zeng, Y., Pathak, P.H., Mohapatra, P.: A first look at 802.11ac in action: energy efficiency and interference characterization. In: 2014 IFIP Networking Conference, pp. 1–9 (2014)
6. Narayan, S., Jayawardena, C., Wang, J., Ma, W.: Performance test of IEEE 802.11ac wireless devices. In: 2015 International Conference on Computer Communication and Informatics (ICCCI), pp. 1–6 (2015)
7. García-Pineda, M., Felici-Castell, S., Segura-García, J.: Do current domestic gigabit wireless technologies fulfill user requirements for ultra high definition videos? In: 2017 13th International Wireless Communications and Mobile Computing Conference (IWCMC), pp. 8–13 (2017)
8. Cheng, R.S.: Performance evaluation of stream control transport protocol over IEEE 802.11ac networks. In: 2015 IEEE Wireless Communications and Networking Conference Workshops (WCNCW), pp. 97–102 (2015)
9. Chang, C.Y., Yen, H.C., Lin, C.C., Deng, D.J.: QoS/QoE Support for H.264/AVC video stream in IEEE 802.11ac WLANs. IEEE Syst. J. **11**(4), 2546–2555 (2017)
10. Szulakiewicz, P., Kotrys, R., Krasicki, M., Remlein, P., Stelter, A.: OFDM interfering signal rejection from 802.11ac channel. In: IEEE 23rd International Symposium on Personal, Indoor and Mobile Radio Communications - (PIMRC), pp. 2015–2018 (2012)
11. Gaber, A., Omar, A.: A study of TDOA estimation using matrix pencil algorithms and IEEE 802.11ac (2012)
12. Perahia, E., Stacey, R.: Next Generation Wireless LANs 802.11n and 802.11ac, 2nd edn. Cambridge University Press, Cambridge (2013)
13. Comer, D.: Internetworking with TCP/IP, 5th edn. Pearson Prentice Hall, New Jersey (2006)
14. Comer, D.: Computer Networks and Internets, 5th edn. Pearson Education Inc, New Jersey (2008)

A Load-Aware Matching Game for Node Association in Wireless Ad-Hoc Networks

Upasana Dohare[✉] and D. K. Lobiyal

School of Computer and Systems Sciences, Jawaharlal Nehru University, New Delhi, India
upasanadohare@yahoo.com, dkl@mail.jnu.ac.in

Abstract. In this paper, a load aware matching game to achieve stable one-to-one matching of senders and receivers is proposed, when distance between sender and receiver, and busyness level of receivers are taken into account. We have formulated matching game for the network formation where the nodes are capable of load sharing, selfish behaviour of node that maximize their individual utility and agreeing to cooperate in pair. Sender keeps changing one hop receiver that assist in load balancing of the network. Busyness level of receiver is introduced into matching game to initiate competition between the proposing senders. Distance is introduced to instigate competition between the receivers. The proposed matching game theoretic models compared with the state of art load balancing model for ad hoc networks in the terms of lifetime of the network and standard deviation of the load. Simulation results have shown that the proposed LAMG performs better as compared with GLBR in the terms of network lifetime and standard deviation of the load.

Keywords: Ad hoc networks · Game theory · Matching game · Load balancing
Lifetime

1 Introduction

Ad hoc networks knows as wireless multi-hop networks formed by a set of mobile nodes in self-organizing manner without need of pre-established infrastructure, in which some pair of nodes may not be able to communicate directly with each other, and have to use multi-hop transmission to forward the packets for each other. In ad-hoc network, nodes can move anywhere any time and can formed arbitrary topology. In common crisis, whole the network belongs to the same authority where nodes forwards the packets unconditionally for each other to complete their common goals. The ad-hoc networks are also deployed in civilian applications where nodes belongs to different authority and may not intent to achieve common goal. The self-organizing ad-hoc networks would be control solely by the operation of end users [1]. The energy efficiency of the network can be increased by allowing packets to be delivered over several short links rather than one long link [2]. The speedup of connection setup, energy efficient, load balancing, and the ease of removal of services are the design objectives of the networks.

Previous works have evaluated the performance of ad hoc Networks analytically without forming a strong theoretical framework. The interaction among nodes in the

G. C. Deka et al. (Eds.): ICACCT 2018, CCIS 899, pp. 247–259, 2018.
https://doi.org/10.1007/978-981-13-2035-4_22

network may be modelled using game theory. Pair wise cooperation in forwarding of the packets in wireless networks has generally considered selfless behavior for all nodes in the network that will improve a network wide utility [3]. However, it is interesting to study how to autonomous selfish nodes are functioning for their own self-interest to maximize their individual utilities than work together to improve network wide utility. The nodes of the network are agreeing for cooperation only if they are instructed to improve the utilities of both parties [4]. Matching game theory is an appropriate tool to study such situations where individual nodes with differing interests that may be agreeing to cooperate in pair for mutual profit [5]. Matching the equal number of men and women from a group men having different preferences for women in another group of women has been modelled by matching game for stable and optimal pairs in [5].

In this paper, we differ in process of formation of network from these aforementioned previous works, which assume optimum load balancing in a given static network topologies. In particular we consider the network formation where the nodes are (i) capable of load sharing, (ii) selfish behavior of node that maximize their individual utility and (iii) agreeing to cooperate in pair. The basis of matching game [5] has been used for one-to-one matching. A load aware matching game (LAMG) to achieve stable one-to-one matching of senders and receivers is proposed, when distance between sender and receiver, and busyness level of receivers are taken into account. Sender keeps changing one hop receiver that assist in load balancing of the network. Busyness level of receiver is introduced into matching game to initiate competition between the proposing senders. Distance is introduced to instigate competition between the receivers. The proposed matching game theoretic models compared with the state of art load balancing model for ad hoc networks in the terms lifetime of the network and standard deviation of load.

The rest of the paper is organized as follows. In Sect. 2, work related to the proposed work is presented. We explained the problem description is Sect. 3. In Sect. 4, we proposed the solution using matching game for node associations, stability analysis of the game and an incentive method. In Sect. 5, some analytical result and simulation results have been presented. In Sect. 6, we conclude the paper.

2   Related Work

Matching games have recently been applied to study the performance of wireless networks in [6–10]. Authors in [6] studies one-to-one and one-to-many matchings for transmitters and receivers according to the rates in ad hoc networks and observed that rates of whole networks are improved with additional nodes along with possibility of energy transfer considering the selfish behavior of the nodes. Author in [7] haves analyzed the problem of resources allocation with one-to-one and many-to-one matchings and concluded that stable matchings for throughput maximization are not always feasible. They have also shown that if nodes preference and resources are strict, then there is uniqueness in the stable matching. A stable matching between primary and secondary users in cognitive radio network for spectrum allocation has been identified in [8], a distributed algorithm has been proposed to solve the matching problem, and that enables both the users to self-organize into a stable and optimal matching. In [9], cooperative spectrum sharing in the cognitive radio network between primary and secondary users using matching theory is presented. The transmission rate and power consumption have optimized for the primary and secondary users as their utilities. Authors in [10] investigate a matching game for caching problem of video downloading between small base station and service provider's servers in a small cell network and provides a pairwise stable matching.

Load balancing has been proposed as way of reducing delay, jitter, and energy consumption in ad hoc network by means of manageable load in the network and non-distortable nodes [12–14]. A cooperative load balancing approach for ad hoc networks has presented in [12], in which nodes ranks their channel access providers based on the availability of the resources, and select the best one to improve performance of the network in terms of throughput, energy consumption and delay. In [13], a game theoretic load balancing routing (GLBR) with cooperative stimulation has been presented to minimize the average end-to-end delay and packet loss. To balancing the traffic over the networks, utility function in the term of delay is used. Authors in [14] also considers minimization of delay and jitter by balancing the load in ad hoc network using quantum inspired game theory.

3 Problem Description

Consider an ad hoc network with a set of sender nodes S and a set of receiver nodes R. All the nodes having same transmitting range at a time constraint t. Each sender can transmit to any receiver. We consider current load at each node, whether it is a sender or a receiver, arises at price and outcomes in an increase in the node's utility. We define normalized load ϕ_{sr} of a node as the ratio of current data rate p_{r_t} at time t to the bandwidth b_r assigned for transmission, and it is given by

$$\phi_{sr} = \frac{p_{r_t}}{b_r} \tag{1}$$

Different values of ϕ_{sr} are taken at different time intervals and the values vary between 0 and 1. A node has maximum possible load when $\phi_{sr} = 1$. It is desirable to associate a sender node with a less busy or free receiving node. the packets of each active node forwarded by their neighbour. For load balancing among the nodes, each active sender node is served by a neighboring node, which offers the fastest service. In other words, by carefully examine individual neighbour nodes, we can identify the node where additional load can be forwarded, and where it cannot be. The load balancing problem in ad hoc networks is defined as an optimization problem in which source nodes are assigned to forwarding nodes ($\mu : S \rightarrow R$), which will maximize the overall sum of utility of the networks.

$$\text{Maximize} \quad \sum_{s \in S} \sum_{r \in R} \phi_{sr} \tag{2}$$

$$\text{Subject to} \, \forall_s, r : \phi_{sr} \leq 1 \tag{3}$$

Since the nature of the combinatorial assignment problem mentioned in (2) and (3) is non-linear. Therefore, we propose a new approach to solve the problem using matching in the next section.

4 Proposed Solution: Node Association as a Matching Game

In a matching game, two sets of players evaluates each other using well-defined preference relation [15]. We formulate our load balancing problem in ad hoc networks as one to one matching game in which we map a set of senders S to a set of receivers R, and each sender will be associated at most one receivers. We assume that multihop packet forwarding is used to send data packets to a destination node. A node have maximum load limit b_r bits per second. Depending on the load at receiving node, each sender node $s \in S$ builds a preference relation $>_s$ over their receiving nodes $r \in R$ and not being matched $\emptyset$. In general, set S is able to form $S \times R$ matrix in which each elements ϕ_{sr} of the matrix will be the busyness level (load) of r measured by s. Moreover each neighbour node r of a sender node has a preference $>_r$ over the subset of S that propose to their most preferred neighbour node s but sender might accept or reject the request for forwarding their data. Nodes of set R prefer s if it is destination for them or the geometrically nearest node s. Based on these assumptions, we define a matching μ between sender and receiver nodes.

Definition 1. A function μ is defined from $S \times R$ to $S \times R$ known as a matching if:

$|\mu(s)| = 1$ for each elements of S and $\mu(s) \in R \bigcup \emptyset$

$|\mu(r)| \leq b_r$ for all r and $\mu(r) \subseteq S \bigcup \emptyset$, and

$s \in \mu(r)$ iff $\mu(s) = r$

Consequently the tuple $(R, S, >_r, >_s, Q)$, defines the node association load balancing matching problem using $>_R = \{>_r\}_{r \in R}$ as a preference set of the R and, $>_S = \{>_s\}_{s \in S}$ as a preference set of the $S \cdot Q$ is a set of quota on the nodes of set R and defined as $Q = \{b_r | \forall r \in R\}$ [11].

4.1 Context-Based Preferences

To describe two side matching μ, we defines the preferences of sender and receiver in the next section.

a. *User's Preferences*

Each node s wishes to forward data packets to maximize its own individual utility. In our assumption, sender nodes ranks the forwarding nodes based on normalized load, therefore, we uses the normalized load ϕ_{sr} as utility function. Let z is the number of elements in R. The $1 \times z$ utility vector of sender node s can be determined. Each member of S ranks the member of R and make a preference list by using g as a load function, and it is defined by

$$L = g(\phi_{sr_z}) = \frac{1}{z}\sum_{r=1}^{z}\phi_{sr_z} = \frac{1}{z}\sum_{r=1}^{z}\frac{P_{z_t}}{b_z} \tag{4}$$

Where L is the average possible load over z nodes, which are directly connected with s. A neighbour node will be acceptable for a sender node if $r \succ_s \emptyset$ if and only if $L < 1$. A neighbour node $u \succ_s v$ if and only if $L_u < L_v$ and $L_u, L_v < L$. Hence a preference matrix P_{SxR} can be originated whose s-th row will be the preference vector of user s and is represent by ρ_s.

b. *Preference of neighbour nodes*

   In neighbour node side game we define a scheme, which gives priority to sender nodes, based on urgency of information. Sender nodes sends their preference vector to each neighbour node and neighbour nodes wishes to associate with a sender node. Therefore each neighbour node form a 1×S vector, we call them chance vector $(Ch_{1 \times S})$ for their sender nodes coming in their transmission range. Whose elements are chosen from the given equation with respect to r,

$$D_s = d_s.T_{s-delay}$$
$$s = 1, 2 \ldots \ldots .S \tag{5}$$

where, D_s is mobility distance factor, d_s and $T_{s-delay}$ is distance and delay between the link r to s. If a link between two neighboring nodes exists then $d_s = 1$, otherwise it equal to 0, d_s equals 1 means node is accepting the proposal and 0 means the node is discarding the proposal.

   Next, we describe the receiver node side matching approach and clarifying assignment procedure. By using (1) the utility function for receiving nodes is defined as follows:

$$U_{sr}(\beta_s, \delta, \phi_{sr}) = \begin{cases} \psi_{sr}(\beta_s, \phi_{sr}) & if, \quad \delta = 0 \\ g(\phi_{sr}) & if, \quad \delta = 1 \end{cases} \tag{6}$$

where U_{sr} is known as the utility of the sender node s given by the receiving node r. As above defined utility is the function of priority coefficients β_s, likeness factor $\delta \in \{0, 1\}$, and ϕ_{sr}. Hence sender node $s_1 \succ_r s_2$ if and only if, utility of $s_1 (U_{s_1r}) >$ utility of $s_2 (U_{s_2r})$. Clearly, every sender node increases their utility, for that it communicates with an appropriate neighbour node. We take $\delta = 1$, when two or more sender nodes are on same priority otherwise, the neighbour node assigns $\delta = 0$ to the utility of those sender nodes. Now the function $\psi_{sr}(\beta_s, \phi_{sr})$ is defined as

$$\psi_{sr}(\beta_s, \phi_{sr}) = V_r(\beta_s, \phi_{sr}) + g(\phi_{sr}) \tag{7}$$

$$= \frac{1}{Z}\sum_{r=1}^{z}\left[\frac{\beta_s\eta_1}{\eta_2 + \beta_s\phi_{sr}} + \phi_{sr}\right] \tag{8}$$

In Eq. (7), function $V_r(\beta_s, \phi_{sr})$ represents the promotional amount to the sender node. Promotional amount is dependent on priority $\beta_s \cdot \eta_1$ and η_2 are the control parameters and used to decide the shape of utility function. Once the sender nodes proposal are sent to an arbitrary receiving node, the following three groups of priorities can be divided as follows.

1st priority: When a sender node and their neighbour node both have their first and only remaining preference. Then this type of sender nodes have been accepted by neighbor node in the first iteration.

2nd priority: In second type of priority we have taken those user nodes for whom neighbour node r is not on first choice but it is the only neighbour node remaining in the preference list.

3rd priority: Those user nodes will come in third priority which user node was rejected by a neighbour node but the user node still have other choices in their preference list.

Matching Algorithm:-

```
Inputs - R, S, Q, Aₛ

Initialize - first we will compute the preference
matrix P with the help of equation (4) and prepare a
provisional rejected vector as W.

While W is nonempty repeat given steps

Step 1:  if a user node s ∈ W then short their
preference vector ρₛ (sᵗʰ row of P_{S×R}) in descending
order and match with preference of next ordered
neighbour node.

Step 2: neighbour node ranks the sender nodes by
their utility, selects first Q(r) node from them, and
discards the rest.

Step 3:  let A_{cc} be an acceptance matrix, update A_{cc}
and W for ∀s ∈ W

If Ch(s) = 0 ,

Then remove s from W and put them in unmatched set if
user node list U.

Output:

Stable matching μ
```

4.2 Stability

In this section we derive some results in the form of theorems and prove them for ad hoc networks.

a. *Existence of stability*

Theorem 1. If sender nodes and neighbour nodes submit their preference lists then our given matching algorithm will produces a non-empty output, which will be stable also.

Proof. We know a matching is a set of ordered pair and there should be at least two nodes required to form a network. With these two nodes, our algorithm gives non-empty output (a matching pair of those nodes). For N number of nodes in networks, each neighbour node r match with q_r choice with its final updated preferences of sender nodes. Since any sender node s whom some neighbour node r initially ranked higher than one of its final assignment, higher in his ranking than r. Hence the final obligation gives s a position that the sender node ranked higher than the neighbour node r. So the final output will stable with respect to any such s and r.

Definitions: - S-Optimal and R-Optimal matching
A stable matching is called S-optimal if every user node like it at least as much every other stable matching.

A stable matching is called R-optimal if every neighbour node like it at least as much every other stable matching.

b. *Common and Conflicting behaviour of network's nodes*

Now we discuss another salient feature of two sided matching, which is common and conflicting behavior of players (nodes) of different sides. When we give our attention to the stable outcome, the conflicting feature will reversely behave. It is natural that there would be competition with one another in sender nodes for desirable neighbour nodes, while neighbour nodes compete with one another for desired sender nodes. However players (nodes) of opposite sides of the game have a common interest in matching with one another but players of the same side of the game interests in conflicting with some angle.

For the given preference vector ρ_s (s^{th} row of $P_{S \times R}$) and chance vector ($Ch_{1 \times S}$) a sender node s and a neighbour node r will be achievable for each other if r forwards s's data for some stable match.

Theorem 2. In the set O(sta) of stable matches, there is a S-optimal stable match s* with the property that every sender node assigned with its most preferred achievable neighbour node and a R-optimal stable match r*with the property that every neighbour node will assigned with less than or equal to q_r most preferred achievable sender nodes.

Proof. let for the first part of the theorem s* and s_1^* are two matches for sender nodes, where s* is most preferable output and s_1^* is lesser preferable match than s*. We have already discussed above that sender nodes compete for better neighbour node therefore, the S-optimal stable match occur with s* because it is better one and hence the result "there is a S-optimal stable match s* with the property that every sender node assigned with his most preferred achievable neighbour node" proved. Similarly we can prove the second part of the theorem.

As our algorithm progresses, results comes out with neighbour nodes dominating but output remains stable.

4.3 Incentive

Now we consider the incentive part of our game when we concentrate on networks mechanism. A node should assigns data packet to its neighbour node to forward or receive the data packet that node should give preferences over its neighbour node's potentials assignments. The acceptance of any such mechanism makes a new game among the nodes, which decides what preferences given to the nodes.

The algorithm proposed for matching process for the networks nodes offered some nodes an incentive to public an order different from their true preferences. In ad hoc networks this problem has occurred because of mobility of the networks nodes and frequent change of networks topology. There should be an incentive for the sender node that is not for providing its first choice neighbour node, but the algorithm gives an opportunity to solve this problem.

"For all players there is no such stable matching technique exists that makes it a dominant strategy to public their true preferences."

If there exist most of the players of the networks public their true preferences then the published preference and true preference coincide, and then there is no problem arises. It could be probable that because of incentives of distortion of preference information the state of collision occur. If distortion exists in the preferences, it means information needed about outer player's preferences to know how too gainfully and securely coincides one's true preference.

"If the networks nodes are highly rational and up-to-date then their submitted preference ordering will coincide with a Nash equilibrium."

It would finish the possibilities for further gainful manipulations. However, according to theorem first, our algorithm give stable results for any preference order and for true preference order both.

5   Results and Discussion

In this section, analytical result in the form of theorem considering the dynamic network topology is presented. We evaluated the performance of the proposed load aware matching game for ad hoc networks by conducting simulation. The simulation results have been compared with the similar type of work carried out in GLBR [13]. Comparison Table 1 presents a qualitative comparison of previously discussed GLBR and the proposed LAMG load balancing protocols using game theory for Ad-hoc networks in terms of game type, assumptions, mobility model, energy balancing, topology type and simulators. GLBR used game theory for cooperation stimulation where as the prosed

LAMG used matching game theory that is non-cooperative game theory for node association based on data rate/load and distance between the sender and receiver. The both the load balancing protocols considered energy consumption balancing, Random Waypoint mobility, and random topology.

Table 1. Comparison between GLBR and LAMG

Load balancing protocols	Game type	Assumptions			Mobility model	Energy balancing	Topology	Network simulator used
		Link capacity	Delay	Distance				
GLBR	Cooperative game	Yes	Yes	No	Random Waypoint	Yes	Random and dynamic	OPNET
LAMG	Non-cooperative game	Yes	Yes	Yes	Random Waypoint	Yes	Random and dynamic	Own simulation script written in MATLAB

5.1 Analytical Results

In ad hoc networks, nodes topology gets change frequently, therefore, some nodes comes to the closer to a node and some goes away. This effects nodes preferences.

Theorem 3. when the topology of the network is not strict or fixed then there may not exist two stable outcome.

Proof. consider a six nodes in the networks in which there are three $\left(S = s_1, s_2, s_3\right)$ sender nodes and three $R = \left(r_1, r_2, r_3\right)$ receiving nodes, each forwards a data packet at a time clock. Preferences are given as-

For neighbour/receiving nodes

$$r_1 = s_1 \succ_r s_2 \succ_r s_3$$
$$r_2 = s_1 \succ_s s_3 \succ_s s_2$$
$$r_3 = s_1 \succ_s s_2 \succ_s s_3$$

For sender nodes

$$s_1 = r_1 \succ_r r_2 \succ_r r_3$$
$$s_2 = r_1 \succ_r r_3 \succ_r r_2$$
$$s_3 = r_2 \succ_r r_3 \succ_r r_1$$

For the given preferences there are exactly two stable outputs are possible, let them name X and Y where

$$X = \begin{cases} X_s = \left((s_1, r_1), (s_2, r_3), (s_3, r_2) \right) \\ X_r = \left((r_1, s_1), (r_2, s_3), (r_3, s_2) \right) \end{cases}$$
$$Y = \begin{cases} Y_s = \left((s_1, r_2), (s_2, r_1), (s_3, r_3) \right) \\ Y_r = \left((r_1, s_2), (r_2, s_1), (r_3, s_3) \right) \end{cases}$$

Neighbour node r_1 does not have difference in between its obligation at X and at Y, while neighbour node r_2 and sender node s_2 prefer Y more than X, and neighbour node r_3 and sender node s_1 and s_3 prefer X more than Y. So each of stable output is preferable by the different set of sender nodes and neighbour nodes. Hence the theorem.

5.2   Simulation

a. *Simulation Environment*

In this section, a simulation has been carried out to evaluate the performance of the proposed load aware matching game for ad hoc networks. A square network area of 500 × 500 m^2 is considered. The number of nodes that are randomly deployed for the simulation is 20–100. The transmission range of nodes is taken to be 100 m. The data packets size of 512 bits is taken. The packets are generated using Poisson point process. The data rate of the traffic is 10 packets per seconds. The maximum bandwidth of 10 Kbps is taken. The Random Waypoint mobility has been used for movement of the nodes with 2 m/s. The energy model that has been used in [16] is employed in this simulation. The total energy e_t consumed for transmitting, and receiving, 1-bits of data is given by

$$\left. \begin{array}{l} e_t = e_{tx} + e_{rx} \\ e_{tx} = e_{el} + e_{am}d^n \\ e_{rx} = e_{el} \end{array} \right\}, \tag{9}$$

where e_{tx}, and e_{rx} denote the energy consumed by a node for transmitting, receiving 1-bit of data between two nodes separated by a distance d respectively. The energy consumed for electrical circuit is $e_{el} = 50$ (nJ/bit), and energy consumed per bit to run the transmitting amplifier is $e_{am} = 100$ $\left(pJ/\left(bit/m^2 \right) \right)$. The initial energy for simulation is taken from 5 mJ to 25 mJ. The path loss $n = 2$, and d = 200 m have been considered. The values of the priority coefficient β_s, the contorting parameters n_1 and n_2 of utility function are equal to 1. Links between two nodes are established if they belong in each other's transmission ranges. We have verified and endorsed the proposed matching algorithm by simulations using our programs implemented in MATLAB.

b. *Evaluation Metrics*

The following matrices have been used to evaluate the proposed LAMG comprehensively.

- *Network lifetime:* The lifetime is defined as time taken in the simulation until first node depleted its energy completely.

- **Standard deviation of load:** It is defined as standard deviation of load ϕ_{sr} where $\overline{\phi_{sr}}$ is the mean of normalize load of N nodes, is given by

$$SD = \sqrt{\frac{\sum_{i=1}^{N}\left(\phi_{sri} - \overline{\phi_{sr}}\right)}{N}} \qquad (10)$$

c. **Simulation Results**

Figure 1 shows the result obtained for the simulation with 100 nodes and with the different initial energy of the nodes. The lifetime versus the number of nodes has been shown for the proposed LAMG and state of the art technique GBLR. It is noticed that as the number of nodes increases from 20 to 100 nodes, the lifetime increases for LAMG, that is 10 to 40 for initial energy 5 mJ and 20 to 75 for initial energy 15 mJ. This is because there will be more number of sender/user are available and, found the best match of receiver nodes with preferable choices. It is also noticed that when the initial energy of the nodes increases from 5 mJ to 25 mJ, the lifetime of the network also enhanced for both the approaches but the lifetime for LAMG is better than GLBR. When the number of nodes and initial energy increase, the lifetime for LAMG is better than that of GLBR, this is because in LAMG the looks for best match that is less loaded receiving nodes and nearest sender nodes from the receiver. Less load node reduces the quick depletion of energy node the node and shorter sender node same the energy of receiver in transmission.

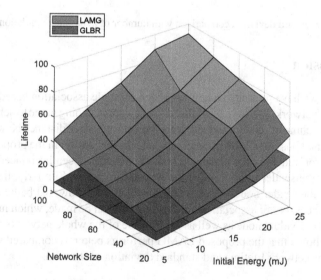

Fig. 1. Lifetime versus the number of nodes and initial energy

Figure 2 shows the results obtained in the simulation for standard deviation of load for different number of nodes. It is observed that as the nodes increases the standard deviation of load increases for both the game techniques. This is because there will be more number of node. The increase in standard deviation is more for GLBR. It is also observed that when the simulation time increases, the standard deviation for both the techniques decreases but the rate of decrement is more for LAMG. It is clear that the LAMG fairly balance the load among the nodes as compared to the GBLR. This is due the fact that LAMG selects the best receiver node based on the current load.

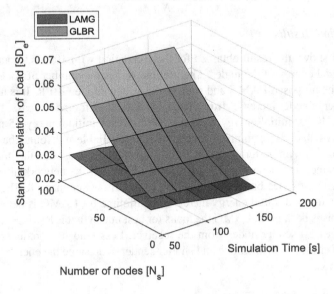

Fig. 2. Standard deviation comparison with number of nodes and simulation time

6   Conclusion

In this paper, we have presented a new approach for node association based on current load in ad hoc network. We have formulated load aware matching game to achieve stable one-to-one matching of senders and receivers is proposed, when distance between sender and receiver, and busyness level of receivers are taken as utility. In the proposed utility, the priorities for matching the players at both the sides has been introduced. Based on the priorities, the sender nodes ranked the forwarding nodes. Similarly, the receiving nodes ranked the sender nodes based on distances. It was show that being aware each others preferences, better association among the node can be made, which increases the lifetime of an individual node as well as the lifetime of the whole networks. Simulation results have shown that the proposed LAMG performs better as compared with GLBR in the terms of network lifetime and standard deviation of the load.

References

1. Aggelou, G.: Mobile Ad Hoc Networks: From Wireless LANs to 4G Networks. Tata McGraw-Hills, New York (2009)
2. Chlamtac, I., Conti, M., Liu, J.J.N.: Mobile ad hoc networking: imperatives and challenges. Ad Hoc Netw. 1(1), 13–64 (2003)
3. Srinivasan, V., Nuggehalli, P., Chiasserini, C.F., Rao, R.R.: Cooperation in Wireless Ad Hoc Networks. In: IEEE INFOCOM 2003, pp. 1–10 (2003)
4. Srivastava, V., et al.: Using game theory to analyze wireless ad hoc networks. IEEE Commun. Surv. Tutor. Fourth Q. 7(4), 46–56 (2005)
5. Gale, D., Shapley, L.S.: College admissions and the stability of marriage. Amer. Math. Monthly 69(1), 9–15 (1962)
6. Varan, B., Yener, A.: Matching games for ad hoc networks with wireless energy transfer. IEEE Trans. Green Commun. Netw. 1(4), 503–515 (2017)
7. Jorswieck, E.A.: Stable matchings for resource allocation in wireless networks. In: Proceedings of the 17th International Conference on Digital Signal Processing, pp. 1–8, July 2011
8. El-Bardan, R,. Saad, W., Brahma, S., Varshney, P.K.: Matching theory for cognitive spectrum allocation in wireless networks. In: Proceedings of the 50th Conference Information Science and Systems, Princeton, NJ, USA, pp. 466–471, March 2016
9. Namvar, N., Afghah, F.: Spectrum sharing in cooperative cognitive radio networks: a matching game framework. In: Proceedings of the 49th Annual Conference on Information Systems and Sciences, Baltimore, MD, USA, pp. 1–5, March 2015
10. Hamidouche, K., Saad, W., Debbah, M.: Many-to-many matching games for proactive social-caching in wireless small cell networks. In: Proceedings of the 12th International Symposium on Modelling and Optimization in Mobile, Ad Hoc, and Wireless Networks (WiOpt), pp. 569–574, May 2014
11. Semiari, O., Saad, W., Valentin, S., Bennis M., Maham, B.: Matching theory for priority-based cell association in the downlink of wireless small cell networks. In: 2014 IEEE International Conference on Acoustics, Speech and Signal Processing (ICASSP), Florence, pp. 444–448 (2014)
12. Karaoglu, B., Heinzelman, W.: Cooperative load balancing and dynamic channel allocation for cluster-based mobile ad hoc networks. IEEE Trans. Mob. Comput. 14(5), 951–963 (2015)
13. Tian, H., Jiang, F., Cheng, W.: A game theory based load-balancing routing with cooperation stimulation for wireless ad hoc networks. In: 2009 11th IEEE International Conference on High Performance Computing and Communications, Seoul, pp. 266–272 (2009)
14. Hasanpour, M., Shariat, S., Barnaghi, P., et al.: Quantum load balancing in ad hoc networks. Quantum Inf. Process. 16, 148 (2017)
15. El-Hajj, A.M., Dawy, Z., Saad, W.: A stable matching game for joint uplink/downlink resource allocation in OFDMA wireless networks. In: Proceedings of the IEEE International Conference on Communications (ICC), Ottawa, ON, June 2012
16. Hou, T.C., Li, V.O.: Transmission range control in multihop packet radio networks. IEEE Trans. Commun. 34(1), 38–44 (1986)

Optimizing and Enhancing the Lifetime of a Wireless Sensor Network Using Biogeography Based Optimization

Ajay Kaushik[1(✉)], S. Indu[2], and Daya Gupta[1]

[1] Department of Computer Engineering,
Delhi Technological University, Delhi, India
ajaykaushik777@gmail.com, dgupta@dce.ac.in
[2] Department of Electronics and Communication Engineering,
Delhi Technological University, Delhi, India
s.indu@dce.ac.in

Abstract. Wireless sensor networks (WSNs) contain tiny sensor nodes which are operated battery and have a limited lifetime. Improving the network lifetime of a WSN by optimal battery usage is an area investigated by many researchers in the past. In this work we propose a new nature-inspired technique Biography based optimization for energy efficient clustering (BBO-C) in a WSN. BBO-C takes into account novel parameters like minimization of Cluster Head (CH) energy dissipation and the transmission distance between both sensor nodes to CH and sink to CH which results in better distribution of sensors and a well-balanced clustering system, thus enhancing the network lifetime of a WSN. BBO-C is simulated using Matlab and provide very good results in terms of network lifetime, packets sent to the base station and load distribution. BBO-C outperforms past works like PSO based clustering, GLBCA, GA and LDC by 38.2%, 53.6%, 58.8% and 62.2% respectively.

Keywords: Gateways · Network lifetime · Energy efficient WSN
BBO · Clustering

1 Introduction

WSNs are extensively used in a wide variety of both indoor as well as outdoor applications. WSNs consist of many tiny sensor nodes in which each individual sensor node senses the useful information from its proximity and sends it to the base station. This individual sensing operation of sensor nodes was very inefficient as a large amount of node energy get dissipated in sensing and transmitting the information individually. WSN clustering was introduced as a solution to this problem [1]. In WSN clustering a group of sensor nodes forms a cluster with each cluster assigned a CH. In WSN clustering an individual sensor node senses the information and transmits the sensed information to its respective CH. The CH aggregates the information from all the sensor nodes and finally transmits the sensed information to the sink. A bottleneck with WSN clusters is that they are battery operated and have limited network lifetime.

© Springer Nature Singapore Pte Ltd. 2018
G. C. Deka et al. (Eds.): ICACCT 2018, CCIS 899, pp. 260–272, 2018.
https://doi.org/10.1007/978-981-13-2035-4_23

Since a WSN is connected therefore entire network structure may get disconnected on the death of a CH.

Since a CH have an additional load of receiving and transmitting the sensed data assigned to it, it is equipped with some extra energy to ensure its long-run operation. The extra energy equipped CH is termed as a gateway. Gateways are a crucial component in the structural hierarchy of a WSN but unfortunately, gateways are also battery operated. The entire cluster will die as soon as a gateway is dead. Since gateways have limited battery lifetime, its battery should be consumed in the most efficient manner. Achieving an energy efficient WSN and extending the lifetime of a gateway is an NP-hard problem.

In the past, energy conservation in WSN is considered to be an optimization problem and solved using nature-inspired techniques like genetic algorithm [2, 3], particle swarm optimization [4] etc. Work done by most researchers in the past focus on optimizing the transmission distance between a gateway and a sink to minimize the energy dissipation but no work in the past have considered the transmission distance between a sensor node and a gateway which is a very important factor in energy dissipation of a WSN. To the best of our knowledge this is the first work that focuses on 3 crucial factors in minimizing the energy dissipation (i) Minimize the transmission distance between a gateway and a sink (θ); (ii) minimize the transmission distance between a sensor node and a gateway (Φ); (iii) minimize the total energy dissipated by a gateway. The proposed algorithm minimizes the above 3 novel parameters using a new nature inspired algorithm BBO [5].

BBO has given good results in many applications like face reorganization [6], remote sensing [7], and travelling tournament problem [8] which encourage the use of BBO to optimize the WSN performance with novel parameters. The BBO-C improves the lifetime of a gateway. BBO-C is compared with PSO clustering [4], GA clustering [3], GLBCA [8], LDC [19]. Related work is presented in Sect. 2. The problem formulation and system model are explained in Sects. 3 and 4 respectively. The proposed BBO-C and the experimental results are presented in Sects. 5 and 6 respectively.

2 Related Work

A lot of work has been done in the past to improve the network lifetime of a WSN. Authors in [8] proposed a clustering algorithm in which a breadth-first tree is used to find the gateway which is least loaded and then sensor node is assigned to that gateway. One big problem with this algorithm is it took a large amount of memory space to store and process BFS. Also execution time while calculating BFS is large. It has a time complexity of the order O (mn 2). In [3], load balancing algorithm of WSN is presented which minimizes the standard deviation of load assigned to the CHs to obtain a load balanced WSN. Authors in [9] presented a fuzzy based clustering algorithm is which 3 fuzzy variables are chosen as node energy, concentration and centrality. This approach suffer a major drawback as it only chose one CH during the clustering process whereas transmission of data, data aggregation and forwarding requires multiple CHs in a WSN scenario. Another fuzzy based WSN routing approach was used in [10]. Authors minimize the energy dissipated in the network but did not consider cluster head to cluster head distance which is a very important parameter in a WSN routing an clustering. Ignoring CH to CH distance may lead to imbalanced CH distribution among the entire network.

Authors in [11] proposed a energy efficient dynamic clustering approach which minimizes the energy consumption in the network by considering only one parameter node's centrality. Authors in [11] did not consider crucial parameters like transmission distance, load of CH, uniform sensor deployment which are important contributing factors in WSN performance. Authors in [12] presented a Distance-Based Residual Energy-Efficient Stable Election Protocol (DRESEP) to achieve a energy efficient WSN. It was an improvement on LEACH algorithm. The basic issue with LEACH was that it chooses CHs on a random basis and a node with low residual energy could become a cluster head resulting in early death of the CH. Early CH death may lead to the disconnection of entire network. DRESEP addressed this problem and chose CH based on the nodes having the maximum residual energy. This approach proved to be successful as it considerably improved the network life but DRESEP does not say anything about the stability and load balancing of a WSN due to which the first CH in DRESEP dies very quickly. Authors in [13] proposed SEECP which was an improvement of DRESEP. In SEECP CHs were chosen in such a way that load is balanced along the nodes and SEECP was successful in obtaining a LOAD balanced and energy efficient WSN. Another routing algorithm is proposed in [8] where authors have presented an algorithm to minimize the communication distance between a CH to another CH using GA. Authors in [14] present a novel algorithm to minimize the distance between a CH and the sink using GA. In both [14, 15] only the transmission distance between CH and sink is emphasized upon. There is no mention of the communication distance between a sensor node to the CH. Authors in [16] used roulette wheel selection for energy efficient routing process. The roulette wheel selection is used to select a set of candidate solution and the fitness function is optimized using GA. In [4] a particle swarm optimization based clustering is proposed to enhance the lifetime of a wireless cluster. They consider network lifetime and CH to sink distance as their fitness function parameters and obtain an energy efficient network using PSO. Unfortunately works in [4] also did not consider sensor node to CH distance and the energy dissipated by the CH. The proposed algorithm uses BBO to minimize all 3 crucial WSN parameters namely sensor node to gateway distance, gateway to sink distance and gateway energy dissipation to achieve a stable and energy efficient network with prolonged lifetime.

3 Problem Formulation

Gateways in a WSN are battery operated and can work as long as the gateway battery is alive. In order to improve the network lifetime of a WSN, battery lifetime of the gateways need to be maximized. Past research works have proved that the battery life of a gateway varies inversely with the increase in sensor nodes in a WSN. A possible solution to this issue is to increase the gateway count in the network so that the increased number of gateways may be able to share the network load.

However, this approach also has a limitation since an increase in gateway count in a network will increase the total network energy dissipation as well (Eqs. 1 and 2). Some of the terminologies used in problem formulation are given in Tables 1 and 2.

$$L_{WSN} \; \alpha \; Life_{gat} \tag{1}$$

$$Life_{gat} \frac{1}{\alpha} Ener_{gat} \tag{2}$$

We have

$$\beta = \sqrt{(N_x - gat_x)^2 + (N_y - gat_y)^2} \, 1 < i,j < N \tag{3}$$

$$¥ = \sqrt{(gat_x - Sink_x)^2 + (gat_y - Sink_y)^2} \quad 1 < i,j < N \tag{4}$$

Let $D_{i,j}$ be a decision variable that assign S to G in a WSN

$$D_{i,j} = \begin{cases} 1 & \text{if sensor node } N_i \text{ is assigned to gateway } gat_j \; 1 < i < N, \; 1 < j < N, \\ 0 & \text{otherwise} \end{cases} \tag{5}$$

We can formulate the objective function as nonlinear programming.

$$\text{Maximize X} = \frac{Life_{WSN}}{\Phi} + \frac{Life_{WSN}}{\theta} \tag{6}$$

Subject to constraint

$$\sum_{j=1}^{N} \left(\sum_{i=1}^{N} D_{i,j} > 1 \right) = G, \quad 1 < i,j < N \tag{7}$$

Table 1. Terminologies used in the paper

Symbols	S	G	$Life_{WSN}$	E_R	$Ener_{gat}$
Description	Node count in a WSN	Gateway count in a WSN	Lifespan of a WSN	Gateway remaining energy	Gateway depleted energy

Table 2. Terminologies used in the paper

Symbols	(N_x, N_y)	(gat_x, gat_y)	$(Sink_x, Sink_y)$	$D_{i,j}$	$Life_{gat}$
Description	Node location	Gateway location	Sink location	Clustering decision variable	Gateway life

$$\sum_{j=1}^{N} D_{ij} = 1, \quad 1 < i,j < N \tag{8}$$

In BBO-C, the objective function (Eqs. 6–8) is maximized using BBO. BBO-C make sure that entire deployment region is covered with adequate sensor nodes and also maximizes the network lifetime.

4 System Model and the Terminologies Used

For the sake of fair comparison, we use the similar system model as used in [4]. We use multipath fading (mp) and free space (fs) channels for data transmission. The condition for the data transmission is given in Eqs. 9 and 10 respectively. Here E_{tr} is the energy consumed in transmission of an m-bit message and E_{el} is the energy dissipated in electronics in the model. K_{diss} is the dissipation constant. E_{amp} is the amplifier for transmission.

$$E_{tr} = E_{el} * K_{diss} + E_{amp} * K_{diss} * d^2 \ for \ d < d_0 \tag{9}$$

$$E_{tr} = E_{el} * K_{diss} + E_{amp} * K_{diss} * d^4 \ for \ d > d_0 \tag{10}$$

E_{rec} is the energy consumed in receiving a m bit packet which is given by Eq. 11

$$E_{rec} = E_{el} * K_{diss} \tag{11}$$

5 Proposed Algorithm

5.1 Overview of BBO

BBO is an evolutionary algorithm that takes inspiration from bio diversity of species and converges to the optimum solution [17]. In BBO an individual is represented by a habitat. A population may contain many habitats like chromosomes in genetic algorithms. For each habitat in the population, habitat suitability index (HSI) value is calculated. A habitat having high HSI value is considered to have higher fitness and more suitable for a population to grow and vice versa for habitat having low HSI value [16, 18]. Based on this HSI value rank of each individual is calculated. Migration operation is based on immigration rate (λ_i) and emigration rate (μ_i) as shown in Eqs. 12 and 13 respectively.

$$\lambda_i = I * \left(1 - \frac{k_i}{n}\right) \tag{12}$$

$$\mu_i = E * \left(\frac{k_i}{n}\right) \tag{13}$$

Here I and E are the maximum immigration rate and emigration rate of an individual. k_i is the rank of a habitat. n is the size of the population. A habitat having high HSI value will emigrate its suitability index variables (SIVs) to habitat having low HSI value and habitat having low HSI value will immigrate SIVs from habitat having high HSI value [19, 20]. Probabilistic mutation is performed based on Eq. 14.

$$m_i = m_{max}* \tag{14}$$

Here m_i is the mutation probability, m_{max} is the maximum m_i, p_i Is the prior probability of existence of a solution. The algorithm stops after achieving the optimum solution.

5.2   Implementation of BBO

To initialize the algorithm, all the sensor nodes and gateways are randomly distributed in the deployment area. The performance of a WSN is measured in terms of its network lifetime and CH energy dissipation. In the proposed algorithm we use BBO based energy efficient clustering to minimize the energy dissipation in the network and extend the operational lifetime of a WSN. Communication distances through which a sensor node or a CH sends data to the sink have a direct impact on the energy dissipated and network lifetime of a WSN. Lesser the communication distance less will be the energy dissipated by the CHs to transmit information to the sink. Therefore in the proposed clustering is done in such a way that clusters with optimum transmission distance are formed which minimize the communication distance and energy dissipated by CH in a WSN.

5.3   Calculation of HSI

For each habitat, we calculate HSI which defines the goodness of a solution. As explained earlier minimization of transmission distance and CH dissipated energy are two crucial WSN performance parameters. HSI is defined in such a way that each sensor node is assigned to its optimum CH and only those nodes are chosen as CH which dissipate minimum energy, ensuring the long run operation of the CHs. Precisely, HSI depends minimizing the sum of all θ,sum of all Φ and minimizing total energy dissipated by the gateways. *HSI* is calculated in Eq. 15.

$$¥ H_i, HSI = K * \left(¥ H_{i,} \sum \Phi\right) + \left(¥ H_{i,} \sum \theta\right) + \left(\sum_{i=1}^{H_i} Ener_{gat}\right) \tag{15}$$

5.4   Migration

By minimizing the fitness function given in Eq. 15 we achieve a network which is stable and has an improved network lifetime due to minimizing energy dissipation.

After calculation of the HSI each habitat is ranked in descending order of their HSI value. Based on the rank of each habitat vector their Immigration (λ) and emigration rates (μ) are calculated using Eqs. 12 and 13. The entire migration operation is performed using MPX crossover.

5.4.1   MPX Crossover

MPX crossover (Table 3) is used in migration step. In MPX crossover we generate a random vector of 0's and 1's. If an entry in the random vector is 1, choose an SIV/CH from immigrating habitat else choose a CH from emigrating habitat.

Table 3. MPX crossover to obtain a modified vector.

Random vector							
1	0	1	0	1	1	0	0

Gateway vector of immigrating habitat							
g2	g1	g4	g2	g3	g4	g1	g3

Gateway vector of modified habitat							
g2	g2	g4	g1	g3	g4	g4	g2

Gateway vector of emigrating habitat							
g1	g2	g3	g1	g4	g3	g4	g2

5.5   Mutation

Mutation operator is performed to randomly modify the solution coming from migration step. The solution is modified from a random gene position in a habitat. Mutation step is an important part of the algorithm framework as it maintains diversity in the population. The solution is mutated as per Eq. 14 [22].

The BBO clustering algorithm is run until the optimum solution is obtained or the maximum numbers of iterations are elapsed. The Pseudo code for the proposed algorithm is given below.

1. Initialize the population Size Pi. Initialize the max numbers of iteration I_{max}.
2. **while** $I < I_{max}$ **for each** iteration **do**
3.   **for each** Habitat H_i **do**
4.   Clone the sensor nodes and gateways to H_i.
5.   Compute the HSI of each habitat using equation 12 and 13.
6.   Perform immigration and emigration for all H_i using equation .
7.   Use Eq. 14 and to perform random mutation.
8.   Choose the habitat with best HSI/Fitness.
9.   **end**
10. **end**
11. Optimum clustering of sensor nodes is obtained after final iteration/convergence.

6 Results

Results are compared with PSO based clustering [4], GLBCA [8], GA [3] and LDC [19]. The simulation parameters used are shown in Table 4. For the evaluation of results, we consider two scenarios in which the base station is placed at coordinates (500, 250) and (250, 250) respectively.

Table 4. Simulation parameters.

Simulation criterion	Measurement
Deployment region	500 * 500
S	200 − 500
G	60 − 90
Location of sink	(500, 250) and (250, 250)
Transmission distance	150 m
Node energy	2 J
Gateway energy	10 J
Communication packet size	4000 bit

Scenario 1 – Sink at (500, 250)
The proposed algorithm is compared with the existing works in terms of network lifetime of sensor nodes as presented in Figs. 1 and 2 respectively. As visible from Figs. 1 and 2 respectively, network lifetime of sensor nodes is considerably increased in BBO-C. This is because BBO-C performs clustering in such a way that every sensor node is able to find its optimum location with respect to the gateway which results in a reduction of total network energy dissipation by minimizing θ and Φ. BBO-C performs better than the existing works for packets sent to the sink as shown in Fig. 3.

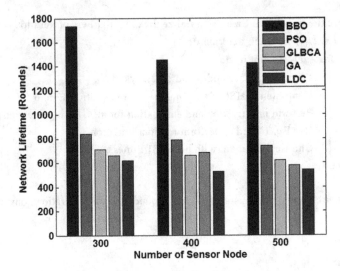

Fig. 1. Network lifetime comparison for 60 gateways

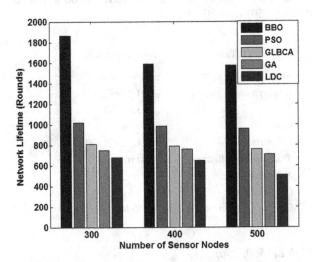

Fig. 2. Network lifetime comparison for 90 gateways.

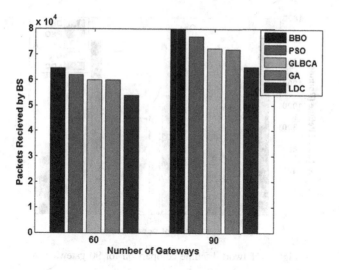

Fig. 3. Comparison of packets sent to sink.

Scenario 2 – Sink at (250, 250)

The proposed algorithm is compared with the existing works in terms of network lifetime and packets sent for new sink location. The comparison of the proposed algorithm with the existing works is shown in Figs. 4, 5 and 6 respectively.

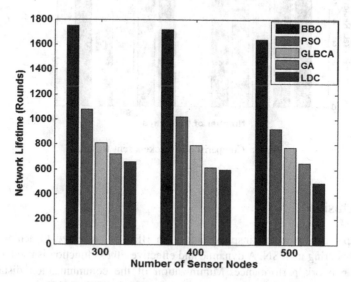

Fig. 4. Network lifetime comparison for 60 gateways.

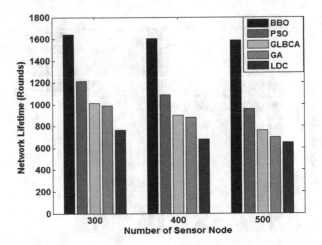

Fig. 5. Network lifetime comparison for 90 gateways

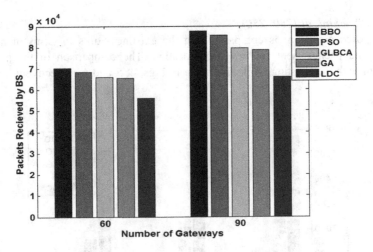

Fig. 6. Comparison of packets sent to sink.

7   Conclusion

In this paper a new nature inspired algorithm BBO is presented to achieve energy efficient clustering in WSN. A dynamic and effective fitness function is used to achieve enhanced network performance. Minimization of the communication distance and maximizing the residual energy improves the network lifetime. Maximizing the network lifetime by minimizing the energy dissipation and the communication distance is solved as an optimization problem using BBO. The cluster thus formed dissipates less energy and improves the network lifetime of a WSN. BBO based clustering outperform many past algorithms like PSO, GLBCA, GA and LDC by 38.2%, 53.6%, 58.8% and 62.2% respectively.

References

1. Zanjireh, M.M., et al.: A survey on centralized and distributed clustering routing algorithm for WSNs. In: IEEE (2015)
2. Kuila, P., et al.: A novel evolutionary approach for load balanced clustering problem for WSNs. Swarm Evol. Comput. **12**, 48–56 (2013)
3. Kaushik, A., et al.: Novel load balanced clustering approach in WSN using BBO. In: International Conference on Energy Engineering and Smart Materials, Lyon, France (2017)
4. Kuila, P., et al.: Energy efficient clustering and routing algorithms for WSNs: PSO approach. Eng. Appl. Artif. Intell. **33**, 127–140 (2014)
5. Simon, D.: Biogeography-based optimization. IEEE Trans. Evol. Comput. **12**(6), 5 (2008)
6. Gupta, D., et al.: An efficient biogeography based face recognition algorithm, pp. 64–67. CSE, Atlantis Press (2013)
7. Goel, L., et al.: Biogeography and geo-sciences based land cover feature extraction: a remote sensing perspective. Appl. Soft Comput. **13**, 4194–4208 (2013)
8. Low, C.P., et al.: Efficient load-balanced clustering algorithms for WSNs. Comput. Commun. **31**, 750–759 (2008)
9. Gupta, I., et al.: Cluster-head election using fuzzy logic for wireless sensor networks. In: 2005 Proceedings of the 3rd Annual Communication Networks and Services Research Conference. IEEE (2005)
10. Tamandani, Y.K., Bokhari, M.: SEPFL routing protocol based on fuzzy logic control to extend the lifetime and throughput of the wireless sensor network. Wirel. Netw. **22**(2), 647–653 (2016)
11. AbdulAlim, M.A., et al.: A fuzzy based clustering protocol for energy-efficient wireless sensor networks. Adv. Mater. Res. **760–762**, 685–690 (2013)
12. Mittal, N., Singh, U.: Distance-based residual energy efficient stable election protocol for WSNs. Arab. J. Sci. Eng. **40**, 1637–1646 (2015)
13. Mittal, N., et al.: A stable energy efficient clustering protocol for wireless sensor networks. Wirel. Netw. **23**, 1809–1821 (2017)
14. Gupta, S.K., Kuila, P., Jana, P.K.: GAR: an energy efficient GA-based routing for wireless sensor networks. In: Hota, C., Srimani, Pradip K. (eds.) ICDCIT 2013. LNCS, vol. 7753, pp. 267–277. Springer, Heidelberg (2013). https://doi.org/10.1007/978-3-642-36071-8_21
15. Ataul, B., et al.: A GA based approach for energy efficient routing in two-tiered sensor networks. Ad Hoc Netw. **7**, 665–676 (2009)
16. Goel, L., et al.: Extended Species Abundance Models of BBO. In: 4th International Conference on Computational Intelligence, Modelling and Simulation (2012)
17. Gupta, D., et al.: Enhanced heuristic approach for TTP based on extended species abundance models of biogeography. In: International Conference on Advances in Computing, Communications and Informatics (2014)

18. Seyed, H.A., et al.: A new BBO algorithm for the flexible job shop scheduling problem. Int. J. Adv. Manuf. Technol. **58**, 1115–1129 (2012)
19. Ataul, B., et al.: Clustering strategies for improving the lifetime of two-tiered sensor networks. Comput. Commun. **31**, 3451–3459 (2008)
20. Gupta, D., et al.: A hybrid biogeography based heuristic for the mirrored TTP. In: IEEE 6th International Conference on Contemporary Computing (IC3), Catalog no. CFP 1381U-CDR, pp. 325–330 (2013)

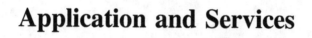

Application and Services

Investigation of Parameters Influencing the Success of Crowdfunded Campaigns

Jaya Gera[1] and Harmeet Kaur[2(✉)]

[1] Department of Computer Science, Shyama Prasad Mukherji College,
University of Delhi, Delhi, India
jayagera@spm.du.ac.in
[2] Department of Computer Science, Hansraj College,
University of Delhi, Delhi, India
hkaur@hrc.du.ac.in

Abstract. Crowd funding is a new ray of hope for entrepreneurs. It is a collective effort of investors, creators and crowdfunding platforms to raise funds for a venture/project over social media. Future of a venture is decided by successful funding that depends on various factors such as project quality, size of network, pattern of pledge money etc. This paper performs statistical analysis and investigates various factors that influence campaign success. Campaigns having video and lower goals are most likely to succeed and hence are better candidates for investment. Sharing campaign via Facebook has a positive impact on success. Pledge money is also a powerful predictor. Posting updates and comments during funding period help in improving success probability of a campaign.

Keywords: Crowdfunding · Campaign success · Kickstarter
Statistical analysis

1 Introduction

The aim of crowd funding is to collect money from large group of people to fund a project, a business or personal loan, and other needs through an online web-based platform [1]. Funds can be raised via an open call on one's webpage or by placing a notice on a public place or through crowdfunding platforms [2]. Since its inception, crowd funding has been progressively adopted as an alternative way for seeking financial assistance by start-ups, entrepreneurs, creative people and others [3]. Crowdfunding Industry experienced 167 percent growth and raised $16.2 billion in 2014, which was $6.1 billion in 2013. In 2015, the industry growth was twice of 2014 and raised $34.4 billion [4]. Over the years, numbers of crowdfunding platforms and campaigns launched have increased at multiplying rate. Some of the well-known platforms are Kickstarter, IndieGoGo, DonorChoose, RocketHub, Kiva.

Campaigns launched on platforms are of diverse nature and greatly vary in both goal and magnitude [5]. Though, diversity and number of campaigns launched has increased with time, but not the success rate. A campaign is successful in raising funds, if it achieves its target amount with in the given time span. Not all are successful in raising funds. On the Kickstarter itself, 3,86,570 campaigns have been launched till

© Springer Nature Singapore Pte Ltd. 2018
G. C. Deka et al. (Eds.): ICACCT 2018, CCIS 899, pp. 275–285, 2018.
https://doi.org/10.1007/978-981-13-2035-4_24

now. Out of which, 1,37,782 i.e. around 36% of campaigns have been successful in raising funds, others were unsuccessful [6].

Why did so many projects fail to raise sufficient funds through crowdfunding? What are the reasons behind success and failure? What factors influence success of a campaign? What is the association between success and these factors? Do these factors have some association amongst themselves? In this paper, we try to understand different dimensions of a project and the factors influencing its success and try to address the questions raised above. This work performs statistical analysis and concludes important results. This work classifies the features as pre-launch and post-launch features and examines their predictive power.

The rest of the paper is organized as follows: Sect. 2 sum ups literature work. Section 3 describes dataset and its characteristics. Section 4 presents analysis and results. Section 5 concludes the work.

2 Literature Review

Evaluation of various aspects of a campaign and its association with successful funding has been examined by various scholars. Over the past years, there has been an increase in literature on campaign success evaluation and prediction. This work is similar to some of the other work in a sense this work also explores campaign's features and their impact on success. But, this work differs too as it helps in identifying nature of features and classifies them on the basis of characteristics and the type of information it communicates. Some of the works from the literature are presented next.

Greenberg et al. [7] design a prediction model based on various campaign features. Etter et al. [8] proposed prediction models that were based on pledge money and social data. Mollick [5] examined factors and its association with success. He identified that project quality and size of networks play important role in success. Belleflamme et al. [9] examined how type of organization is associated with success and concluded that non-profit organization tends to attract funds successfully compared to other form of organization as initiatives are not driven purely by profit. Other dimensions too have been explored by research scholars. Kuppuswamy and Bayus [10] analysed the backer dynamics over the project funding cycle. Chung [11] analysed characteristics of successful projects, behaviour of users and dynamics of the crowdfunding platform. He suggested a prediction model based on campaign, social and user features. Xu et al. [12] analysed campaign updates and comments posted on campaign page and correlated them with campaign success. Mitra and Gilbert [13] proposed a prediction model based on the linguistic features derived from campaign description. Agarwal et al. [14] examined role of geography in fetching funds for a campaign. Ordanini et al. [15] investigated how the role of consumer is changing in present scenario and converting to an investor role. Giudici et al. [16] concluded individual social capital has a significant positive effect on the success probability, while geo-localized capital has no significant effect.

This paper too investigates various campaign features with the aim to understand the underlying nature of features, to categorize them and understand their correlation with success.

3 Dataset

Kickstarter is a well-known reward based crowdfunding platform. It allows creators to launch creative projects and raise funds by creating a dedicated project page on the site. Project page is a well-defined structured page that outlines objective, goal amount, deadline, product description, associated risks and challenges, commitments, reward tiers etc. The information communicated via the project page has an effective and valuable contribution on project outcome and provides help to backers in taking decision about funding.

This analysis was performed on the dataset extracted from the Kickstarter platform. This dataset consists of data about 4121 campaigns launched in the month of April 2014. Out of 4,121 projects, 1,899 (46%) are successful and 2,232 (54%) are unsuccessful. This dataset comprises of projects in all fifteen categories as classified by Kickstarter such as music, dance, etc. This dataset consists of a number of features. Analysis of these features helped in identifying their nature and purpose. On the basis of features nature and purpose, they are categorized into two classes: pre-launch and post-launch (shown in Table 1). Pre-launch features are features that are decided by creator prior to its launch. These features are less likely to change. Pre-launch features comprise of campaign features, creator experience, funding history and social status of creator. Features such as category, currency, goal amount, number of rewards, duration in days etc. define a campaign's characteristics. So, they are grouped under Campaign features. Number of campaigns backed and number of campaigns created prior to launch of current campaign tells about the creator experience of the platform. So, they are classified as creator experience. Social status tells whether the creator is active on Facebook and other media. Features such as connection with Facebook, number of friends defines social status.

Table 1. Variables used in analysis

	Type of features	Variables	Description
Pre-launch features	Campaign features	Cat(p)	Category of project p
		Subcat(p)	Sub category of project p
		Goal(p)	Target amount to be raised
		Duration(p)	Number of days for which project is live on platform
		Rewards(p)	Number of reward levels
		HasVideo(p)	Does the project have any video(s)?
		#Video(p)	Number of videos
		#Image(p)	Number of images
		#wordDesc(p)	Number of words in the description of the project
		#wordRisk(p)	Number of words in the risk and challenges section

(*continued*)

Table 1. (*continued*)

	Type of features	Variables	Description
	Creator experience	Created(*p*)	Number of projects creator has created previous to the launch of this project
		Backed(*p*)	Number of projects creator has backed previous to the launch of this project
	Social status	Frnds(p)	Number of Facebook friends of the creator
		Conn(*p*)	Yes, If creator shares Facebook connection
		Shares(p)	Number of times campaign is shared over Facebook
Post - launch features	Support	Pledge$_t$(p)	Pledge amount at time *t*
		Backer$_t$(p)	Number of backers backed pledge amount at time t
	Communication	Updates$_t$(p)	Number of updates posted by creator at time *t*
		Comments$_t$(p)	Number of comments posted by backer at time *t*

Post launch features are features that are generated after the launch of campaign and are a result of various activities carried out by different types of users. These are time series data and may change frequently. It includes support and communication. Backers support the campaign by contributing funds to the campaign. Kickstarter page displays the amount pledged and the number of backers who pledged it. This status changes with every additional contribution. Dataset contains records of the amount pledged by backers during the funding cycle. It consists of each day's status of pledged amount and number of backers during funding cycle of campaign. During the funding period, creators may post updates to inform backers about various activities of the campaign. Backers may post comments to ask something or add something more about the campaign. The dataset also contains each day's status of updates and comments posted on the campaign page. This is one of the various ways creators and backers interact with each other. Hence, these are grouped under the communication features.

4 Analysis

The proposed work tries to understand the nature of these features to use them for predicting success. The features those are available at the time of launch or prior to launch, have been termed as pre-launch features. These features are stable in nature and less likely to be edited. Some features are available after launch and are time series data i.e. dynamic in nature, are referred as post launch features. Due to differences in nature, they are examined separately.

4.1 Pre-launch Features

Pre-launch features are features that are stable in nature and less likely to be modified during funding period. They basically provide information regarding project, creator and social media usage. As shown in Fig. 1, Features are classified as campaign features, creator experience and social status. This section investigates association of success with these three groups of pre-launch features.

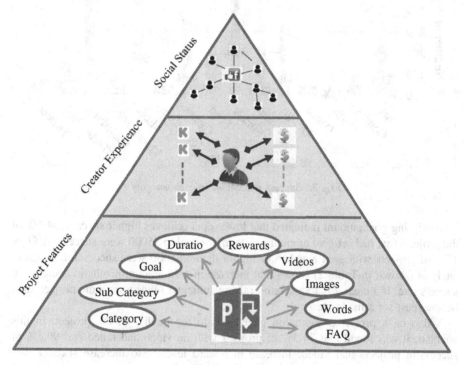

Fig. 1. Pre-launch features

Impact of Project Aspects. Statistical analysis was done using frequency count, grouping and crosstab analysis and logistic regression. Results of logistic regressions were compared with the base model. Base model is the model with only constants and no feature is used in the base model. Base model performed with an accuracy of 54.2% as these are the number of campaigns unsuccessful in the dataset.

Analysis revealed interesting facts about some of the features of the dataset. In the sample dataset 54.2% projects failed to raise goal amount. Maximum number of projects (around 20% of total projects) was launched in the category of film and video. Next, two popular categories music and publishing comprised of 15% and 11% of the total projects, respectively. Journalism, crafts and dance categories in all constitute 3% of the total projects. Dance category had maximum success at 75%. Theatre had 63.8% success and comics had 57%. Crafts had maximum failure at 67.4%. Fashion and Technology had also seen many failures, 66.8% and 66% respectively (shown in Fig. 2).

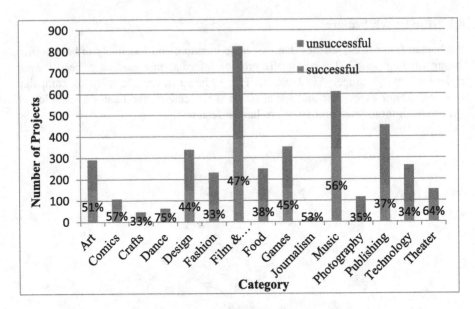

Fig. 2. Success percentage in each category

Analysing goal amount indicated that lower goal achieves higher success. 54.6% of the projects that had set goal amount less than or equal to $5000 were successful. Only 17% of projects with goal equal to or higher than $50,000 were successful. Crosstab analysis (shown in Table 2) shows that increase in goal amount results in decrease in success rate. If a creator is focusing on raising sufficient funds to execute project, then he/she must set a moderate goal.

Video on a project presentation page adds to the quality of the project. In this analysis, it was found that 74.3% of projects with no video had failed and 90.3% of successful projects had video. Increase in reward levels also increase success rate. Projects having more than 20 reward levels had 71.4% of success rate.

Impact of Creator Experience. A creator's previous experience with the platform is expressed by two control variables: Created(p) and Backed(p). Created(p) tells how many projects has the creator launched previously. And Backed(p) tells how many projects the creator has backed earlier. Adding them one by one to the base model of logistic regression helps in understanding the predictive nature of these variables. Adding Backed(p) increased the accuracy of the base model by 6% and then adding created(p) to this model did not improve the accuracy. Adding created(p) as single parameter to base model resulted in increased accuracy of 3%. This means backing other creator's project brings more benefits than the experience of creation. This means to say that a creator should explore the platform and back potential projects of other creators before creating their first project. This may help them in becoming more visible on the platforms and may inspire other creators (whom they had backed) to back and promote it on their social circle. Thus, creator having previous creation and backing experience has a positive influence on success.

Table 2. Cross tab analysis for goal amount

State			Goal amount in $ <=5000	5000–10000	10001–15000	15001–20000	20001–25000	25001–30000	30001–35000	35001–40000	40001–45000	45001–50000	>=50001	Total
Failed	Count		882	468	187	130	82	77	39	32	18	79	238	2232
	% within State		39.5%	21.0%	8.4%	5.8%	3.7%	3.4%	1.7%	1.4%	0.8%	3.5%	10.7%	100.0%
	% within Goal		45.4%	56.9%	53.7%	58.6%	59.9%	67.0%	63.9%	65.3%	64.3%	73.8%	82.9%	54.2%
	% of Total		21.4%	11.4%	4.5%	3.2%	2.0%	1.9%	0.9%	0.8%	0.4%	1.9%	5.8%	54.2%
Successful	Count		1062	355	161	92	55	38	22	17	10	28	49	1889
	% within State		56.2%	18.8%	8.5%	4.9%	2.9%	2.0%	1.2%	0.9%	0.5%	1.5%	2.6%	100.0%
	% within Goal		54.6%	43.1%	46.3%	41.4%	40.1%	33.0%	36.1%	34.7%	35.7%	26.72	17.1%	45.8%
	% of Total		25.8%	8.6%	3.9%	2.2%	1.3%	0.9%	0.5%	0.4%	0.2%	0.7%	1.2%	45.8%
Total	Count		1944	823	348	222	137	115	61	49	28	107	287	4121
	% within State		47.2%	20.0%	8.4%	5.4%	3.3%	2.8%	1.5%	1.2%	0.7%	2.6%	7.0%	100.0%
	% within Goal		100.0%	100.0%	100.0%	100.0%	100.0%	100.0%	100.0%	100.0%	100.0%	100.0%	100.0%	100.0%
	% of Total		47.2%	20.0%	8.4%	5.4%	3.3%	2.8%	1.5%	1.2%	0.7%	2.6%	7.0%	100.0%

Impact of Social Status. Social Status here includes whether creator has shared link of Facebook or not (Conn(p)), number of friends (Frnds(p)) of the creator, and how many shared the project over Facebook (Shares(p)). If a creator does not provide Facebook link on the project page, then, field Frnds(p) (number of Facebook friends) is Null i.e. this field has some value only in case creator share his/her Facebook link. The predictive nature of these control variables was tested separately by creating a model in stepwise manner. Adding Conn(p) and Frnds(p) to the base model (where none of the feature is present) does not improve prediction much, but adding Shares(p) improves the prediction accuracy drastically and it increases by 13%. This means whether creator shares Facebook account or not on the project page does not impact project success. Moreover, adding number of friends improved base model marginally. But, adding the number of Facebook shares changed the scenario and indicates that sharing a project on the social media and promoting it among social community has a great impact on the success of the project and helps in making it successful.

Analysis on the Basis of Combined Features. Earlier analysis tells the impact of individual feature on success. There are some other strange facts about the features of projects. There are 2795 projects with Facebook connection and out of that 1492 (53.4%) have failed i.e. more than half of projects with Facebook connection have failed. Out of 3404 projects having video, 1699 (49.9%) projects have failed i.e. probability of success is half even if a project has video. These statistics provide useful insight but do not discover all facts. This means that studying impact of features individually on success is not sufficient; there is a need to assess interaction among two or more features and its impact on success. To investigate association of two potential features, two-way crosstab tables were generated. 70.6% successful projects have both Facebook connection as well as video.

Addition statistical analysis helped in understanding nature of campaigns, but could not assess predictive power of these features in combination. So, logistic regression was performed stepwise. Multiple models were created and compared by adding a subset of relevant attributes in each step. Base model, a model with no features, provided accuracy of 54.2%. All other models were built upon the base model. First, a model was built using the goal amount only. This model predicted with an accuracy of 59.1%. Adding HasVideo in the second step improved accuracy to 61.6%. Adding Facebook Connection in the third step resulted in no improvement. This implies that having Facebook connection only does not have any impact on success. Adding Facebook friends (in case of having connection) had resulted in an accuracy of 64.9%. Adding creator attributes resulted in 66.9% accuracy and adding the remaining attributes yielded an accuracy of 74%. But, adding one more relevant feature Facebook shares yielded a model with great improvement and having an accuracy of 82.6%. Facebook shares is a dynamic and time series data, to study the impact of sharing during the funding cycle precisely, each day Facebook sharing status of a project is required. It is not available in the dataset, so, the analysis of its dynamic impact was not possible, but above statistics tells that promoting a project on social media is a big advantage for project success. This may also help in improving visibility of the project and expanding the network.

4.2   Post-launch Features

Post-launch features are time series data that keep on changing as time passes. They are classified as support and communication as shown in Fig. 3.

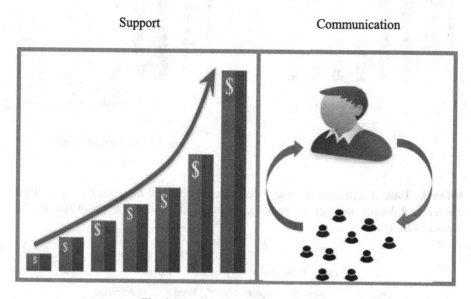

Fig. 3. Post launch predictors' features

Support features include pledged money and number of backers. Communication feature comprises of number of updates and comments. All these features were explored separately and it was found that pledge money status is the most powerful predictor. Incremental models were developed by adding features one by one to the base model (with no features) and evaluated and compared them. Adding number of comments increased the accuracy of the base model (54.2%) on an average by 4% (i.e. 58.2%), then adding the number of updates resulted in an average improvement of 6% (i.e. 64%) to the previous model, then adding the number of backers resulted in average improvement of 8% (i.e. 72%) and finally adding the pledge money status resulted in an average improvement of 18% i.e. post-launch predictor achieved average accuracy of 90% that is better than all the models proposed in various studies. A model using pledge money status only was also developed and it achieved the same performance. This indicates that the analysis can be performed with only one feature i.e. pledge money status if the other features are not available for experimental purpose.

Additional analysis using updates and comments tell how they help in promoting projects. Figure 4 shows that 78.7% (1331) of the projects with no updates had failed. 63% of the projects with one or more updates were successful.

Similarly, 69.2% (1594) of projects with no comments failed and 65% of projects with one or more comments were successful (shown in Fig. 5). This indicates that the updates and comments play vital role in making a project successful. Statistics shown

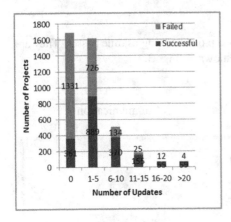

Fig. 4. Update analysis

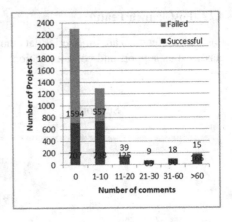

Fig. 5. Comments analysis

below in Table 3 indicates that the successful projects had high amount of pledged money and higher number of backers, updates and comments compared to the unsuccessful projects.

Table 3. Statistics for post-launch features

Feature	Category	Min	Max	Total	Average
Pledged	ALL	0	23,999	4,69,53,780	11,393.78
	Successful	21	23,999	4,18,72,172	22,166.32
	Unsuccessful	0	5,194	50,81,608	2,276.71
Backers	ALL	0	23,999	5,75,734	139.71
	Successful	1	23,999	5,15,334	272.81
	Unsuccessful	0	5,194	60,400	27.06
Comments	ALL	0	4,225	80,879	19.63
	Successful	0	4,225	73,590	38.96
	Unsuccessful	0	1,654	7,289	3.27
Updates	ALL	0	47	13,105	3.18
	Successful	0	47	9,929	5.26
	Unsuccessful	0	43	3,176	1.42

5 Conclusion

This paper evaluates the probability of success not only by an ensemble of features but studies the impact of features individually as well. This paper also highlights the prediction power of individual features and when combined with each other. Campaigns having video and lower goals are better candidate and become successful. Sharing campaign via Facebook has a positive impact on success. Pledge money is a powerful predictor. Posting updates and comments during the funding period helps in improving the success probability of a campaign.

Acknowledgments. A portion of the dataset used in this work was taken from the web site: http://www.kickspy.com/. This was released by owner of this website. We are thankful to the owner of this website for releasing this dataset and making it available for others.

References

1. Kirby, A.E., Worner, S.: Crowd-funding: an infant industry growing fast. Iosco, pp. 1–62 (2014)
2. Wash, R.: The value of completing crowdfunding projects. In: Proceedings of the 7th International Conference on Weblogs and Social Media, ICWSM, pp. 631–639 (2013)
3. Hemer, J.: A snapshot on crowdfunding. Enconstor, p. 39 (2011)
4. Massolution: 2015CF-The Crowdfunding Industry Report (2015). http://www.crowd-sourcing.org/editorial/global-crowdfunding-market-to-reach-344b-in-2015-predicts-massolutions-2015cf-industry-report/45376
5. Mollick, E.: The dynamics of crowdfunding: An exploratory study. J. Bus. Venture **29**(1), 1–16 (2014)
6. Kickstarter: Kickstarter Stats (2018). https://www.kickstarter.com/help/stats?ref=global-footer. Accessed 14 Jan 2018
7. Greenberg, M.D., Hariharan, K., Gerber, E., Pardo, B.: Crowdfunding support tools: predicting success & failure. In: CHI 2013, Changing Perspectives, Paris, pp. 1815–1820 (2013)
8. Etter, V., Grossglauser, M., Thiran, P.: Launch hard or go home!: predicting the success of Kickstarter campaigns. In: Proceedings of the First ACM Conference on Online Social Networks - COSN 2013, pp. 177–182 (2013)
9. Belleflamme, P., Thomas, L., Schwienbacher, A.: Individual crowdfunding practices. Venture Cap. **15**(4), 313–333 (2013)
10. Kuppuswamy, V., Bayus, B.L.: Crowdfunding creative ideas: the dynamics of project backers in Kickstarter. J. Chem. Inf. Model. **53**(9), 1689–1699 (2013)
11. Chung, J.: Long-term study of crowdfunding platform: predicting project success and fundraising amount. In: HT 2015 26th ACM Conference on Hypertext and Social Media, pp. 1–10 (2015)
12. Xu, A., Yang, X., Rao, H., Fu, W., Huang, S., Bailey, B.P.: Show me the money! An analysis of project updates during crowdfunding campaigns. In: Proceedings of 32nd Annual ACM Conference on Human Factors in Computing Systems, pp. 591–600 (2014)
13. Mitra, T., Gilbert, E.: The language that gets people to give: Phrases that predict success on Kickstarter. In: Proceedings of the 17th ACM Conference on Computer Supported Cooperative Work & Social Computing, pp. 49–61 (2014)
14. Agrawal, A.K., Catalini, C., Avi, G.: The geography of crowdfunding. NBER Working Paper (2011)
15. Ordanini, A., Miceli, L., Pizzetti, M., Parasuraman, A.: Crowd-funding: transforming customers into investors through innovative service platforms. J. Serv. Manag. **22**(4), 443–470 (2011)
16. Giudici, G., Guerini, M., Rossi-Lamastra, C.: Why crowdfunding projects can succeed: the role of proponent's individual and territorial social capital. SSRN Electron. J. (2013). https://ssrn.com/abstract=2255944

Rise of Blockchain Technology: Beyond Cryptocurrency

Hasil-E-Hayaat[1], Anu Priya[1], Aanchal Khatri[2,3(✉)],
and Prashant Dixit[1]

[1] CSE Department, Manav Rachna International University, Faridabad, India
hasilsadar@gmail.com, anu396priya@gmail.com,
prashant.fet@mriu.edu.in
[2] Jawaharlal Nehru University, New Delhi, India
[3] Accendere KMS Pvt. Ltd., New Delhi, India
aanchal.khatri@accendere.co.in

Abstract. This paper highlights how block chain technology will help in innovation and transformation of business and service sector. To solve the issue, the paper presents the architecture and benefits of blockchain technology. Further it discusses the implication of using blockchain technology in banking, transport sector, Internet of things (IoT), and in enterprises consisting of global commodity chains. The technology helps to bring a shift from technology driven to need driven approach. With all the advancement and benefits, there is further research to be done to fit the model in other areas like e governance which will benefit the society and public values.

Keywords: Blockchain · Finance · IoT · Architecture

1 Introduction

We stand on the edge of a new digital revolution. With the advent of internet, a new phase began for the human race. And now after many years of scientific research and experiments, we have reached a stage where science and technology continue to find newer ways to improve our lifestyles and bring more and more people into the mainstream. A manifestation of these attempts has been validated in technologies such as the Blockchain which implores upon finding solutions like decentralization and removal of third-party-authenticators. The Blockchain is encrypted, shared and distributed database that provides an irreversible and tamper-free public record keeping system. With this technology, digital property can be transferred and digital transactions can be carried out without the need of backing by a financial middleman [1]. This is a reason why this technology has capabilities that when explored to the right extent, it can provide utilities beyond the scope of what has been done till date. In the future we expect more digital markets working free from any regulation because it can take care of itself on its own based on self-emerging and approving techniques. We would also see decentralized communication platforms and internet based assets and properties that are freely exchanged [2].

G. C. Deka et al. (Eds.): ICACCT 2018, CCIS 899, pp. 286–299, 2018.
https://doi.org/10.1007/978-981-13-2035-4_25

The blockchain is the name given where each consecutive data and transactions are recorded on blocks. Each block is linked to a previous block, and this length keeps on growing continuously. Hash functions are used that are stored in the header. This continuous and ever-growing blockchain length [3] is distributed over a public ledger and is available to all the mentioned nodes in the network. The data once entered in the various transactions are not possible to tamper with. Blockchains can also be described as blocks of information connected together in long chains of validation. Any point in the node cannot be altered without changing the entire network of blocks and hence falsification attempts can be easily detected.

Various important features that describe the blockchain mechanism are decentralization that rules out the need for third-party authenticators thereby saving organization and maintenance costs related to establishing and running these huge institutions. Transaction procedures also get simplified. Another important feature is the persistency in procedures. Data once stored is visible to everyone in the network and it cannot be tampered or disturbed unless making a change at all nodes. This ensures security of transactions. Anonymity is also a feature as users at various nodes can generate multiple private addresses to ensure secrecy and privacy as required. Auditability is also a useful feature as with this facility, information about all previous transactions can be easily retrieved from the network and the data can be put to required use. In this manner, by using blockchains many complex day to day transaction activities can be simplified. Blockchains employ a few consensus algorithms, such as Proof of Stake, Proof of Work being more important among others [4, 5]. Explanation of these algorithms has been given briefly. Often pertaining to any given condition a hybrid solution consisting of a mixture of one or more consensus procedures suits more aptly to blockchain mechanism. Different environments have different suitability of algorithms (Fig. 1).

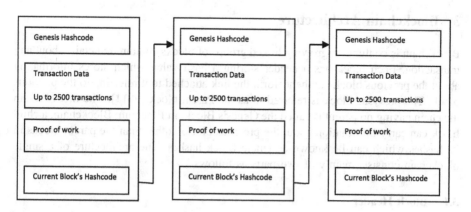

Fig. 1. General blockchain model

Bitcoins are namely the most extensive application of the blockchain technology. Digital Currency was almost on the verge of collapsing and getting out of the market scenario until blockchain mechanism came to its rescue. As for today, we know that digital currencies such as bitcoins and other forms of digital currencies are giants in the financial world and also serve as major investment options. New areas of research and studies have also sprung up consequently such as Cryptoeconomics. Blockchains solve the double spending problem and ensure agent to agent transaction communication without the need for any intermediate body. Further in this extract, various applications of blockchains have been discussed. We will come to know that not only are block-chains enormous role players in the financial sector but also they can serve many different sectors including maintaining social status records of different persons if employed with proper referencing.

2   Related Work

Blockchain technology has validated its applicability in numerous instances. Security of digital identities of citizens using blockchain is much safer as compared to other methods like using ids and passwords in insecure environments. In today's world where cryptocurrency is making headlines in its favor is based on the blockchain. Bitcoin is an example. Blockchain can be used to store legal documents where there is influence of the third party, thus leads to secure storage of the data. Blockchain eliminates the role of the third party and hence maintenance cost is minimized. One such example is the role of election commissions. Election based on blockchain technology can banish the influence of any political parties and thus leads to secure and cost-efficient elections. It will serve as the missing link to settle the privacy and reliability concerns of people in the internet of things. Vast usage of IoT techniques will come into place by the usage of the blockchain technology. There are lots of use cases and applications of blockchain technology [24–27].

3   Blockchain Architecture

Blockchain is continuous growing linked groups of blocks containing details about any transaction. Each block has a header storing a hash value which stores information about the previous block and henceforth the link attached to it referring to the previous block. The previous block is referred to as the Parent block [9–11]. The first block in the chain having no parent is called the Genesis Block. In Ethereum Blockchain, a child block can carry information about the previous blocks, other than the parent blocks in its hashes which can be known as Uncle Block hashes. The architecture of a single blockchain consists mainly of two parts as follows.

3.1   Block Header

Under block header following four components exist:
   Block Version: It will comprise of all the rules (hashing rules) that a block has to follow in order to be validated.
   Parent Block Hash: This hash stores the values which are used to indicate the link to previous record block.

Merkel Tree Root Hash: It will store the hash value of all the transactions in the block.

Timestamp: It is a recorded information storing unit which records the order in which transactions occur in the blocks, given by the reference of time.

N-bits: It refers to the current hashing target in the list.

Nonce: It is a 4-byte field which increases in value after each consecutive transaction or calculation.

3.2 Block Transaction Body

This is the lower second part of the blockchain. We can describe the Block transaction body to consist of the following features. It will consist of transaction counter and transactions. Maximum limit of the number of transactions will be determined by thesize of each block as well as thesize of each transaction. Block body will store the number of validated transactions. This information once stored cannot be changed later on. This is the crude step where data storage procedure is carried out. All the other components are simply needed to maintain the overall blockchain mechanism (Fig. 2).

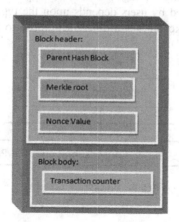

Fig. 2. Blockchain architecture

3.3 Digital Signature

In the diagram below, the exchange of confidential message takes place between A and B. In order to ensure the message confidentiality and to ensure that only receiver can open the message, the sender uses the public key of the receiver. Here, A encrypts the message using B's public key. This ensures that message can be decrypted only by B. In order to verify that the message is sent by A, A uses his private key in the hash function. This is called digital signature. B can verify that the message is sent by A by using A's public key and decrypt the message by using his own private key (Fig. 3).

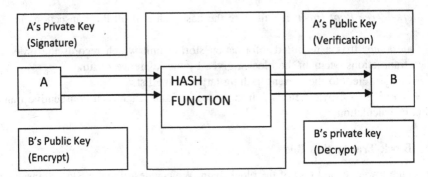

Fig. 3. Digital signature

3.4   Domains of Blockchain

Blockchains are divided into three categories on the basis of authorization of access that an organization or community can have the records stored under any particular blockchain. This categorization springs from sources applied in its creation. Whether or not records can be accessed by users depends upon the type of domain that a chain belongs to. Different blockchain has a different purpose to fulfill. Following are the types of blockchain (Fig. 4):

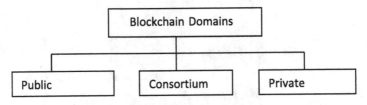

Fig. 4. Blockchain domains

- Public
- Private
- Hybrids (Consortium).

3.4.1   Public Blockchains

This is the domain of blockchains in which all miners participate in consensus determination. The read permissions are not required as they are all public with decentralization, without the need of any central trusted agency. These blockchains are nearly impossible to tamper and all members can participate in the consensus determination procedures.

3.4.2   Private Blockchains

In this domain the consensus determination mechanism can take place only within an organization. The read permissions here could be either public or restricted. There is centralization within this domain as the blockchain participants are restricted to within an organization. The consensus determination process will require permission.

3.4.3 Hybrid Blockchains

Only a selected segment of nodes that are allowed can participate in the consensus determination process. Here the read permission could be either public or restricted. With this, the security is reduced and this network will be more likable to tamper in comparison to public ones. There is partial centralization (Table 1).

Table 1. Properties of blockchains

Property	Public blockchains	Private blockchains	Hybrid blockchains
Consensus determination	All miners	Selected set of nodes	One organization
Read permission	Public	Could be public or restricted	Could be public or restricted
Efficiency	Low	High	High
Centralization	No	Partial	Yes
Consensus process	Permission less	Permission needed	Permission needed

4 Features

Blockchain is a continuous growing list of records in the form of blocks which are linked together. Blockchain provides a secure medium for storage of data. It eliminates the participation of the third party making it more reliable, Secure and safe from influence of any organization or the participant. Several features of the blockchain are discussed below:

4.1 Decentralization

A very important feature enabled by blockchain mechanism is decentralization. Before bitcoin many research resources were employed to achieve this feature. Decentralization refers to absence of a central ruling body to supervise financial transaction. The network operates on a user to user (peer to peer) basis. With this costs incurred to organize and maintain such large central institutions end at once. Further, it empowers the users also, as they carry out their transaction mechanism with ease and control. The transaction mechanism also simplifies blockchain creates as a whole new model of platform intermediation (Fig. 5).

4.2 Persistency

Once a record stored on a block, a new block is generated with a connection to the previous block. Thus blockchains maintained and grow in size. Every transaction in the

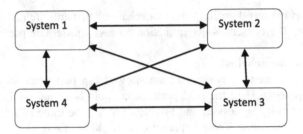

Fig. 5. Decentralized blockchain platform

network is confirmed, recorded and distributed in the whole network and it becomes impossible to temper.

4.3   Immutability

It refers to the feature where once data has been written to a blockchain, no one can change it. However, immutability is only relative to ensure security and incase where data has to be changed in its core, such as modification can be carried out. If any attempt to change the data is carried out, it will have to be done at all the nodes in the network at the same time. This feature enhances security.

4.4   Auditability

Each and every transaction in the blockchain is recorded and maintained with a timestamp which means that we can exactly determine at what point of time a trans-action was made to occur. Every record has this data with itself. With the help of this feature all previous records related to theparticular transaction can be traced and retrieved as and when required. This is a very important feature as with of help of this, transparency of data stored in the various records improves greatly and further, the trust of the users also increases.

5   Approaches to Consensus

These approaches describe mainly how the blockchain technology actually works. The entire setup is based on these procedures and consensus approaching techniques. They serve as the backbone on which functionality of all data and authenticity of storage methods in blockchains depends [21, 22]. Such methods are more than one which is designed to serve different scenarios adequately. They are discussed as below.

5.1   Proof of Work

In proof of work protocol, there is acomplicated calculation in which each node of the network calculates the hash value of the changing block header. The calculated hash value should be equal or smaller than a specific given value. In decentralized blockchain, all the participants calculate the hash value. When one of the validators calculates the required given value, all the other validators approve the calculation. The next block generated contains all the transaction used in the calculation. All the validators that calculate the hash value are called miners. And all the proof of work procedure is called mining. When (Nakamoto) proposed the idea of Bit coin, he added that the miners would be given a small amount of bit coin after every successful transaction. Multiple validators can generate valid blocks simultaneously. In order to make the validation of the block, next generated block is taken into consideration. It is very unlikely that the next block would be generated simultaneously by the validators. The block with valid calculation is taken as the approved one and the other block is called asorphan block because no further blocks can be added to it. Calculations for the validation of the block are a time as well as energy consuming process. Bitcoin blocks are generated after every 10 min and Ethereum block is generated after every 17 s.

5.2 Proof of Stake

In order to combat the time as well as power consuming POW, POS was introduced. In POS, the participants with more currency could be chosen as the creator of the new block as it assumes that the participants with more currency would be the least likely to attack the network. Since it is quite unfair to declare the next generator on the basis of currency, a combination of other factors are often introduced like size of stake, age of stake to declare the next block creator. In peer coin to coin age is taken into consideration for the declaration of next block creator. As POS is more energy efficient and less time consuming than POW many blockchain adopt POW at the beginning but later transform to POS.

5.3 Practical Byzantine Fault Tolerance

In PBFT every validator is known to the network. In PBFT there is no calculation of the hash values. A new block is selected in a round. In each round a primary would be selected and is responsible for the ordering of transaction. This process is divided into three phases: pre-prepared, prepared and commit. In each phase a validator has to get approval from at least 2/3 of all the validators.

5.4 Delegate Proof of Stake

It is like representative democratic in which each stakeholder choose their candidates to generate and validate a block. The transaction is validated quickly as there are fewer validators to verify and validate it. Other factors such as block size and block interval can also be combined. Security wise it is safe as dishonest validator could be removed. Bit share follows the DPOS protocol.

6 Applications of Blockchain Technology

Blockchains are known to have the widest usage in the form of being the technology behind cryptocurrency and digital token market. But besides this wide applicability, this technology serves as an important instrument today for digitizing and decentralizing other fields as well [16, 17, 19]. The future is near where blockchain will be associated with all forms of data storage and validation media. This, in turn, will help achieve the idea of living in smart environments which will be equipped to respond as per our desires and generate suggestions for us as well (Fig. 6 and Table 2).

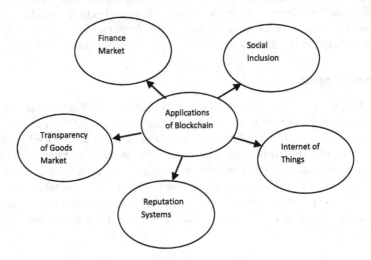

Fig. 6. Major applications of blockchain technology

Table 2. Applications of blockchain

	Application areas	Utility
1.	Private securities	Expenses on a company being made public can be reduced with them releasing shares via the blockchain
2.	Content distribution	Artists become empowered as media distribution systems are made more transparent and easy to use
3.	Market prediction	Users can trade on predictive trends information and outcomes based on blockchains
4.	Private equity	Equity exchanges are being implemented on blockchains and made simpler to operate
5.	Insurance	Unique asset identifiers can be maintained on blockchain. Owner and Seller information can then be extracted as required
6.	Data management	Blockchain based identity ledgers are used for date management and data analytics

(continued)

Table 2. (*continued*)

	Application areas	Utility
7.	Diamonds	A usually high-risk sector can be made counterfeit proof by implementing the features of blockchain
8.	E- Voting	Transparent voting systems can be created to facilitate fair elections
9.	Gaming	Virtual gaming platforms are being created where activities score points with data stored in background blockchain based databases
10.	Organizational governance	This technology helps to automate procedures related to taking decisions within the company, forming committees and raising funds
11.	Authorship and ownership	Artists and content creators can attribute digital art
12.	Government	Citizen interaction with the officials of the government can be documented using this technology
13.	Commodity market	Investors can carry out business transactions related to money and gold safely
14.	Internet of Things	Blockchain here accelerates safe transactions, reduces Cost and builds trust
15.	Energy	Value chains in the energy industry can be upholder using blockchain
16.	Digital identity and authentication	Blockchain technology used for creating and maintaining online authentic social profiles
17.	Cannabis (cash-heavy business)	Entrepreneurs can create and maintain their business legitimacy
18.	Decentralized storage	Cloud file storage options can be decentralized using blockchain. Traditional data failures and outages will disappear
19.	Notary Public (Non-financial)	Legal documents can be safeguarded using blockchains as they are tamper free
20.	Internet applications	Current DNS servers are controlled by governments. With blockchain this will be decentralized and no misuse of this power shall happen

6.1 Finance

The traditional business services have witnessed great impact with the advancement of blockchain technology. Many financial analysts are of the opinion that blockchain technology has the potential to replace the banking sector completely at some point in time in the future. Banking systems could be reshaped altogether, and the improved changes can take better care of the individual and organizational needs in the world. It will result in enhanced integrity, auditability governance and transfer of ownership capabilities. Not only the large institutions will be affected but blockchain can be a major role player to help smaller enterprises to transform into bigger players smoothly.

They can introduce their own set of digital coins, differentiated from the others, while still retaining their status as a trusted public authority. In this way, they can expand their business and provide more advanced services.

6.2 Transparency of Global Commodity Chains

Blockchain technology has the potential to rebuild transparency in transactions, reestablish product authenticity verification standards, build newer relationships of consumers with consumer goods manufacturers, and ethical standards in global commodity chains. The decentralized, shared, consensus based public ledger that the blockchains are, people can use them to track all the transformations that goods have gone through as well as information about the authenticity of the origin of the end products. A consumer can be assured of the quality of the products and this can change the entire market scenario. The consumer will know that they are receiving the correct end products and this will all be possible by employing blockchain technology. Entire history related to the end products can be verified as and when desired. Fraud players who sell contaminated or fake products shall be thrown away immediately (Fig. 7).

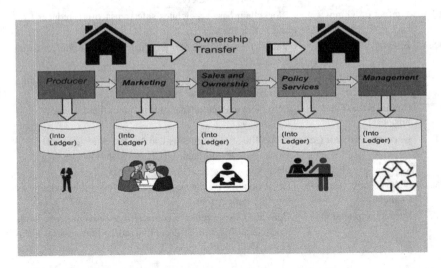

Fig. 7. Blockchain for global community

6.3 Internet of Things

Blockchain that initially started off with applications in the digital money market has since then found enormous application in areas other than cryptocurrency roots. Blockchains could be used to store information about how devices would communicate with each other. Key benefits of using blockchains for the Internet of Things would be that it would build trust between the parties and devices and reduce risks of collusions and tampering. It would also reduce costs incurred, by removing overheads associated with middlemen and intermediaries. It will accelerate transactions and reduce the time needed for the settlement to complete, from days at theend to nearly complete in only an instant. However, the challenges faced here are those related to legal and compliance issues. Security is also an issue that has to be better dealt with.

6.4 Reputation Systems

Since blockchains are a public ledger any and almost every information about a person can be stored and accessed as and when desired. It could be employed to build reputation systems, where a person's previous transaction records would enable to evaluate his or her trustworthiness. It would erase all fraud personal reputation records. Such false reputationrecords maintained by organizations could be removed. All forms of academic, intellectual as well as social work done by an individual or an organization could be awarded using some form of digital currency or rather account keeping mechanism. Their transactions would be stored on blockchains and all this information could be accessed as a proof as well. Reputation model blockchain networks could also help build a person's online creditability. This could serve as the persons work history detail record as well as other social and charitable activity record holder.

6.5 Social Inclusion in the Developing World

Another farseeing application related to this technology pertains to its social inclusion capabilities in the developing world. Blockchain could one day be in a position to be used in many days to day services and activities. How this will be received by people at the end of the day is something many await to see. Blockchains can be very favorable towards achieving bigger economic scenarios such as universal financial access and hence achieving social progress. Many underprivileged people might one day be able to make small payments and transactions through just a mobile device. This will let people gain purchasing power potential and will connect millions of people to the mainstream. Blockchains can be used to influence people to make use of green energy. The concept of thesolarcoin has been proposed to encourage usage of solar energies. Online educational markets could be expanded using this concept.

7 Conclusion

Blockchains are a very powerful technology. Only today it has removed many disadvantages in transaction procedures in many fields. The scope of tomorrow is yet to be realized. For sure there is going to be it's wide and many new applications in the future in which we need to work today. Blockchain features such as decentralization are going to make the user gain power and control. Auditability will ensure that any kind of fraud workers are immediately removed from the scenario. We need to work more and make more advancements as this technology has the capability to bring about a vast change in the way we work and lead our lives.

Acknowledgement. We would like to express our sincere gratitude to Accendere Knowledge Management Pvt. Ltd. for providing us the platform and opportunity to pursue the research.

References

1. Bonneau, J., Narayanan, A., Miller, A., Clark, J., Kroll, J.A., Felten, E.W.: Mixcoin: anonymity for Bitcoin with accountable mixes. In: Christin, N., Safavi-Naini, R. (eds.) FC 2014. LNCS, vol. 8437, pp. 486–504. Springer, Heidelberg (2014). https://doi.org/10.1007/978-3-662-45472-5_31
2. Zheng, Z., Xie, S., Dai, H., Chen, X., Wang, H.: An overview of blockchain technology: architecture, consensus, and future trends. In: 6th International Congress on Big Data. IEEE (2017)
3. State of blockchain q1 2016: Blockchain funding overtakes bitcoin (2016)
4. Peters, W., Panayi, E., Chapelle, A.: Trends in crypto-currencies and blockchain technologies: a monetary theory and regulation perspective (2015)
5. Akins, B.W., Chapman, J.L., Gordon, J.M.: A whole new world: income tax considerations of the bitcoin economy (2013)
6. Antshares: Antshares digital assets for everyone (2016). https://www.antshares.org
7. Bentov, I., Lee, C., Mizrahi, A., Rosenfeld, M.: Proof of activity: extending bitcoin's proof of work via proof of stake. ACM SIGMETRICS Perform. Eval. Rev. **42**(3), 34–37 (2014)
8. Biryukov, A., Khovratovich, D., Pustogarov, I.: Deanonymisation of clients in bitcoin p2p network. In: Proceedings of the 2014 ACM SIGSAC Conference on Computer and Communications Security, pp. 15–29 (2014)
9. Bruce, J.D.: The mini-blockchain scheme, July 2014. http://cryptonite.info/files/mbc-scheme-rev3.pdf
10. Buterin, V.: A next-generation smart contract and decentralized application platform. White paper (2014)
11. Chepurnoy, A., Larangeira, M., Ojiganov, A.: A prunable blockchain consensus protocol based on non-interactive proofs of past states retrievability. arXiv preprint arXiv (2016)
12. Christidis, A., Devetsikiotis, M.: Blockchains and smart contracts for the internet of things. IEEE Access **4**, 2292–2303 (2016)
13. Decker, C., Seidel, J., Wattenhofer, R.: Bitcoin meets strong consistency. In: Proceedings of the 17th International Conference on Distributed Computing and Networking (ICDCN), Singapore, p. 13. ACM, Singapore (2016)
14. Dennis, R., Owen, G.: Rep on the block: a next generation reputation system based on the blockchain. In: 2015 10th International Conference for Internet Technology and Secured Transactions (ICITST), pp. 131–138. IEEE (2015)
15. Devine, P.: Blockchain learning: can crypto-currency methods be appropriated to enhance online learning?. In: ALT Online Winter Conference (2015)
16. Eyal, I., Gencer, A.E., Sirer, E.G., Renesse, R.V.: Bitcoin-NG: a scalable blockchain protocol. In: Proceedings of 13th USENIX Symposium on Networked Systems Design and Implementation (NSDI 16), pp. 45–59 (2016)
17. Habib, K., Torjusen, A., Leister, L.: Security analysis of a patient monitoring system for the Internet of Things in eHealth. In: The Seventh International Conference on eHealth, Telemedicine, and Social Medicine (eTELEMED) (2015)
18. Hardjono, T., Smith, N.: Cloud-based commissioning of constrained devices using permissioned blockchains. In: Proceedings of the 2nd ACM International Workshop on IoT Privacy, Trust, and Security, pp. 29–36. ACM (2016)
19. Jaag, C., Bach, C., et al.: Blockchain technology and cryptocurrencies: opportunities for postal financial services. Technical report (2016)
20. Kraft, D.: Difficulty control for blockchain-based consensus systems. Peer-to-Peer Netw. Appl. **9**(2), 397–413 (2016)

21. Mazieres, D.: The stellar consensus protocol: a federated model for internet-level consensus. Stellar Development Foundation (2015)
22. Meiklejohn, S., Pomarole, M., Jordan, G., Levchenko, K.: A fistful of bitcoins: characterizing payments among men with no names. In: Proceedings of the 2013 Conference on Internet Measurement Conference (IMC 2013) (2013)
23. Aliyu, A., Abdullah, A.H., Kaiwartya, O., Khatri A.: Mobile cloud computing energy-aware task offloading (MCC: ETO). In: Proceedings of ICCCS, Taylor & Francis, 10 September 2016
24. Miau, S., Yang, J.M.: Bibliometrics-based evaluation of the Blockchain research trend: 2008–March 2017. Technol. Anal. Strateg. Manag. **30**(9), 1–17 (2018)
25. Islam, A., Chae, S., Shin, S.Y.: Social Internet of Things (SIoT) and Blockchain: research opportunities and challenges. 한국통신학회 학술대회논문집 326–327 (2018)
26. Berg, C., Davidson, S., Potts, J.: Some Public Economics of Blockchain Technology (2018)
27. Lewison, K., Corella, F.: Backing rich credentials with a blockchain PKI. Technical report, Pomcor 2016 (2018). https://pomcor.com/techreports/BlockchainPKI.pdf

Smart Healthcare Based on Internet of Things

Dhruv Rohatgi[1], Siddharth Srivastava[1], Simran Choudhary[1],
Aanchal Khatri[2(✉)], and Vaishali Kalra[2]

[1] CSE Department, Manav Rachna International University, Faridabad, India
dhruvrohatgi53@gmail.com, ssiddharth1204@gmail.com,
simranchoudhary0096@gmail.com
[2] Department of Computer Science, Accendere KMS,
Jawaharlal Nehru University, New Delhi, India
aanchal.khatri@accendere.co.in,
vaishaliarya.fet@mriu.edu.in

Abstract. With the advancement in technology, Internet of Things (IoT) enabled solutions are gaining lots of attention. The change in lifestyle of people leads to increase in health problems, which demands a need for ubiquitous healthcare system. In this paper, the work of various contemporary authors has been reviewed in different healthcare sectors. Further, smart bed model is proposed for addressing acute health problem of pressure ulcers or bed sores. The sensor based platform will collect and analyse the data using learning algorithm and accordingly will activate the actuators to distribute the pressure along the patient bed sores from time to time.

Keywords: Healthcare · Intensive Care Unit · Bed sore · Internet of Things

1 Introduction

Internet of things (IoT) is emerging in probably every area of life. It is such a pioneering communication technique which aims to bring together different kind of digital devices with the internet. This is envisaging making the internet more ubiquitous. The IoT market is expanding rapidly as manufacturers, companies, vendor, etc. has recognized the potential it offers. According to reports, the worldwide Iot market will hit around US$2 trillion by 2020. The devices in itself account for 32% of total IoT market worldwide. The IoT is joining most of the industries these days like smart city, smart healthcare, smart building, and lot more. These concepts have offered advancement in the quality of life of peoples, but also on the other hand improves the efficiency and asset management like smart grids, smart lightning, smart transportation system (e.g., smart mobility, smart traffic control), smart services, etc.

Internet-of Things (IoT) based smart healthcare systems will allow continuous, cheap and remote monitoring of patients with several chronic conditions like pressure ulcer, hypertension, heart failure, depression, obesity, diabetes, elderly care and other preventive wellness measure. The IoT is promising a significant role for improving the health and wellness of patients by providing the availability of service at the right time and also further reducing the treatment cost and other travel charges. The IoT based

G. C. Deka et al. (Eds.): ICACCT 2018, CCIS 899, pp. 300–309, 2018.
https://doi.org/10.1007/978-981-13-2035-4_26

healthcare system basically uses various kinds of biosensors for collecting the respective physiological signals. Further, the sensors are connected to internet for transmitting the collected information. The data collected are transmitted to the cloud server from where it is analysed for clinical reviews.

The IoT has its vast applications [5] in various domains but we are focusing on its usage in healthcare domain. Although various applications have been developed in health care also, but still there is scope of improvement and future work. In the paper, the work of various contemporary authors in different healthcare sector has been discussed. Further, a model for smart bed is proposed for patients suffering from pressure ulcer. Bed sores also called as pressure ulcer are kind of abrasion to the skin and underlying tissues as a consequence of prolonged pressure. The sores mostly occur on skin of bony areas of the body like ankles, back, hips, heel, etc. People with the sores are at limit with the ability to change their positions. Due to confining on the bed for long period of time will lead to pressure ulcers which are difficult to treat. One of the most important cares for a bed sore patient is to reduce the prolonged pressure. A common practice in the care is to reposition the patient after every two hours. A preventive measure based on the need of ulcer position will reduce the need of nursing strength. In the paper, the model is proposed for developing a pressure mapping based bed that analysis the risk of developing pressure ulcers. Further, a learning algorithm will be designed to find out how various positions can reduce the pressure on affected area.

2 Literature Review

In this paper we are going to shed light on current usage of IoT in healthcare technologies such as using RFID to connect patients and doctors, transfer patient's condition using Zigbee mesh protocol, using cloud to store information collected through various sensors used for medical treatment. The sensor network has been used in every field of life, so for the improvement of lifetime and its efficiency the work has been done by contemporary author [13–15].

[7] discusses the importance of IoT in healthcare systems. The Paper defines various prospects of Internet of things in providing ubiquitous healthcare system. The IoT He discussed that, [7] The IoT brings the usage of sensing devices and using those sensing devices the information can be collected about the patient, doctor and the equipment with which the device is connected. Doctors Equipment such as oxygen cylinder, ERT machine, etc. are all facilitated with sensors, actuators, and RFID tags which they can access anytime from anywhere. IoT has the immense potential to connect various devices to machines, objects to objects and also at the same time patients to doctors as well as to machines. Sensors, RFID, Tag reader, Mobile devices which ensure effective healthcare system for medical assets monitoring, medical waste management, etc. In the Table 1, the author has given the description of usage of sensing devices in sensing the information and its usage in real applications. This article tries to give a new direction to healthcare system by automating the various activities like processing of patient admit form, in knowing patient location and the determining the amount of drug given to the patient etc. which helps in giving the on

time and quality service to the patient. The paper stresses on a healthcare system which consider different aspects of healthcare including traceability, accounting and effective healthcare control.

Table 1. IoT in healthcare

Tracing/tracing	Sensing	Identification and authentication	Real time data collection
Patients inflow and outflow management	Automatic medication management for both sick, elderly and pregnant women	Maintaining patients privacy	Intelligent data collection and transfer mainly aimed at minimizing the effort and processing time
Detection of patient's location	Home	To identify Patients, for preventing any harmful incidence	Automated care and procedure auditing, and medical information management
Management of drug supply and treatment procedure done on patients	Sensor and RFID tag will allow monitoring real time conditions of patients. Parameters such as blood pressure, glucose levels, heart and breathing rate	Clean wrong patient/wrong surgery	Relates to integrating IoT, RFID technology with other health information and clinical application technologies
Detailing of patient arrival in emergency department	Sensor allows the devices to be patient specific as well, according to the disease and condition of the patients	Accurately identifying the Patients to avoid wrong drug, dose, time, procedure	Integrating state-of-the- art physiological parameters monitoring time interval in order to determine actual time period

[8] defines the IoT based Healthcare system using ZigBee mesh protocol. ZigBee protocol used in IoT for many applications such as smart home, smart building, healthcare and Industrial automation, etc. there exist a IoT of wireless communication protocols such as 802.11 and Bluetooth. But these networks face a lot of shortcomings like power consumption, reliable, and scalability. Therefore, ZigBee has been proposed to solve the issues faced by WLAN and Bluetooth. [8] Mostly, Zigbee is defined as WPAN (Wireless Personal Area Network) having low data rate, and can operate at low power and low cost [8]. The power can be efficiently saved using sleep mode operations. For example: To find out the temperature of patient. Temperature sensor is used. It estimates the hotness or coldness of any body. If temperature is more than or less than certain threshold the physician can be alerted with the details of patient. Corresponding sensor are interconnected to appropriate Zigbee modules using ADC pin and the temperature is sampled by 10-bit ADC according to the configured sample rate and the same is transmitted to the gateway at every 5 s (sample rate). "These transmitted

samples are collected by the gateway through UART and required calibrations are performed to get the temperature value corresponding to the transmitted ADC value. Then, this gateway runs a web server to serve this temperature data to the cloud. IoT based medical device is a combination of Zigbee S2 module interfaced with LM35 temperature sensor. Intel Galileo board is integrated with Zigbee S2 module. This architecture acts as a portal for overall healthcare system. This architecture is used to collect, analyse, store and communicate the data to the cloud on a secure network.

[9] presents the application of IoT and addresses some essential parameter and characteristics of each of the applications of IoT. In this paper, they have deeply elaborated the use of IoT in health sector and its technical aspects that are helpful in healthcare sector. They propose a Cloud-IoT framework that can be used for health monitoring of patients with the suggested healthcare solutions. This platform can also be used by doctors for treating depressed patients and improve their conditions in a better way. The framework consists of a network that collects various parameters from different sensors used for monitoring the health of a patient and use the collected data to perform various task on a single platform. The proposed framework can be implemented on various applications such as E-prescribing system, EHR, personal health records, clinical decision system, pharmacy system etc. The doctors can use this framework for clinical study of a patient and can produce improved results.

[10] presents a model for monitoring the health of patients using IoT based technologies for intelligent and cheap observation. The paper discusses the model for structural monitoring in which smart sensors are used with the integration of big data. As the data generated by sensor are too much therefore the techniques of big data help to analyse the solutions generated. The big data and IoT based application will help to monitor the events or any subsequent structural change in the health of patient which will help to improve the healthcare infrastructure of country (Fig. 1).

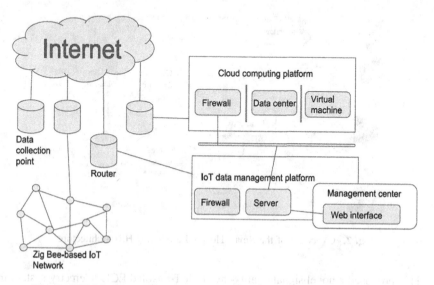

Fig. 1. SHM framework overview based on IoT using Zigbee protocol [10]

In this paper "Luca Catarinucci proposes a novel, "IoT- aware, smart architecture for automatic monitoring and tracking of patients, personal, and biomedical devices within hospitals and nursing institutes. Staying true to the IoT vision, they propose a Smart Hospital System (SHS) which relies on different, yet complementary, technologies, specifically RFID, WSN, and smart mobile, interoperating with each other through a CoAP/6LoWPAN/REST network infrastructure. [11] The SHS is able to collect, in real time, both environmental conditions and patients' physiological parameters via an ultralow-power Hybrid Sensing Network (HSN) composed of 6LoWPAN nodes integrating UHF RFID functionalities. Sensed data are delivered to a control centre where an advanced monitoring application makes them easily accessible by both local and remote users via a REST web service. The simple proof of concept implemented to validate the proposed SHS has highlighted a number of key capabilities and aspects of novelty which represent a significant step forward compared to the actual state of art. In this work, a novel, IoT-aware, Smart Hospital System (SHS) architecture for automatic monitoring and tracking of patients, personnel, and biomedical devices within hospitals and nursing institutes has been proposed. With the IoT vision in mind, a complex network infrastructure relying on a CoAP, 6LoWPAN, and REST paradigms has been implemented so as to allow the interoperation among UHF RFID Gen2, WSN, and smart mobile technologies. In particular, taking advantage of the zero-power RFID-based data transmission, an ultra-low- power Hybrid Sensing Network (HSN) has been implemented." (Fig. 2)

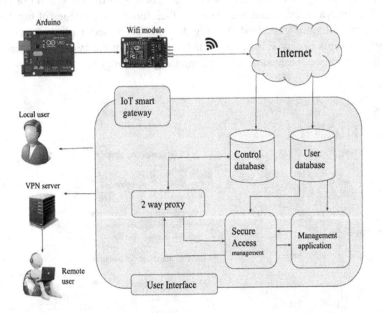

Fig. 2. Overview of the Smart Hospital System (SHS) architecture

[12] proposed a novel signal quality- aware IoT-enabled ECG telemetry system for continuous cardiac health monitoring applications. The proposed ECG setup consist of

ECG module, automated signal quality assessment module and signal-quality aware ECG analysis and transmission module. The objective was to make a light-weight ECG signal quality assessment method for identifying and classifying the input ECG signal into acceptable and unacceptable class and real time implementation of the proposed system using ECG sensors, Arduino board, android enabled smartphone, Bluetooth module and cloud server.

The various trials generated congruent results that Software quality assurance method improves the quality in identifying the unacceptable ECG signals and outperforms existing methods based on the morphological and RR interval features and machine learning approaches. After the completion of various trails, the author further concludes that transmission quality of ECG signals can significantly improve the battery lifetime of IoT-enabled devices." (Fig. 3)

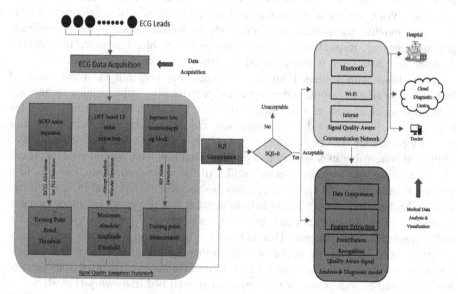

Fig. 3. Proposed signal quality-aware IoT framework for energy and resource-efficient ECG telemetry system [6]

[16] proposed a system which is expected to reduce costs, increase the quality of life, and enrich the user's experience. This system reduces the headache of patient to visit to doctor every time he/she needs to check ECG and temperature and pulse oxygen in blood. Doctors and hospitals could make use of real-time data collected on the cloud platform to provide fast and efficient solution [13]. It is impossible for the huge population of elders to follow the traditional health care. This IoT based system not only provides an accurate diagnosis of the user's condition, but rather a solution that detects and prevents health episodes by carefully following, capturing, and describing the health trends recorded from physiological and contextual sensors.

3 Smart Beds for Pressure Ulcer

There are innumerable solutions to cure bedsore [17, 18] present in the market for hospital beds given by various govt and non govt agencies. But, till now there has not been any solutions to cure bedsores in a cost-efficient manner. One such way is, to reduce the labour cost involved in monitoring patient illness through physical means.

The focus of this model is to build up a product equipment stage that tends to a standout amongst the most exorbitant, intense wellbeing conditions, weight ulcers - or bed bruises. Looking after weight ulcers is amazingly exorbitant, expands the length of healing centre stays and is extremely work concentrated. The solution/bed proposed will cater to 4 dimensions of curing and monitoring bedsores in a cost-efficient manner i.e. data collection, learning, reasoning and deciding, and acting. When we implement these 4 dimensions, the ability of the bed to cure bedsores in a cost-effective manner magnifies. Wide variety of sensors have been used which will accelerate the beds ability to monitor the patient very accurately in various aspects, which are body pressure imaging, respiration rate, heart rate and even blood pressure information. A signal processing unit is often needed to extract the desired information.

Interactions with various hospitals concludes that beds are the main cause of bedsores. The simplest solution that one could propose is by implementing technology in the bed which can act as a first line of defence. Biological data collection from the hospitals can be considered as the best way for our system to learn and monitor patient's conditions. The objective of this work, as a rule, is to improve the capacities of the bed concerning its scholarly and physical qualities, with the end goal that it can give subjective help to healing centre staff. All the more particularly, the mix of a sensor organize, machine knowledge, a morphable, tiled surface, and PC control can create a brilliant bed fit for offering help to the staff that altogether enhances the care, epidemiological investigation and aversion of weight ulcers. The savvy bed lessens the staff expected to turn patients. That implies the medical attendant can invest more straightforward care energy at the bedside evaluating for difficulties or antagonistic occasions as opposed to searching for help to turn the patient. There are four parts of intrigue identified with a weight ulcer mindful shrewd bed framework (Fig. 4).

3.1 Data Collection from Mat

In order to measure pressure over the entire body, a pressure mat is developed over the bed's surface in an array format. The surface is developed using a material known as Velostat which act as a resistance between the two conducting surfaces. This material is used with copper wire to track the body position and movements. The Velostat acts as a pressure mat which is perfect for tracking various activities of the patient such as analysing sleep pattern, monitoring the limbs, body mapping, predicting the location of pressure ulcer. The collected data is then send to the microcontroller which transfers the collected data to the cloud for further analysis.

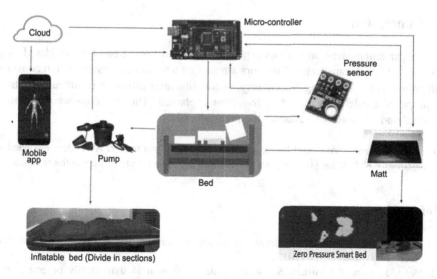

Fig. 4. Flowchart of the system [7]

3.2 Process After Data Collection

After the collection of the data, the collected information is used to conclude various aspects of the patient's health such as the position of the patient and limbs, temperature of the body of patient, breathing pattern, sleeping analysis and much more. This information is used by the doctors for various conclusions.

3.3 Working of the Bed

First the patient uses the smart bed application which has a 3D human obj. built in. The patient marks the areas where he/she is affected. After the inputting of data, the bed starts to inflate and fills up completely in about 7 to 8 min. The pressure of the inflation is monitored using pressure sensors. The bed is divided into multiple sections which inflated and deflates independently. After that the patient lays down on the bed and the pressure mat tracks the body of the patient. The complete body of the patient is mapped and various parameters for monitoring the overall health of the patient are collected using different sensors. After the tracking of the body, the pump starts to inflate and deflate following the different patterns depending upon the condition of the bedsore which is determined using the input from the application of the patient. The inflation and deflation in different pattern results in the improvement in the flow of blood which in turn cures and decreases the chances of bedsore. Other than curing the bed sore, the bed is capable of predicting the possible locations on the body of the bedsores. This intensive information of the patient body is very essential for the doctors to treat patients in a better, cheaper and faster way.

4 Conclusion

This paper emphasizes on various aspects of IoT and how it can be considered as a boon to the health care sector. The work stresses on a healthcare system which consider different aspects including traceability, accounting and effective healthcare control. A proposed model for smart bed has been explained. The bed consists of velostat material and biosensors to analyse the pressure points.

Acknowledgement. We would like to express our sincere gratitude to Accendere Knowledge Management Pvt. Ltd. for providing us the platform and opportunity to pursue the research.

References

1. Miorandi, M.D.: Internet of Things: vision, applications and research challenges. Ad Hoc Netw. **10**(7), 1497–1516 (2012)
2. Deng, J., Han, R., Mishra, S.: Secure code distribution in dynamically programmable wireless sensor networks. In: Proceedings of the 5th International Conference on Information Processing in Sensor Networks (IPSN), pp. 292–300 (2006)
3. Minoli, D., Sohraby, K., et al.: IoT considerations, requirements, and architectures for insurance applications. In: Hassan, Q. (ed.) Internet of Things. CRC Press, Boca Raton (2017)
4. Zorzi, M., Gluhak, A., Lange, S., Bassi, A.: From today's intranet of things to a future internet of things: a wireless- and mobility-related view. IEEE Wirel. Commun. **17**(6), 44–51 (2010)
5. Darianian, M., Michael, M.: Smart home mobile RFID based Internet-of-Things systems and services. In: Proceedings of the International Conference on Advanced Computer Theory and Engineering, pp. 116–120 (2008)
6. Chunli, L.: Intelligent transportation based on the Internet of Things. In: Proceedings of the International Conference on Consumer Electronics, Communications and Networks, pp. 360–362 (2012)
7. Talpur, M.S.: The appliance pervasive of internet of things in healthcare systems. computer Science, Cornell university library (2013)
8. Kodali, R., Boppana, L.: An implementation of IoT for healthcare. IEEE, December 2015
9. Tyagi, S., Aggarwal, A., Maheshwari, I.P.: A conceptual framework for IoT based healthcare system using cloud computing. IEEE (2016)
10. Tokognon, C., Gao, B., Tian, G., Yan, Y.: Structural health monitoring framework based on Internet of Things. IEEE IoT J. May 2015
11. Catarinucci, L., et al.: An IoT-Aware architecture for smart healthcare systems. IEEE IoT J. (2014)
12. Satija, U., Ramkumar, B., Manikandan, M.: Real-Time signal quality-aware ECG telemetry system for IoT-based health care monitoring. IEEE, pp. 73–80 (2015)
13. Khatri, A., Kumar, S., Kaiwartya, O., Abdullah, A.H.: Green computing in wireless sensor networks: huffman coding and optimization approach. Peer-to-Peer Networking and Applications. Springer, US (2016)
14. Khatri, A., Kumar, S., Kaiwartya, O.: Towards green computing in wireless sensor networks. controlled mobility aided balanced tree approach. Int. J. Commun Syst **31**(7), e3463 (2017)

15. Khatri, A., et al.: Optimizing energy consumption and inequality in wireless sensor networks using NSGA-II. In: Proceedings of ICCCS. Taylor & Francis, Boca Raton, 10 September 2016

16. Nerker, R., Salunke, P.: IoT driven healthcare for remote monitoring of patient. Int. J. Mod. Trends Sci. Technol., **3**(6), June 2017

17. Smith, D.: Pressure ulcers in the nursing home. Ann. Intern. Med. **123**(6), 433–438 (1995)

18. Hsia, C., Liou, K., Aung, A., Foo, V., Huang, W., Biswas, J.: Analysis and comparison of sleeping posture classification methods using pressure sensitive bed system. In: Annual International Conference of the IEEE Engineering in Medicine and Biology Society, EMBC 2009, pp. 6131–6134. IEEE (2009)

Blockchain Technology in Fund Management

David Doe Fiergbor[(✉)]

KBF Centre for International Studies, Bortianor - Accra, Ghana
daviddoef@gmail.com

Abstract. Technological application in business is enormous as corporate institutions are striving to reduce operational cost and to maximize profit as well as to create enabling environment for efficiency and effectiveness. One of the disruptive technologies for business application is Blockchain Technology. Emerging markets are taking advantage of Blockchain technology's integration and application in the financial service industry to break new grounds for better service delivery. The integration of Blockchain technology in fund management business would enhance data credibility, transparency, accuracy, accountability and immutability between fund managers and investors. This is due to the security features of data storage in Blockchain technology that make data alteration difficult. This paper discusses about the mutual funds management in Ghana. The paper also introduces the prospects of Blockchain Technology in Fund Management in Ghana.

Keywords: Mutual funds · Performance evaluation · Blockchain technology
Ethereum · Smart city

1 Introduction

Many research works had been done on fund management in recent times in assessing fund management integration into other areas of business interest. Notable among them was conducted by Van Duuren, Plantinga and Scholtens on ESG Integration and the Investment Management Process. The studies revealed three things which were; first, many conventional fund managers have adopted features of responsible investing in their investment process. The second was that in many respects ESG investing seems to resemble fundamental investing. The third was that the domicile of the portfolio manager has a distinct impact on responsible investing: US-based managers tend to be skeptical about its benefits, whereas European managers are outright optimistic (Van Duuren et al. (2016)). However, not much work had been researched on the prospects and application of Blockchain technology in fund management in Ghana. It was against this background that the author sought to evaluate the prospects of Blockchain technology, its integration and application in fund management.

Over the last decade, there has been the emergence of mutual funds in Ghana. These fund managers have intense influence in the money market and capital market of the economy. They serve as agents to the unit holders, they select the stocks that will bring forth good returns to their unit holders, and also provide good financial advisory services

© Springer Nature Singapore Pte Ltd. 2018
G. C. Deka et al. (Eds.): ICACCT 2018, CCIS 899, pp. 310–319, 2018.
https://doi.org/10.1007/978-981-13-2035-4_27

to their clients. A mutual fund is a collective investment that pools funds and resources from different investors with the same investment objectives in order to gain greater buying power (Hall 2010). It can be seen as the pool of funds invested in accordance with a specified objective. Mutual funds are professionally managed investment schemes that allow small investors to invest in order to gain some returns. Money collected from investors is invested in diversified portfolios in the capital market and money market. Investors who invest their funds in mutual funds are called unit holders. The investment gains gotten from the mutual funds are shared amongst the unit holders in proportion to the number of units or shares owned by each of them. The investment returns are received in the form of capital gains and dividends. In view of this, each shareholder shares in the capital gains and capital losses in the fund. Simply put, mutual funds are means of investing in something with a group of people (Northcott (2009)).

Rest of the paper is divided into 4 Sections. Section 2 is a literature review. While Sect. 3 is Research methodology, Sect. 4 is a Case Study about the Mutual Fund management in Ghana. Section 5 Prospects of Mutual Fund management in Ghana by Blockchain Technology, finally, the Conclusion Section concludes the paper.

2 Literature Review

The evolution of mutual funds to the modern state was welcomed with the arrival of the Massachusetts Investor's Trust which was formed in 1924 (Bogle (1994)). The fund went public in 1928 which eventually emanated into the mutual fund firm MFS investment management. The Massachusetts Investor's Trust was the first to have an open-end fund structure that allowed for shares to be continuously issued and redeemed by the investment company at a price that is proportional to the value of the underlying investment portfolio.

Whiles there is no legal definition of mutual funds; it can be defined as a professionally managed investment scheme that pools fund from investors with the main aim of purchasing securities to create more wealth for its investors. Mutual funds are flexible investment schemes that are made public to the general public and are also classified as open-ended. They provide investments schemes that are safe and lucrative. The combined securities of the mutual fund are known as portfolio. Mutual funds are managed by professional fund managers, who invest the fund's money in order to generate income and capital gains for the unit holders of the fund. Mutual funds allow investors to pool their investments together in order to participate in a larger and diversified portfolio (Russell (2007)).

Mutual funds' investments avoid the usual restrictions on individual investments. This would increase their ability to diversify and lower the costs of buying and selling shares. The proportion of tradable shares possession has inhibitory effect toward the rate of return as the current managerial fees and previous managerial fees affect the funding rate of return positively (Yi et al (2016)). The profits of mutual funds usually consist of capital profits, profits resulting from an improvement or change in the prices of the invested securities in addition to the securities distribution if any. The fund can face losses in case the value of the securities' that make up the fund's assets decreased. The definition has been further extended by allowing mutual funds to diversify their activities in the following areas:

- Portfolio management services
- Management of offshore funds
- Providing advice to offshore funds
- Management of pension or provident funds
- Management of venture capital funds
- Management of money market funds
- Management of real estate funds

A mutual fund serves as a link between the investor and the securities market by mobilizing savings from the investors and investing them in the securities market to generate returns. As data becomes the bedrock for fund managers for their decision making, the essence of Blockchain technology as a distributed ledger comes into picture. A Blockchain is a type of distributed ledger, which enables records to be stored and sorted into blocks (Deloitte (2016)).

As cloud computing had been successfully integrated into businesses, Blockchain technology could also be invariably integrated in fund management which would enhance data credibility, transparency, accuracy, accountability and immutability between fund managers and investors. This is due to the security features of data storage in Blockchain technology that make data alteration difficult. Benefits of the Blockchain Technology are:

- Saves time - Transaction time from days to near instantaneous
- Removes cost overheads and cost intermediaries
- Reduces risk, Tampering, fraud & cyber crime
- Increases Trust through shared processes and recordkeeping

3   Research Methodology

The research instrument employed for this study was the unstructured interview guide. The interview guide was used to collect date from randomly selected staff of fund management companies.

The sources of data employed in the research were based on both primary and secondary data. The primary data were sourced with the aid of interview guide from clients and the staff of fund management companies. The secondary data was based on published information, journals and reports found on the internet. The following table shows the field used for capturing data in this research work (Table 1).

Table 1. Research methodology used in this work

Structure of the interview guide	Issues to explore
Part 1 and 2; Organizational profile and work	(i) Organization's profile (ii) Nature of the organization's work and (iii) Target and prospective clients
Part 3; Mutual funds in Ghana	(i) Investment instruments in Ghana (ii) Mutual funds (iii) Awareness of mutual funds in Ghana (iv) Public understanding of mutual funds (v) Public perception of mutual funds (vi) Applications of technology in mutual funds
Part 4; Funds risk, performance and evaluation	(i) Performance of mutual funds (ii) Evaluation of mutual funds performances (iii) Risk associated with mutual funds (iv) Relationship between risk and returns on mutual funds (v) Methods used in assessing mutual fund performance
Part 5; Conclusion	(i) Investment prospects of mutual funds (ii) The way forward for mutual funds (iii) Future technological prospects of mutual funds

i. Classification of Mutual Funds

A scheme can also be classified as growth scheme, income scheme, or balanced scheme considering its investment objective. Such schemes may be classified mainly as follows:

- Growth/Equity Oriented Schemes
- Income/ Debt Oriented Schemes
- Balanced Funds
- Liquid Funds
- Gilt Funds
- Index Funds

(a) Issues & Challenges
i. Awareness of Mutual Funds in Ghana

Mutual funds are not well known to the "average Ghanaian". Most Ghanaians do not know about the existence and benefits of investing in mutual funds. Most Ghanaians do not invest in mutual funds. It is only a minimal percentage of the working population that has investment in the fund schemes. The lack of awareness of mutual funds among Ghanaians is mostly due to the high level of financial illiteracy among Ghanaians. Most Ghanaians are "financial illiterates" due to the low level of knowledge exhibited in financial matters.

ii. **Public Understanding of Mutual Funds**

The high level of financial illiteracy among Ghanaians permeates into most of the financial instruments which mutual fund is not an exception. A chuck of the Ghanaian populace has little to negligible knowledge and understanding of mutual funds. Even this challenge does not exclude the elite. Hence most people who want to invest do not consider mutual funds as investments avenues. However, the low level of understanding of mutual funds among the Ghanaian populace is as a result of inadequate public education on finance. For instance, in most of the specialized institutions such as the Nursing Colleges and the Colleges of Education, there are virtually no finance, accounting or economics courses in their curriculum where students' knowledge will be expounded on the various aspects of financial and investment products available in the country.

(b) **Challenges Faced by Fund Managers**

Mutual fund managers face the following challengers;

- High Cost
- Inadequate Knowledge on Investment
- Fluctuation in Share Price Movement
- Expenses and Fees Charge by Fund Managers
- Sales Charges
- 12 b-1 Fees
- Management Fees
- Trading Costs

(c) **Fund Administration Methods Implored by fund managers**

The following methods of the fund administration were itemized by the fund managers:

- Calculation of the fund's net asset valuation on every day, month to month, quarterly, semiannual or yearly basis.
- Maintenance of investment portfolio including securities valuation.
- Calculating of management and performance fees.
- Profit allocation on series or shares equalization methods.
- Monitoring the investor register of the fund.
- Accepting investor subscription, transfer and redemption applications.
- Maintaining client bank accounts for receipt of subscription funds and payment of redemption proceeds.
- Issuing investor statements, confirmations, contract notes, call notices and investment manager's reports.
- Online access for investors and managers to view reports.
- Finally, providing reports to enable the preparations of the audited annual financial statement in accordance with IFRS.

(d) **Fund Performance Using Composite Measure**

The use of these indexes requires that, the Beta and the Standard deviation of the funds are known (Fig. 1).

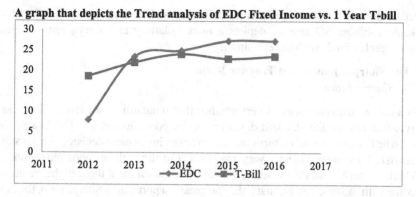

Fig. 1. Trend analysis of EDC Fixed Income vs. 1 Year T-bill (Source: Researcher's work)

Additionally, Market return, Portfolio return, and risk free return will also be specified (Table 2).

Table 2. Trend analysis of EDC Fixed Income vs. 1 Year T-bill

Year	EDC	T-Bill
2012	8	18.63
2013	23.4	21.94
2014	24.9	23.97
2015	27.3	22.9
2016	27.3	23.5

Source: EDC Fixed Income annual reports

(e) Net Asset Value (NAV)

The performance of a particular scheme of a mutual fund is denoted by Net Asset Value (NAV). Mutual funds invest the money collected from the investors in securities markets. In simple words, Net Asset Value is the market value of the securities held by the scheme. Since market value of securities changes every day, NAV of a scheme also varies on day to day basis. The NAV per unit is the market value of securities of a scheme divided by the total number of units of the scheme on any particular date. NAV is required to be disclosed by the mutual funds on a regular basis - daily or weekly depending on the type of scheme.

(f) Standard Deviation and Beta of Investment Funds

The Standard Deviation (SD) measures the volatility of the fund's returns in relation to its average. It shows how much the fund's return can deviate from the historical mean return of the scheme.

The beta measures a fund's volatility compared to that of a benchmark. It determines how much a fund's performance would swing compared to a benchmark. The low SD and beta average values of the funds accounted for their growth over the years as they attracted more investors to grow the customer base and the size of the funds. This contributed massively for the more reason the funds always out-performed the bench-mark. As a higher SD number depicts a more volatility in a fund's returns. Hence investors prefer funds with lower volatility.

(g) **The Sharpe, Jensen and Treynor Ratio**
   i. *Sharpe Index*

Is a risk-adjusted measure of performance that standardizes the return in excess of the risk-free rate by the standard deviation of the portfolios return. The Sharpe ratio shows whether a portfolio's returns are due to smart investment decisions or a result of excess risk. This measurement is very useful because although one portfolio or fund can reap higher returns than its peers, it is only a good investment if those higher returns do not come with too much additional risk. The greater a portfolio's Sharpe ratio, the better its risk-adjusted performance has been. A negative Sharpe ratio indicates that a risk-less asset would perform better than the security being analyzed.

The Sharpe performance index (Si), is

$$S_i = \frac{r_p - r_f}{\Sigma p} \tag{1}$$

Where,
r_p = portfolio return r_f = risk free rate
σp = standard deviation of the portfolio

(h) **Jensen Index**

Jensen's alpha (or Jensen's Performance Index, ex-post alpha) is a measure of performance that compares the actual return with return that should have been earned for the amount of risk borne by the investor. Jensen alpha is given by the formula below;

Jensen's alpha = Portfolio Return - [Risk free rate + portfolio Beta * (Market Return - Risk Free Rate)]

ii. *Treynor index*

The Treynor index is a risk-adjusted measure of performance that standardizes the risk premium of a portfolio with the portfolio's systematic risk or beta coefficient. Treynor's index is given by;

Treynor index = (portfolio return - risk-free rate)/portfolio beta coefficient

$$T_i = \frac{R_p - R_f}{B} \tag{2}$$

4 Case Study - Mutual Funds in Ghana

The most popular application of Blockchain technology is Bitcoin, a cryptocurrency. 1 Bitcoin is created in every 10 min. Bitcoin is used by more than 375,000 people world-wide every day. Bitcoin is accepted by more than 50 thousand merchants worldwide.

The following are some of the prominent use cases of Blockchain Technology (IEEE Spectrum (2017, September 29)) Srinivasa and Deka (2017).

i. IBM and Intel are collaborating on an open source Blockchain initiative called Hyperledger.

ii. TenneT Holding records and Coordinates several thousand residential energy storage is built on a variant of Blockchain technology called Fabric-a product of Hyperledger a collaborative Blockchain project run by Linux Foundation

iii. Consensys System, a Blockchain studio in Brooklyn, has an application very similar to TransActive Grid in the works of the Ethereum Blockchain.

iv. Enel, a multinational utility in Rome is developing a Blockchain based market for energy wholesalers in Europe.

v. Dubai city Government to support public Blockchain Ethereum and a distributed ledger code base Fibre (Open source Linux Foundation project Hyperledger). The city to go paperless by 2020. Under Smart Dubai, 25 city agencies to begin a pilot before the end of 2017.

vi. Similar projects are already under way in Sweden and Republic of Georgia.

vii. Illinois Department of Commerce and Economic Opportunity, the state is launching 5 separate Blockchain pilot projects.

viii. Blockchain has the potential to reduce infrastructure cost up to $20 billion a year.

ix. P2P money Transfer across international borders - segment worth $500 B.

Anderseen Horowitz (VC firm) has invested over USD $100 million into Blockchain technology There are over 4000 active fintech startups in the NY arena and investment in the sector tripling last year to $12 Billion. Research scholars and scientists are meticulously working for identifying and pinpointing the prospects as well as barriers of this technology.

There are high prospects for mutual funds in Ghana as there are a lot of potential markets for fund managers to explore and attract more investors locally and globally. With the discovery of oil and the IMF bailout policy which the central government has rolled unto, there are future prospects of economic stability as the central bank is also taking prudent measures to ensure long term stability of the cedi (A unit of currency of Ghana) which is the local currency against the major foreign currencies. Yields on investment are expected to rise which is more likely to attract more investors into the mutual fund industry.

There are enormous opportunities for mutual funds to thrive in the Ghanaian economy in the coming years. This is due to the analysis that the industry is young and the market is huge. However, there are certain measures to be taken to exploit these opportunities which include but not limited to public education on mutual funds.

In many parts of the world, collective investment schemes are becoming more and more popular in recent time and more accessible to the individual investor. Investors are thus looking beyond traditional investments for such opportunities that will give them higher return on their capital. However, it is very important for investors to realize that there is no guarantee that one particular scheme will give them an above average return. They need to carefully evaluate all facts concerning a particular scheme. Most investors are tempted into believing that a scheme will do well because it did well in the past and as such invest in such a scheme. It is not certain that a scheme will in future repeat its past performance. The share prices might have already reached their peak with no prospect for further significant growth. It is recommended that investors consider investing in funds when their share prices are not already at their peak by evaluating and analyzing growth prospects of the fund as opposed to just past performance.

(a) **Discussion of Findings:** Investment Instruments in Ghana

The financial industry is still young in Ghana as there are still many viable prospects to explore. However, in the researcher's quest to explore some of the investment instruments implore by mutual funds to grow their assets, the following investment instruments came to light;

- Pension fund
- Asset management
- Unit trust

5   Prospects of Mutual Funds Management in Ghana by Blockchain Technology

Emerging markets such as Ghana, due to:

- their higher mutual fund management risks
- lower penetration, and
- Greater presence of digital financing, are an ideal backdrop for the adoption of Blockchain-based financial solutions, and benefits could include a technological leap forward and a boost to financial inclusion and growth.

There are vast prospects for rapidly developing Blockchain technology into a full range of financial services, beyond just digital payments of which its application in mutual fund is a viable avenue. The Blockchain system when carefully and properly exploited with it enormous prospects can reach previously unexploited markets and the huge unreached customer (investor) base in the Ghanaian economy. Blockchain application in mutual fund management where reconciliations of records relating to transactions especially between fund managers and investors can be costly and time consuming, when performed via traditional channels will be rapid, effective and efficient. As transactions become more efficient and effective, profitability increases thereby reducing liquidity and operational costs.

Blockchain technology when integrated into mutual fund management in Ghana has the following prospects;

- Investors will be connected on a platform that enables them to monitor the performance of their investment pool
- Fund managers will be opened to attract more investors based on the performance of their funds

Accurate and reliable information accessibility by prospective investors will not be a challenge as data entries into the blocks cannot be tempered.

6 Conclusion

The fund administration technique employed by the fund managers was such that recording transactions involved complex financial and investment reporting. Seasoned and well-skilled professionals were employed to manage the fund. Fund managers made the effort of keeping customers abreast with the performance of the fund and through the use of the print media, online and printable tracts. Investors invest in mutual funds for various reasons such as its liquidity nature, safety of their principal, high expected returns and because of regular information investors receive on fund performance. It is only a fraction of the elite who are abreast with appreciable level of knowledge on mutual funds. There is also high cost involved in investing or saving with mutual fund companies. The role of mutual funds in the capital market cannot be overemphasized. They form an integral part of the capital market. Hence there is the need for all stakeholders in the market to boost investors' confidence in the market. This could be achieved by way of organizing seminars and trainings to educate the Ghanaian populace. Future prospects of Blockchain technology in fund management are bright as the resultant effect would be investor confidence in data security and ease of doing transactions online without third party intervention.

References

Bogle, J.: Bogle On Mutual Funds-New Perspective For The Intelligent Investor. Dell publishing group Inc., New York (1994)

Deloitte: Bitcoin, Blockchain & distributed ledgers: Caught between promise and reality, Centre for the Edge, Australia (2016). Accessed 13 Jan 2017

Hall, A.D.: Getting Started in Mutual Funds, 2nd edn. Wiley, Hoboken (2010)

Northcott, A.: The Mutual Funds Book: How to Invest in Mutual Funds & Earn Higher Rates of Returns. Atlantic Publishing Group Inc., Ocala (2009)

Russell, R.: An Introduction to Mutual Funds Worldwide. The Atrium (Southern Gate). Wiley, Chichester (2007)

Van Duuren, E., Plantinga, A., Scholtens, B.: ESG integration and the investment management process: fundamental investing reinvented. J. Bus. Eth. **138**(3), 525–533 (2016)

Yi, J., Lu, D., Deng, Y.: Empirical study under the encouraging model to managerial fees of social security fund investment. Am. J. Ind. Bus. Manag. **6**(05), 649 (2016)

IEEE Spectrum: Special Report: Blockchain World, 29 September 2017 https://spectrum.ieee.org/static/special-report-blockchain-world. Accessed 17 Mar 2018

Srinivasa, K.G., Deka, G.C. (eds.): Free and Open Source Software in Modern Data Science and Business Intelligence: Emerging Research and Opportunities: Emerging Research and Opportunities. IGI Global, Hershey (2017)

Performance Analysis of Time Series Forecasting Using Machine Learning Algorithms for Prediction of Ebola Casualties

Manish Kumar Pandey[✉] and Karthikeyan Subbiah

Department of Computer Science, Institute of Science,
Banaras Hindu University, Varanasi 221005, India
pandey.manish@live.com, karthinikita@gmail.com

Abstract. There is an immense concern on our vigilance for controlling the spread of pandemics such as Ebola, Zika, and H1N1 etc. through state of art technology. The dynamics become very complex of epidemics in sweeping population. Efficient descriptive, predictive, preventive and prescriptive analyses on the huge data generated by SMAC are very crucial for valuable arrangement and associated responsive tactics. In this paper, we have proposed the use of machine learning techniques for performance evaluation of time series forecasting of Ebola casualties. By experimenting without lag creation, we achieved the best results in the MAE of 7.85%, RMSE value of 61.14%, and Direction Accuracy of 85.99% with Random Tree Classifier. Thus we can conclude that by using these models for forecasting epidemic spread and developing public health policies leads the health authorities to ensure the appropriate actions for the control of the outbreak.

Keywords: SMAC · Epidemic Forecasting · Ebola · Time series forecasting
Random tree

1 Introduction

Globally infectious diseases are the major cause of human mortality. The six deadliest infections are pneumonia, tuberculosis, diarrhea, malaria, measles and HIV/AIDS. The occurrences of infectious diseases can be unearthed as far back as the middle ages. Disease Outbreaks from Middle Ages to 21st Century are illustrated in the Fig. 1 [1].

The word epidemic was derived from the Greek words: epi (upon) and demos (people) meaning "upon people." It is an event in a population, of cases of a sickness, particular health behavior or other health-related events in a surplus of what would be normally possible. A pandemic is an epidemic that sweeps a population, such as the H1N1 eruption in 2009, whereas, an endemic disease is one in which new infections are regularly happening in the residents.

The 2014–2016 outbreaks in West Africa were the largest and most complex Ebola outbreak since the virus was first discovered in 1976. It has more confirmed cases and casualties in this outbreak than the rest combined. It has started from Guinea and spread between Sierra Leone and Liberia. Key facts and Chronology of previous Ebola virus outbreaks are given in Fig. 2 and Table 1 [2].

© Springer Nature Singapore Pte Ltd. 2018
G. C. Deka et al. (Eds.): ICACCT 2018, CCIS 899, pp. 320–334, 2018.
https://doi.org/10.1007/978-981-13-2035-4_28

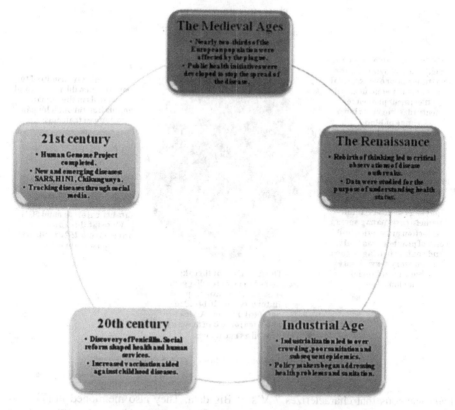

Fig. 1. Disease outbreaks from the middle Ages to 21st Century

The study of the distribution and determinants of the events related to health across specified populations and its application for description, prediction, prevention and prescription of health problems is defined as *Epidemiology* [3]. The Main concern of Epidemiologists is public health which includes the efficient analytics of descriptive public data and maintenance of its collection. They do it by exploring the spatial extent of the outbreak, progress chart of the disease, mode of controlling the disease, the origin of disease and how it is different than the previous outbreaks.

2 Big Data Analytics in Epidemiology

History of Epidemiology goes long back to 1760. In 1760; Daniel Bernoulli [4] has given the first mathematical model and established that inoculation could facilitate an increase in the life expectancy in France. A British physician, John Snow analyzed a cholera outbreak in London in 1854. He had attributed it to a supply of polluted water [4]. In the current era of SMAC [5, 6] platforms, a huge amount of data is getting generated from various sources like social networking sites, real time streams of outbreaks etc. In [7], authors had mentioned how Healthcare data are so varied and

Ebola virus disease (EVD), formerly known as Ebola haemorrhagic fever, is a severe, often fatal illness in humans.

Early supportive care with rehydration, symptomatic treatment improves survival. There is as yet no licensed treatment proven to neutralize the virus but a range of blood, immunological and drug therapies are under development.

Community engagement is key to successfully controlling outbreaks. Good outbreak control relies on applying a package of interventions, namely case management, infection prevention and control practices, surveillance and contact tracing, a good laboratory service, safe burials and social mobilisation.

The virus is transmitted to people from wild animals and spreads in the human population through human-to-human transmission.

The average EVD case fatality rate is around 50%. Case fatality rates have varied from 25% to 90% in past outbreaks.

The first EVD outbreaks occurred in remote villages in Central Africa, near tropical rainforests. The 2014–2016 outbreak in West Africa involved major urban areas as well as rural ones.

Fig. 2. Key facts about Ebola disease outbreak

heterogeneous that characterizes 7 V's of Big data. They also mentioned in [7], how Disease Outbreaks comes under social health category of healthcare data. These huge data make the computational Epidemiology more complex and became *Big Data Computational Epidemiology which* is a rising interdisciplinary field that uses intelligent big data analytics methods for understanding and controlling the spatiotemporal transmission of disease throughout populations. Following are the reasons for the need of big data computational epidemiology:

1. Mathematical models have become increasingly complex for which big data analytics tools are required.
2. The model representing the affected population creates a complex interaction network. These network models are real scenarios based which makes it more computational and data costly. As mentioned in [6, 8], the analysis of such data sets requires powerful computing resources and big data analytics tools.
3. New methods of disease surveillance and detection are required for collection of huge data generated.
4. With the SMAC era, where everyone is connected to the internet, there is a growing demand for developing web-based tools that can be accessed by epidemiologists in a pervasive manner. This clearly indicates the role of big data epidemiology [9].

The Big Data computational epidemiology involves four basic classes of problem analysis based upon the network created in the places where the disease has spread.

Table 1. Chronology of previous Ebola virus disease outbreaks

Year	Country	Ebolavirus species	Cases	Deaths	Case fatality
2015	Italy	Zaire	1	0	0%
2014	DRC	Zaire	66	49	74%
2014	Spain	Zaire	1	0	0%
2014	UK	Zaire	1	0	0%
2014	USA	Zaire	4	1	25%
2014	Senegal	Zaire	1	0	0%
2014	Mali	Zaire	8	6	75%
2014	Nigeria	Zaire	20	8	40%
2014–2016	Sierra Leone	Zaire	14124*	3956*	28%
2014–2016	Liberia	Zaire	10675*	4809*	45%
2014–2016	Guinea	Zaire	3811*	2543*	67%
2012	Democratic Republic of Congo	Bundibugyo	57	29	51%
2012	Uganda	Sudan	7	4	57%
2012	Uganda	Sudan	24	17	71%
2011	Uganda	Sudan	1	1	100%
2008	Democratic Republic of Congo	Zaire	32	14	44%
2007	Uganda	Bundibugyo	149	37	25%
2007	Democratic Republic of Congo	Zaire	264	187	71%
2005	Congo	Zaire	12	10	83%
2004	Sudan	Sudan	17	7	41%
2003 (Nov–Dec)	Congo	Zaire	35	29	83%
2003 (Jan–Apr)	Congo	Zaire	143	128	90%
2001–2002	Congo	Zaire	59	44	75%
2001–2002	Gabon	Zaire	65	53	82%
2000	Uganda	Sudan	425	224	53%
1996	South Africa (ex-Gabon)	Zaire	1	1	100%
1996 (Jul–Dec)	Gabon	Zaire	60	45	75%
1996 (Jan–Apr)	Gabon	Zaire	31	21	68%
1995	Democratic Republic of Congo	Zaire	315	254	81%
1994	Côte d'Ivoire	Taï Forest	1	0	0%
1994	Gabon	Zaire	52	31	60%
1979	Sudan	Sudan	34	22	65%
1977	Democratic Republic of Congo	Zaire	1	1	100%
1976	Sudan	Sudan	284	151	53%
1976	Democratic Republic of Congo	Zaire	318	280	88%

Table 2. Algorithms used in the proposed work

Linear-Regression	Class for using linear regression for prediction
MLP	A Classifier that uses back-propagation to classify instances
SMOReg	SMOreg implements the support vector machine for regression. The algorithm is chosen by setting the RegOptimizer. [29, 30]
Ensemble-Selection	Several classifiers can be integrated using the ensemble selection method. [31]
Bagging	Class for bagging a classifier to decrease variance. [32]
Random-Forest	Class for building a forest of random trees. [33]
RepTree	Fast decision tree learner. Builds a decision/regression tree using information gain/variance and prunes it using reduced-error pruning (with backfitting). Only sorts values for numeric attributes once. Missing values are dealt with by splitting the corresponding instances into pieces (i.e. as in C4.5)
Random Tree	Class for constructing a tree that considers K randomly chosen attributes at each node. Performs no pruning. Also has an option to allow estimation of class probabilities (or target mean in the regression case) based on a holdout set (backfitting)

Descriptive Analytics: This step describes the extent of the disease outbreak, thus helps in identifying the duration and other properties of the epidemic. Actual visualization of the spread and other related features could be helpful in the next step.

Predictive Analytics: This step determines the quantitative attributes of the epidemic. Machine Learning techniques can be used for efficiently forecasting the spread based on the output of the previous step.

Preventive Analytics: With the help of forecasting result obtained in the previous step, we can put a check on the spread of the epidemic. This can be done in this step by identifying the spread network, initial condition and the model that can be applied.

Prescriptive Analytics: This includes strategies for controlling the spread of epidemics, e.g., by vaccination or quarantining, correspond to making changes in the node functions or removing edges so that the system converges to configurations with few infections. We could use the result of preventive analytics for an efficient delivery model of production, transportation and distribution of vaccines, doctors and other resources. In this paper, we propose predictive analytics techniques about the recent outbreak of Ebola for casualties forecasting using training as well as testing set.

Predictive analytics include problems of determining quantities, such as the number of casualties, no of suspected cases, number of infections over time, etc. Epidemic Forecasting in terms of casualties, location, etc. is an important topic in big data computational Epidemiology. It involves collecting and combining data from nontraditional sources like Social Media, Wikipedia, and World Health Organization's surveillance systems and processing them with statistical models and machine learning techniques to now cast and forecast the occurrence of diseases in the host population. Nsoesie et al. [10] has made a literature review with the case study of Influenza outbreak. Nishiura [11] have given a discrete time stochastic model and applied as a case study of the weekly incidence of pandemic influenza in Japan. Ohkusa et al. [12] have demonstrated real-time estimation and prediction of the entire course of a pandemic of ILI (influenza-like illness) in Japan. Hall et al. [13] have predicted the spread of the H5N1 influenza virus in birds by fitting a mass-action epidemic model to the surveillance data from standard regression analysis. Tizzoni et al. [14] have proposed Global Epidemic and Mobility Model to generate stochastic simulations of epidemic spread worldwide using a Monte Carlo Maximum Likelihood analysis. Shaman et al. [15–17] has developed forecast for flu occurrences by applying Bayesian ensemble methods. Chakraborty et al. [18] has analyzed temporal trends of flu activity. Pandey et al. [19] has conducted the experiments for Ebola outbreak forecasting using machine learning.

In [20], the authors have worked to recognize premature warnings of dengue outbreaks through analysis of a relative set of forecast models. In [21], the authors have proposed a Bayesian belief network (BBN) technique to evaluate disease outbreak risks. In [22], the authors have proposed a relevance vector machine classification of the dataset based on the death toll from the epidemic outbreak of Ebola virus. In [23], authors have discussed the state of the art in computational networked epidemiology. In [24], the authors have made a relative learning from the perspective of forecasting an influenza epidemic. In [25], the authors have performed computations of Time Series analysis using Autoregressive Moving Average (ARMA) Model to produce values based on the current circumstance of the outbreak. In [26], the authors have proposed a hybrid prediction algorithm (EMD-GRNN) that combines empirical mode decomposition (EMD) as a time series decomposition method and the generalized regression neural network (GRNN) as a prediction model to improve the quality of diarrhea prediction.

We have selected Ebola outbreak data from duration 29-08-2014 to 29-12-2015 that is available in the WHO sitrep [27] which provide updated data for countries with an active Ebola outbreak. Total number of instances are 4112 that contains details about the cumulative no of confirmed Ebola cases and cumulative no of confirmed Ebola Deaths. Figure 3 describes the statistics of the dataset. The data were available in csv format and we have converted into Attribute-Relation File Format (Arff) that is required to be used in Weka [28]. We have merged the duplicate data from the original data for data cleaning.

2.1 Proposed Methodologies

Experiments are conducted for time series forecasting using 10 different machine learning algorithms, which are applied to prediction task. A brief description about the best performing algorithm is given in this study under Table 2. The flow diagram of the proposed methodology can be depicted from the Fig. 4. Random tree was found to be better performing algorithm among all machine learning algorithms for the proposed problem prediction.

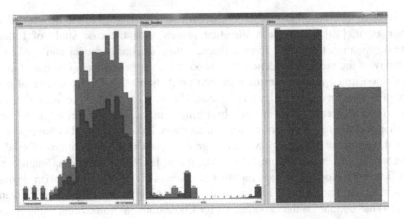

Fig. 3. Graphical display of the distribution of various attributes between the two classes as Cumulative Confirmed Ebola Cases and Cumulative Confirmed Ebola Deaths

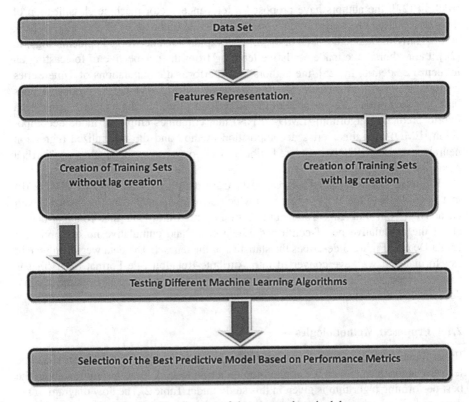

Fig. 4. Flow diagram of the proposed methodology

2.2 Performance Evaluation Metrics

The relative performance of time series analysis and forecasting through different machine learning algorithms is evaluated by using following three metrics.

Mean Absolute Error (MAE): The MAE measures the average magnitude of the errors in a set of forecasts, without considering their direction. It measures accuracy of continuous variables. The MAE is the standard over the confirmation model of the absolute values of the differences between forecasts and the equivalent observation. The MAE is a linear score, which means that all the individual differences are weighted equally in the average.

$$MAE = \frac{\sum |Predicted - Actual|}{N} \tag{1}$$

Root Mean Squared Error (RMSE): The RMSE is a quadratic scoring rule which measures the average magnitude of the error. The RMSE is the divergence between forecast and equivalent observed values are each squared and then averaged over the sample. Finally, the square root of the average is taken. Since the errors are squared before they are averaged, the RMSE gives a relatively high weight to large errors. This means the RMSE is most useful when large errors are particularly undesirable.

$$RMSE = \frac{\sqrt{\sum (Predicted - Actual)^2}}{N} \tag{2}$$

Direction Accuracy (DA): Percentage of correctly predicted positive and negative examples using the formula

$$DA = Count(sign(actual\_currenr - actual\_previos)) = \frac{sign(pred\_current - pred\_previous)}{N} \tag{3}$$

The relative measures give an indication that how well the forecaster's predictions are performing compared to just using the last known target value as the prediction. They are articulated as a proportion and lesser values (not Direction accuracy) designate that the forecasted values are enhanced predictions than just using the last known target values.

The open source Java based machine learning platform WEKA [28] was used to perform all the experiments in this study.

3 Result

We experimented with ten different algorithms, namely: (1) Linear Regression, (2) Multilayer Perceptron, (3) Support Vector Machine for Regression, (4) Ensemble Selection, (5) Bagging with Reptree, (6) Bagging with Random tree, (7) Bagging with Random Forest (8) Reptree, (9) Random tree and (10) Random Forest on the training data and the values of different performance metrics for these algorithms are given in Table 3.

Table 3. Performance evaluation parameters for the machine learning algorithms on time series forecasting in training and testing set

Machine Learning Algorithms	Without Lag Creation						With Lag Creation					
	Training			Testing			Training			Testing		
	MAE	RMSE	DA	MAE	RMSE	DA	MAE	RMSE	DA	MAE	RMSE	DA
Linear Regression	448.17	669.75	61.94	653.36	892.52	57.64	259.80	474.91	63.91	362.1	551.21	56.42
MLP	157.44	302.31	72.09	163.27	314.13	67.41	142.26	263.07	74.35	267.24	456.51	70.88
SMO Reg	317.80	774.56	69.07	744.45	1256.64	51.53	194.42	512.54	64.63	264.09	555.70	59.88
Bagging-Reptree	111.06	297.42	84.76	136.04	306.19	71.49	145.37	325.53	67.60	167.04	320.83	71.28
Bagging-RandomTree	50.53	167.32	83.08	118.30	335.31	83.30	60.53	165.74	80.38	150.08	380.02	82.28
Bagging-Random Forest	65.16	189.43	79.56	118.41	326.48	79.62	79.77	193.88	78.31	152.92	342.84	72.70
Ensemble Selection-Forward	173.92	367.26	81.15	411.97	675.53	48.68	210.27	471.15	72.10	503.43	828.78	51.53
RepTree	142.20	354.42	83.35	142.507	305.449	71.49	138.74	339.64	73.63	144.81	362.74	71.49
RandomTree	7.85	61.14	85.99	113.57	352.97	85.74	3.77	22.08	66.77	120.07	420.02	85.74
Random Forest	44.43	136.47	82.03	112.83	338.45	83.30	54.74	128.25	80.20	150.04	341.00	78.41

We have used both, with Lag formation and without Lag formation to measure the performance of various machine learning algorithms. It was also observed that the performance of Random Tree was superior to the rest of the nine other machine learning algorithms in terms of the different evaluation parameters. It is clear from the Table 3 and Figs. 5, 6, 7 and 8 that Random tree has performed superior in both the cases, i.e. with lag creation and without lag creation. The Lag creation permits the creation, manipulation as well as the control of the lagged variables. With lagged variables, the relationship between past and current values of a series can be captured by propositional learning algorithms. They create a "window" or "snapshot" over a time period. Fundamentally, the number of lagged variables created determines the size of the window.

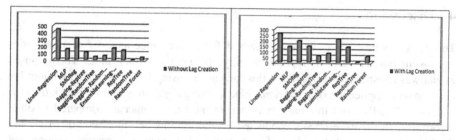

Fig. 5. Mean Absolute Error with/without Lag Creation

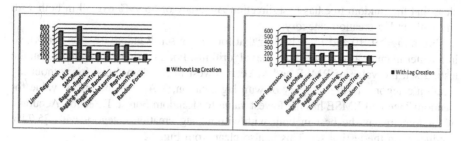

Fig. 6. Root Mean Squared Error with/without Lag Creation

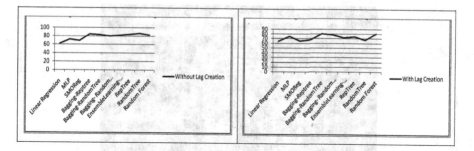

Fig. 7. Direction Accuracy with/without Lag Creation

4 Discussion

The present study has proposed a method for performance analysis of time series forecasting based on crudely reported weekly Ebola outbreak incidences. The proposed model was constructed using time series forecasting using lag creation and without lag creation with application of various machine learning algorithms. From Figs. 5, 6 and 7, it is clear that Random tree has performed in the best manner as compared to other algorithms. In the experiments conducted on the training set, the value of MAE and RMSE is lower in both the cases of with/without lag creation. Direction Accuracy of Random tree is the best in the training set for without lag creation category, while with lag creation Bagging-Random tree has performed in the best manner. From Fig. 8, it is clear that the random tree has best direction Accuracy of 85.99% overall in both with and without lag creation category.

From Figs. 9, 10 and 11, it is clear that for testing set, Random tree has performed in a better manner as compared to other algorithms. For experiments conducted on the testing set, the value of RMSE and MAE is lowest in Random forest for without lag creation category. In the category of with lag creation, MAE has the lowest value for Random Tree and RMSE has the lowest value for Random Forest. Direction Accuracy of random tree is the best in both with/without lag creation category with 85.74% conducted on the testing set. This is also clear from Fig. 12.

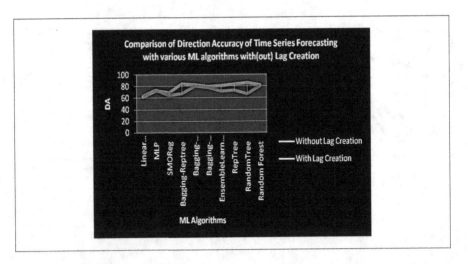

Fig. 8. Comparison of Direction Accuracy with/without Lag Creation

Figures 13 and 14 show a comprehensive comparison of MAE, RMSE and DA in training set as well as testing set with/without lag creation. It is quite clear from these graphs that performance evaluation metrics of training and testing models performed in a similar manner. This provides the confirmation of the validity of our proposed approach. Table 4 presents a comparison of current work with that of existing work. This clearly shows that the result of current work is better than the existing work.

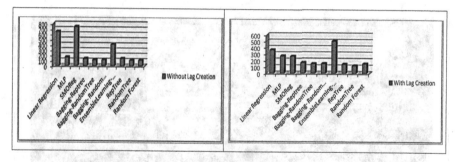

Fig. 9. Mean Absolute Error with/without Lag Creation

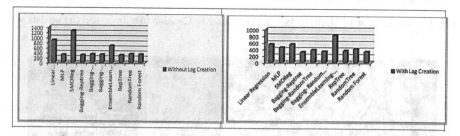

Fig. 10. Root Mean Squared Error with/without Lag Creation

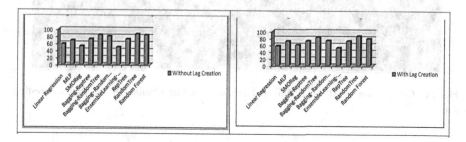

Fig. 11. Direction Accuracy with/without Lag Creation

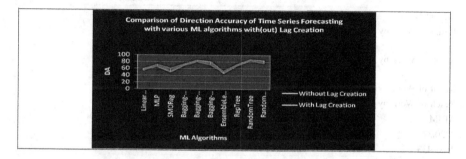

Fig. 12. Comparison of Direction Accuracy with/without Lag Creation

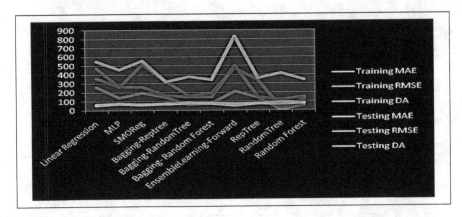

Fig. 13. Comparison of MAE, RMSE and DA with Lag Creation in training and testing data set.

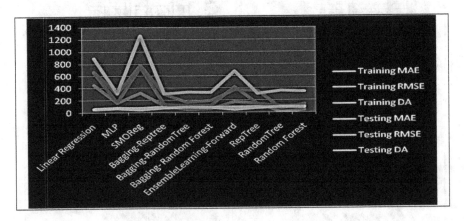

Fig. 14. Comparison of MAE, RMSE and DA without Lag Creation in training and testing data set.

Table 4. Comparison of results of current work with that of previous work

Metrics	MAE (With/Without Lag Creation)	RMSE (With/Without Lag Creation)
Current Work	**7.85(3.77)**	**61.14(22.08)**
Result of Work by [10]	Review of studies on forecasting the dynamics	
Result of Work by [12]	Prediction of total Quantity of Ill Patients is done	
Result of Work by [19]	5.39(6.5824)	42.41(53.22)
Result of Work by [26]		
ARIMA	GRNN	EMD-GRNN
3330.324	2123.084	664.361
4437.433	3049.842	811.925

5   Conclusion

In this paper, we have applied Machine Learning techniques in time series forecasting for performance evaluation. With this result, we could say that performance of time series forecasting could be improved with the help of machine learning algorithms. Forecasting of casualties could help health officials in preparing themselves to encounter this outbreak, supply of medicines, food supply, doctors etc. to the location where prediction of casualties are more.

References

1. Pyne, S., Vullikanti, A.K.S., Marathe, M.V.: Big Data applications in health sciences and epidemiology. In: Handbook of Statistics, vol. 33, pp. 171–202 (2015). ISSN 0169-7161
2. WHO. Ebola virus disease: Fact sheet (2018). http://www.who.int/mediacentre/factsheets/fs103/en/
3. Last, J.: A Dictionary of Epidemiology, 4th edn. Oxford University Press, New York (2001)
4. Brauer, F., van den Driessche, P., Wu, J. (eds.): Mathematical Epidemiology. LNM, vol. 1945. Springer, Heidelberg (2008). https://doi.org/10.1007/978-3-540-78911-6
5. IDC. IDC predictions 2013: Competing on the 3rd platform (2012). http://www.idc.com/research/Predictions13/downloadable/238044.pdf
6. Gartner. The Nexus of Forces: Social, Mobile, Cloud and Information (2012). http://www.gartner.com/technology/research/nexus-of-forces/
7. Pandey, M.K., Subbiah, K.: A novel storage architecture for facilitating efficient analytics of health informatics Big Data in cloud. In: IEEE International Conference on Computer and Information Technology (CIT), pp. 578–585 (2016). https://doi.org/10.1109/cit.2016.86
8. Bisset, K., Chen, J., Feng, X., Vullikanti, A., Marathe, M.: EpiFast: a fast algorithm for large scale realistic epidemic simulation s on distributed memory systems. In: Proceeding of 23 ACM International Conference on Supercomputing (ICS-2009). ACM Press, New York (2009a)
9. Salathé, M., et al.: Digital epidemiology. PLoS Comput. Biol. **8**(7), e1002616 (2012)
10. Nsoesie, E.O., Brownstein, J.S., Ramakrishnan, N., Marathe, M.: A systematic review of studies on forecasting the dynamics of influenza outbreaks. Influenza Other Respir. Viruses **8**(3), 309–316 (2013)
11. Nishiura, H.: Real-time forecasting of an epidemic using a discrete time stochastic model: a case study of pandemic influenza (H1N1-2009). BioMed. Eng. Online **10**(1), 15 (2011)
12. Ohkusa, Y., Sugawara, T., Taniguchi, K., Okabe, N.: Real-time estimation and prediction for pandemic A/H1N1(2009) in Japan. J. Infect. Chemother. **17**(4), 468–472 (2011)
13. Hall, I.M., Gani, R., Hughes, H.E., Leach, S.: Real-time epidemic forecasting for pandemic influenza. Epidemiol. Infect. **135**(3), 372–385 (2007)
14. Tizzoni, M., Bajardi, P., Poletto, C., Ramasco, J., Balcan, D., Goncalves, B., Perra, N., Colizza, V., Vespignani, A.: Real-time numerical forecast of global epidemic spreading: case study of 2009 A/H1N1pdm. BMC Med. **10**(1), 165 (2012). ISSN 1741-7015
15. Shaman, J., Karspeck, A.: Forecasting seasonal outbreaks of influenza. Proc. Natl. Acad. Sci. U.S.A. **109**(50), 20425–20430 (2012)
16. Shaman, J., Goldstein, E., Lipsitch, M.: Absolute humidity and pandemic versus epidemic influenza. Am. J. Epidemiol. **173**(2), 127–135 (2010)

17. Shaman, J., Pitzer, V.E., Viboud, C., Grenfell, B.T., Lipsitch, M.: Absolute humidity and the seasonal onset of influenza in the continental United States. PLoS Biol. **8**(2), e1000316 (2010)
18. Chakraborty, P., Khadivi, P., Lewis, B., Mahendiran, A., Chen, J., Butler, P., Nsoesie, E.O., Mekaru, S.R., Brownstein, J.S., Marathe, M.V., Ramakrishnan, N.: Forecasting a moving target: ensemble models for ILI case count predictions. In: Proceedings of the 2014 SIAM International Conference on Data Mining, 28 April 2014, pp. 262–270 (2014b)
19. Pandey, M.K., Karthikeyan, S.: Performance analysis of time series forecasting of ebola casualties using machine learning algorithm. In: Proceedings ITISE 201, Granada, 18–20 September (2017). ISBN 978-84-17293-01-7
20. Ramadona, A.L., Lazuardi, L., Hii, Y.L., Holmner, Å., Kusnanto, H., Rocklöv, J.: Prediction of dengue outbreaks based on disease surveillance and meteorological data. PLoS ONE **11** (3), e0152688 (2016). https://doi.org/10.1371/journal.pone.0152688
21. Liao, Y., et al.: A new method for assessing the risk of infectious disease outbreak. Sci. Rep. **7**, 40084 (2017). https://doi.org/10.1038/srep40084
22. Sharma, S., Mangat, V.: Relevance vector machine classification for Big Data on Ebola outbreak. In: 2015 1st International Conference on Next Generation Computing Technologies (NGCT), Dehradun, pp. 639–643 (2015). https://doi.org/10.1109/ngct.2015.7375199
23. Marathe, M.: Assisting H1N1 and ebola outbreak response through high performance networked epidemiology. In: 2015 IEEE International Parallel and Distributed Processing Symposium, Hyderabad, India, p. 831 (2015). https://doi.org/10.1109/ipdps.2015.121
24. Ristic, B., Dawson, P.: Real-time forecasting of an epidemic outbreak: Ebola 2014/2015 case study. In: 2016 19th International Conference on Information Fusion (FUSION), Heidelberg, pp. 1983–1990 (2016)
25. Buendia, R.J.M., Solano, G.A.: A disease outbreak detection system using autoregressive moving average in time series analysis. In: 2015 6th International Conference on Information, Intelligence, Systems and Applications (IISA), Corfu, pp. 1–5 (2015). https://doi.org/10.1109/iisa.2015.7388087
26. Wang, Y., Gu, J.: A hybrid prediction model applied to diarrhea time series. In: 2015 12th International Conference on Fuzzy Systems and Knowledge Discovery (FSKD), Zhangjiajie, pp. 1096–1102 (2015). https://doi.org/10.1109/fskd.2015.7382095
27. https://data.humdata.org/dataset/ebola-cases-2014
28. Hall, M., Frank, E., Holmes, G., Pfahringer, B., Reutemann, P., Witten, I.H.: The WEKA data mining software: an update. SIGKDD Explor. Newsl. **11**, 10–18 (2009)
29. Shevade, S.K., Keerthi, S.S., Bhattacharyya, C., Murthy, K.R.K.: Improvements to the SMO algorithm for SVM regression. IEEE Trans. Neural Networks **11**(5), 1189–1193 (1999). https://doi.org/110.1109/72.870050
30. Smola, A.J., Schoelkopf, B.: A tutorial on support vector regression (1998)
31. Caruana, R., Niculescu, A., Crew, G., Ksikes, A.: Ensemble selection from libraries of models. In: The International Conference on Machine Learning (ICML 2004) (2004)
32. Breiman, Leo: Bagging predictors. Mach. Learn. **24**(2), 123–140 (1996)
33. Breiman, Leo: Random forests. Mach. Learn. **45**(1), 5–32 (2001)

Impeccable Renaissance Approach:
An e-Village Initiative

Danish Faizan[1] and Shaheen Ishrat[2(✉)]

[1] National Informatics Centre, Ministry of Electronics and IT,
Government of India, Chandauli, UP, India
danish.faizan@nic.in
[2] Department of Computer Science, Shyama Prasad Mukherji College
for Women, University of Delhi, New Delhi, India
shaheen.ishrat7@gmail.com

Abstract. This paper proposes to first identify the basic requirement of common citizens in their day to day life, as their attachments are mainly with the crucial documents such as lands records and basic certificates which are needed to avail government facilities and services. The essential information are collected and stored in verified form to make them available 'Over the Counter' through 'under one roof unit' concept. It can be done through digitizing 'Parivar Register' to generate results using artificial intelligence with the help of designed algorithms for the same and this public record can be stored through block chain technology for the management of government trusted information. This will help them to curtail time loss component in service delivery mechanism, avail needed certificates, gather information about their queries and eligibility for different government and non-government benefits, at one single point, and will give a perception of a smart e-village.

Keywords: e-Village · Smart village · Block-chain · Artificial Intelligence
Parivar Register · Over the Counter · Common service centre
Under one roof unit

1 Introduction

Digitizing the village with the vision to develop a G2C 'over the counter' (OTC) platform to demonstrate the information technology (IT) infrastructure capability. It has the twin objective of providing relevant information to the rural population and acting as an interface between the district administration and the general rural population. It is a big step towards building an interoperable system which provides data and information in the form of deliverables to the general rural population [6, 7]. And for this purpose we need to use technologies like block-chain and artificial intelligence in a very efficient and effective manner.

In reference to the above, the basic entities like name, age, gender, address, religion, caste, disability (if any), education qualification, bank details etc. along with the recorded records of government were collected and clubbed for gathering the details of a family or a person. These recorded records are namely *Parivar Register and Land*

© Springer Nature Singapore Pte Ltd. 2018
G. C. Deka et al. (Eds.): ICACCT 2018, CCIS 899, pp. 335–346, 2018.
https://doi.org/10.1007/978-981-13-2035-4_29

Record (area) which can be used to serve the purpose. However, collection of records alone cannot ensure the desired results. Service oriented architecture (SOA) using artificial intelligence algorithms can generate critical information like individual income, family income, eligibility for particular facility based on land type and crops, types of services or job, weather impact etc., which can be used for over the counter (OTC) service delivery under one roof unit concept. It has many advantages over current manual system as mentioned in Table 1.

Table 1. Advantages of data digitized system over manual system

Manual system	Data digitized system
Less reach of Govt. services to villagers & their information	Connecting villagers & their information
Indirect & Less Transparent to rural citizens to connect with Govt. services	Direct & more transparent medium to connect rural citizens with Govt. services
Slow delivery of services	Fast delivery of services
Villagers are uninformed	Villagers become more Informed
Errors are more	Less errors
Slow & no accuracy in analysis	Fast & accurate analysis of the records
Less awareness/reluctant	Increase awareness/less fear

Apart from this, other things which are of prime objective are health system, and education system. And at this front as well, the 'under one roof unit' concept is very useful. Now to understand it in better way, let's first discuss few jargons like Parivar Register, Over the counter, Under one roof concept, Land Records, Block-Chain Technology, Artificial Intelligence and SOA, IoT (Internet of Things).

Parivar Register: It is a basic record of any village which includes the family holder's name and address along with the basic details as mentioned in Fig. 1, which ensures persons eligibility for different central and state government schemes, as per there presence in any particular village. As mentioned above, some fields are needed to be added and some are needed to be generated to get an enhanced form of parivar register (discussed later) to have the desired deliverables as per the need and requirements to serve the cause of smart e-village. And, as if this basic record were collected in the proper fashion, so the family tree information can be used in many forms, like family wise group of aadhaar, land property successor and owner list, election process etc.

Under One roof Unit: It is a compact premise designed for information and communication (ICT) activities to provide increased opportunities for progression in life of citizens living in rural expanse [9]. It helps to manage the resources up to optimal level as mentioned below:

(1) Through solar panel grid supply to curtail power consumption.
(2) Easy to manage ICT applications in term of manpower and infrastructure through multitasking IT staff.

परिवार रजिस्टर

ग्राम सभा .... पोस्ट ....

रूप पत्र 'क' (नियम 2 देखिये)

न्याय पंचायत .... विकास खण्ड ....

तहसील ....

क्रम सं.	मकान नम्बर	परिवार के प्रमुख का नाम	परिवार के सदस्यों का नाम	पिता/पति का नाम	पुरुष/ महिला	वर्ग अनुसूचित जाति की दशा में जाति	जन्मतिथि यदि ज्ञात हो सम्भाव्य में जाति	धन्धा	साक्षर निरक्षर साक्षर होने की दशा में अर्हता का ब्यौरा दें	सर्विस छोड़ देने मृत्यु की दिनांक	अन्य विवरण

Fig. 1. Basic record of Parivar Register

(3) One point Centre to handle multiple domains like health, education, training etc. which enhances the adaptivity.

(4) Knowledge and awareness among the citizens about the importance of digitization.

(5) Digital India campaign which results in the formation of digital village or e-village.

Over the counter (OTC): Over the counter, as the name suggests, on the basis of queries received of various types are entertained and disposed instantly or in due time, as the case may be. Types of queries includes:

(1) Information related to government schemes, agriculture, and tele-medicine for human being as well as for animals.

(2) Demand of different types of certificates like caste, domicile, income, differently able etc.

(3) Apply for different applications like LPG (Ujjwala Yojana), Ration Card, PMGAY, etc. and certificates.

(4) Schedules of e-learning sessions, health camp, election camp etc.

In this e-village system, apart from the front end peripherals as discussed above, lots of field work is to be carried out for the types of data which are needed to be processed through SOA mechanism for desirable results and future analysis as per the need and requirement It should be further cross verified by the concern officers and readily signed through digital signatures before creating block-chain blocks for individual and/or family having their information. It will help the system to disperse most of the certificate related query instantly over the counter. It also curtails the time consumption of officers as well which they will consume for eligibility verification and validity of candidate information, as that is readily available through the block-chain proposed system [1, 17].

Land Record (Area): It gives details about the statistics of land which include size, type like agricultural land or barren land etc., types of crops if any, natural conditions during the period of time, to calculate the probable income of individual and/or family, which is based on predefined algorithm using artificial intelligence, to evaluate deliverables in the form of certificates and other facilities which can be extended to them.

Block-Chain Technology: It can simply be understand as management of trusted information, which make it easier for government agencies to access and use critical public-sector data along with the security of said information. It is an encoded digital ledger that is stored on multiple locations in a public or private network. It comprises of data records, named as "blocks" [15, 16]. Once these blocks are collected in the form of chain, they cannot be changed or deleted by a single authority; instead, they are verified and managed using automation and pre-defined governance protocols. Basically, it is not a new-technology but it is just a combination of established components in a new way. So, in the nutshell it can be understood as:

(1) Ledgers record transactions – the passing of value from authority to authority.
(2) Transactions are time bound.
(3) Once a Transaction is recorded you cannot alter it.
(4) You are able to detect, if your ledger has been altered.

Artificial Intelligence and SOA: Service Oriented architecture (SOA) has gained considerable popularity as SOA paradigm promotes the reusability and integrability of software in heterogeneous environments by means of open standards. Most software development capitalizes SOA as per their organizations need for internal control of applications and develops new services with quality-attribute properties tailored as per requirement [10]. Therefore, based on architectural and business requirements, developers can elaborate different alternative solutions within a SOA framework to design software. Artificial Intelligence (AI) can assist developers in dealing with service-oriented design with the positive impact on scalability and management of generic quality deliverable results with the help of generated attributes [11]. In this, real time algorithm is a critical component which records the real time variable and cal-culates the result and also trigger the event based on that. For example, if one farmer has two crops a year, and one is destroyed due to weather condition, so the system can re-calculate the income by calculating the probable income from one crop and losses from second crop and it also initiates the benefits through facilities like 'Kisan Bina Yojana', 'Disaster relief fund' etc.

Internet of Things (IoT): It is an idea from computer science to connect ordinary things like doors and lights to a computer network to make them "intelligent". An embedded system which connects each thing together in a network and to the internet. The connections allow each thing to collect and exchange data, and we can control them remotely with the help of set of rules and/or chain of actions. It is a very fast growing idea and will be a major component of daily life by 2020. With the help of this, we can trigger many activity related to reporting of update, scheme eligibility etc. through mobile message under e-village ecosystem for different facility. As now a days mobile-governance is also a major reform in the digital world. We are using it to initiate many activities, log of activities are performed in various domains and many information are also available in the form of mobile apps.

The application work flow process, is depicted in Fig. 2 In this firstly, work is performed for 'parivar register' information gathering and validation, which is pushed to server for storage and information formation as per requirement, and serve the need through 'over the counter', which is again connected with national repository for storage as cold-site and also acts for different kind of purposes.

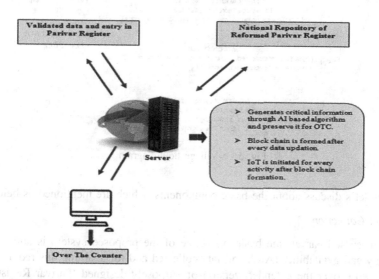

Fig. 2. Application work flow process

2 Proposed System

In proposed e-village system, two basic components are mass volume of verified data in structured form and other one is under one roof/building unit to accommodate the facilities for one single point 'over the counter' concept to deliver desirable results to the society. The e-Village flow diagram is depicted in Fig. 3. For attaining the same, data collection and its feeding and information generated on the basis of collected data, is the key component. As all the success of the system is based on the quality of data and its proper infringe free storage. So, we need such a technology supported system which can serve the purpose of government i.e. accountability, reliability, security, verifiability, auditability etc. It can be served through the block-chain as the data of one family (parivar) is formed with the help of data collection and calculation through algorithms based on artificial intelligence under SOA.

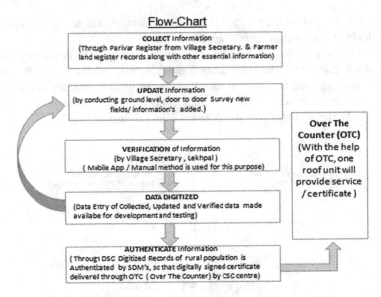

Fig. 3. e-Village flow diagram

Now let's discuss about the basic components, which are mentioned as below:

A. *Data Collection*

As discussed earlier, the basic backbone of the proposed system is authenticity, reliability and availability (ARA) of data collected and for attaining this requisite, we have to work over the extended version of purposely designed 'Parivar Register' to satisfy the QoS parameters like Scalability, Reliability, Security, throughput etc. to make it a sustainable, secured and trustworthy model.

For this Purpose 'Parivar Register' is taken into account as basic information. Extensive door to door survey has to be carried out in order to get precise information with minimal error. Since 'Parivar Register' is made to fulfill its own objectives, we have taken data from it but for the e-village model we need more information. For that we have added some fields and modified few of existing fields in family information sheet in Fig. 4.

With this we have 37 fields in Fig. 5 of information in total, which can be used for different type of deliverables, as mentioned below:

(a) SSN_ID - Generated by concatenating unique fields in itself for every rural citizen in Parivar register i.e. Revenue_Village_Code, Village_Code and House_Code. It is unique for each family.

(b) Readily availability of certificates like domicile, caste, differently able etc. can be generated.

(c) Applications related to ration card, widow/handicap pension, BPL status etc. along with its eligibility can be filled.

Fields Added	Fields Modified
Address field	Widow/Widower in Marital Status field
Mother's Name field	Muslim/Hindu/Sikh/Christian/Others in Religion field
Sub-Caste field	General/OBC/SC/ST/Others in Caste field
Educational Qualification field	Pakka/Kachcha in House condition field
Voter-ID detail	
Ration Card detail with category APL/BPL/Antyodaya	
Adhaar Card field.	

Fig. 4. Details of modified and added field in Family information sheet

e-Village

Sr.no	Vill_Name	Revenue_Vill_Code	Vill_Code	House_Code	Address	House_hold SNo	Head of Family Name	Family members name	Relation with head of family	Husband/Father name	Mother name	Male/Female	Marital Status (Married/Unmarried/Widow)	Religion (Hindu/Muslim/Sikh/Christian etc)	Caste (General/SC/ST/OBC/Others)	Sub Caste	Date of Birth
1	2	3	4	5	6	7	8	9	10	11	12	13	14	15	16	17	18
1																	
2																	

Educational Qualification (illiterate/5th /8th/10th/12th/Graduate/Post Graduate)	Differently Abled	Date of Death	Business	Income from Business	Voter ID Sr no	Ration Card Sr no	Types of Ration Card(APL/BPL/Antyoday)	Type of Home(Kacch a/Pakka)	if Agriculture land(Size in Rakba)	Income from Agriculture	Note	Date of leaving Village ,if any	Aadhar Card No	SSN ID (concatenation of colum 3,4 SS)	Mobile No.	Account No.	IFSC code	Bank, Branch
19	20	21	22	23	24	25	26	27	28	29	30	31	32	33	34	35	36	37

Fig. 5. An e-Village record containing required information fields

(d) Land Records and job information helps government officials to calculate income through artificial intelligence algorithm for identifying eligibility for different schemes and support which can be extended as per the requirement.

(e) An education detail helps them to offer jobs and various trainings, which can also be given to them by identifying the eligibility through the reports generated with the help of SOA.

(f) SSN_ID, AADHAAR Card can be used to define family set for different analysis and usage.

B. *One Roof Unit*

As the name suggests, it will be a well equipped and planned service point to serve and act as the intermediate between the citizen and government.

It is easy to maintain resources and made optimal use of it. Desired services delivery is served along with group activities, social support, public information, and other purposes.

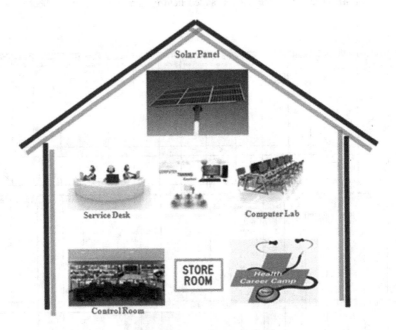

Fig. 6. Concept of one roof unit

List of facilities in one round shaped roof unit with 4–5 rooms can have, which is depicted in Fig. 6 are mentioned as below:

(a) One solar panel over roof for additional power supply
(b) One 'Over the Counter' service desk(s)
(c) One theater for ICT training, e-leaning and support purpose
(d) One Computer Lab for Digital India Awareness

(e) One common room for any other purposes, like blood donation camp, health camp etc.

(f) One Control room for supervisor

(g) One store room

Above setup uses ICT as a powerful element for educational development in rural arena as three quarter of Indian population live in rural area and majority of rural people are underprivileged in term of facilities and education. It has the tremendous potential to solve the problem of mass literacy in rural India. It gives a platform for sharing information and knowledge for promoting teaching and learning process. Setting up E-learning centers in rural area helps in crafting E-learning program which will work as an efficient tool of reaching technology in rural India. It provides an enormous motivation for learning and awareness as well. ICT focuses on student centric learning process which gives a great advantage as the availability and accessibility of skilled teachers are very difficult to manage in rural area. Promoting computer literacy projects and focusing on online education in which smart classes and phones plays a vital role to disseminate education in the form of recorded lectures and e-books. It is user friendly and anytime available resource and helps in proliferating the adoption rate of ICT.

And, apart of it, this 'one roof unit' model can be used as working model for different other non-ICT activities as well like:

(a) Biogas Plant, as a initiative for LPG free campus

(b) Soak Pit may be constructed near by, for displaying as drainage free campus

(c) Rain harvesting units, for water conservation, for maintaining water level

(d) Model toilets, as a model for 'Swach Bharat Abhiyan' and display its importance

(e) Cleanliness drives can be carried out, to show the importance of it.

This initiative can give the sense of security and availability to citizens that the district administration is in their reach, which resolve most of the issues of their day to day life. It display as a working model of various government initiatives and at the same time rush to government offices will reduce which will help them to concentrate over other development, law and order matters.

C. *Over the counter*

Viability of any project depends on the quality of data, quantitative analysis of data on regular basis, maintaining the security of data from any breach/mischief and imprinting of trust mark over the data. For ensuring this, entire work-flow should be thoroughly designed with security features like digital signature (this means that no certificate can be generated, nor any application can be moved, until the data is digitally signed, and once the data is digitally signed, no modification is allowed, until and unless, it was permitted otherwise again through administrator of data, and on the basis of this verified data, other information which is needed to be generated were generated through artificial intelligence, and it is also made available as deliverables) and as an additional feature Quick Response (QR) code can be printed as a facility to verify the legitimacy of data through mobile phones, which enhance the system towards m-governance as well. Work flow for 'Over the Counter' mainly focuses on:

(a) To maintain record's authenticity, reliability and its availability to counter the basic requirement of rural citizens.

(b) Enabling Integrated Service Delivery and a Service Oriented Architecture leading to joined up government.

(c) Help easily to protect the legacy investments in software and hardware.

(d) Integrating them with other technology platforms and software implementation, as per the requirement to enhance the delivery service.

(e) De-link the back-end departments/Service Providers (SP) from the front-end Service Access Providers thereby Ensuring re-engineering in service implementation i.e. separates the Portal, CSC, Kiosks etc. from the government services.

This multi-purpose desk is the key point of the entire process, and the model is taken from multitasking kiosk's or common service centre, which is used for many government and non-government service to general public in villages and town areas as well, through private persons. But, here dedicated work force preferably under PPP model can be deployed for government services exclusively to the citizens and educate them to the usage and importance of ICT in there life.

3 Impact

National agencies are supposed to manage and maintain the records that include information about individuals, organization, assets and activities, like birth and death dates, information about marital status, business income, property transfers, criminal records etc. Managing and using these data can be complicated, even for digital governments. Some records exist only in paper form, and if changes need to be made in official records, citizens often must appear personally to do so. All government agencies tend to build their own silos of data and information-management protocols, which preclude other parts of the government from using them. And, of course, these data must be protected against unauthorized access or manipulation, with no room for error.

So, this re-designed 'parivar register' using artificial intelligence algorithm SOA, preserved through 'block-chain' technique, simplifies the management and also ensures the authenticity of recorded data, and also helps in maintaining the traces of activities performed on every block of information. And, in this manner many information related to different entities of government can be accumulated and used vice-versa as per the requirements.

And, lastly the 'Aadhar field' is taken for further extension with the technologies with biometric authentication, as it helps for ensuring the genuineness and uniqueness of any person and also helps to retrieve the related data of one person across the various domains. It also helps to club with other services to increase the volume of benefits without hassle and help to be identified as unique voter at one desired constituency as well.

4 Conclusion

As, this type of innovative initiatives in information technology in rural areas helps the government to minimize the 'digital divide' and also narrow the gap between village and town. ICT is the only tool for connecting rural areas to the promising future of India through various measures like preserving the required records in digital form for referencing as and when needed by ensuring its viability, availability and authenticity. New technological changes in computer science help in designing and implanting the e-village system in executable mode and will be an asset in long run for the 'Digital India' initiative, in terms of service delivery, distance learning, telecommunication for health and other social information. And guide a road map to 'Digitized India' and 'Developed India'.

References

1. Katara, S.K.: Envisioning smart villages through information and communication technologies – a framework for implementation in India. In: Chugunov, A.V., Bolgov, R., Kabanov, Y., Kampis, G., Wimmer, M. (eds.) DTGS 2016. CCIS, vol. 674, pp. 463–468. Springer, Cham (2016). https://doi.org/10.1007/978-3-319-49700-6_46
2. AadhaarStars Social Media Campaign (n.d.). https://uidai.gov.in/. Accessed 13 Apr 2017
3. ABOUT DIGITAL INDIA | Digital India Programme (n.d.). http://www.digitalindia.gov.in/. Accessed 28 Jan 2018
4. Public Private Partnerships in India (n.d.). https://www.pppinindia.gov.in/. Accessed 28 Jan 2018
5. Jain, A.K., Nandakumar, K.: Biometric authentication: system security and user privacy. IEEE Comput. **45**(11), 87–92 (2012)
6. Patankar, R., Vyas, S.K., Tyagi, D.: Achieving universal digital literacy for rural India. In: Proceedings of the 10th International Conference on Theory and Practice of Electronic Governance - ICEGOV 2017, pp. 528–529. ACM (2017)
7. Shanker, D.: E-governance in rural India. In: Proceedings of the 2nd International Conference on Theory and Practice of Electronic Governance - ICEGOV 2008, pp. 268–273. ACM (2008)
8. Ahram, T., Sargolzaei, A., Sargolzaei, S., Daniels, J., Amaba, B.: Blockchain technology innovations. In: 2017 IEEE Technology & Engineering Management Conference (TEMSCON) (2017)
9. Mertens, E., Spark, R., Houten, M.A., Rutten, P.G.: Enable the growth of a smart energy and information network in rural India today. In: IEEE PES ISGT Europe 2013, pp. 1–5 (2013)
10. Clement, S.J., Mckee, D.W., Xu, J.: Service-oriented reference architecture for smart cities. In: 2017 IEEE Symposium on Service-Oriented System Engineering (SOSE), pp. 81–85 (2017)
11. Rodríguez, G., Soria, Á., Campo, M.: Artificial intelligence in service-oriented software design. Eng. Appl. Artif. Intell. **53**, 86–104 (2016). https://doi.org/10.1016/j.engappai.2016.03.009
12. Kaur, R.: Digital signature. In: IEEE International Conference on Computing Sciences (ICCS), pp. 295–301 (2012)
13. Computing Now - IEEE Computer Society (n.d.). https://www.computer.org/web/computingnow. Accessed 13 Apr 2017

14. Danish, F.: Usability of AADHAR in election process: new paradigm. J. Adv. Comput. Commun. Technol. (ISSN:2347-2804) **5**(5) (2017)

15. Foth, M.: The promise of blockchain technology for interaction design. In: Proceedings of the 29th Australian Conference on Computer-Human Interaction - OZCHI 2017, pp. 513–517 (2017)

16. Li, C., Zhang, L.: A blockchain based new secure multi-layer network model for internet of things. In: 2017 IEEE International Congress on Internet of Things (ICIOT), pp. 33–41 (2017)

17. Emerging Opportunities with Blockchain (n.d.). Decentralized Computing Using Blockchain Technologies and Smart Contracts Advances in Information Security, Privacy, and Ethics, pp. 80–96 (2017)

Bot Development for Military Wargaming Simulation

Punam Bedi, S. B. Taneja, Pooja Satija$^{(\boxtimes)}$, Garima Jain,
Aradhana Pandey, and Aditi Aggarwal

Department of Computer Science, University of Delhi, Delhi, India
punambedi@ieee.org, sbtaneja@yahoo.co.in,
poojas.mcs.du.2015@gmail.com,
garima.mcs.du.2015@gmail.com,
aradhana.mcs.du.2015@gmail.com,
aditi.mcs.du.2015@gmail.com

Abstract. Over the years many techniques have been used by the decision makers to test their theories in a near real world simulated situation. Military war games are one such platform where these theories can be tested and the outcome is recorded. War gaming has evolved from its starting as a board game to now widely played as a computer game. This paper focuses on a military war game simulation which is being used to develop a bot using artificial intelligence techniques. Various modules are developed for working of the bot. Route planning is one of them which is used by units to find a path in the game. Thus, an algorithm is proposed using the A* algorithm as a base. A* algorithm is modified to use influence maps in order to find a safe path for the units which helps the bot succeed in the game. The modified A* algorithm is implemented and compared with a traditional A* algorithm and modified algorithm is found to be more optimal.

Keywords: Real Time Strategy · War game · Bot · Routing · Planning
Path finding · A* search algorithm · Influence maps

1 Introduction

Decision making and planning is an integral part of many real world activities. The planning process involves and utilizes the knowledge in the respective domains. The problem becomes challenging when many interdependent events, constraints, time and many other factors influence the current and future state. Many techniques and tools are used to train the decision makers in integrated near real world simulated situation to try out their planning and execution processes. Military war games are one of the platforms where the decision makers at various hierarchies are put in assuming a real time situation and see the effect of the strategies and action in the real time constraint environment. In the early days, AI was used in board games which led to the development of many heuristic-based search techniques, but with the development of RTS (real time strategy) games now these techniques are being refined so that they can be used for RTS games as well [1]. Laird & VanLent suggested the use of Strategy game

G. C. Deka et al. (Eds.): ICACCT 2018, CCIS 899, pp. 347–360, 2018.
https://doi.org/10.1007/978-981-13-2035-4_30

as a test bed for artificial intelligence research. Strategy games were seen as potential area for advancement in sophisticated scenarios, which led to the development of human-level artificial intelligence. Game state in RTS (real time strategy) game is huge which set them apart from simpler board games. In RTS games, players will not have enough time to plan their move due to many constraints [2]. A war game is a strategy game that is similar to military operations but in reality it is fiction. Over the years, war gaming has evolved from its starting as a board game to now widely played as a computer game. With coming of artificial intelligence, computers are now used as opponents against human player where different strategies can be tried and results are recorded. To develop the bot against whom humans can play many techniques have been used in the past. Since game domain is huge, problems are divided into parts and solved independently [3].

The war game simulation is designed for two players. One player is the Red team and the other side is the Blue team. The bot is designed for the Red team. Aim of Red team is to do destruction and create chaos. Blue team is responsible for protecting the terrain and neutralizing the Red team. Mind behind the Red team in the game is that of the Mission Planner. Working of the game is divided into two parts: Planning and Execution. Planning includes the selection of mission type and the target by the mission planner. Based on the mission, targets are assessed and a plan is formed for each target. Based on priority one target is chosen and others are kept as contingency plans. A team is chosen for the mission and the units are equipped with resources. Once a target is selected, mission planner passes the work to OGW (Over Ground Worker) who foresee the mission on ground level. There can be two types of mission: Strike and Disrupt. Strike mission involves violence, destruction and causing maximum casualties. Disrupt mission involves creating chaos and panic but does not focus on casualties. Once a team is chosen for the current target, team members are prepared, so they can carry out the mission efficiently. Units provided to the player initially may not be ready for the execution so many of them may have to be trained for their roles. Every unit requires different training, resources and time to train. So after training the units and supplying them with the required resources, they are ready to carry out the mission. For every decision made by the Mission planner or OGW, there are some set of rules that are discussed in the Sect. 4.

With the help of scouting, some information about the target can be gathered. To carry out the mission some hideouts and escape route are also required. The hideouts are area having a good support base for the Red team and are located near the target. After this a route with minimum detection can be found from the base camp to the hideout or the target. Once there is a target, a plan, a team, some routes and hideouts the planning part is over and execution can be started. Execution mainly involves carrying out the mission. During execution, the units move to the desired location and kill as many members of the Blue team as they can. The units try to move undetected throughout the terrain but if they encounter some Blue units, they can either attack or escape.

The bot designed is capable of making intelligent decisions and carryout the task at hand. The interaction between the simulation and bot takes place with the help of text files. Simulation generates certain text files that are fed to the bot as input and in turn bot generates some text files that are read by the simulation. The bot acts as an agent that uses its input files to sense the environment and after taking a decision, it issues commands for the simulation. This cycle goes on until one team is declared the winner. This paper focuses on the routing algorithm used by the bot for path finding. To achieve the goal it is important that the units move through the terrain easily and for that an efficient routing algorithm is needed, that provides a route with minimum detection. To achieve the route with minimum detection influence maps are used for path finding.

This paper is divided into six sections. Section 2 reviews the literature survey of RTS games for bot development and various techniques used for path finding. The war game scenario is shown in Sect. 3. Functional components of the bot are covered in Sect. 4. The proposed routing model is presented in Sect. 5 followed by the conclusion and future works in Sect. 6.

2 Literature Review

Research work has been done in the field of RTS (real time strategy) games for developing a bot. "StarCraft" (RTS game) [2, 4] is being used by many researchers to explore AI problems and is also used as a test bed for their theories. Various challenges like planning, learning, uncertainty, domain knowledge exploitation and task decomposition were discovered and detailed understanding was gathered [3, 5]. Over the past years there has been a huge amount of work done in the field of RTS games. Different people have used different approaches to solve RTS game problems and some have enhanced already existing techniques. Ontanon et al. divided the problem into five parts: Strategy, Tactics, Reactive control, Terrain analysis, Intelligence gathering. Most popular among these are Strategy and Tactics [3]. Strategy refers to long term planning whereas tactics refer to short term planning. Hard-coded approach is an AI technique extensively used in commercial RTS games for solving high-level strategic reasoning. Planning is also used for solving high-level strategic reasoning and makes use of case based planning [3, 6]. Tactical and micromanagement decisions uses reinforcement techniques which are an area of machine learning where an agent must learn, by trial and error, to take optimal actions in a particular situation in order to maximize an overall reward value that can be used for tactical decision making [3]. Resource control is also one of the important aspects of strategy in RTS games.

The state space is so large in RTS (real time strategy) games that traditional heuristic-based search techniques do not work efficiently because of the presence of fog of war. In these games, path finding is needed which simply means finding the shortest distance between two points. A path-finding algorithm could, for example, give a straight line path to the destination, and have the algorithm controlling unit behavior take care of avoiding obstacles along that path. Influence mapping is a tool used for terrain analysis and it also provides three different types of information that are useful for decision making: situation summary, historical statistics and future predictions [7]. Influence map is essentially a 2D array representing the playing field, or parts of the playing field. The value at any given coordinate is the damage that the enemy immediately is able to inflict there. This specific use of influence maps is referred as threat maps. Threat maps have been used for path finding to avoid unnecessary conflicts while travelling towards a destination [7]. Then there is the concepts of path planning and re-planning where path planning is the art of deciding which route to take and which target to attack, which is an unusual but effective way of solving the problem of allocation of military resources and re-planning is the concept of discarding a previous plan for the benefit of a new plan from the current state to the goal state when the current state is not the expected state [7].

In the field of robotics, Wavefront planning algorithm is used to move the robot avoiding the obstacles but it has high time complexity [8]. A* algorithm is one of the algorithm for estimating the best path in RTS games [9, 10]. Partial-Refinement A* (PRA*) can fully interleave between planning and actions and uses path abstraction and refinement [11, 12]. For abstraction, resolution of the map is reduced and instead of refining complete path they refine the partial segment of the abstract path at each step. Windowed Hierarchical Cooperative A* (WHCA*) [13] broke down multi-agent path planning problem into single-agent and searches to find non-colliding paths for different agents travelling to different destinations. In [14] WHCA* and PRA* are combined to form Cooperative Partial-Refinement A* (CPRA*). It is faster than WHCA* and also uses less memory. Using CPRA*, they were able to find routes for multiple objects simultaneously without any collisions. Two heuristics for estimating distance between two locations on the map are given in [15]. Firstly, the map is divided into several smaller areas which then connected to form a high-level graph. Dead-end heuristics eliminates areas from search map that are of no use for current route. It only explores the areas which are relevant. Gateway heuristic is used to pre-calculate the distance between starting/ending of the area [15].

A routing model using A* search algorithm and influence maps is proposed which gives the optimal path from the source to the destination. This algorithm repeatedly examines the most promising unexplored location it has seen.

3 War Game Scenario

The game simulation takes place in a terrain of size 20 × 20 km. Terrain in the simulation is divided into cells of equal length and breadth. It is treated as a two dimensional matrix of equal number of rows and column. The terrain is divided into a two dimensional matrix with 'N' number of rows and columns. Length is the total length of the terrain and resolution is the size of one cell on the terrain. N is computed as

$$N = \text{Length/resolution} \tag{1}$$

Each cell has certain properties or attributes associated with them. These attributes are Area Type, Population Type, Number of Supporters and Security Level. Area Type tells about the area of that cell whether it is Urban or Rural area. Population type says about the population in that cell. Population can be supportive, neutral or non-supportive. Security Level can be High, Moderate or Low. Supportive or non-supportive population is with respect to the Red team as is the security. In the scenario, the borders of cells are colored based on the security in the cell. Blue signifies neutral; green signifies low and red signifies high security. Some cells have no color associated with them. They are barren lands where no one lives. Figure 1 shows one of the scenarios for the game. The game scenario can have multiple possible targets available for possible disruption. The final target is chosen by the mission planner after prioritizing them based on their ultimate aim. Air Field, Helicopter Base, Command & Control Centre, Religious Places, Market Places, Schools, Hospitals and Government Offices are the list of possible targets.

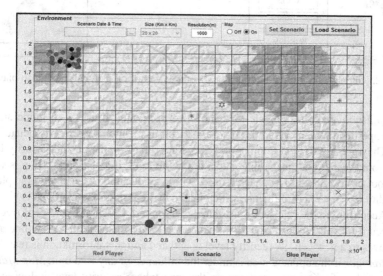

Fig. 1. Game Scenario with scale of 10^4 for X and Y axis (Color figure online)

4 Bot Components

Some static information is provided to the bot for initialization purpose. This information is given in the configuration file. There are four sections in the configuration file. Section one gives the name and location of files that are fed as input to the bot. Section two gives the mission details like aim and day to carry out the mission. Section three is target specific information. It gives a list of targets and their properties. Along with target properties it also gives an ideal team size for the mission. It specifies the quantity of each unit for every target. This information is used to select an ideal team for the mission based on the units provided initially. These are mere guidelines and not exact rules for team selection. Section four gives guidelines for resource allocation. It gives quantity of each resource a unit should ideally have. But it may vary in the simulation depending on initial resources provided. There are many components in the game, so various managers are made to handle each of these components as shown in Fig. 2. Game Commander is the main module responsible for invoking all other modules. If a certain module is to be turned on or off, it should be done from the Game Commander.

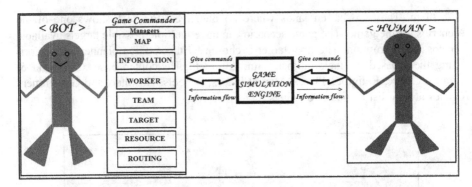

Fig. 2. Interaction between the functional components of the bot and the human player

Map Manager is responsible for handling terrain data. It uses a dynamic array to store properties of each cell in the map. Each cell has some properties associated with them. They are Area Type, Population Type, Supporter Population and Security Level. Apart from these properties, a flag is maintained to mark if a cell on the map is visited by the bot or not. Since fog-of-war is used, whole map cannot be visible to the players. Every unit has an area of influence which marks the region on the map that is visible to them. According to the rule set of the game, areas where Blue forces are deployed have high security level. Figure 3 shows influence region of a Blue unit. Every time a Blue unit moves to a new cell, its security level is updated and this information is read by the *Map Manager* if the updated area is under the influence of any Red unit. *Map Manager* is also used to find secure locations on the map where security level is low and the population is supportive to the Red team so that hideouts can be made. Hideouts are generally made near the target area and are used to store resources. Hideouts are used by Red team to hide near a target area so that they can easily reach the target without any problem.

Information Manager is used to handle unit related functions. There are nine types of units in Red team: OGW, OGE_SA (Over ground executor with small arms), OGE_MG (OGE with machine gun), OGE_Expl (OGE with explosives), Informer, Guide, Driver, Doctor and Supporter. Firstly, there is an Over Ground Worker who identifies the target location and is responsible for team selection and training. It monitors the hideouts and guides the other entities. Next, there is an Over Ground Executor (OGE) whose task is to attack and repulse. It is also responsible for explosions and demolishing various targets. Informer's role is information gathering and passing the gathered information to OGW (Over Ground Worker). Reception Guide is responsible for receiving the entities at some location and then guiding them to the target location or hideout location. Driver helps in escaping and moving from one place to another. Doctor provides treatment to the injured entities involved in mission. Supporters create interference to facilitate the mission. For Blue team, there are patrolling teams and a QRT (Quick Response Team). *Information manager* is used to update data for the Red units. Units of Red team have some attributes associated with them so that they can be controlled by the bot. Each unit has a unique id associated with it. Units also have a status value that can be given training, trained, moving, and

LOW SECURITY	LOW SECURITY	LOW SECURITY	LOW SECURITY	LOW SECURITY	LOW SECURITY	LOW SECURITY
LOW SECURITY	MODERATE SECURITY	MODERATE SECURITY	MODERATE SECURITY	MODERATE SECURITY	MODERATE SECURITY	LOW SECURITY
LOW SECURITY	MODERATE SECURITY	HIGH SECURITY	HIGH SECURITY	HIGH SECURITY	MODERATE SECURITY	LOW SECURITY
LOW SECURITY	MODERATE SECURITY	HIGH SECURITY	Blue Unit	HIGH SECURITY	MODERATE SECURITY	LOW SECURITY
LOW SECURITY	MODERATE SECURITY	HIGH SECURITY	HIGH SECURITY	HIGH SECURITY	MODERATE SECURITY	LOW SECURITY
LOW SECURITY	MODERATE SECURITY	MODERATE SECURITY	MODERATE SECURITY	MODERATE SECURITY	MODERATE SECURITY	LOW SECURITY
LOW SECURITY	LOW SECURITY	LOW SECURITY	LOW SECURITY	LOW SECURITY	LOW SECURITY	LOW SECURITY

Fig. 3. Influence region of a Blue unit (Color figure online)

raw. There is a resource vector for each unit that tells the quantity of each resource a unit is carrying. There is also a health value that can be excellent, fair, good or poor. There is also age, training level, current location which is x, y coordinate on the map and a team id.

Target Manager manages the target information. Each target has some properties associated with it like location, security level, population type, media impact, defence potential, chances of success and a target value. Security level and population type are taken from the *Map Manager*. Media impact gives a value for how the media will be impacted if the given target is chosen. Defence potential measures the value of how much a target is secure on the inside. Target value is computed using all the other values and is used for target selection and prioritization. A complete target list is given before the start of the game, but all of them may not be placed in the current scenario. Rules for target prioritization are as follows: After analyzing the population type, and the defense potential of an area near or at the target place, a target value is calculated. Higher this value better is the probability of selecting that target for a strike or disruption. The security level of the target area should be low. Higher the chance of success, higher is the probability of selecting it for the mission.

Once the target is selected for the mission, *Team Manager* starts creating the team according to the target. Unit types and their count are taken from the configuration file and a team is created. If sufficient units are not present then, re-planning is done. A different target can be chosen according to the priorities. While forming the team, a team id is associated with every team member. *Resource Manager* is responsible for providing resources to all the units which are selected for the mission. Each entity is provided with some resources to facilitate the mission. The resources are radio set,

GPS, mobile, small arm, binoculars, machine gun, grenade, rocket launcher, explosives. Initially, OGW has all the resources. List of all the resource types and their count required by the units, is provided in the configuration file. Using this information, the resources are allotted to the units involved in the mission. *Worker Manager* allots work to idle units. There are eight kinds of work: Idle, Gather, Drive, Support, Plan, Treatment, Attack and Guidance. Each unit type performs different type of work. For example, Informer gathers information; Driver's work is to drive the vehicle, etc. Initially, all the units are idle. To execute the mission, each unit in a team is allotted work according to its capability.

Routing Manager follows the routing model proposed in the next section. It provides an optimal path from the source to the destination cell following the A* search algorithm using influence maps. To move from one cell to another, routing manager provides the path to each moving unit, considering the security of the cells in its area of influence.

5   Routing Model

Analysing the map is a former step for path finding to gather information about influence areas and cell properties. The routing model used by the bot is a modified A* algorithm which is an A* path finding algorithm using influence maps. A* searches all possible paths to the destination and chooses the one that incurs least cost. The cost is calculated as a penalty of travelling from a region of no detection to a region of possible detection. A* selects the path that minimizes $f(n) = g(n) + h(n)$, where n is the path's end location, $g(n)$ is the cost of the path from the source to n, and $h(n)$ is a heuristic that estimates the cost from n to the target [9, 10]. All the red marked regions, i.e. area of high security level are those cells on the map which this algorithm will avoid because of high chances of detection. Also, because of the dynamicity of the game, the cells may change their current properties. For example, if the Blue team is enforced in a region of low security level while playing the game, the cell value changes from low security to high security. Thus, the algorithm re-routes the path of the unit so that it remains undetected. The goal of the route planning algorithm will be to have an optimal path that leads the unit to its destination without detection and with minimum penalty.

The cost g (n) can be easily calculated as each unit has an influence area associated with it. If the unit is located at position (x, y), it can move in eight possible directions $(x - 1, y + 1)$, $(x, y + 1)$, $(x + 1, y + 1)$, $(x + 1, y)$, $(x + 1, y - 1)$, $(x, y - 1)$, $(x - 1, y - 1)$, $(x - 1, y)$. In the algorithm, only these possible locations are explored as the next node, as shown in Fig. 4. Out of these, the cell that has the minimum penalty is selected as the next node.

Proposed Experimentation

The influence maps are used to keep track of threat in each cell. It is in a form of 2D array filled with security levels: high, moderate and low. After prioritizing the target according to the target value, the bot selects the target for the mission. It then looks for possible hideouts (safe locations near the target) to hide. To reach the target cell or a

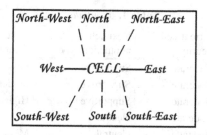

Fig. 4. Possible directions a unit can go to

particular hideout from the unit's location as quickly as possible, the bot uses modified A* search algorithm which chooses the safest path very efficiently. Modified A* star algorithm picks up a cell according to the value 'f' where:

$$f(x, y) = g(x, y) + h(x, y) \tag{2}$$

where

g (x, y) = Cost of moving from the source point to location x,y on the grid, following the path generated to get there.

h (x, y) = Estimated cost of moving from location x,y on the grid to the final destination, referred as the **heuristic.**

Calculation of h(x, y): The Euclidean Distance is used as the heuristic function. It is the distance between the current cell [cur_x, cur_y] and the destination cell [dest_x, dest_y]

$$h = \sqrt{\left((cur\_x - dest\_x)^2 + (cur\_y - dest\_y)^2\right)} \tag{3}$$

Using the Table 1, the value of g (x, y) is computed.

Table 1. Calculation of g (x, y)

Current cell population type	Current cell security	Next cell population type	Next cell security	Cost g(x, y)
Supportive	Low	Supportive	Low	0
Supportive	Low	Supportive	Moderate	5
Supportive	Low	Supportive	High	10
Supportive	Low	Neutral	Low	5
Supportive	Low	Neutral	Moderate	5 + 5 = 10
Supportive	Low	Neutral	High	5 + 10 = 15
Supportive	Low	Non supportive	Low	10 + 0 = 10
Supportive	Low	Non supportive	Moderate	10 + 5 = 15
Supportive	Low	Non supportive	High	10 + 10 = 20

(*continued*)

Table 1. (*continued*)

Current cell population type	Current cell security	Next cell population type	Next cell security	Cost g(x, y)
Supportive	Moderate	Supportive	Low	0
Supportive	Moderate	Supportive	Moderate	0
Supportive	Moderate	Supportive	High	5
Supportive	Moderate	Neutral	Low	5
Supportive	Moderate	Neutral	Moderate	5
Supportive	Moderate	Neutral	High	5 + 5 = 10
Supportive	Moderate	Non supportive	Low	10
Supportive	Moderate	Non supportive	Moderate	10
Supportive	Moderate	Non supportive	High	15
Supportive	High	Supportive	High	0
Supportive	High	Neutral	High	5
Supportive	High	Non supportive	High	10

The algorithm uses a function *Calculate_Cost (u, v)* where u is the current cell location and v is the next cell location.

```
Calculate_Cost ( Current Location , Next Location )
    Set Cost = 0 units
    if( Current Location(Security) == Low)
        if(Next Location(Security) == Moderate)
            Cost = Cost + 5
        else if(Next Location(Security) == High)
            Cost = Cost + 10
    else if( Current Location(Security) == Moderate)
        if(Next Location (Security) == High)
            Cost = Cost + 5
    if( Current Location(Population Type) == Supportive)
        if(Next Location (Population Type) == Neutral)
            Cost = Cost + 5
        else if(Next Location(Population Type)==NonSupportive)
            Cost = Cost + 10
    else if( Current Location(Population Type) == Neutral)
        if(Next Location(Population Type) == NonSupportive)
            Cost = Cost + 5
    return Cost
```

Two list are created to implement modified A* algorithm. Open List to maintain the nodes which are currently used to find the next suitable node for finding the path. Closed List contains nodes which are already travelled by the algorithm and are maintained to facilitate backtracking in case re-routing is considered.

> **Modified A* search algorithm for Bot Development**
> Initially set the open list and closed list.
> Insert the source cell (source_x, source_y) on the open list.
> Set f=0 for the starting cell.
> while (open list != empty)
>   pop the cell having minimum f in the open list. Let it be 'p'
>   generate p's 8 adjacent cells (adj) and set their parents to 'p'.
>   for each adjacent_cell (adj_x, adj_y)
>   if adjacent_cell == goal
>   stop search
>   adj.g = Calculate_Cost(p, adj)
>   adj.h = Euclidean distance (adj, goal)
>   adj.f = adj.g + adj.h
>   if the adj is present in the closed list
>   skip this adjacent cell
>   if the adj is present in the open list with lower 'f' value
>   skip this adjacent cell
>   else
>   insert the cell to the open list
>   end
>   Insert p on the closed list
> end

In case the algorithm fails to find a secure path from the location of the unit to the destination, two possibilities arise. Either the mission planner changes the plan and chooses another target from the list of possible targets to cause disruption or the mission fails. If the mission planner chooses another target, the bot re-initializes the hideouts and form a new team for new target and new routes are found for the new destination.

6 Experimental Results

The routing algorithm was tested for different combinations of source and destination. All experiments were run on 2.2 GHz CPU personal computer.

Initially the distance was used for calculating the cost of moving from one cell to another. For heuristic function the straight line distance was used. This traditional A* gave the shortest path but given path was not safe and had obstacles on it. When the influence maps were used for calculating travelling cost between two cells and straight line distance was used for heuristic function, path obtained was safe.

Table 2 shows the result of the experiment where traditional A* is compared with the modified A*. Both the algorithms were compared in term of cost that is calculated using influence maps. The traditional A* algorithm provided the shortest path with minimum distance, but fails to do so in minimum time. Time taken is very crucial in the war game simulation which is frame specific. The modified A* algorithm significantly improved the time taken to find the path from the source till destination because of less intermediate nodes explored which are included in the closed list. This algorithm smartly prims the nodes which are not required thus saving time to find the path. Thus, the modified A* algorithm not only gave a path with minimum cost but also do so quickly. Using influence maps for calculation of g(x) takes the safety factor into account while finding the path. The size of closed listed for traditional A* is also bigger than the modified A*.

Table 2. Route analysis

Source & destination	Scenario 1	Traditional A*	A* using influence maps
Source: 2,17	Time (ms)	83	48
Destination: 8,13	Cost	30	25
	Distance	21.799	25.213
	Closed list	54	30
	Nodes	17	20
Source: 6,17	Time (ms)	96	33
Destination: 0,0	Cost	40	5
	Distance	19.485	21.142
	Closed list	95	28
	Nodes	18	18
Source: 15,10	Time (ms)	72	58
Destination: 2,3	Cost	35	10
	Distance	15.9	16.728
	Closed list	56	14
	Nodes	14	14

Figure 5 shows the optimal path found using modified A* in magenta line and path found by traditional A* in blue dashed line from the unit location to the destination location.

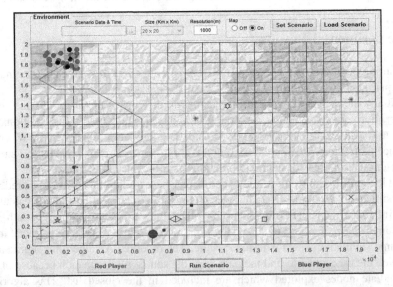

Fig. 5. Path for Traditional A* and modified A* (Color figure online)

7 Conclusion

A framework is developed for a test game wherein the bot is able to interact with a scenario given. This paper gives a brief introduction of various modules developed for the working of the bot. Also a brief introduction of the military war game simulation is presented. Route planning being the core part of the bot has to be effective and efficient. The routing model presented uses the A* search algorithm as a base and is a modified using influence maps. This algorithm successfully gives the optimal path considering the safety of the units. When compared with the traditional A* algorithm, the modified A* algorithm gave better results. The bot is also capable of dynamically changing the path using this model if it encounters threat on the path chosen. Other than route planning the bot can successfully form a plan for execution. Planning includes selecting a target, forming a team, allocating resources to the units.

Acknowledgement. The authors duly acknowledge I.S. Sharma (Scientist, ISSA, DRDO), Colonel Mukul Dhobal and University of Delhi for the support provided.

References

1. Adil, K., Jiang, F., Shaohui, Z.T., Fu, Y.: State-of-the-art and open challenges in RTS game-AI and Starcraft. IJACSA **8**, 16–24 (2017)
2. Robertson, G., Watson, I.D.: A review of real-time strategy game AI. AI Mag. **35**(4), 75–104 (2014)
3. Ontanón, S., Synnaeve, G., Uriarte, A., Richoux, F., Churchill, D., Preuss, M.: RTS AI: Problems and Techniques (2015)
4. Farooq, S.S., Oh, I.-S., Kim, M.-J., Kim, K.J.: StarCraft AI competition: a step toward human-level AI for realtime strategy games. AI Mag. **37**(2), 102–107 (2016)
5. Ontanón, S., Synnaeve, G., Uriar, A., Richoux, F., Churchill, D., Preuss, M.: A survey of real-time strategy game AI research and competition in starcraft. IEEE Trans. Comput. Intell. AI Games **5**(4), 293–311 (2013)
6. Aha, D.W., Molineaux, M., Ponsen, M.: Learning to win: case-based plan selection in a real-time strategy game. In: Muñoz-Ávila, H., Ricci, F. (eds.) ICCBR 2005. LNCS (LNAI), vol. 3620, pp. 5–20. Springer, Heidelberg (2005). https://doi.org/10.1007/11536406_4
7. Stene, S.B.: Artificial intelligence techniques in real-time strategy games-architecture and combat behavior, Institutt for datateknikk og informasjonsvitenskap (2006)
8. Wojnicki, I., Ernst, S., Turek, W.: A robust heuristic for the multidimensional a-star/wavefront hybrid planning algorithm. In: Rutkowski, L., Korytkowski, M., Scherer, R., Tadeusiewicz, R., Zadeh, L.A., Zurada, J.M. (eds.) ICAISC 2015. LNCS (LNAI), vol. 9120, pp. 282–291. Springer, Cham (2015). https://doi.org/10.1007/978-3-319-19369-4_26
9. Russell, S.J., Norvig, P.: Artificial Intelligence: A Modern Approach. Prentice-Hall, Egnlewood Cliffs (2010)
10. Rich, E., Knight, K.: Artificial Intelligence. McGraw-Hill, New York (2008)
11. Sturtevant, N., Buro, M.: Partial pathfinding using map abstraction and refinement. AAAI **5**, 1392–1397 (2005)
12. Barnouti, N.H., Al-Dabbagh, S.S.M., Naser, M.A.S.: Pathfinding in strategy games and maze solving using A* search algorithm. J. Comput. Commun. **4**, 15–25 (2016)

13. Silver, D.: Cooperative pathfinding. In: AIIDE, vol. 1 (2005)
14. Sturtevant, N., Buro, M.: Improving collaborative pathfinding using map abstraction. In: AIIDE (2006)
15. Björnsson, Y., Halldórsson, K.: Improved heuristics for optimal path-finding on game maps. In: AIIDE, vol. 6 (2006)

Author Index

Printed in the United States
By Bookmasters